Neither Saints nor Sinners

Neither Saints nor Sinners

WRITING THE LIVES OF WOMEN

IN SPANISH AMERICA

Kathleen Ann Myers

UNIVERSITY PRESS

2003

OXFORD
UNIVERSITY PRESS

Oxford   New York
Auckland Bangkok Buenos Aires Cape Town Chennai
Dar es Salaam Delhi Hong Kong Istanbul Karachi Kolkata
Kuala Lumpur Madrid Melbourne Mexico City Mumbai Nairobi
São Paulo Shanghai Taipei Tokyo Toronto

Published by Oxford University Press, Inc.
198 Madison Avenue, New York, New York 10016

www.oup.com

Oxford is a registered trademark of Oxford University Press

Library of Congress Cataloging-in-Publication Data
Myers, Kathleen Ann.
Neither saints nor sinners : writing the lives of women in Spanish America.
p. cm
Includes bibliographical references (p.) and index.
ISBN 0-19-515722-2; ISBN 0-19-515723-0 (pbk.)
1. Nuns—Latin America—Biography—History and criticism.   2. Latin American
literature—To 1800—History and criticism.   I. Title.
BX4225 .M94 2003
271'.900228—dc21
[B]   2002071519

9 8 7 6 5 4 3 2 1

Printed in the United States of America
on acid-free paper

For Bob

Preface

In the beginning was the Word and the Word was God.
—John 1 (Rev. Std. Bible)

By the early modern period hundreds of women wrote about their experience of the divine in Italy, France, Spain, and Spanish America. In the Spanish-speaking world in particular, in the wake of the famous mystic author Saint Teresa of Avila (1515–1582), hundreds of religious women were asked by their spiritual directors to write about their lives. They spoke of visionary experience of God rather than book knowledge. Spiritual directors mixed sincere concern for the salvation of their "spiritual daughters'" souls with a desire to create new texts aimed at inspiring Christian readers.

The use of the written word to further the Word of God is as ancient as literacy and religion. Beginning in the fourth century with the compilation and canonization of certain texts to create the Bible, the Roman Catholic Church privileged the written word as the physical locus of God's presence and will and the one "true Book." Within a few centuries, a new narrative tradition—the lives of the saints—was promoted to instruct Christian communities. Written records made of saints' life stories formed a narrative tradition that was intended to inspire emulation by listeners and readers. Over time, Christianity equated not only the Bible but also the narrative lives of the saints with the Word of God. The most popular collection of saints' lives in the Spanish-speaking world notes: "The saints' lives are a sure declaration of Holy Scripture."*

By the sixteenth and seventeenth centuries in the Hispanic world, the hagiographic tradition had become intertwined with religious women's own spiritual writings and with clerical biographies of these women. Scholarly awareness of early modern women's spiritual autobiographical accounts has increased dramatically in the last two decades. Studies often examine these writings for evidence of self-representation and narrative authority, without regard to the different religious genres and the church's requirements for first-person narratives in the period. Other studies examine the relationship between genre and life representation, but they usually focus on a single author and do not place these writings in the larger context of other women writers and clergy.

In this volume, my goal is to illuminate the different church practices that led to religious conventions for confessional autobiography and hagiographic biography and their roles in formulating identity. I focus on early modern life writings by or about holy women (known as *vidas*). The two main forms of *vidas* were confessional, autobiographical accounts written by the women themselves and reverent

---

*"La vida de los santos es declaración cierta de las sagradas escrituras." Pedro de Ribadeneyra, "Al Cristiano lector," *Flos Sanctorum*, paragraph 2.

biographies (also called hagiographies) written by others about saints and holy people after their death. I study a single period, continent, and religious phenomenon: the life writings by and about six religious women living in seventeenth-century Spanish America. I show the lively interaction between rules for behavior and between women's own lives and the church's reinterpretation of these lives, a process I call "rescripting." This approach uncovers the widespread cultural religious codes that established models both for a life and for the life narrative, and it shows how these were key to the building of many people's identity in the colonial period. Looking at dozens of autobiographical texts, which in most cases are just now coming to light, and at scores of published biographical texts, we see that religious women played an important part in establishing a spiritual-cultural colonial power. They were considered icons of heroic virtue who brought blessings to their cities, to the New World, and ultimately to Christendom itself. The texts I consider here are part of an intricate process by which women formulated their own identities—identities that reflected expectations for women, but at times deviated quite significantly from them.

My own process of coming to understand the essential interrelationship between individuals and the colonial church and society that emerged through life writing practices began in 1984, when I rediscovered the colonial Mexican nun María de San José's twelve-volume confessional journals, which had been lost, and the hagiographic biography about her.* I began to examine why there were so few known writings by religious women in the early modern period and what the lives of women who lived hundreds of years ago could tell us. My work coincided with general interest in the study of life writings by anthropologists, historians, and literary critics, who began to publish research that filled in enormous gaps in our knowledge about how people lived and thought in the early modern period. The new research gave us glimpses, often for the first time, into the lives of slaves, native Americans, and visionary women. I spent years piecing together the roles of church rules, confessors, and family. As my ears became more accustomed to the language of religious texts, I began to recognize in María's journals narrative echoes from the life stories of Sts. Teresa of Avila, Rose of Lima, and Catherine of Siena, among many others. I became aware of the strong network that existed between Spanish America's leading church officials and religious women. María and her famous counterpart Sor Juana Inés de la Cruz, for example, wrote for the same bishop (Fernández de Santa Cruz). Sor Juana was compared to her contemporary, the infamous transvestite Catalina de Erauso, known as the "Lieutenant Nun" (La Monja Alférez). Catalina had audiences with the king of Spain and the pope. Clearly, these women were central to colonial and European society. I realized that to understand this intricately intertwined religious, literary, and historical context, I needed to study these religious women both as historical subjects and as authors of a growing tradition of life writing.

Looking to critical studies about early modern religious women and their writings, I saw three general approaches to Hispanic texts. The first is reflected in a group of pioneering studies or anthologies of nuns' writings by Asunción Lavrin (1978),

---

*The manuscript was not cataloged but was in the collection owned by the John Carter Brown Library, Providence, Rhode Island. See chapter 3 of this book for more information.

Josefina Muriel (1982), Electa Arenal and Stacey Schlau (1989), and Isabel Poutrin (1995). These works exposed us to a variety of authors, although at times they confused male biographical rescripting and quoting of nuns' writings with the women's own words.* The second approach is taken by a cluster of monographic studies and critical editions of individual women writers—in particular, Alison Weber's and Carol Slade's studies of Teresa of Avila (1990, 1995), Mary E. Giles on María de Santo Domingo, and Ronald Surtz on Juana de la Cruz (1990)—and, on nuns in America, such as Kathryn Joy McKnight's work on the Colombian mystic Madre Castillo (1997). These studies examined mystic women's use of religious precepts and narrative strategies to gain authority. A third approach has been used in the last few years as more nuns' writings have been brought to light from the archives and studied as a corpus. The valuable work of Sonja Herpoel on Peninsular nuns (1999) and Kristine Ibsen's study of Spanish American nuns (1999) have synthesized previous work on the confessional *vida* genre and the dynamics of authority and added new authors to the list. Much of this work has been informed by groundbreaking studies in other areas, such as medieval women mystics and seventeenth-century Protestant and New French women life writers. (I am thinking here, in particular, of the work by Caroline Walker Bynum, Elizabeth Petroff, Karen Scott, and Natalie Zemon Davis.)

This book paints another part of this canvas: the role of religious women in the development of the literary genres we now call autobiography and hagiographic biography (*vidas*). The project brings together a survey of the church processes that sought to identify saints and sinners—in particular, the processes of canonization and the Inquisition—with the study of the sacrament of confession, which required the telling of one's life story. I argue that the categories of saint and heretic set the extreme limits for self-representation, while confession served as a catalyst for life writings. In between the two extremes and through the vehicle of confession, we see a surprising variety of life paths, among them, those of a mystic, a soldier, and a poet. In all, I examine six representative women, their writings, and their historical circumstances.

Although I began this specific project only three years ago, it has been a long time incubating. My teachers Alan S. Trueblood, Stephanie Merrim, Roberto Gónzalez-Echevarría, Geoffrey Barrow, and William Woolley, and my students Grady Wray, Kristin Routt, Galen Brokaw, Mónica Díaz, Rebecca Marquis, and Mario Ortiz, among many others, have all taught me how to better hear the voices of the past. To Nina Bosch I am grateful for her cheerful and efficient help on the preparation of this manuscript. My wonderful colleagues Amanda Powell, Antonio Rubial, Frank Graziano, Asunción Lavrin, and Cathy Larson all played a very significant part in the formulation of this project and urged me on to its completion. I am particularly indebted to Mary E. Giles for her input on this project, to Nina Scott for many of the translations, and to my readers Mark Feddersen and Kathryn Joy McKnight, who provided me with valuable suggestions on the manuscript.

---

*Some twentieth-century scholars have taken biographers' quotes from the women's accounts to be verbatim. Often the citations are altered by the biographers and therefore represent a blending of the nun's own words with her confessor/biographer's. See chapter 3 of this book for a study of this process.

I have also benefitted greatly from the aid of many archivists and librarians—in particular, my thanks to Becky Cape at the Lilly Library, the staff at the John Carter Brown Library, Manuel Ramos Medina at CONDUMEX in Mexico City, the staff at the Archbishop Archives in Lima, Peru, and Padre Angel Martínez at the Augustinian Archives in Rome. And, as always, my deepest gratitude goes to my friends, especially Jenny, Kelly, Suzy, and Judy, and to my family, the Myers and the Feddersens.

Research for this project has been funded in part by fellowships from Rotary International, the American Philosophical Society, and Indiana University.

Contents

A Note about the Translations

Although the primary aim of this book is a reconstruction of the lives and life narratives of a half dozen colonial Latin American women, I include in the appendixes a sample life writing in translation for each woman studied. The dominant genre is the autobiographical confessional *vida* and its permutations, and so the selections reflect this focus. When possible, the selections center on two significant elements shared by most of these life stories: (1) the narration of the writer's upbringing, which was essential for establishing the Christian background for canonization and inquisition testimony, as well as hagiography; and (2) the call to a specific vocation, reflecting the idea of God's will and authority over life paths. A third element, the moment of judgment, in which a church superior, a confessor, or, often, a bishop asks for an account of the woman's life, typically setting into motion the chain of events that led to a formal, lengthy confession and, later, the writing of the life story is included in the chapter studies. In the cases of Rosa de Lima and Catarina de San Juan, we must depend on alternate autobiographical forms and secondhand testimony (canonization inquiry and hagiographic biography) that filters their own words.

Nina M. Scott has provided all translations in the chapter studies and appendixes, except where otherwise noted. My thanks go to the following individuals and presses for permission to reprint previous translations: Jodi Bilinkoff, Kenneth Mills, and Scholarly Resources for material on Rosa de Lima; Peg Hausman and the Johns Hopkins University Press for translations of Alonso Ramos's biography of Catarina de San Juan; Amanda Powell and Indiana University Press for selections on María de San José; Electa Arenal, Amanda Powell, and the Feminist Press for selections from Sor Juana's *Respuesta*; Nina M. Scott and the University of New Mexico Press for selections from Catalina de Erauso's *Vida i sucesos*.

Neither Saints nor Sinners

Introduction

It has been a truism of historiography to say that a large part of Spanish America was conquered by soldiers and missionaries in search of gold and souls. The colonization of the New World, however, as differentiated from its conquest, depended in large part on the successful implantation of sacred and secular Spanish institutions and practices on American soil. The Roman Catholic Church, in particular, initiated a spiritual conquest and colonization of America by converting native populations. As Christianity took hold, Spanish urban centers developed around a central church or cathedral, and vast sums of money were donated to the founding of monasteries and convents. By some estimates, one in every four women lived in a religious house in seventeenth-century Lima.[1] In addition, printing presses were established in the two viceroyalties: in New Spain (Mexico City) in 1535 and in Peru (Lima) in 1582 (see figure I.1). The majority of the texts published were religious in nature—catechisms, sermons, devotional guides, and saints' lives—and were aimed at shaping a new Roman Catholic community in America.

When compared with traditional historiography and literary histories from the nineteenth and twentieth centuries, one particularly popular colonial genre—biography of local saints and holy people—tells a significantly new story. Instead of a focus on conquest, we see the essential role of holy people in colonization. During a century and a half, Mexico City produced dozens of sacred biographies of local spiritual heroes.[2] Some of the most popular subjects of these biographies were Spanish American religious women, who were lauded as exemplary individuals and models of virtue, and who brought fame to the founding of Spanish rule in the Americas. Sometimes based on the subject's own writings, biographers' *vidas* detail intimate aspects of the person's journey to God. A typical biographer of the period exclaims, for example, that his subject is a better symbol for his city (Puebla) than the coat of arms given by Carlos V: "From the time the Handmaid of the Lord entered this city it had two paired coats of arms: those of the emperor, which ennoble it, and those of Catharina, which defend it; the Handmaid of the Lord was the most efficient weapon Puebla had, for many times she defended it from enemies."[3] These biographies are important because of the new perspective they give to the role of holy people, especially women, in the New World. They form a *petite histoire* for Spanish America and give insight into how religious women—who are almost entirely absent in traditional historiography and literary canons of the colonial period—were, in fact, central to the building of America's Christian identity.

FIGURE I.1   Map of Seventeenth-Century Spanish America (Courtesy of the Lilly Library, Bloomington, Indiana)

After a hundred years of Spanish and mestizo chroniclers documenting their experience of the conquest of America, some seventeenth-century nuns joined the ranks of nonprofessional authors writing about living in America. Drawing on two key European religious narrative forms, the autobiographical confessional account and biographical hagiography, socially privileged white women were trained to examine their lives and write about them for confessors who would use the accounts to guide their spiritual daughters. Later, these unpublished confessional accounts often became the basis for sacred biographies by clerics that were published in both the New World and Spain. The biographical *vidas* were evidence of the important role of the colonies in the Universal Roman Catholic Church.

Sacred biographies, along with corresponding funerary sermons and devotional guides, became foundational narratives of the colonization process in Spanish America. The Mexican philosopher Edmundo O'Gorman noted how midcolonial thought and identity focused less on the economy and politics than on news of its holy people. As O'Gorman explains, "New Spain is a period in which a nun's spiritual flight, a terminally ill person's miraculous cure, a sinner's repentance, or a holy woman's vaticinations [prophecies] are more important news than the rise in prices in business or the imposition of a sales tax; a period in which a spiritual journey to the interior of the soul is more momentous than the expeditions to California and the Philippines. . . . The historian who ignores this hierarchy of period values, might offer us an exhaustive and well-documented narrative of the historical events, but he will never penetrate the secret interior of the most signficant events."[4] O'Gorman's observations are supported by the fact that eight out of every ten works printed in Mexico and Peru were religious texts.[5] Literate families often read these works aloud to each other, while others heard them cited in daily and weekly Mass. The texts filled convent and monastery libraries and were exported to Europe to spread the word about the vitality of Roman Catholicism in America. By the second century of colonization, new generations of readers and listeners began a new cycle of reading, imitation of the holy lifestyle, and writing.

The complexities of the interrelationship between hagiographical narratives and confessional accounts, and between church practices and individual lives, are vividly apparent in the midcolonial Mexican nun María de San José's journals as she describes her life for a confessor. As a young girl living in the mid–seventeenth century, María recounts, she sat in the living room of her family's rural hacienda every evening and listened attentively to the readings of the lives of Catholic saints. María, her sisters, and mother did needlework, while her father and brother took turns reading aloud the heroic stories of martyrs, hermits, and virginal women who had dedicated their lives to God. Some saints had sacrificed their lives for the faith and evangelic missions and, like Jesus Christ, were often subjected to cruel deaths. Other holy people sought out extreme solitude and penances, hoping in this way to purify themselves and serve as vessels for prayer and redemption. Like many seventeenth-century European and American Catholics, María could fly in her imagination to exotic lands and remote times as she contemplated the saints' lives. From their examples she created her own spiritual life and path to salvation. Taking to heart the stories' exhortation to total devotion to God, María and one of her sisters began to imitate Christ and his saints. In the family's garden, María built a hut where she spent several hours a day engaged in prayer and penances, while her sister wore a crown of thorns and walked barefoot with a cross on her shoulder. Although they lived in a world with a relatively short Christian history and in households filled with native American servants and slaves of African descent, many families of Spanish descent (*criollos*) continued the popular European hagiographic tradition. The genre originated in the early years of Christianity, but it was still thriving—albeit with a distinct register and structure—in the century after Luther's reform had vigorously attacked the Catholic practice of venerating saints.

Spanish Americans not only read and imitated the lives of Old World saints, they aspired to promote their own. In fact, María de San José herself became a nun and wrote her own autobiographical account. Later, her spiritual autobiography served as the basis for a posthumous sacred biography by a local Dominican friar in an attempt to initiate her canonization.[6] Eager to bridge the geographical and spiritual gap between Europe and America—between the Old World that boasted hundreds of years of Catholic practice and the New World that threatened to taint European settlers' virtue through exposure to "infidels" and "idolatrous" practices—criollos sought to prove that the New World was a paradise for a new and pure Catholic order. Local holy people were depicted in Spanish American hagiographies for a dual purpose: they served as models to emulate and as symbols for the building of a local history and identity. Significantly, upon María's death, the girl who had been transfixed by the saints' lives and had ardently followed the path of several became a model of holiness for other women to follow and a symbol for New Spain when her hagiographic biographer describes her as a mystic conquistador for America, one who helped accomplish a spiritual conquest.[7]

A complex process emerged out of the central Catholic spiritual practice of imitation (*imitatio*) and the inherently repetitive forms this practice took in the saints' lives. María's story of reading, emulating, writing, and being rewritten as a hagiographic subject to be read by others, however, is not a phenomenon unique to Spanish America or to women. Religious sisters in Italy, France, New France, and Spain also took part in this spiritual/textual cycle, as did male clergy whose designated roles as "physicians of the soul" and bearers of the keys to salvation required them to identify and judge extraordinary women subjects. For the most part, however, it was women who were required to write a history of their lives. A woman's confessor frequently worked in conjunction with his superiors to judge the worthiness of the account. Although religious and lay men also served as subjects for hagiographic biographies, they were rarely required to write the full-fledged confessional *vidas* that were often an essential intermediary step for women. Religious men and women collaborated on this project of autobiography, but only male clergy at the highest levels had the authority to judge whether the journey a woman described was that of a potential saint or a sinner.

By the mid–sixteenth century, gathering first-person testimony about spiritual experiences and comparing it to the testimony of others began to be a relatively common practice by the church in an effort to control orthodoxy and power. In turn, people began to internalize the testimonies as a kind of narrative code to represent their own spiritual legitimacy. As a result, the legalistic structures for determining spiritual orthodoxy became increasingly apparent in life stories. Because any deviation from the models of sainthood required explanation, narratives often used conventional rhetorical forms to describe the traditional path to sanctity, but then argued for a new interpretation of God's will to propose alternative models for sainthood. This complex situation raises questions about what lies at the heart of these life stories, which often contradict official models and practices, and how the church not only reconciled difference but turned these at times deviant lives into paradigmatic hagiographic biographies for a new age and a New World.

The Counter-Reformation and Life Stories

Perhaps the core source of inspiration for the life stories we study is the early Christian precept of *imitatio Christi*. The ultimate goal of devout individuals and of the church was to create lives that imitated Christ. A central tenant of the Catholic faith set into motion this life-modeling process. Based on the doctrine of the Incarnation, Christianity avers that God became a man, Jesus Christ, in order to save humankind. By following Christ's human example of love and sacrifice, Christians could achieve salvation. The early saints and martyrs were witnesses to and practitioners of Christ's way. Soon they became valid models to follow and were considered valuable intercessors between heaven and earth.[8] But over the centuries, this simple spiritual precept, by which imitations of the holy original produced holiness in the imitator, became more complex as Christianity spread and Rome attempted to control the definition of holiness.

By the early modern period studied here, the church and its ministers had come to disagree about rules for judging a person's life and what constituted signs of divine mercy and Catholic behavior. Teachings established by the Council of Trent (1545–1563) on the sacrament of confession, the rules for canonization, the role of the Inquisition, and the distinct roles for women and men in the church, deeply affected the interpretation of holiness and the articulation of self-identity. In the following chapters I outline the religious ideology and institutional practices that set in motion a four-part process of hagiographic reading, imitation, confessional writing, and "rescripting" (or reinterpreting holy lives). I suggest that the process contains an inherent tension as authoritative "canonized" models and texts of saints were adapted to particular historical circumstances and individual experience. The interplay between official models and individual interpretation illustrates how the narrow parameters of the ideal religious woman were variously followed or reformulated as new experiences led to new interpretations of the standard models for a holy life.

Within forty years of the conquests of Mexico and Lima, Spain and Rome began a vigorous counterattack against a more proximate threat than the "infidel" native American—the Protestant Reformation. The Counter-Reformation reformulated Catholic doctrines in order to work toward internal renewal and to respond to Luther's attack on Catholicism. Prescriptions were given to reform religious orders and clergy, and new documents reaffirmed the role of the sacraments and the intercessory powers of the saints. The Catholic Church not only redefined the importance of these doctrines, but it instituted ways to more carefully regulate the practices of the faithful. Redirecting the *devotio moderna*—the idea that had developed at the turn of the fifteenth century about an individual's direct access to God—the Catholic Church now began to require frequent confession, to prohibit books that promoted individual spiritual practices without church monitoring, and to construct new models of holiness in which heroic virtue, defined as obedience to the church and active participation in the sacraments, was a key factor in determining sainthood. As both lay persons and religious members sought new avenues for religious expression, the church sought to control and codify them.

When Counter-Reformation initiatives began to clash with individual spiritual practices, many of Spain's most notable holy people and authors, such as St. John of the Cross and Fray Luis de León, were brought before the Catholic Church's newly revived institution for determining heresy, the Holy Office of the Inquisition. Besides going after suspects for Judaism, Lutheranism, and witchcraft, the Inquisition attempted to control religious fakery and heretical sects such as the illuminists (*alumbrados*), who claimed to have direct access to an understanding of divine will without the need for church mediation. In the 1550s, the Inquisition also established the *Index of Prohibited Books*, which banned books that dealt with individual spiritual exercises. For example, one of sixteenth-century Spain's most noted saints, Teresa of Avila, complained that the *Index* had censured most of the books that she had used in learning about the spiritual life.[9]

As Counter-Reformation practices took hold in Spain and Italy, the main colonization of Spanish America was taking place. The European prescriptions for Catholics designated at the Council of Trent were followed in the New World. In Lima, for example, the Concilio Limense of 1567 and 1582–1583 established rules that echoed those of Trent, such as the prohibition of public preaching by lay men and women. During these same decades, the Inquisition's largest public spectacle, the autos-da-fé, took place in Mexico and Lima. By the turn of the seventeenth century, the viceroyalties of both New Spain and Peru were sending stories of their holy people to Rome and Madrid. And yet, because of America's radically different racial, geographical, and historical circumstances, European standards were necessarily localized and often altered. For example, a series of Inquisition edicts, at least in theory, severely limited the reading of popular Spanish secular texts, such as *Don Quijote*, in America. And the majority of hagiographic biographies published in America promoted local holy people rather than European models.

To understand the relationship between Counter-Reformation teachings and the production of life narratives in Spanish America, it is helpful to understand the extreme limits established for Catholic behavior—the saint and the heretic—and to study the process by which the church examined people's lives and judged them. In general, the post-Tridentine church (the Catholic Church after the Council of Trent) created a more centralized role for itself in the supervision of individual spirituality through the use of three specific processes: confession, canonization, and inquisition. All three processes sought to monitor and promote spiritual orthodoxy. The church set the two end points for judging a person's behavior through the codification of sanctity in the process of canonization and of heresy through the Inquisition. Confession—whether sacramental or juridical—was the vehicle through which an individual articulated his or her religious identity. In private encounters during mandatory confessional exchanges, priests guided confessants' lives. In church chambers, inquisitors and bishops took testimony about people's behaviors and beliefs. Through the public spectacles of an auto-da-fé and through the veneration of a holy person, the church produced positive and negative exemplars. Whether a confession, canonization process, or Inquisition trial, church authorities often required first an oral account and later a written one of the subject's life. The Holy Office of the Inquisition required first-person juridical narratives; confessors asked for full life accounts; and the organization charged with determining holiness, the Congregation of Holy Rites, sought autobiographical writings, third-person testimony, and biographies. Each of these oral and written life narratives was governed by a set of rules and conventions that evolved over time. (For examples of these documents, see Figures I.2 and I.3.)

Although in the early church, confession was conceived of as an infrequent and public act that could lead to great transformation it became an increasingly private and frequent act after the Lateran Council in the thirteenth century made it a yearly requirement.[10] Soon, the production of confessors' manuals began to guide the confessional act toward an examination of both actions and intentions. According to the Roman Catholic Church (and vehemently attacked by Luther) as God's official intermediary on earth the confessor held the keys to salvation. While the Council of Trent reinforced the requirement and frequency of confession, the recent

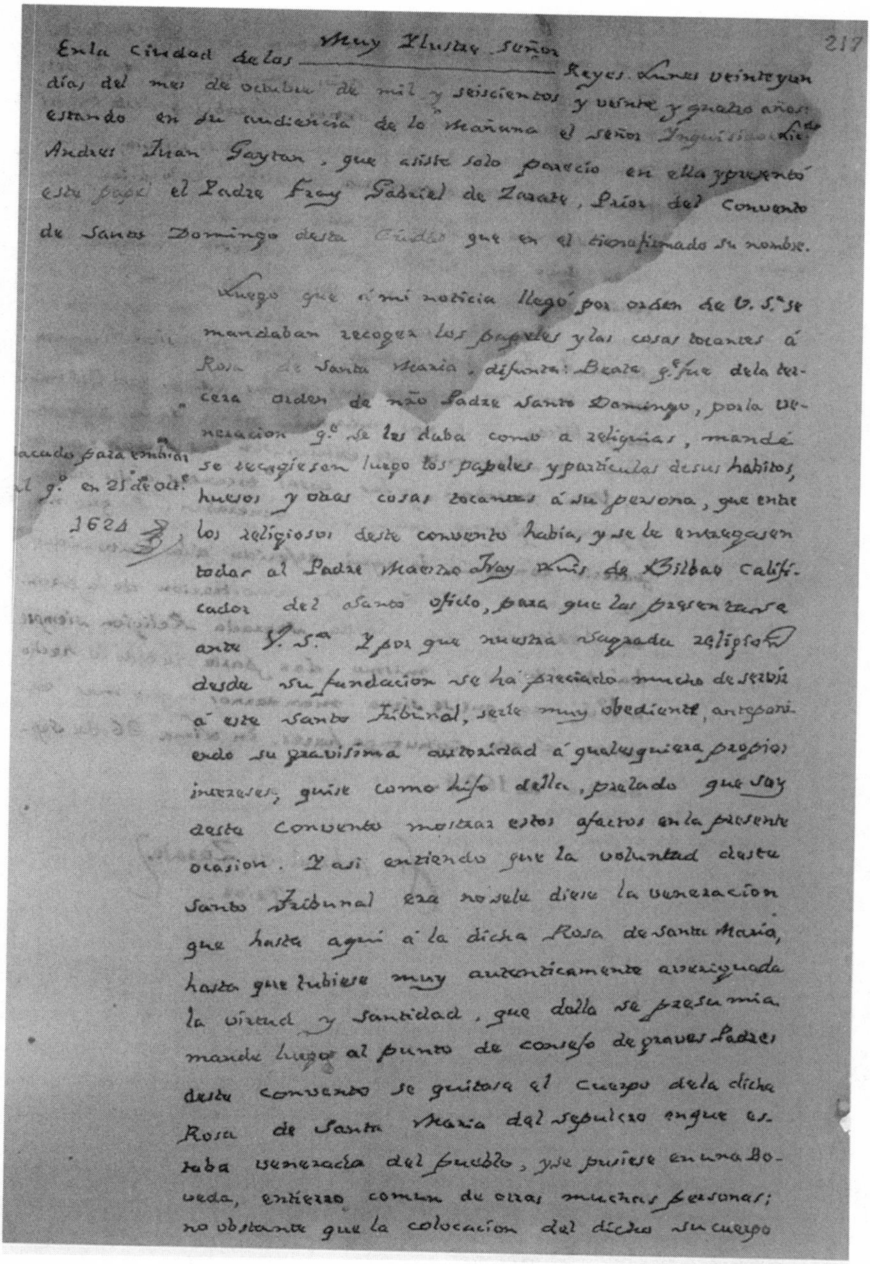

Muy Ilustre Señor

En la Ciudad de los [...] Reyes Lunes veinte y un
días del mes de octubre de mil y seiscientos y veinte y quatro años
estando en su audiencia de la mañana el señor Inquisidor Lic[enciado]
Andrés Juan Gaytán, que asiste solo pareció en ella y presentó
este papel el Padre Fray Gabriel de Zarate, Prior del Convento
de Santo Domingo desta Ciudad que en el tiempo firmado su nombre.

Luego que a mi noticia llegó por orden de V. S.ª se
mandaban recoger los papeles y las cosas tocantes á
Rosa de Santa María, difunta Beata q.e fue de la tercera orden de n[uest]ro Padre Santo Domingo, por la veneración q.e se les daba como a reliquias, mandé
se recogiesen luego los papeles y particulas de sus habitos,
huesos y otras cosas tocantes a su persona, que entre
los religiosos deste convento había, y se le entregasen
todas al Padre Maestro Fray Luis de Bilbao Calificador del Santo Oficio, para que las presentase
ante V. S.ª Y porque nuestra Sagrada religión
desde su fundación se ha preciado mucho de servir
a este Santo Tribunal, serle muy obediente anteponi-
endo su gravísima autoridad a qualesquiera propios
intereses, quise como hijo della, prelado que soy
deste convento mostrar estos afectos en la presente
ocasión. Y así entiendo que la voluntad deste
Santo Tribunal era no se le diese la veneración
que hasta aquí a la dicha Rosa de Santa María,
hasta que tubiese muy auténticamente averiguada
la virtud y santidad, que della se presumía
mandé luego al punto de consejo de graves Padres
deste convento se quitase el cuerpo de la dicha
Rosa de Santa María del sepulcro en que estaba venerada del pueblo, y se pusiese en una Bo-
veda, entierro común de otras muchas personas;
no obstante que la colocación del dicho su cuerpo

Figure I.2 Canonization Process for Rosa de Lima, 1617 (Courtesy of the Lilly Library, Bloomington, Indiana)

NOS LOS INQVISIDORES
CONTRA LA HERETICA PRAVEDAD, Y A-
POSTASIA, EN LA CIVDAD DE MEXICO, ESTADOS, Y
Prouincias de la nueua España, nueua Galicia, Guatemala, Nicaragua, Yucatan, Verapaz, Honduras,
y las Philipinas, y su distrito, y jurisdicion, por authoridad Apostolica, &c.

POR Que sin enbargo de las muchas ordenes, que estan dadas, para occurrir
à los graues daños, que resultan de los libros hereticos, y prohibidos, por los
Cathalogos del Santo Officio, y de que no esten expurgados, los que confor-
me al nuebo expurgatorio sean de expurgar, no dejan de entrar en estos Reynos mochos libros prohibidos, ni los libreros, y las demas personas cuidan,
de hazer la expurgacion de los que han de ser expurgados, como esta ordenado
se haga. Por tanto por el tenor de la presente mandamos, que dētro de seis me-
ses que se quenten desde el dia de la publicaciō de este Edicto, tengan los libreros, y las demas personas (de qualquier grado, dignidad, ò peheminencia q̃
sean) obligacion de expurgar los libros que tubieren, y estan mandados expurgar. Y pasado este termino, y
hallandoseles sin la expurgacion, los pierdan, y sean condenados por cada autor, en cinq enta ducados, y
los que no fueren libreros, y se les hallaren los dichos libros por expurgar, los pierdan, y esto, demas y a-
liende de las penas, y censuras puestas por el Cathalago, y Appendix de este Santo Officio. Y que de aqui
adelante, no pueda ninguna de las dichas personas, meter los libros, que tubieren qualquiera expurgaciō
en estos Reynos, ni en ningun puerto dellos, si no estando expurgados sopena de tener perdidos los dichos
libros, y de ducientos ducados por cada vez. Y debajo de las dichas penas mandamos à los Comissarios,
Calificadores, y otras personas, que hizieren la dicha expurgacion, que con tal cuidado borren lo que se
expurgare que nose pueda leer en ninguna manera:
Yten habiendose visto la Regla, y mandato que esta enel dicho expurgatorio, y tiene por titulo
MANDATO A LOS LIBREROS. Y luego comiença TODOS LOS QVE HA-
ZEN OFICIOS DE LIBREROS, &c. Mandamos, que demas de el memorial, que tie-
nen obligacion los dichos libreros de hazer al principio de cada año, la tengan tambien, de añadir enel
inuentario todos los libros que entre año entraren en su poder, como no sean de los mesmos que estan pu-
estos enel dicho inuentario, y que despues de escritos enel no los pueda vēder, sin mostrarlos à la persona
que por nos fuere diputada, debajo de la pena puesta en la dicha Regla, y mandato contra los dichos libreros, Corredores, y tratantes de libros, y para que vēga a noticia de todos, y nadie pueda pretender ignorancia, mandamos dar la presente. Fecha en la Ciudad de Mexico, en la Sala de nuestra Audiencia, à
doze dias del mes de Iunio de mil, y seiscientos, y veinte y vn añ os.

FIGURE I.3   "Nos los inquisidores," Edict of the Mexican Inquisition, 1621 (Courtesy
of the Lilly Library, Bloomington, Indiana)

innovation of the confessional box allowed for a more private experience and a more
detailed accounting of thoughts, as well as deeds. As the priest guided the confessant,
often with a series of provocative questions about sexuality and faith, the confessant
was encouraged to interpret his or her own story in light of church codes for Christian behavior. New confessional practices led to the development of a formal system
of introspection.[11]

As the process of confession became more complex, individuals began to prepare for confession by taking notes and using confessional guides as a narrative
matrix.[12] The colonial Spanish American women studied in this book call these informal notes *cuentas de conciencia*. They were used as an aid to confession and even in
lieu of confession when the confessor was absent. At a significant turning point in
an individual's life—particularly after taking a vow as a religious, beginning to work
with a new confessor, or having experienced a prolonged period of visionary activity—an individual might be asked to make a general confession, one that included

the origins of a call to a holy vocation. The confession often started with birth and childhood and ended at the present moment of the confession. This spoken account could be followed by a formal written report of the life story, variously called a *vida espiritual* or a confessional *vida*, which evolved into the predominant narrative form used by early modern women to write about their lives. These confessional *vidas* carefully negotiate the codes for confession and feminine behavior.

Until recently, post-Romantic readers often failed to read these narratives as part of a sacramental process in which the value of the author's life was at stake. As a result, these readers did not understand that religious women wrote highly codified narratives that guided the confessor's interpretation and judgment of the account. New scholarship demonstrates how we have at times been reading texts like Teresa of Avila's "canonized" *Libro de la vida* (1588) in the wrong genre, as a post-Romantic autobiography. As Carol Slade demonstrates, Teresa's *vida* both responds to the requirements of juridical confession for the Inquisition, such as information about family genealogy and the nature of visionary activity, and alters them by incorporating narrative elements from a previously canonized life model, St. Augustine and his own *Confessions*.[13] Kate Greenspan suggests that, in fact, most medieval religious women wrote "autohagiographies."[14] These accounts frequently discuss the saints' lives that autobiographers read in their youth, which often became the indirect narrative model. The confession of sin became a didactic confirmation of God's grace and goodness in the subject's life and a story of her doctrinally pure response to those divine gifts. Confessional accounts often were informed by the rules established by the Inquisition and canonization.

The Catholic Church established the Holy Office of the Inquisition in order to "defend the faith." Although it was first instituted in Spain during the thirteenth century, the Inquisition was reestablished by the Catholic monarchs, Isabel and Ferdinand, in 1480 to help unify the kingdom and to preserve orthodoxy among recently converted Jews. By the mid–sixteenth century it actively persecuted a number of heretical groups, most notably Protestants (*lutheranos*) and illuminists (*alumbrados*). Soon the Inquisition was transferred to America, and by 1571 it was formalized with the founding of two tribunals—one in Mexico City, the other in Lima. Unlike its Spanish counterpart, however, the New World Inquisition was relatively ineffective at completing its charges: to protect religion and culture against heresy and immoral behavior. Native Americans (more than 75 percent of the population in Spanish America) were exempt from the Inquisition's rulings, and it was impossible for the two tribunals to control the vast territory that stretched from modern-day northern California to the southern reaches of Chile. In fact, as one scholar notes in her study of women denounced to the Mexican Inquisition, only 6 percent were actually tried ("processed");[15] in general, the charges were dropped. As we will see in chapter 2, the Inquisition exercised more control over the cultural production of books—but even then, restrictions and prohibitions were often unevenly met. Nonetheless, the threat of being tried, or even informally examined by the Inquisition, was enough to motivate many people to internalize the codes that distinguished orthodox practice from heterodoxy. The information a witness gave and the words used to describe his or her life and spiritual activity often followed norms published in guidebooks and edicts about what constituted good Catholic practices and customs (*buenas costumbres*).

Whether it was an informal examination or a formal confession taken from an imprisoned individual after being denounced, statements made to the Inquisition generally moved from information about the confessant's age, place of residence, and profession to a genealogy of the family and proof of Catholic training and education. Inquisitors also frequently asked for a more general story of the subject's life (a juridical confession) and then followed up with more specific questions about spiritual practices and contacts. The juridical confession was a parallel to the penitential sacrament of confession. Because the subject typically was not informed of the charges made, the confessant had to respond to imagined accusations. Interrogation about spiritual practices often focused on exposing Jewish practices or *alumbrado* tendencies.[16] The questions and responses were documented by a notary and usually witnessed by at least one other church official.

The process of canonization—of recognizing sanctity, a quality of living that was similar to that of Jesus Christ—falls at the other end of the spectrum of church practices for defining Catholic behavior. The role of the saints had always been key to the promotion of Christianity from its earliest years. These exemplary individuals inspired others to imitate Christ and were believed to possess intercessory powers between man and God. First recognized in the early church by local public veneration, by the thirteenth century, the process of proclaiming a person worthy of canonization became more formalized and was reserved for the Holy See. The Council of Trent increased the requirements for sanctity, and a few years later, in 1588, the process became yet more bureaucratic and centralized with a ruling that required all canonizations to be overseen by the Congregation of Holy Rites. Cases now had to include materials and witnesses that proved the candidate's heroic virtue and documented miracles. Ecclesiastical tribunals set up trials (*procesos*) with judges, advocates, and witnesses to try the cases of potential saints. Soon after, Pope Urban VIII further codified the canonization process (1623–1644) with more rulings about when a candidate could be considered and how biographies presented the life of a holy person. The construction of sanctity became an increasingly elaborate and centralized process. By controlling the type of saint venerated, the church hoped to further control the spiritual activity of its faithful.

The narrative codification of sanctity is most clear in the hagiographic production of life stories about saints and individuals being promoted for sanctity. The church authorized certain types of narratives and information while censoring others. The church's campaign after the Council of Trent focused on saints who illustrated doctrinal purity and heroic virtue more than the performance of numerous miracles. The hagiographic campaign emphasized narratives that seemed more historical, based like humanist histories on documentable facts. Urban VIII's reforms of the canonization process further codified these requirements.

Religious Women and the Church

For our purposes, it is important to note that the increased control over the definition of official sanctity and the production of hagiographic narratives resulted in a yet more

narrow area of sanctity allowed for women. Peter Burke notes post-Tridentine requirements resulted in far fewer canonizations, the demotion of saints who contradicted
new models, and the promotion of mystics associated with religious orders.[17] Weinstein
and Bell observe that only 17 percent of all saints were women, but of these 40 to
50 percent were mystics.[18] Mystic piety revitalized the reader's own love for God,
while the saint's association with a religious order ensured that individual spiritual experience was guided toward the collective good of Catholicism (and promoted the religious order). Official models of sanctity greatly influenced the
hagiographies of contemporary noncanonized individuals in America and religious
women's own self-portraits.

As Gerda Lerner, Jo Ann McNamara, Elizabeth Petroff, and Caroline Walker
Bynum have established, in the middle ages one of the few avenues of power within
the church open to women was that of the visionary.[19] Theories about the physical and spiritual capacities of men and women led to a belief that women were
important conduits for divine will. By the period of the Counter-Reformation,
Catholic teachings about individual spirituality were highly gender-specific. While
men could engage in a wide range of religious roles that would lead to holiness,
women's options were limited. The variety of possibilities for religious men reflected the variety of social roles they could engage in: they could live cloistered in
a monastery or out in the world as priests, missionaries, theologians, and bishops.
According to mystical guides, men often pursued truth through the intellect, whereas
women pursued truth through love. María de San José's biographer explains that
women tended toward emotional states (*incendios*), whereas men tended toward
reasoned discourse (*discurso*).[20] By training the faculty of the will to love God, women
could become more virtuous ("virile") and were said to have manly hearts (*corazones
varoniles*) or to be manly women (*mujeres varoniles*). This active preparation could
then be met with God's divine grace in the form of visionary experiences. The
affective path was highly valued by the church, as a sermon preached in María de
San José's Augustinian Convent of Santa Mónica declared: Saint Monica rivaled
her son Augustine because she experienced God through tears of love, while he
used the intellect to love God.[21]

A belief in the value of experience over theory and speculation lies at the heart
of mysticism. By decreasing the reliance on the three faculties of the soul—reason,
understanding, and will—the mystic sought to become like Christ through the use
of her senses and higher faculties, especially through love. But only God could grant
the rare gift of mystical union—of transforming the soul and uniting with him.
Participating in the sixteenth-century rift between *letrados* (often scholastics) and
experimentados (relying on direct experience), the Hispanic mystic movement involved
both men and women. But women in particular found mysticism an important
avenue for spiritual expression, no doubt because the *letrado* route was generally closed
to them. Many religious women desired to be mystics, and many had visions that
could either aid or hinder their spiritual progress. Yet according to Catholic doctrine, true mysticism requires God's grace and few visionaries actually become mystics. As we will see in the chapters that follow, as confessors, inquisitors, and canon
lawyers examined testimony about spiritual practices in an attempt to distinguish

the true mystic from the false visionary or *alumbrada*, they asked women to detail in oral and written accounts their religious experiences and lives.

Mystics and visionaries could both help and hurt the church. As highly affective experiences, mysticism and visions could inspire others to renew their faith. But as highly individual experiences, it could threaten the church's authority. Therefore, the Counter-Reformation established a system of controls that influenced most visionaries. Because women were considered to be more open and available to divine contact through visionary experience, as well as more vulnerable to temptation of all sorts, they were closely monitored by clergy. To better control religious women's spirituality, the Counter-Reformation required nuns to take a vow of perpetual enclosure, and, in theory at least, began to limit the spheres of influence of *beatas*, lay religious women who had devoted their lives to God but still lived "in the world." This careful restriction of religious women's roles extended into the confessional and the production of written confessional accounts. Nuns like Teresa of Avila and María de San José were often *escritoras por obediencia*, required to write in obedience to a confessor or another clergyman, who would then determine the orthodoxy of their spiritual practice. Confessors looked, in particular, for evidence of heroic retreat from the world, penitential practices, obedience to the church, and personal knowledge of God that had not been learned from books.

Orthodox visionary experiences had important consequences when women began to write their own autobiographies. Such experiences were clear evidence of the divine hand at work in a humble life. Whereas church fathers had recourse to books for judging their spiritual daughters, these visionaries used their own experience of the divine as their source of knowledge—and their authority. Teresa of Avila's writings about the mystic path—and her *Libro de la vida*, in particular—allow us to see how her mystic experience ultimately served as the cornerstone for creating a church-approved life and narrative. Throughout her narrative she posits the authority of her own direct experience of God and prayer over that of poorly trained confessors who would condemn her spiritual path. She even argues that because some of her favorite spiritual guides had been put on the *Index of Prohibited Books*, she had no recourse but to listen to God himself: "When they took away many books written in the vernacular, so they would not be read, I was very sorry, because some of them gave me pleasure, and I could not read them in Latin. But the Lord said to me, 'Don't be distressed, I will give you a living book.'"[22] Using a subtle manipulation of conventional topics of ignorance, humility, and obedience and the hagiographic unfolding of a soul's call to God, Teresa details her method of prayer, her work with different confessors, and the divine mercies God had granted her. Teresa's strategy for convincing doubtful clergy of God's presence in her life was a success. Although the *Libro de la vida* passed in and out of the hands of the Inquisition for a period of time, by 1622 Teresa was canonized and many of her writings had been published. Her life writings galvanized Catholic women to follow her instructions for prayer and to imitate her as a literary model for their own journals. Teresa became the archetype for religious women writers. She was an instrumental figure in all but one of the women's life paths and writings discussed in this volume.

The authority for these women's texts came from their individual experience of God, from the confessor's request for a narrative, and from their use of hagiographic-confessional genre as established by Teresa. Life narratives had both sacramental and doctrinal implications. Linking an account to this specific genre type was not just literary play; it was essential to personal salvation and to the promotion of church agendas. Narratives required specific structures and rhetoric. Religious-literary genres—whether confessional *vidas*, hagiography, or sermons—focused the material narrated, the reader's expectations, and the ideological ends of the account. A multileveled system for representing and judging sanctity and heresy created a surprisingly rich range of feminine *vidas* in Spanish America.

Spanish American Lives and Life Stories

This volume examines six representative seventeenth-century women whose lives and life narratives serve as case studies that illustrate how a single church role for women to be saintlike *perfecta religiosas* in fact generated multiple life paths: America's first official saint wrote poetry, a Hindu slave prophesied royal succession, a mystic found herself preaching to a town of blacks, a nun wrote copiously about love, another nun delighted in deceiving men, and a girl fled the convent to become a soldier. In addition, I show how these women's lives and texts were integral to the building of colonial society: most of them were heralded as symbols of America. I have chosen these six women as suggestive of the possibilities found in colonial Spanish American women's life writings.[23] While they include both several of the most famous and a few relatively unknown religious women, taken together they represent the range and interrelatedness of women's life representation. The six included here share a core set of historical, social, and generic circumstances, but they work through them in very different ways.

To reflect this diversity of life paths and writings within a single institutional model, I have organized the book into two parts. Part I examines three women, two lay holy women and a nun, in order to elucidate the inner workings of the processes of canonization, inquisition, and confession vis-à-vis the visionary woman. In all three cases, we see how local veneration of holy women could later lead to conflicting official interpretations about the sanctity of the subject; they often became the focal point of church and civic debates. In addition, we see how the confessional process was the cornerstone upon which inquisitors and hagiographers would build their cases about the subject's spiritual life.

Part II studies three women who spent time in the convent, but instead of being exemplars of heroic virtue, they are women who in one form or another redefine—or reject completely—the path of the *perfecta religiosa*. Although none was questioned by the Inquisition or considered for canonization, all three at one point in their lives had to temporarily curb their nonconforming activities because of punishments imposed on them by bishops or archbishops. All three write accounts about their lives, and they do so at least in part by adapting the confessional *vida*.

Chapter 1 examines the saint-making process of America's first saint, Rosa de Lima (1586–1617). Through a reconstruction of her life story as an ascetic third-order

Dominican in Lima and an examination of the vicissitudes of her canonization process from 1617 to 1691, we glimpse the often inconsistent observation of rules for sainthood in the century after the Counter-Reformation had revised the Catholic Church's official guidelines for sanctity. In many ways, Rosa's choice to remain outside the convent as a lay religious woman and to follow extreme penitential practices reflected a largely unchanged expression of feminine affective piety from that of the popular medieval model St. Catherine of Siena and directly undermined the Counter-Reformation's attempts to curb individual spiritual practices and to cloister women. How was it that a woman whose life in many regards contradicted the Council of Trent's recommendation that religious women be enclosed in convents and practice moderate penances was America's first saint? By examining the canonization processes of 1617 and 1630, several hagiographic *vidas*, reports on an inquiry by the Inquisition, and Rosa's own works, we will see the strong interrelationship between politics and sanctity, between the interviewing of witnesses and the writing of official hagiography, and between spiritual guidelines and life practices. A desire to disassociate Rosa from several followers who were being examined by the Inquisition for evidence of *alumbradisimo*, combined with new rules for canonization in the first half of the century, heavily influenced the representation of Rosa's life story for future generations.

Chapter 2 looks at the subject of a hagiographic biography, Catarina de San Juan (ca. 1607–1688). Her case reveals more about post-Tridentine guidelines on sanctity and their textual representation. In addition to the Congregation of Holy Rites' rules for holiness and hagiography that I study in Rosa's case, I examine the rules set out by the Holy Office of the Inquisition for books and doctrinal purity. Catarina de San Juan was in some respects like Rosa. She was a lay holy woman. Although first brought to America as a slave, she was central to local citizens' lives because of her intercessory powers. Upon her death in Puebla, she had throngs of followers from all walks of life and was promoted by the powerful Jesuit order. In fact, one eager Jesuit wrote a hagiographic biography of Catarina that would become the longest work published in the colonial Americas—Alonso Ramos's *De los prodigios. . .* (1689, 1690, 1691). New Spanish clergy further advanced her cause by heartily approving the three-volume tome, while the laity began to venerate a painted portrait of her. Soon, from the other side of the Atlantic, the Spanish Inquisition attempted to suppress her developing cult and prohibited further publication and reading of her biography. Significantly, the Mexican Inquisition seems to have ignored the Spanish ban for four years. Catarina de San Juan's case, like Rosa's, illustrates the contradictions in the interpretation of holiness and heresy and the myriad of mitigating factors that—depending often on sudden changes in policy, leaders, and power struggles—could catapult a sinner into an elevated status or send a saintly person to the Inquisition's jails or narrative oblivion.

The last chapter in this triad of saintly women focuses on the Mexican nun María de San José (1656–1719). Here I investigate a third important institutional practice that shaped the outcome of many lives with similarly paradoxical results: the role of confession, both as a sacrament promoted by the Council of Trent and as a practice for religious women that could produce autobiographical and biographical life stories. The extensive confessional journals and Stations of the Cross (a guide to Christ's Passion and death) written by María and her posthumous biography by Sebastián Santander y Torres serve as the basis for this study. As we saw in the opening pages of this introduction, if ever there was a woman who longed to be a saint, it was Madre María. As a mystic and founder of a prestigious reformed convent, she carefully followed the path of the model nun, the *perfecta religiosa*. The unusual variety and length of her life writings are a valuable tool for tracing the interdependent roles of nuns and confessors, of *escritoras por obediencia* and clerics who judged and at times rewrote the life story for didactic purposes. The history of Catholic confession and hagiography inform the structure and ideology of María's spiritual writings. Her writings reveal a central tension between "canonized" church texts and learned authorities and individual spiritual experience, often "authorized" by divine intervention. María de San José illustrates the delicate process of simultaneously casting herself as repentant sinner and chosen saint, and she carefully negotiates a path between self-will, divine will, and the confessor's will. She became a visionary scribe, an unofficial medium for the divine word, which she passed on to her confessor, as her official intercessor between heaven and earth. María's accounts reveal the dynamics of a profoundly gender-specific role as a mystic woman author. We see how her story was recast by clergy to represent the new spiritual conquistador, as evidence of the flowering of Christianity in America. In summary, Part I presents women who were promoted by the institutional church—at least locally—as potential saints, regardless of race or religious status.

Part II looks at the creation and reworking of established rules and genres to effect very different outcomes on the lives of the women and their texts. Each of the three women studied in these chapters created a hybrid text that blends elements from the confessional *vida* with other first-person narrative genres in order to defend an alternate path to God. The use of the *vida* form was essential because the church demanded it. And yet, these women subverted the form by using irony, satire, and parody, as well as the competing ideologies borrowed from such secular narrative structures as the picaresque narrative and soldier's story. Despite diverging from the model church script, upon their deaths two women were "rescripted" by clergy into accounts that borrow hagiographic elements. While neither was promoted as a potential saint per se, they both were co-opted for the building of America's fame. They were rewritten as curiosities (*casos singulares*), as examples of extraordinary women who overcame the limitations of their sex to become more *varonil* and, therefore, worthy subjects of biographical narratives in a different light.

Chapter 4 surveys the autobiographical writings of Spanish America's most famous nun, Sor Juana Inés de la Cruz (1648–1695). In a series of letters to New Spanish clergy from 1682 to 1691, Sor Juana used the epistolary genre, the letter, to define her own role and beliefs about religious vocation vis-à-vis church authorities and texts. Highly structured as a genre by the seventeenth century, the letter could serve as a public or private document and as a legal or spiritual aid. It is only with the most famous of these letters, the *Respuesta* to the bishop of Puebla, however, that Sor Juana combined the rhetorical possibilities of the letter with those of the confessional *vida*. She redefined the model nun to be one who used God's gifts, which in the case of the intellectually gifted meant following a life of study. Because the path to salvation required using one's gifts, the *perfecta religiosa* for Sor Juana became the *religiosa letrada*, a learned nun. Such an audacious rewriting of the traditional role, genre, and ideology for nuns provoked a crisis. It appears that the archbishop of Mexico commanded Sor Juana to sell her library and renew her religious vows. To change the influence of her story on others, upon her death he ordered a hagiographic biography written about her. In so doing, he effectively turned a rebellious daughter of the church into a more saintly, noncontroversial nun. We learn from this, once again, how high the stakes were in the church's rescripting of its extraordinary women's lives. Relatively new archival finds suggest that while Sor Juana was subjected to punitive measures, she unofficially continued her literary career, and several churchmen continued to support her. As in the case of the lives studied in Part I, there was no unilateral clerical response to Sor Juana's case. That the image of Sor Juana spending her final days with scourges and prayers instead of pens and books endured until the mid-1990s tells us much about the powerful effect of official church narratives on our perceptions of women.

Sor Juana's Chilean counterpart, the talented nun Ursula Suárez (1666–1749) employed humor in the account of her call to the religious life. In chapter 5 we study Ursula's use of humor to criticize norms that dictated women's subordination to men and that made many—whether as wives or nuns—economically dependent on men. Writing a *vida* at the behest of her confessor, Ursula employed the convention of the divine call and authorship, but only to redefine sanctity: she quotes God as saying he gave her a good wit and that he wanted an entertaining actress and preacher among his saints. Just as Sor Juana had reworked the *vida* genre by combining it with the epistolary tradition, Ursula wove into her narrative elements from popular literature, in particular the scenes and ideology from picaresque tales. Ursula's style is so strikingly different from that of a nun like María de San José that it raises the question of how Ursula managed such open attacks on men in general and their treatment of religious women in particular without being censored. Although Ursula was punished by one bishop, she was later promoted to abbess. Significantly, however, it seems that upon her death, no church official stepped forward to recast her life as a saintly one deserving emulation. Perhaps living in relatively provincial Santiago and in the mid–eighteenth century affected her account and her chances of being used as the subject of a posthumous biography.

In chapter 6, the questions raised by the differences in time, place, and form in Ursula's and other nuns' accounts are heightened by the more dramatic divergence of the Lieutenant Nun (La Monja Alférez), Catalina de Erauso (1582–1650). This final case study brings us full circle to Lima, Madrid, and Rome in the 1620–1630s, the very same decades that Rosa's case for canonization was halted as her circle of followers was examined by the Inquisition. Catalina deliberately rejected the religious life: she escaped the convent, dressed as a man, and became a soldier and even a murderer. Yet when her true identity was discovered by a bishop, she somehow avoided both religious and civil censure. Catalina's petitions to the Crown and pope, the autobiographical *vida* attributed to her, and several posthumous accounts serve as the sources for studying her seemingly paradoxical case. Most likely, moving from her birthplace in urban Spain to the far reaches of the Spanish American frontier allowed Catalina to reject the role as a model nun. In the frontier, "civilized" rules were often ignored. But how was it that she could petition for a reward for her military valor and a license to remain dressed as a man upon her return to the centers of European secular and sacred power? Catalina's success at these levels probably was due in large part to her skill in playing off the different expectations for men and women. The autobiographical account attributed to her combines a portrait (albeit brief) of the highly prized virginal woman with that of the valiant soldier. Moreover, as in Ursula's account, Catalina weaves into this blurred identity the negative example of a rogue. In so doing, she creates a hybrid first-person narrative, drawing on the conventions and ideology of the confessional *vida*, the soldier's story, and the picaresque narrative to create a new identity of a woman living as a man. Not surprisingly, no official church hagiography was written about Catalina. But other period genres—the broadside, the *comedia*, and a Jesuit history of Chile—retell the extraordinary life story of the "Monja Alférez." In these rewritings we see society's thirst for titillating stories balanced against the impulse to reject deviation. Each text fictionalizes the life story to make it fit better with societal codes for behavior. Catalina's life underscores how the analysis of period life writings needs to take into account the role of gender, genre, geography, and chronology.

The life stories of these six colonial women encourage us to reconsider our notion that women in colonial times were forced to choose the role of obedient wife or perfect nun. Although many no doubt followed these traditional models, others found alternate paths. Men and women worked together to construct a new society—though in distinct gender roles—and were important collaborators in the colonization process. In the chapters that follow, the voices of these women can be heard. Also evident is the esteem in which they were held by their own society. The complex interplay between church practices of confession, canonization, and Inquisition, and individuals' lives and narratives becomes apparent. These life writings by and about religious women in colonial Spanish America reveal a dynamic, multivalent process that had strong implications for individual and societal identity.

I
Potential Saints

I

Redeemer of America

Rosa de Lima (1586–1617)—The Dynamics
of Identity and Canonization

*Here is a Rose, new flower of a new world, that from the Pacific Ocean of the
Indies exudes peace, springtime, and joy. Could it be that it exudes sanctity as well?*
—Leonard Hansen, "Dedicatoria," *Vida admirable de Santa Rosa*

On April 29, 1671, bells rang throughout Lima, Peru, to announce the arrival of
the papal bull from Clement X that proclaimed America's first saint, Rosa de
Santa María. A criolla woman who was born less than a century after Columbus's
voyages to America, Rosa was elevated to the highest ranks of the Roman Catholic
Church. A contemporary Dominican chronicler, Juan de Meléndez, describes the
celebration that followed in Lima.[1] Religious brotherhoods dedicated to Rosa displayed their floats, churches brimmed over with flowers and candles for the event,
and Limeños of all classes and races poured into the streets to follow the procession.
Even the highest ranking state officials, the viceroy and vicereine, attended the Mass
in Rosa's honor and received the official Roman hagiography and portrait of the
saint. Meléndez goes on to report that when a miraculous voice spoke to the assembled
crowd, witnesses interpreted the event as yet another sign that Lima had indeed received God's favor.

Rosa de Santa María (1586–1617) had been a popular figure for Limeños for
over half a century, with mass veneration beginning almost at the moment of the
mystic's death at the age of thirty-one. Throngs of people fought to catch a glimpse
of Rosa in her open casket at the Church of Santo Domingo, where this lay holy
woman associated with the Dominican order had so often been seen in the past,
praying for Lima's inhabitants. Chronicles of the period record that the viceroy summoned the civil guard to control crowds that were clipping pieces of her clothing to
keep as holy relics.[2] Soon Limeños were adorning their houses with portraits of Rosa
in order to honor her and to invoke her protection. They also began to form religious brotherhoods and to found the Dominican Convent of Santa Catalina, whose
establishment Rosa had prophesied.[3]

Ecclesiastical officials in Lima responded immediately to this popular devotion
by taking testimony from witnesses as to Rosa's life and miracles. This first local

"diocesan process" (*proceso arzobispal*) aimed at documenting Rosa's saintly qualities for canonization took two years to complete (1617–1619). By 1625, however, the attitude of the church seems to have changed: the Inquisition in Lima had confiscated her writings, and some of her lay followers were prosecuted ("processed") by this same office. These actions reflect growing concern about the rise in local lay religious movements. In the meantime, Rosa's cause had crossed the Atlantic: in 1624 the king of Spain supported her case, and in 1630 Rome initiated a second official "apostolic process" (*proceso apostólico*) to gather further testimony about her life. But her cause came to a halt once again when Pope Urban VIII's new requirements for sanctity tabled the discussion for nearly twenty years. By the middle of the seventeenth century, a dramatic exception to the new rules allowed the case to be resumed against the backdrop of a series of hagiographic biographies whose intent was to promote the Peruvian woman. Her case now moved quickly, and Rosa was canonized in exceptionally rapid order (1656–1671). Soon, Catholics throughout the Spanish empire invoked the saint's protection, and young girls emulated Rosa's life of prayer and penance, as depicted in sacred biographies.

Until recently, critics never questioned why a young woman noted for her extreme penitential practices became an American and a European heroine, exalted equally by king and pope, Spaniards and Limeños, Dominican clergy and young girls. The more than four hundred works published about her before the twentieth century simply recount the hagiographic elements of Rosa's life that had been established in the seventeenth century. But that uniformity has been shaken since then, with the publication of primary texts that cast Rosa's life in a new light. Domingo Angulo published several of Rosa's letters (1917), Bruno Cayetano and Luis Millones published significant portions of the canonization testimony (1992, 1993), and Luis Getino rediscovered and published Rosa's iconolexic collages about her spiritual life (1937). Significantly, Getino argues that Rosa's intellectual ingenuity matched that of Saint Teresa.[4] More recently, with the emergence of new cultural histories and the study of *mentalités*, critics have begun to examine the broader contexts of Rosa's life: the role of the Counter-Reformation, the extirpation of idolatrous practices in Peru, and the development of a criollo identity. Scholars such as Luis Galve, Frank Graziano, Teodoro Martínez Hampe, Fernando Iwasaki, Luis Millones, and Ramón Mujica Pinilla pose the question of why Rosa de Lima was America's first saint. Although their arguments differ, all agree that she became a valuable symbol of identity for Lima during a time of dramatic changes, in both the city and the Catholic Church.[5] A recent study of the politics, dogma, and iconography involved suggests that Rosa was in the right place at the right time and that her image could be molded to fit the changing the needs of the faithful.[6]

Building on the work by Galve, Iwasaki, and Mujica Pinilla, in particular, I propose to reformulate the question of why Rosa was the first New World saint and pose some additional questions: What role was played by the changing church standards for sainthood? Why did some clerics promote hagiographies about Rosa's life, while others limited access to the spiritual writings and public works of Rosa and her friends? What was omitted in the process of representing Rosa as an official saint? Responding to these questions may further our understanding of the process of defining official sanctity, which affected individual spiritual practices and popular culture; it may also shed light on attempts to control lay spirituality and to regulate the role of women within the church. Before these questions can be addressed directly, a brief biographical account is in order.

The Holy Portrait of America's Rosa

By the time of Rosa's birth in 1586, Lima, named by conquistadors as the City of the Kings and founded by Francisco Pizarro fewer than fifty years earlier, was a place of extreme contrasts and rapid growth. Innovations in silver production and the establishment of Spanish institutions had created a densely populated and racially mixed city of both splendor and squalor; moreover, Lima was vulnerable to the dangers of earthquakes and pirates, as well as the deep political and religious rifts that ran through the entire viceroyalty of Peru. Struggles over Indian labor, native rebellions, civil wars, factions within religious orders, and unrest due to the extirpation movement of native religions in the Andes characterized the civil and ecclesiastical politics of the period. The opulence of city architecture and the wealth of the criollo elite stood in stark contrast to the increasing numbers of American-born vagabonds, displaced indigenous peoples, and African slaves.[7]

In this cauldron of social and economic unrest, religious fervor and asceticism flourished. With the arrival of the new archbishop Toribio de Mogrovejo in 1581, the Peruvian church took new initiatives, setting up a printing press to publish catechisms and devotional works and establishing a council, the Concilio Limense (1582), to centralize the process of evangelization. Men and women flocked to religious houses, giving their lives to the church. By 1614, at least 10 percent of the estimated 25,454 inhabitants were members of religious orders.[8] A significant number of these men and women would subsequently receive special recognition from the church. Besides Rosa, three Limeños from the early seventeenth century would later be canonized by Rome, not to mention a substantial list of aspirants whose cases were to receive serious consideration.[9]

In this city that was filling with both riches and ascetic saints, Rosa lived, died, and was later proclaimed a saint. Most of the information about her life comes from the two canonization processes (in 1617–1619 and 1630–1632) and hagiographic stories of her heroic Christian behavior.[10] Briefly, Rosa was born Isabel Flores de Oliva to María de Oliva and Don Gaspar de Flores, one of eleven children. Divine favor reportedly blessed the infant when a servant saw the baby's face transformed into a rose, a symbol of a European flower transplanted to the New World. From that day forward, the child was called Rosa. At age five, the girl heard the life story of the popular Italian saint, Catherine of Siena (1347–1380), and soon she began to imitate her ascetic practices. One source states that Rosa soon memorized the complete life story of Catherine.[11] Like the Italian holy woman, Rosa built a hut in her backyard for prayer and penitential practices.

Rosa's parents were criollos of modest means. Although her father had received a post as an arms-maker (*arcabuquero*) for the king, at times he worked at several modest occupations, including that of dyer. Rosa's mother and sisters supplemented the family's income by sewing and running a home school for girls learning needlework. During her adolescent years, Rosa moved to the Andean mountain town of Quives, where her father worked for a period as overseer of an *obraje* (textile factory employing conscripted Indian labor).[12] Biographers say little about these years, but they do mention Rosa's compassion for indigenous laborers and her confirmation by the bishop and future saint, Toribio de Mogrovejo.

By the time of her return to Lima, Rosa, like her exemplar Catherine of Siena, had received the spiritual gift of mystic marriage to Christ. She then chose a lifestyle that was appropriate to her spirituality, that of a lay holy woman, and became known only by her religious name of Rosa de Santa María. Not surprisingly, this choice set her in conflict with both her mother (who wanted her to marry) and with her confessor (who wanted her to enter a convent). Biographers report that Rosa undermined her mother's efforts to present suitors for marriage by putting hot chili peppers in her eyes, and her confessor's efforts to make her a nun by freezing in place when she was on her way to the Convent of Santa Clara.[13] Later, Rosa became a tertiary—first informally associated with the Franciscan order (ca. 1603–1607)—and then the Dominican order (ca. 1607), like her model Catherine. She took simple religious vows, which required chastity, poverty, and obedience, but did not require perpetual enclosure.

During this time Rosa followed a rigorous schedule of work, prayer, and penance. The proceedings for her canonization state that she generally worked ten hours a day, prayed twelve hours, and slept two.[14] Much of her workday consisted of sewing for her mother. To keep herself awake at night and pray, she was given to hanging herself by her hair. Other severe penances included wearing a crown of thorns (later, of metal) and sleeping on a bed that was designed to cause suffering. Her first biographer, Pedro Loayza, elaborates:

> From a tender age she slept on beds made for penitents. The first one that she had was made of three wide planks, one wider than the others, and the one that served as the headboard had a hole into which she inserted her head; in this way was her body broken in or yoked like a burro, and when she woke up, she would place these planks under the bed. This saintly woman also made another bed out of seven sticks, latticed in the form of a grill, out of some cattle horns, which she placed on a board, and between the joints she placed many sharp ceramic shards, and she would lay down on them, not in order to sleep but, rather, to suffer. The board was set so that the shards stayed in place and would not fall to the floor, and the sticks, so that they would not lean against her body. She slept on this bed for fifteen or sixteen years.[15]

Rosa's most famous biographer, Leonard Hansen, depicts her self-mortification in yet more detail. She walked barefoot in the garden with a heavy cross on her shoulders, suffered painful illnesses, and whipped herself as atonement for the sins of the world:

> Every night she whipped her back bloody so hard and cruelly that blood splattered the walls, the floor and her clothing, for the innocent maiden

believed that she deserved all these punishments for her sins. In addition to these, filled with compassion in times of public calamities, she endeavored to imitate her Teacher [Catherine of Siena] with acts of penitence, placating the wrath of God and mitigating His justice, for which she would wound her body, sometimes for the troubles afflicting the entire Holy Mother Church, other times for the anguish and dangers suffered by her homeland, mercilessly making of herself a bloody sacrifice, in order thereby to gain the mercy of Heaven and to heal the common wounds with wounds of her own.[16]

Rosa's fasts were equally rigorous. Again like Catherine of Siena, she tried to subsist by eating nothing but the Communion host, although she added a New World element to the regimen: Indian servants helped with her special diets and mortifications. The belief was that fasting and penances helped to purify the person and redeem humankind.

Rosa's spiritual practice included active prayer for souls and for the city of Lima. Biographers report she was graced with divine gifts such as intercessional powers, mystical union with Christ, and prophecy. According to Counter-Reformation doctrine and popular belief, such powers were the physical manifestation and outgrowth of Rosa's chosen status before God. She spent hours in solitary prayer beseeching God's intervention to cure a variety of community ills that ranged from natural disasters to suffering souls in purgatory. As the intermediary for miracles, Rosa tamed both earthquakes and disease-carrying mosquitoes as God responded to her appeals to save her native city from destruction.

By 1613, Rosa took up residence with a neighboring family, the Gonzalo de la Mazas, whose home was a haven for pious local lay people. There Rosa developed her spiritual gifts as she advised Jesuits and Dominican friars, visited prominent women, established a circle of religious followers, and taught her patron's two daughters. She also formed prayer groups when the city was in danger. Hagiographers credit her group's intercessory powers with saving Lima in 1615 from the Dutch Protestant pirate Janis van Speilberg. Although she was active in the local community, as a woman Rosa was prohibited from carrying her evangelism beyond the city to the Andean foothills where native Americans lived. As one confessor noted, Rosa lamented these limitations: "'Oh, I wish I were a man, just so I could participate in the conversion of souls,' and to this end she exhorted all the preachers she knew to convert many souls and to go out and make all the idolaters of this land surrender to God. And she urged that they make this the primary goal of their studies."[17] A visible yet at times reclusive figure within Lima, Rosa became popularly known as one of its protectors during her own lifetime.

Even though Rosa was recognized for her spiritual gifts and compassion, she was nonetheless scrutinized by the Inquisition. In 1614, Rosa was examined informally by several members of the Inquisition, but the consensus was that Rosa was following an orthodox path. Within three years of her examination and after years of extreme fasts and penances, Rosa was dead. In his testimony, Gonzalo de la Maza reports: "The health and constitution of the said blessed Rosa was by then so wasted by so many ailments and pains that she could not produce anything of note at her labors nor help her parents in the way that she had done during the course of her life."[18] Upon her death, a number of her closest followers reportedly experienced flights of spirit (*arrobamientos*), several of which are transcribed in the canonization processes as a sure sign of Rosa's holiness.[19] In the years following her death, Catholics in places as far away as Antwerp and Sicily were interviewed as witnesses to Rosa's miraculous intercessions.[20]

The first stage in Rosa's canonization process began immediately upon her death and was initiated by at least three sections of Limeño society: city officials, the Archbishop of Lima, and the Dominican order.[21] For two years, from 1617 to 1619, an official council took testimony from witnesses close to Rosa, including some seventy-five family members, members of her religious circle, and various clergymen, mostly Dominican friars and Jesuits.[22] More than half the witnesses were male religious. Included in this canonization file is a short biography written by her Dominican confessor, Pedro de Loayza.[23] During these years, popular veneration of Rosa grew so rapidly that the Dominicans decided to exhume Rosa's body and move her tomb to a more visible place in the Church of Santo Domingo (1619). A second Dominican confessor, Luis de Bilbao, delivered a panegyric sermon to celebrate the occasion.

Given this evidence of Rosa's spiritual stature among the laity and the Dominicans, the suspension of her cult in Lima five years later comes as a surprise. A reason for the suspension may rest with the Dominicans themselves, who were experiencing a schism in their order, occasioned in part by a dispute over the choice of a candidate to promote as a Dominican saint.[24] Not only was the cult suspended, but the censor of the Inquisition, Luis de Bilbao—one of Rosa's own confessors—demanded (in compliance with the Inquisitor General's orders in 1622) that Rosa's works and personal effects be turned over to his office.[25] The Inquisition also examined many of Rosa's followers for evidence of the heretical practice of illuminism (*alumbradismo*).[26] Her lay spiritual guide, Juan del Castillo, and her close companion, María Luisa Melgarejo, had their writings censured, and a handful of lay holy women were publicly processed by the Inquisition. Ironically, while Limeños were debating the spiritual practices of Rosa and her group, officials in Spain began to promote her case. King Philip IV sent the 1617 *Proceso* to the Council of the Indies, which then forwarded it to the Spanish ambassador in Rome in 1624. The king was so enthusiastic about Rosa's sanctity that he soon named her patron of his armed forces, even though she was not yet a saint.

Although the case stagnated for several years, by 1630 the Holy See in Rome had opened an official inquiry into canonization.[27] Now out of the hands of Limeños, local Dominicans, and the Crown, the case was solely under the jurisdiction of the highest ecclesiastical office. In this *Proceso apostólico*, officials interviewed a larger and broader cross-section of society: of the 147 witnesses about half were women, and many were ordinary citizens. Spurred perhaps by the immense popular devotion to Rosa, the church increasingly shifted its focus from associating Rosa with the Dominican order to making her a symbol for the city of Lima. The complete apostolic document for Rosa's canonization was presented to the Vatican's Sacred Congregation of Holy Rites in 1634.

But Rosa's case came to another halt because of Pope Urban VIII's reforms. Responding to Protestant attacks on Catholic veneration of saints, the pope added new rules to the Council of Trent's stated criteria for sanctity. The new rules encouraged more historical documentation about a candidate's life and required that fifty years elapse between the death of a candidate and consideration of the individual's case for sanctity. Rosa had died only seventeen years earlier.

In 1656, a new pope, Alexander VII, made an exception to the fifty-year rule, and heavy lobbying by the Dominicans in Rome and the Spanish Crown helped to reactivate Rosa's candidacy. A rapid succession of events ensued. A year later, King Philip IV sent his ambassador to Rome, again to promote the case. The influential English Dominican, Leonard Hansen, was asked in 1664 to write a biography of Rosa. His four-hundred-page Latin text, *Vita Mirabilis Mors Pretiosa Venerabilis Sororis Rosa de S. Maria,* became the most successful hagiography of her life. Written by someone who never knew her, the account, which drew on the two *procesos,* nonetheless offers a compelling portrait of Rosa as the Catherine of Siena of the New World. Although initially written for a Roman audience, the biography was quickly translated into several languages and widely disseminated, hence becoming a valuable tool for promoting Rosa's cause.[28] In spite of several competing biographies, Hansen's work became the classic life of Rosa over the course of the next few centuries. In addition to the commission of Leonard's hagiography, the Dominican González de Acuña was sent to Rome to oversee Rosa's case (1661), and the queen of Spain, Mariana of Austria, sent a petition to Rome on Rosa's behalf (1665). Reports of local miracles and celebrations in Lima and miraculous apparitions of Rosa in Europe further pressured Rome. In 1668 Rosa de Santa María was beatified; in 1669 Pope Clement IX declared Rosa patron of Lima and Peru; in 1670 Pope Clement X extended this title to patron of America and the Philippines; and in 1671 Rosa became a saint.

During the next century, dozens of hagiographic representations of Rosa emerged in paintings and texts.[29] Popular images of the saint include Rosa holding the city of Lima in her hand; appearing as a double for the beloved Virgen del Rosario; carrying an anchor to symbolize her faith; and practicing severe mortification.[30] (See figures 1.1 and 1.2.) Rosa became a symbol for a Catholic America and a reason for celebration. As part of the festivities held in Lima upon Rosa's canonization, for example, a poetry contest (*certamen*) was held.[31] More traditional religious works, such as prayerbooks, novenas, and sermons based on the saint's life and prayers, also were published extensively in Lima and Mexico. In increasingly grandiloquent, symbolic language, criollos and Spaniards alike turned Rosa into a religious and political icon. For the latter, she often represented a new type of conquistador, while for the former, the saint proved America's parity with the Old World.[32] For both, Rosa was a powerful symbol of America's triumphant Roman Catholic Christianity.

The Spanish Count Oviedo y Herrera, previously posted to Peru, wrote a lengthy epic poem in 1711, portraying the saint as being integral to the conquest and evangelization of America.[33] In a license to publish a sermon preached to celebrate Rosa's beatification, the censor for the Inquisition represents Rosa as converting the American "jungle": her "virtuous fragrances . . . have converted into a paradise of holy delights the previously barbarous jungle of our South America."[34] Whereas Rosa's model,

FIGURE 1.1 "Los pueblos rinden culto a la Bienaventurada Rosa of Santa María" by Lázaro Baldi, 1668, in the Iglesia Santa María Sopra Minerva, Rome (Courtesy of Ramón Mujica Pinilla)

FIGURE 1.2 "Penetencias para vencer el sueño" by Laureano Dávila, eighteenth century, in the Monasterio de Santa Rosa, Santiago de Chile (Courtesy of Ramón Mujica Pinilla)

Catherine of Siena, had labored among Christians to reform and further Dominican causes, Rosa, her devotees insisted, had sought to convert pagans to Christianity. Through her, Rome itself was to be brought to an acceptance of America's essential role in the history of the Universal Catholic Church. Rosa became the symbol for a New World that had been saved—evidence that the idolatrous practices of natives had been conquered and Catholicism firmly implanted. The Dominican chronicler Juan Meléndez once again captures the common sentiment as he calls her "our heroic criolla," the "redeemer" of the New World, in a world in which there are "two spheres," Lima and Rome.[35]

Hagiography and Rescripting a Life Story

An examination of the canonization process and hagiographies suggests that ideology and practice with regard to sainthood changed in the Counter-Reformation Catholic Church of the seventeenth century. The early church's original definition

of saint as any holy person became more complex as church bureaucracy and centralization grew.[36] By Rosa's time, Rome orchestrated all canonization processes in
its struggle to balance popular veneration of local holy people with the new requirements for official recognition of a saint. As a result, there was a long hiatus from
1629 to 1658 when no new saints were added to Catholic altars.[37] Besides demonstrating doctrinal purity and the theological virtues of faith, hope, and charity, a
Counter-Reformation saint had to demonstrate heroic virtue in the faithful imitation of Christ through asceticism, contemplation, and active service to Christianity.
As the renunciation of worldly passions and possessions, asceticism strengthened the
individual in stamping out vices and following Christ in suffering for the sins of others.
Contemplation and prayer also drew a person closer to God, by developing the art
of spiritual dialogue and the readiness to receive divine messages. A saint might then
witness divine grace working through her in the form of such miracles as healings,
prophecies, and intercessions, as well as corporeal, imaginary, and intellectual visions.[38]
Unlike saints from earlier periods, however, Counter-Reformation saints needed only
a few miracles to prove their sanctity, while proof of heroic virtue carried far more
weight. Such heroic lifestyles had to reflect post-Tridentine guidelines that advocated subordination to the guidance of ecclesiastical hierarchy and observance of the
sacraments—in particular, confession and communion.

    These official requirements for sainthood influenced the *procesos* and the hagiog-
raphies about Rosa's life. All texts accentuate Rosa's ascetic, prayerful, and heroic
life. The hagiographies also seek to inspire emulation in readers. The standard questions asked of most witnesses in the processes of 1617–1619 and 1630–1632 elicited
critical biographical information, as well as evidence of Rosa's moral qualities and
the special merits she received through divine action. A second set of questions from
the 1630s documented miraculous intercessions.[39] Closely following the structure and
information of the two *procesos*, hagiographies delineate the life of Rosa according to
ideals of heroic virtue and God's grace; individual aspects of her life story are far less
important than proving her conformity within the community of saints. Following
a two-part organization, the hagiographies generally recount the chronological life
and death of the subject, and then examine the virtues. (A variation was to narrate
the life, the virtues, and then the death of the subject.) The life narrative sets forth
examples of moral behavior, prayer and penance, observance of the sacraments and
dogma, and evidence of God's hand working directly in the subject's life. Leonard
Hansen's popular hagiography of Rosa clearly demonstrates his awareness of these
guidelines for the representation of sanctity: the preliminary pages explain his historical method and emphasize his close observation of the guidelines established by
the Congregation of Holy Rites: "This history was not taken from apocryphal accounts lacking weight and authority, but rather from the proceedings that by order
of the Holy See were held in Lima, in order to list her in the catalogue of the saints."[40]
Serving as proof of sanctity (before 1671) and exemplary models for the faithful,
hagiographical narratives of Rosa were the church's public representation of a holy
life according to post-Tridentine rules.

    The question arises, however, as to whether material was omitted in the process
of establishing Rosa's conformity with the criteria for sanctity. Probably there were

not-so-holy elements in Rosa's life—or at least, elements that the church did not want to promote publicly. Two topics recur in the *procesos* and hagiographies that are polemical yet carefully controlled for meaning: the fact that Rosa had been questioned informally by several members of Lima's Inquisition and the fact that she wrote about her spiritual life. Although Hansen presents the interrogation as proof of her orthodoxy and her poetry and prayers as spontaneous compositions for God,[41] the historical record of events between 1622 and 1625 indicates that Rosa's group threatened goals the church had set in Lima and that she may have been an accomplished mystic writer. Like Teresa of Avila, Luis de León, John of the Cross, and Ignatius of Loyola in sixteenth-century Spain, Rosa appears to have been the subject of Inquisitorial scrutiny, and her spiritual writings and public teachings were censored because the orthodoxy of her beliefs and behavior were suspect. At the time, the political and ecclesiastical climate in Spain was such that this censorship was generally overturned, and subsequent hagiographies silenced or reinterpreted the Inquisitorial interventions in the lives of saints. In Rosa's case, her 1614 examination by the Inquisition ultimately served to help build a saintly portrait of her.

The first *proceso* records the 1614 examination of Rosa as a dialogue among the lay doctor employed by the Holy Office in Lima, Juan del Castillo, her confessor, the Inquisitor Fray Juan de Lorenzana, and Rosa, with her mother observing the encounter.[42] When Castillo asked Rosa about her "interior impulses," including her prayers, visions, and penances, she responded by speaking of her spiritual practice and supernatural encounters with the divine. He continued the exploration of her spirit by asking if she had experienced authentic mystic union with the divine (*oración de unión*), characterized by the highest level of visionary activity ("intellectual visions"), or whether she had brought these supernatural occurrences on herself, perhaps by fasting too severely. More important, Castillo and Lorenzana wanted to differentiate her spiritual practices from those of the *alumbrados* and thus define them as orthodox. Castillo based his inquiry on Teresa's mysticism, which he had studied for his own book of commentaries on the Spanish saint's writings. The verdict was that Rosa was privy to the highest form of religious experience, thus making her a bonafide mystic.[43]

In quoting passages from this dialogue with the inquisitors, most biographers describe the process as the rustic talking to learned men about divine mysteries. Hansen places the examination in the context of the popular dialogue genre—which focused on drawing out an essential truth—and presents the place, interlocutors, and theme of the dialogue. He argues that the examination provided proof of her sanctity,[44] because Castillo was a well-known authority on mysticism and Lorenzana—in his triple role as prior of a Dominican monastery, university professor, and censor for the Inquisition—was an expert on discerning people's spirits. The series of questions posed to Rosa moved quickly from an examination about suspect spiritual activity to using her as a springboard to discuss the authentic mystic path. The dialogic process ultimately uncovers a fundamental truth and serves as a vehicle to further church doctrine. Rosa becomes the unlettered authority about divine mysteries: "All were astonished by the responses of a simple, unlettered girl, when asked about the secret mystery of the Holy Trinity . . . and the fact that so many matters hidden from wise and prudent men, are revealed and made manifest to the humble, to children, and to the unlettered. . . . It seemed to Lorenzana that he was seeing not a woman, but rather a mature professor of one branch or another of theology."[45] They all concluded "[that] the spirit of God worked through her, that she was filled with the gift of wisdom, that she was led by infused wisdom from Heaven."[46] Rosa had intuitive knowledge of God.

What hagiographers like Hansen tended to ignore is that within ten years of this inquiry this same office severely undermined access to Rosa's own words and those of her followers. Biographers and witnesses rarely mention the Holy Office's second intervention in the 1620s when it confiscated Rosa's works and began a systematic silencing of lay religious people close to her. This may appear to be a contradictory church response, but it served the single purpose of controlling direct public access to powerful lay people's spiritual works. Ironically, the man who was instrumental in establishing Rosa's orthodoxy in the 1614 examination, and who had been a key witness in the first *proceso*, was now censored by the Inquisition on two counts. As Mujica Pinilla has shown, Juan de Castillo's commentaries on the mystic process, which were based primarily on Teresa's *Vida* and *Interior Castle*, were proclaimed in 1624 to be "heterodox" because he "corrected" Teresa.[47] More significantly, he was accused of overstepping his bounds as a lay person ("for he is a mere lay person and not a theologian") and of inciting pious lay women (*beatas*) to have visions: "By confusing them he controls all their spiritual affairs, by which means he seeks to deceive many simple little women [and] seeing how for others this is a hot commodity he has written a book of his own revelations and four notebooks about the synopsis and revelations of Mother Teresa."[48] Castillo himself received a light sentence, but his works fared less well: they were removed from circulation.[49] Notably, when Hansen wrote his biography forty years later, he did not mention Castillo's encounter with the Inquisition. Hansen presents the doctor as one of the most learned men in Lima, who, despite his lay status, was considered an expert on mystical theology; he argues that Castillo's knowledge was not just a matter of "speculative discourses," but was based rather on his own spiritual experiences and treatises ("tratados"). Because Castillo had officially authorized Rosa's mystical vocation, it was important to portray him as an authority on the topic and emphasize that his "life was a mirror of virtue."[50]

The Inquisition also questioned Rosa's close companion, María Luisa Melgarejo, who had been a key witness for promoting Rosa's sanctity in the 1617 *proceso*. In 1623, Inquisitors were particularly concerned about María Luisa's prolific spiritual journals (by some counts there were at least fifty-nine). The notebooks had begun to circulate in manuscript, and some clergymen feared they would be misinterpreted as *alumbradismo*. Although María Luisa's confessor had already censored the notebooks before turning them over to the Holy Office, they were later confiscated and may have been burned.[51] Nonetheless, María Luisa was called on as a witness again for the 1630 *proceso*, and upon her death several decades later she became the subject of hagiography herself.[52] The most public messages about curbing Rosa's influence included the actions taken against some *beatas* who claimed to follow Rosa's example; they were processed by the Inquisition and convicted as *alumbradas* in the auto-da-fé that took place in Lima's Plaza Mayor in 1625.[53]

During these same years, the Inquisition confiscated Rosa's own writings, including letters, poetry, and spiritual notebooks.[54] In one of her few extant holographs, the future saint mentions that she had written spiritual texts ("which on various occasions I have written for the glory of God"; "the divine mercies that I have written in this way in the notebooks").[55] Several sources state more specifically that Rosa had written at least several notebooks (*cuadernos*), one containing religious poetry and another her spiritual autobiography.[56] In the struggle to define sanctity and heresy, a 1624 edict of the Inquisition required that these documents be turned over to the Holy Office for scrutiny.[57] A document from the Lima office sent to Madrid registers her "book manuscript" as receiving a severe "going-over" (*calificación*).[58] New research at the Convent of Santa Rosa in Lima may uncover some of these lost texts.[59] Until such time, however, two autograph documents are significant. One of Rosa's letters, published for the first time in 1917, reveals that she was a capable organizer and worked hard to found a convent in spite of resistance from the Dominican order. She mentions marshaling support from Juan del Castillo, collecting funds, and arranging for a statue of the patron saint to be brought from Seville, and she notes that four women were already wearing Dominican nuns' habits.[60] Yet more revealing is the collage housed at the Dominican Monasterio de Santa Rosa and published for the first time in the 1930s: it suggests that hagiographic representations of Rosa focused on her penitential practices and downplayed her knowledge of the mystical life and texts.[61]

From the first, Hansen's biography downplays the extent of Rosa's learning. In a chapter dealing with her upbringing, he mentions "education" in the very title,[62] but the narrative only develops Rosa's physical suffering from an early age: she patiently endured deafening earaches, illnesses, and cuts. A handful of chapters later we find out that Rosa did know how to read, but Hansen mentions it strictly in the context of Rosa learning how to imitate the lives of Catherine of Siena and the famous Mexican hermit and ascetic, Gregorio López. He privileges her mortification over her learning: "It is amazing that a body so emaciated and consumed by so many fasts had enough room to receive lashes, and enough blood to flow from these. Nevertheless, so great was the desire and care that Rosa had in punishing her body that it was necessary that her confessors restrain her in this."[63] When talking about the prayers and songs Rosa composed, Hansen presents them only briefly and as spontaneous compositions inspired by God.

Other biographers and witnesses also describe Rosa's penitential practices and record Rosa's spontaneous composition of rather simple religious songs and prayers. Confessors and family members note Rosa's habit of singing devotional couplets and accompanying herself on guitar:

Leave me, little bird
flee the agile singer,
but you are always with me
my sweet Redeemer:
Gentle nightingale,
let us praise the Lord;

you extol your Creator,
I sing to my Savior.[64]

She also made word plays on her names (Flores y Oliva, flowers and olive trees):

Oh, Jesus of my soul!
How wonderfully you appear
among the flowers and the roses
and the olive groves of green.[65]

The prayers attributed to Rosa mention divine love, gratitude, and God's magnificence. Based on the rosary, her "Angelic Exercise," for example, praises the Holy Trinity.[66] Some of these devotional prayers were edited (and perhaps significantly changed) by church officials and then published as official texts.

Rosa's more elaborate work, the two-part iconolexic collage, "The Mercies" (Las mercedes) and "The Mystical Stairway" (La escala mística), however, was not published or mentioned in colonial texts. Through a series of cutout hearts pierced by arrows, crosses, and lances, each surrounded by a written motto, the collage expresses Rosa's understanding of the mystic's journey of purgation, illumination, and union with the divine. Based on the early modern use of emblems to unite words with images to convey concepts, Rosa's work echoes ideas developed by Teresa and John of the Cross. The Mercedes consists of three hearts placed in a column to represent the stages to mystic union with God: the heart wounded by love for God, the heart that carries the cross and Jesus, and the heart in ecstatic flight to God and living in him. Mottos accompany each heart, and a lengthier written explanation frames the lower part of the page. (See figure 1.3.) The Escala mística continues the representation of the heart's journey to God. The center of the page has a cutout of a symbol of the fifteen "Levels of Divine Love," conceptualized as a stairway based, as the image states, on "humility" and "perfection." Thirteen hearts on either side of the steps depict how continual prayer leads to illumination and union with God. At the bottom of the page, a note in another hand (perhaps her Dominican confessor's) explains: "Favors that Our Mother and Holy Patron Saint Rosa de Santa María received, what they mean is written in her own hand."[67] (See figure 1.3.) Not only does the collage have an admirable primitive artistry, but also it reveals a significant ingenuity and understanding of mystic theology and the emblematic tradition.

Like Teresa, Rosa opens her text on a paradoxical note: she is a woman writing under obedience to a confessor but who claims authority for her own mystical experience. The collages are part of the confessional process: "[Here is] that which I submit to Our Father as my only spiritual director, so that he might correct my errors, and emend that which the present work might lack or my ignorance. Many errors and faults you will find being explained by my own hand and if you find anything that is good, it will only be because of the grace of God."[68] Rosa explains further that God, rather than books, is the source of her mystic process: "I confess in all truth in the presence of God that all the mercies which I have recorded in this way in notebooks as engraved and painted on these two pieces of paper I have neither seen nor read about in any book, they are only worked through this sinner by the powerful hand of the Lord in whose book I read what is Eternal Wisdom."[69] This posture of holy ignorance and obedience to church superiors was essential for any woman mystic who sought to justify writing about her spiritual path. She further inscribed the work into the confessional process by saying that, after making a general confession with the Dominicans (ca. 1608), she composed the text:

> Out of divine mercy I received these three graces before a great tribulation that I suffered in the general confession [that I made] by order of that confessor, and it gave me so much that I deserved after having made the general confession and having suffered nearly two years of severe pains, tribulations, desolation, despair, temptations, battles with demons, the lies of confessors and of ordinary people. Illnesses, pains, fever, and, in short, all the greatest torments of hell that can be imagined during those final years, it would be five years since I received graces from the Lord that I have set down on this half sheet of paper, by the inspiration of my heart, although unworthy.[70]

Typical of most autobiographical spiritual writing by religious women in the period, this text is a result of its author enduring a period of suffering and working closely with a spiritual director. Rosa's work, although a hybrid artistic text that included both drawings and writing, is inscribed within Teresian mysticism and the "rhetoric of femininity."[71]

Yet Rosa's insistence on holy ignorance, confession, and obedience does not mean that she was literally unschooled. Again, like Teresa, Rosa had worked closely with many learned men and listened carefully to church sermons and readings. One confessor testified that Rosa memorized entire sermons after hearing them only twice.[72] She studied doctrinal works in the *Devotio moderna* tradition by the sixteenth-century Spanish author Fray Luis de Granada, consulted with the learned Juan del Castillo, and participated in extended dialogues with well-educated Jesuit and Dominican confessors, several of whom were associated with the founding of Peru's first university, the University of San Marcos.[73]

In fact, the fifteen-step "stairway" or "ladder" and the imagery of the heart participate in long iconographic and textual church traditions.[74] The idea of a ladder to the divine originated in the story of Jacob (Genesis 28:12). The two women mystics Rosa most admired, Catherine of Siena and Teresa of Avila, had both used the heart as the central metaphor for the soul flying to God.[75] Iconographic images frequently depicted Catherine with a cross embedded in a heart and Teresa with an arrow (*dardo*) piercing her heart; they symbolized the intimate relationship between the experience of divine love and the pain of surrender to it. In addition, meditation guides from the period, such as Ignatius of Loyola's *Spiritual Exercises*, encouraged the use of visual imagery in prayer, which, in turn, inspired the production of allegorical emblem books. Many of these books include images of the human heart.[76] By Rosa's time, the human heart had become the key symbol for affective piety and mysticism. Rosa may have borrowed the imagery from her Limeño contemporary, Alvárez de Paz, who published a work about a fifteen-step process of movement toward God and who had been one of Castillo's authorities in determining Rosa's orthodoxy.[77]

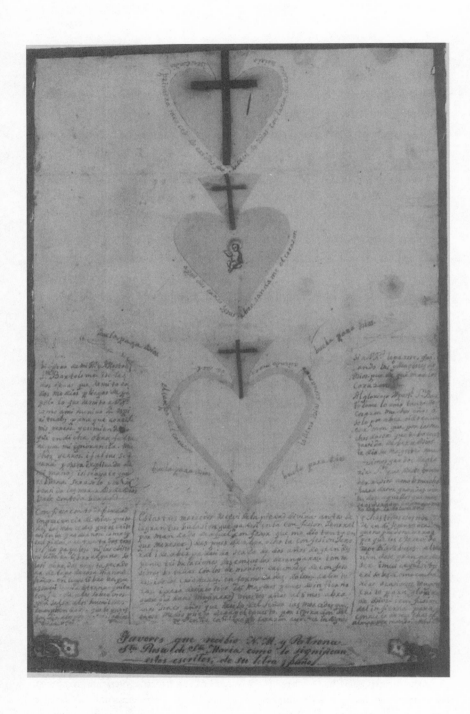

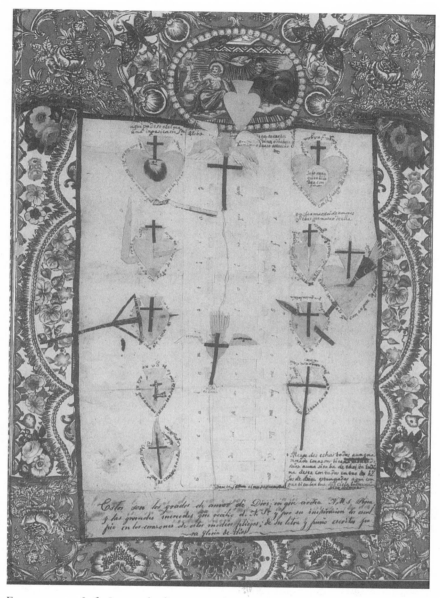

FIGURE 1.3   Left: *Las mercedes*, first page; right: *La escala mística*," second page, both by
Santa Rosa de Lima, ca. 1608, in the Monasterio de Santa Rosa, Lima (Courtesy of Ramón
Mujica Pinilla)

Or she may have read or heard about Granada's popular translation in 1562 of the seventh-century San Juan Clímaco's "Spiritual Ladder" (*Escala espiritual*) about a thirty-step spiritual process.

Rosa's conceptualization of the prayer of union and ascent to God as a mystic marriage between a bride and bridegroom came directly from church interpretations over the centuries of the biblical text, *The Song of Songs*.[78] The *Mercedes* quotes *The Song of Songs* in Latin. Because of the prohibition against lay persons reading the Bible, Rosa's source again may have been Teresa or John of the Cross. Using the spiritual analogy of God as a lover wounding his beloved in order to prepare her for union with him, Rosa's winged heart moves through the stages of being "wounded by an arrow of love," receiving the nails of Christ's painful Passion on the cross, being "sick with love, unto death," and, yet more deeply wounded by a "a fiery spear" and "arrow of divine love." These stages open the way for the purification of the heart, the recognition that one must follow the way of the cross ("life is the Cross") and finally the "spiritual betrothal" in which the winged heart flies to God in a mystical union of the soul with the Holy Spirit in divine marriage.[79] As promised in the biblical source, and reiterated by both Teresa and John, this final stage is a sort of drunkenness and loss of self in a moment of ecstasy: "Ecstasy. Intoxication in the wine cellar. Secrets of divine love. Oh happy union, in the close embrace of God!"[80]

One of the confessors who later would be instrumental in the Inquisition cases of the 1620s claimed that Rosa's understanding of church doctrine was so extensive that he would classify her as a "consummate theologian," able to speak the dogma of the Trinity and Incarnation, among other sacred topics.[81] If Rosa was indeed an accomplished mystic and writer, the question why she has been represented primarily as a woman who practiced extreme mortification is all the more insistent.

Although the hybrid artistic rendering of the mystic process in the *Escala* may have marked the text for marginalization, a more likely cause was that the church wanted to control the representation of female sanctity and to redirect the growing lay religiosity that threatened to detract from the power from of the institutional church. The Council of Trent had mandated the perpetual enclosure of nuns and encouraged women with strong religious vocations to seek the safety of the convent where confessors and rules for daily life and spiritual practice monitored their spirituality. Although often ineffective in its efforts, the church wanted demonstrations of extraordinary feminine piety to be carefully controlled and reserved for established institutions. Confessors often ordered their spiritual daughters to write about their spiritual experiences, which clergy later used as the basis for posthumous male-authored biographies about religious women. As a result, after Teresa's time, women's words rarely were published directly. In fact, Teresa's own *Vida* was in the hands of the Inquisition for many years before it was released for publication.[82]

Nancy E. van Deusen and Fernando Iwasaki argue that popular lay religious movements in Lima undermined church efforts to set limits on spiritual behavior and lay authority.[83] In fact, it is the setting of limits that differentiated saintly behavior from heretics. The church recognized the power of Rosa's life for claiming a Christian identity for America, but it also reacted to an implicit threat to post-Tridentine church efforts to enclose religious women, curb lay people's access to theological books, and limit circulation of women's—and particularly pious lay women's—writings.

Although the church considered women's spiritual texts to be valuable aids to confessors, the writings were dangerous to the welfare of both woman and church if they were made public without the editing (and censorship) of trained church clergy. Thus, the more widely the news of a holy woman spread, the more control was needed over access to her works. Rosa's works caused alarm only after the first *proceso* was completed and popular veneration and emulation of her spread throughout Lima. As her case moved up the hierarchical ladder of the church, her original words were carefully selected and reinterpreted through hagiography and the process of canonization. The events of 1623–1625 were recast. As one witness in 1630 explains, women were using Rosa's good name to authorize spiritual paths that the church did not allow: "Until today . . . although there had appeared in the said city certain women of whom it was said that they dedicated themselves to spiritual matters, it appeared afterward that they were not on the right path for the service of God because some were punished and these women conversed with the said Sister Rosa in order to see if by chance this would authorize their actions and after their sins had been revealed this discredited somewhat the said Rosa . . . and after the noise died down and the said women were punished Sister Rosa's reputation was restored."[84] The portrayal of Rosa as a writer and a lay woman with a religious vocation was downplayed as posthumous representations fixed an image of her as the Catherine of Siena of the New World. Hagiographies omitted mention of Rosa's learning and emphasized her spontaneous experience of divine love and knowledge as the outcome of her penance and prayer and of God's mercy. The church that promoted Rosa was at the same time the church that codified and controlled her.

Just as Rosa had emulated the image of Catherine of Siena that had been promoted by the latter's influential confessor/biographer Raymond of Capua, so did girls attempt to emulate Rosa after her death.[85] Girls would model their lives on Rosa's extreme penances and preparation for mystical union. And just as Rosa's case often provoked contradictory official responses, her imitators often encountered ambiguous dictates about holiness. Speaking to *beatas* about to become nuns at the new Convent of Santa Rosa in Puebla, Mexico, the Dominican Sebastián de Santander y Torres warned of the dangers of imitating Rosa's life. Using the metaphor of the mustard seed for women with a religious vocation, he says that three out of four seeds thrown into the ground outside the cloister will waste away, "as the most appropriate place for a virgin is the cloister of a convent."[86] Well aware of post-Tridentine efforts to enclose religious women, he is in a quandary as to how to exalt the virtues of the convent's patron saint, recognizing that she did not enter a convent. The women he addresses were to imitate their patron, but only to a point. Although enclosure ensured an easier road to virtue, it seemed to foreclose the possibility of achieving heroic virtue, for nuns would never be as sorely tested as their lay sisters. Only one nun from Spanish America, the Puebla Carmelite María de Jesús Tomelín (1574–1637), advanced to the first stage of consideration for sainthood. The only other American woman to become a saint was Mariana de Jesús (1618–1645), a *beata* who imitated Rosa in the city of Quito. But she was only canonized in 1950 (beatified in 1853), centuries after the threat of lay female piety had disappeared. Even Teresa of Avila, who became the Counter-Reformation female saint par excellence, who had upheld the mandate for moderate penances and had advocated strict enclosure, did not herself always remain enclosed.[87] She frequently had to break enclosure in order to travel and set up new houses. These contradictory models for female holiness permeated the period.

Rosa de Lima's case illustrates the complex and intimate connections between hagiography, emulation, confessional life writings, and canonization and Inquisition practices. There was a dynamic interplay among local agendas, the court in Madrid, the institutional church in Lima and Rome, individual confessors, hagiographers, and women's spiritual experiences and writings. At each level, the rules for holy behavior underwent reinterpretation. Hagiographic representation of Rosa's life united America with the Universal Catholic Church and attempted to control local lay movements. But the changing portrayals of her life over time also reflect the shifting official line between sanctity and heresy and the ever-narrowing role for religious women outside the cloister. The same circumstances that provided Rosa with an opportunity to undertake spiritually heroic acts also made her, or her imitators, a threat to the church. In the process of dissecting this elaborate weave, we gain a richer understanding of how holy individuals—in particular, this Peruvian lay woman—played an essential part in defining the identity of the Counter-Reformation church and of Spanish American colonial society.

Chronology of Rosa de Lima

1586	Born Isabel Gaspar y Flores Oliva, in Lima, Peru.
ca. 1593	Moves to the Andean town of Quives.
ca. 1596	Returns to Lima.
1603	Dons the third-order Franciscan habit.
1606	Becomes associated with third-order Dominicans, makes a general confession, and writes spiritual accounts.
ca. 1608–1611	Creates *Las mercedes* and *La escala mística*.
ca. 1613	Moves to the de la Maza household.
1614	Examined by the Inquisition.
1615	Dutch siege of the Port of Callao.
1617	Dies.
1617–1619	*Proceso ordinario* is begun in Lima by the archbishop; includes the first *Vida* of Rosa by Pedro de Loayza
1619	*Sermón solemne* by Luis de Bilbao is given and published.
1622	The Inquisition begins an inquiry into the lives of Rosa's followers. The Inquisition confiscates Rosa's texts and belongings. The Convent of Santa Catalina de Siena is founded in Lima.
1624	Rosa's cult is suspended; internal conflict appears in the Dominican order.
1625	Auto-da-fé punishes *alumbradas*.

1630–1632	The Holy See in Rome initiates and oversees the *Proceso apostólico*.
1633	King Philip IV sends material about Rosa's case to Rome.
1634	Rosa is formally proposed for sainthood. Her case is blocked by the new fifty-year rule established by Pope Urban VIII.
1656	The process is reopened.
1664	Leonard Hansen's *Vida* of Rosa is published for the first time.
1668	Rosa is beatified.
1670	Rosa is named patron of America and the Philippines by Pope Clement X.
1671	Rosa is canonized Rosa de Santa María and popularized as Rosa de Lima.

2

La China Poblana

Catarina de San Juan (ca. 1607–1688)—

Hagiography and the Inquisition

Everything your ministers and your Christians tell me I fail to perceive, nor to understand, because I am a simpleton, a little creature with no memory, nor understanding; speak to me in my tongue, Lord, so that I will know Your will; let Your voice sound sweetly in my ears, for I am ready to hear You and obey You.
—Alonso Ramos, quoting Catarina de San Juan, *De los prodigios*, vol. 3, 68

[De los prodigios] contains revelations, visions, and apparitions that are useless and improbable and full of contradictions and improper, indecent, and dangerous comparisons . . . [and] dangerous doctrines that contradict the understandings of the Doctors and practices of the Universal Catholic Church on no more grounds than the author's vain beliefs.
—1692 Edict of the Spanish Inquisition

Some fifteen years after bells had called Limeños to the streets to celebrate the canonization of their first saint, people living in the other Spanish viceroyality, New Spain, and its second largest city, Puebla de los Angeles, heard the death bells toll for a visionary woman from Delhi, India, who had lived in their midst for nearly seventy years. Hoping to catch a glimpse of her and to participate to some degree in her holiness, crowds descended on the house where Catarina de San Juan's body was displayed on January 5, 1688.[1] Over the next two days, the line of people waiting to enter the house grew to be four blocks long. Although she was brought to America as a slave by Portuguese pirates and sold to a couple in Puebla, Catarina had been a free woman for nearly half a century and had become a popular if reclusive visionary. The widespread recognition of her holiness earned Catarina the sort of farewell that was usually reserved for the highest elite: most of the city's ranking ecclesiastical and civic officials attended an elaborate funeral mass, and she was buried in the Jesuit Church of the Colegio del Espíritu Santo. The laudatory biographical sermon delivered at Catarina's funeral and two hagiographic biographies about her were published within four years of her death. In addition, several portraits of her went into circulation, and the little room (*aposentilla*) where she had spent much of her time praying was converted into an altar dedicated to her memory. Like Rosa, Catarina was deemed by her local community to have led a saintly life worthy of veneration.

The outpouring of popular devotion to Catarina de San Juan and the initial ecclesiastical support for it exemplifies the rise of spontaneous religious devotions in seventeenth-century Spanish America, and in Puebla in particular. Equally illustrative of the interplay between individual lives, society, and the role of the church is the denouement of Catarina's story as a local religious heroine. It provides a case study for what could go awry with cults, canonization, and hagiography. Within three years of her death, the Mexican Inquisition had prohibited the display of her portrait; by 1692, the Spanish Inquisition had banned one of the biographies on the grounds that it was blasphemous; and by 1696, eight years after Catarina's death, the Mexican Holy Office had followed suit, demanding that the biography be confiscated throughout the viceroyalty and ordering the altar dedicated to her to be boarded up. What caused the sudden campaign against devotion to Catarina de San Juan? What definitions and guidelines did church leaders use to determine sanctity and blasphemy, orthodoxy and heterodoxy?

Despite church efforts to control the dissemination of Catarina de San Juan's life story, she has been a popular local figure in Puebla and in Mexican history. Studied mostly for her strong association with the construction of Puebla's identity—first as a local hero at the end of the seventeenth century and later as a nineteenth-century Romantic figure, as the China Poblana (all peoples from Asia were called "chinos" and "poblana" refers to people living in Puebla)—such notable Mexican scholars as Francisco de la Maza, Nicolás León, and, more recently, Antonio Rubial have explored the development of Catarina de San Juan as an almost legendary figure. Rubial, in particular, highlights the role of hagiography in this process. A recent dissertation by Ronald J. Morgan further explores the relationship between one hagiographic biography on Catarina and the ambitions of her Jesuit biographer-confessor. What has not been examined in depth is the dynamic relationship between the literary hagiographic representation of Catarina and the shuffling of rules and regulations between Europe and Spanish America as the latter sought to write foundational narratives about saintly local heroes.

In theory, the same rules established by Pope Urban VIII and used for Rosa's canonization and hagiograhies were in effect for Catarina de San Juan. And yet, we saw that the line between Rosa's holiness and her followers' heresy was a thin and mercurial one: church and Crown politics, Counter-Reformation dictates, and the textual representation of sanctity played important roles in determining holiness. Like Rosa, Catarina was a lay *beata* who lived among the people of her city. Unlike Rosa, however, she was a non-white foreigner and associated with the particularly powerful—if at times problematic—religious order of the Society of Jesus, the Jesuits. Whereas biographies of America's first saint became a staple for every Spanish American convent and were widely imitated, as we will see, dissemination of Catarina's life story was curbed. Despite local efforts, her case was never heard by the Congregation of Holy Rites: while Poblanos struggled to sanctify one of their own, edicts from the Peninsula and Rome blocked their attempts. What was at stake in the posthumous literary representation of Catarina's life? The transatlantic exchanges about her case illustrate another side of the Inquisition's regulation of spirituality: for rather than conducting first-hand inquiries into lives and personal writings, the Inquisition in this case scrutinized and controlled books, specifically official church texts such as *vidas*, sermons, and religious chronicles about holy people.

By 1600 the Holy Office was firmly rooted in American soil, where like its Peninsular counterpart, it fought daily to maintain the religious and social status quo by controlling people, books, and ideas. Although the Holy Office was first run by monks and later by bishops, in 1571 the king of Spain himself took control of the Inquisition, in response to perceived abuses and ineffective administration on the part of local ecclesiastics. Striving to decrease mistreatment of the Spanish and Indian populations (the latter, in fact, became exempt from the Inquisition's control), as well as conflicts between regular and secular clergy, the 1571 edict put into place a new bureaucracy that included expert prosecutors and *calificadores* who were to examine and prepare reports about both people and printed matter of questionable orthodoxy.

As Richard Greenleaf notes, the majority of studies about the Mexican Inquisition have focused on heretics tried by the Holy Office rather than on how heresy itself was repressed.[2] Yet, the restriction of reading materials and of the circulation of ideas among New Spanish inhabitants occupied a major portion of the Inquisition's efforts—indeed, it is in this area that the Holy Office was most successful until the eighteenth century.[3] American colonists were seen by the Counter-Reformation Church as Christians living among hoards of neophyte Indians who were more vulnerable than those of European extraction to heretical ideas and to the poor examples set by fiction; as a consequence, in theory the colonists were allowed to read only books that had passed the inspection of the Inquisition. A 1571 edict made it a crime to read prohibited books, while another ordered that all such books be turned in to the Holy Office. Two years later, the Inquisition distributed the official Index of Prohibited Books to the population and created an infrastructure to search ships arriving in New Spain and to monitor book dealers and publishers in major cities. Although many books slipped through the cracks of this system, it is a telling example of the ideological hegemony the church tried to impose.[4]

The vicissitudes of the biographical portraits of Catarina de San Juan illustrate the often complex dynamics involved in determining the orthodoxy of texts and the representation of holy women in New Spain. Surprisingly, the 1689 publication of the first volume of the Jesuit Alonso Ramos's biography of Catarina, *Primera parte de los prodigios de la omnipotencia. Y milagros de la gracia en la vida de la Venerable Sierva de Dios Catharina de S. Joan ...* [First part of the Almighty's wonders and miracles that graced the life of the Venerable Servant of God Catharina de S. Joan][5]—the volume that would later be banned by the Inquisition—was at first approved by many of New Spain's highest-ranking ecclesiastical officials, even including a *calificador* for the Inquisition. Published within a year of the first part, the second volume also met with success. But soon the tide turned, and in the same year the final volume was published (1692), the first had been put on the Index of Prohibited Books in Spain. (See figure 2.1.) In a strikingly slow response, New Spain followed suit four years later. And yet, in the same year that Ramos's first volume was censored in the Peninsula,

PRIMERA PARTE
DE
LOS PRODIGIOS
DE LA OMNIPOTENCIA;
Y MILAGROS DE LA GRACIA.
EN LA
VIDA DE LA VENERABLE SIERVA DE DIOS

CATHARINA DE S. JOAN.
NATURAL DEL GRAN MOGOR, DIFUNTA
EN ESTA IMPERIAL CIUDAD DE LA PUEBLA DE
LOS ANGELES EN LA NUEVA ESPAÑA.
ESCRITA

*POR EL PADRE ALONSO RAMOS PROFESSO
de la Compañia de IESUS su vltimo Confessor, Natural de Santa
Eulalia en la Vega de Saldaña, y Reynos de Castilla la Vieja.*

DEDICALA
AL ILL.ᴹᴼ Y REV.ᴹᴼ SEÑOR
DOCTOR DON MANUEL FERNANDEZ DE
SANTA CRVZ, COLEGIAL, QVE FVE EN EL MAYOR DE
QVENCA DE SALAMANCA, Y CANONIGO MAGISTRAL
DE LA SANTA IGLESIA DE SEGOVIA. CONSAGRADO
DESPVES EN LA PRELACIA DE QVATRO IGLESIAS,
PRIMERO DE LA DE CHIAPA: DESPVES DE GVADALA-
XARA, Y ACTVAL OBISPO DE LA PVEBLA DE LOS AN-
GELES, HABIENDO SIDO ELECTO ARZOBISPO DE
✠ MEXICO: DEL CONSEJO DE SV MAGESTAD. ✠

CON PRIVILEGIO
En la Puebla, en la Imprenta Plantiniana de Diego Fernandez de Leon. Año de 1689.

FIGURE 2.1   Title page of *De los prodigios de la omnipotencia . . . en la vida de . . . Catharina de S. Joan* (vol. 1), by Alonso Ramos, 1689 (Courtesy of the Lilly Library, Bloomington, Indiana)

a much shorter version of Catarina's life story, *Compendio de la vida y virtudes de la venerable Catarina de San Juan* [Compendium of the life and virtues of the venerable Catarina de San Juan],[6] was allowed to be published in Puebla by the cleric José Castillo de Graxeda. Why should a biography of a woman who was never brought before the Inquisition for questioning about her visions and prophecies be first approved and then prohibited by the Holy Office? What did Ramos's version contain, or possibly omit, that condemned it while Graxeda's was allowed to stand? Do the *Prodigios* contain troublesome elements that "canonized" biographies, like Hansen's *Vida* of Rosa, did not? If not aimed at the circumstances of Catarina's life, why was the Inquisition concerned about the written representation of her life?

As we will see in this discussion, new rules established by the Counter-Reformation requiring historical documentation for the canonization process and new practices for representing holiness had as much to do with Ramos's failure and Graxeda's success as the Inquisition's rules for determining blasphemous books. As mentioned in chapter 1, the Council of Trent revamped the guidelines for sainthood to combat criticism of Catholicism's emphasis on affective spirituality and its cult of the saints. The new rules were heavily influenced by Renaissance humanist theories about historical truth. Ramos's extravagant claims and exclamations about the candidate's holiness clashed with the hagiographic requirements. The inclusion of somewhat unorthodox material, coupled with local politics, further tipped the scales against Ramos's work. Graxeda's text, however, attempts to balance the exotic appeal of Catarina's story with the historical rigor demanded by the church.

Catarina de San Juan and Puebla de los Angeles

History confirms few facts with regard to Catarina de San Juan, but her biographers concur on the general chronology and significant events of her life. All accounts plot a compelling story that echoes elements from the most popular forms of baroque narrative, including captive's tales, picaresque novels, and, of course, hagiographic biography. A composite account follows: born of pagan royal parents in the Mogul empire of India, Catarina (born Mirrha) was singled out at birth for special favors by the Virgin Mary. Among other incidents, she was miraculously saved as a toddler after having fallen into a river more than three days before. Within a decade of her birth, however, local wars forced Catarina and her family to flee to the coast, where the child was kidnaped by Portuguese slave traders.[7]

Catarina was taken first to Cochín and then to Manila, where she came into contact with Jesuit missionaries for the first time and converted to Christianity. In 1619, she was chosen as a house slave for the viceroy of New Spain, and the Portuguese took the adolescent girl to Acapulco. Here a change in fortune resulted in the childless couple, Margarita Chávez and Miguel Sosa, buying her and making her a privileged domestic servant. Upon Miguel's death in 1624 and her mistress's subsequent decision to enter the convent, Catarina was given her freedom and offered a place in the convent as a lay servant, which, like Rosa before her, she chose not to accept. Soon she took a position as a domestic servant for the noted priest, Pedro Suárez, who at one time had served as confessor for Puebla's most famous local holy woman, the nun María de Jesús Tomelín. Although Catarina had already taken a vow of chastity and had prayed (successfully, according to the accounts) to look old and ugly in order to ward off men's advances, Suárez ordered her to marry his "chino" slave, Domingo. She now fought heroically to maintain a chaste marriage with an abusive husband.

By the 1640s, both husband and master had died, and Catarina at last was free to devote her life to Christ as a lay holy woman, a *beata*. She took no formal religious vows, but lived a life of reclusion, prayer, and penance in a small room that a wealthy neighbor had given her across from Catarina's favorite church, El Colegio del Espíritu Santo, run by the Jesuits. She appears to have supported herself by sewing and making chocolate. Later, an elite couple, Captain Don Hypólito Castillo y Altra and his wife Doña Juana Mexia Moscoso, took Catarina under their wing. As in Rosa's case, Catarina's benefactors provided her with room and board while she provided spiritual benefits to the household. Within these confines, Catarina exemplified Christian virtue. She dedicated her life to works of charity and prayer. Biographers report her generosity with beggars, her supernatural gift for reviving moribund dogs, and her wise counsel to people who sought her guidance. Yet the majority of her time was spent praying for the larger Christian community, experiencing visions of a host of heavenly figures, and making prophecies about Jesuit souls, important political and ecclesiastical figures, and events in the Spanish empire, such as the arrival of ships from Spain and battles in Europe. During these years in Puebla, Catarina was under the guidance of a noted Jesuit, Miguel Godínez, the author of an important guide about mysticism. He even gave her several devotional books, although others had to read them to her since she was illiterate. Significantly, Godínez and other local clergy considered Catarina a bonafide mystic, blessed with God's special mercies and visions. Local townspeople knew Catarina because she could often be seen praying at the Jesuit church or performing acts of charity. She lived the last four decades of her life under the protection of the Jesuits, following this charitable, contemplative, visionary path.

Nearly blind and half-paralyzed by a stroke, Catarina de San Juan died in 1688. Her last will and testament provide a glimpse of her poverty and devotion, as she donated her few belongings to the poor: a statue of Christ, a few paintings and devotional books, a small box, and her clothing.[8] Upon her death, commoners and high-ranking officials alike declared that the octogenarian China Poblana had died in the "odor of sanctity." As mentioned, crowds fought to see her one last time before her burial; many reportedly tried to tear off a bit of her tunic in order to have a personal relic that might provide a powerful link to this charismatic woman.

As these highly charged scenes of popular devotion suggest, Catarina de San Juan lived in a deeply religious society that believed in the importance and efficacy of local holy people bringing special divine favor to their community. The biographies written about Catarina contribute to this broader religious and spiritual phenomenon occurring in Puebla; the city tops the list of colonial Spanish cities devoted to publishing the life stories of its holy people. In many ways, Puebla was the criollo center of Spanish America, and its publication efforts reflect this status. Unlike the two viceregal centers in Lima and Mexico City, Puebla elite prided themselves on having the largest percentage of criollo population, riches, and religious institutions. Located on the Royal Road that led from the key port of Vera Cruz to Mexico City, Puebla was a rich center for farming, trading, and the textile industry. Local merchants and landholders of Spanish descent were eager to establish the importance of their city to the Spanish Empire and Christian history. Promoting local religious heroes was key to the process. Like the other mostly feminine subjects of these hagiographic *vidas*, Catarina is lauded for continuing the spiritual conquest of America that had begun more than a century before by the conquistadors: through creating a virtual paradise of Christian virtue in the "New World," she served as a valuable example to both the New World and the Old.[9]

Curiously, although Catarina de San Juan was clearly not a criolla, she was intimately linked from her first years with the most significant criollo male and female church members in seventeenth-century New Spain. The founder of the Carmelite convent in Puebla, Isabel de la Encarnación, and the Conceptionist María de Jesús Tomelín, who was heavily promoted for beatification, had been informal spiritual teachers for Catarina; she had talked with both women, particularly with the latter, through convent grilles, as well as by supernatural communication.[10] Of the host of notable seventeenth-century clerics who had been involved in creating these exemplars of holiness, four men became especially involved in Catarina de San Juan's spiritual path. Juan Palafox y Mendoza, the controversial bishop of Puebla from 1640 to 1649, was himself entered into the canonization process. His successor, Manuel Fernández de Santa Cruz, is well known in our century for his role as the real addressee of Sor Juana Inés de la Cruz's *Respuesta*, but he was famed in his own epoch for founding many religious institutions and promoting María de Jesús's case in Rome. The Jesuit Antonio Núñez de Miranda had been Sor Juana's antagonistic confessor, as well as a noted theologian and *calificador* Miguel Godínez, as noted above, was the influential Jesuit author of several manuals on mysticism. Although Spanish law prohibited the non-white Catarina from being a nun, a prestigious status that required full Spanish ancestry and often a hefty dowry, race did not keep her from intimate contact with prominent religious figures.

Hagiographies and Biographies

With all the attention that Catarina received from male and female spiritual leaders, it is not surprising that she was an important figure in society and the subject of no fewer than three biographies. What is surprising, perhaps, is that a city that prided itself on its criollismo would arduously promote a non-white, non-native woman as a symbol for their city. One of her biographers proclaims:

> The Lord could not have designated the purpose or the glory of this work except to the very Illustrious and Imperial City of Puebla de los Angeles; for the great Emperor Charles V . . . had desired to ennoble it with his own coat of arms. . . . From the time the Handmaid of the Lord entered this city, it had two paired coats of arms: those of the Emperor, which ennoble it, and those of Catharina, which defend it; the Handmaid of the Lord was

the most efficient weapon Puebla had, for many times she defended it from enemies.[11]

Although there are a fair number of other *vidas* published about exemplary native American men and women, none are as extensive as the works on Catarina de San Juan.[12] In fact, Ramos's three-volume *De los prodigios* weighs in as the longest work published in New Spain.[13] And yet, it is the only *vida* that I have found to date that was censored by the Inquisition; because so many licenses were required for publication, most problematic texts were censored before they even went to press. A closer look at the narrative construction and content of the biography of Catarina de San Juan reveals a complex, dynamic process in which literary representation and doctrine were perhaps as important as religious affiliations and race.

Although this discussion focuses on the portraits of Catarina de San Juan in Ramos's and Graxeda's full-length biographies, the Jesuit Francisco de Aguilera's hagiographic *Sermon en que se da noticia de la vida... de la Venerable Señora Chatharima de San Joan* [Sermon reporting the life . . . of the Venerable Senora Chatharima de San Joan] (1688) deserves mention as the founding narrative for her story; he sketches themes that will show up full-blown in Ramos's biography. First delivered shortly after her death to an emotionally charged group of Poblanos attending her funeral, the sermon introduces the China Poblana as an exotic woman with prolific miraculous powers. Relying on baroque literary paradoxes and antitheses to inspire wonder and emulation in the listener/reader, Aguilera provides paradigmatic incidents as clear evidence of her chosen status. Catarina's rescue from the river parallels Moses's beginnings; her kidnapping reads like a Byzantine novel; and her undying desire for chastity persuades God to grant Catarina her wish to turn her beautiful white face into that of an ugly, old dark woman. As far as available records demonstrate, this biography written for Catarina's funeral was banned by the Inquisition only when it was republished with Ramos's third volume.[14] The style is concise and dramatic, employing a fair amount of reported dialogue between Catarina and others. As the title indicates, Aguilera's narrative develops the conventional tri-part hagiographic narrative: a chronological life story (*vida*), a list of virtues (*virtudes*), and exemplary death (*muerte*). Several elements might raise eyebrows, such as his story of the Virgen de Loreto and the Virgen de la Congregación being jealous of each other because of Catarina's simultaneous devotion to both.[15] More notably for our purposes, Ramos extravagantly develops what we would call today a discourse on race, but in colonial times would have been referred to as *castas* and the question of "purity of blood" (*limpieza de sangre*). Perhaps echoing in part *The Song of Songs*, where the bride is lovely for her blackness, Aguilera recreates a dialogue in which God reveals to Catarina his preference for "wheat-colored" (*trigueño*) brides over white saints like St. Inés: "Look how white and beautiful St. Inés is; this other beautiful and white one is St. Catherine the Martyr; this wheat-colored one is you. You are the most beautiful."[16] Surprisingly, Catarina is compared with white saints and comes out on top.

In contrast to Aguilera's relatively brief hagiographical sketch, Ramos's three-volume *De los prodigios* is a physical testimony to his efforts to prove beyond a shadow of a doubt the case for his spiritual daughter's sanctity. An influential figure within the powerful Jesuit order, Ramos occupied for a period of time the position of rector of the order in Puebla and had served as Catarina's confessor for nearly fifteen years. Both positions help explain how he could publish a triple-decker comprising over five-hundred pages printed on high-quality paper—a fact that graphically illustrates the expense the Jesuits and their benefactors were willing to incur in order to promote the woman whom they hoped would make their order and Puebla famous. Obviously not meant for private consumption, *De los prodigios* functions as an epic story of New Spain's identity. In fact, Ramos opens his dedication to the third volume by thanking his benefactor for footing the bill for the previous and present volumes. The expense, he explains, glorifies Puebla.[17] The epic, however, went overboard even by the baroque standards of the time, when narratives frequently celebrated exuberantly awe-inspiring stories that juxtapose the spirit and the flesh, vice and virtue, licentiousness and virginity, the exotic and the familiar.

Depicted in an affective, florid style in Ramos's biography, Catarina de San Juan becomes an anagram of a marvelous, exotic, deeply holy ascetic. Like Hansen's biography of Rosa, Ramos reveals a fascination with his subject's virginal body and the heroic tests of virtue it had to endure on both the human and supernatural planes; but Ramos delves into elaborate, "prodigious" detail. Upon her kidnaping by pirates, for example, the prepubescent Catarina becomes the target of men's lust, barely surviving with chastity intact a series of assaults by men who either want to own her or to marry her. In one of the first scenes, Ramos describes how Catarina's Portuguese kidnappers begin a brawl that injures her. Expanding on Aguilera's depiction of the event, Ramos draws a scriptural parallel with the spilling of Christ's blood:

> The disagreements and disputes among the pirates grew to such a pitch that, dividing into factions, they fell to swordplay and spear-throwing; until one of the soldiers, seeing the quarrel turn so bloody, said (speaking to his comrades), "It is better for one person to die, rather than that all of us perish." Similar counsel was spoken by Caiaphas the High Priest to the Jews in the council that their malice had formed against Christ. But this soldier, speaking and acting without advice, hurled a pike or lance toward that innocent young girl with the intention of ending her life, so that the life of an innocent ewe lamb would become a rainbow of peace among so many criminals. But the thoughtless and cruel pirate did not succeed in his design, for either because the girl dodged or because a hand from above lessened the thrust of the lance, it pierced only her thigh; and the blood that flowed from the wound was enough that, saddened and compassionate, they dropped their anger and their dispute; and that, leaving all their weapons, they went to dress her wound; and thus her innocent blood so spilled became a bond of harmony and concord. They then returned to the *Bageles*, and one of the principal captains, having won her, kept her, with the obligation to heal her and to treat her as a daughter and not as a slave.[18]

Saved by a bloodied leg, the young girl moves from one bad situation to another. A merchant falls in love with her beauty, buys her, and shelters her in a woman's house, planning to marry the girl when she becomes of age. These plans collapse when the insanely jealous woman beats Catarina in order to make her ugly and thus herself marry the merchant. When this ploy fails, the woman attempts to drown Catarina. Ramos depicts with flourish the abuse the young girl endures:

> This jealous woman decided to vent her anger on the beauty that she judged to be the cause or the occasion of her own rejection; undertaking to rob her of her natural loveliness, she mistreated her in word and in deed, often seeking to wear her down to nothing, disheveling her bit by bit, dragging her by the hair, flogging her, cudgeling her, and disfiguring her cheeks with the blood flowing from her wounds. She saw to it that hunger withered away the color and the pleasing qualities of her face: and finally she became the drudge of a vindictive, excessively jealous woman, for no other crime but that of being the beautiful and beloved Mirrha, and with no other prospect than that of being the object of an invidious loathing. This last grew to such a height that, unable to sufficiently avenge her anger and appease her wrath with the blood of an innocent ewe lamb, she tried time and again to take her life. Her anger prepared knives, with the resolution of killing her; but her fear lest the blood so spilled should cry out, like that of Abel, which clamored against invidious fratricide, curbed her and held her back. It seemed to her that killing her bloodlessly and out of sight would hide her wickedness; and thus she resolved on another, more treacherous deed, which was to fling her into the sea weighted down by a stone, so that the studied cunning of her rage might be taken for a possible mishap. In a fury she carried out this perfidy, but by Mirrha's good fortune, an anchor had already been set by Divine Providence at the place where she had fallen, so that raising herself by the cable she was able to pull her head out of the water and cry out for help, succor, and Baptism, which was her principal and only concern; she was rescued by a Portuguese nobleman who was near the seaside, like a foreordained instrument of Divine Omnipotence, to liberate her from the shipwreck and preserve her life as in other dangers. Through this lucky mishap this young girl was settled in another house, where, when her Mogul suitor saw her loveliness and beauty emaciated and disfigured, his love passed over to the Mogul lady who had so anxiously sought him.[19]

After Catarina is deserted by the Mogul merchant, yet another man enamored of her beauty goes mad when he cannot have Catarina, but another change in fortune takes her to New Spain, where she was sold as a house slave. Even en route to New Spain, however, Ramos paints the titillating scene of a sailor who desires her, even though (or, perhaps, because) she is now disguised as a young man (*mancebo*) as a ruse to elude the viceroy's messenger who awaits her at the port in Acapulco to take her to Mexico City. The disguise a success, Catarina makes her way to Puebla where under her new masters she enjoys a few years of relative peace from men's sexual advances until her owner dies and she is forced by her new master to marry his slave, Domingo. Frustrated and jealous because Catarina insists on remaining faithful to her Divine Spouse, Domingo subjects her to years of physical abuse. Later he takes a mistress with whom he has a child, and at his death Catarina is left with not only his debts but also the child.

If Ramos's version of Catarina's relationships with men is melodramatic and serves to create a portrait of Catarina as a sort of martyr, the treatment of her prophetic nature and supernatural encounters is perhaps even more theatrical and daring. The title itself, *De los prodigios de la ominpotencia. Y milagros de la gracia en la vida...*, suggests the first deviation from acceptable seventeenth-century hagiographic convention. Although there was a degree of variation, most titles included something to the effect of Aguilera's tri-part *vida, virtudes y muerte*. According to the guidelines established after the Council of Trent and Pope Urban VIII's reform, authors were to refrain from judging events as miracles or their subjects as saints: this was now the domain of the Congregation of Holy Rites and the pope himself. Clearly Ramos rejects a straightforward, humble title and claims from the start the singularity of his subject's life. The first two volumes, published within a year of each other (1689, 1690), comprise more than five-hundred pages.[20] Recounting the chronological life of Catarina and enumerating her heroic virtues, they spill over with elaborate accounts of Catarina as the wonder of the Spanish empire.

Like Rosa, Catarina intercedes on Spain's behalf in its European conflicts and commerce, comes to the aid of a troubled monarchy, and at times even is mystically transported to aid the Jesuit missionary project in the Mexican borderlands and in the Philippines. She is clearly inscribed into a story of the Jesuit and New Spanish contribution to the empire. Ramos's flair for descriptive symbolism and scriptural parallels comes through in an account of Catarina's vision of Carlos II's royal wedding and her subsequent prophecy about royal succession. Catarina sees a monstrous creature: "A monstrous fish, whose ugliness and ferocity caused her horror, and which she was unable to describe, calling it now a shark, now an alligator, now a sea monster; for it had a peculiar and abominable shape, with scales so spotted and mottled as to make it horrible to see."[21] It circles around the queen and threatens to deform the child she was to carry. With her fervent supplications, God grants Catarina's wish that the queen give birth to a healthy child. Catarina emerges as having a divine connection—one powerful enough to play a part in the Crown's destiny. Ramos concludes the passage with a scriptural parallel to authorize his tale:

> Reader, to see that this vision was worthy of the most profound and lengthy explications, compare it with what St. John the Evangelist has left us written in the twelfth chapter of his Apocalypse, and you will discover how uniformly God speaks and communicates his secrets in all ages to his servants and chosen ones; you will also see that everything could not but be verified that he showed to his Chosen Benjamin about his sacred lastborn, the Catholic Church, always persecuted and always victorious in the shape of a prodigious woman.[22]

In situations dealing with Catarina's ability to intercede and change the outcome of historically documentable incidents, Ramos occasionally interjects a short statement about his methodology, even citing secondary sources or including letters from other clergy that confirm his own account (for example, volume 1, chap. 28).

But once he moves outside the realm of historical events, Ramos often includes rather shocking tales of encounters with the divine and adds little authorial reflection on the veracity of the content. In recounting these scenes, Ramos often discusses hearing Catarina talk of these incidents in the confessional and, at times even quoting her, in language that sounds more like scripted speeches transferred into simple language than real conversations.[23]

In one recurring case, he takes the mystical commonplace of the husband-bride relationship to such an extreme that several critics view it as the basis for the censorship of the entire book. The biographer describes how Catarina endured a series of amorous struggles (*luchas amorosas*) with Christ, engaging for years in debates with a nearly naked Son of God who reveals himself to his beloved:

> On one occasion, the Lord showed himself to her in that same form of a child, but almost naked, much as we are accustomed to dress his images on the feast of his Resurrection, or of his Nativity in the manger: in the latter season Catharina was always most solicitous to clothe Christ, naked in his most holy birth, and with the above-mentioned apparition, it appears that the Lord responded to her wishes, saying to her, like someone longing to throw himself into her lap and her chaste embrace: "Catharina, will you dress me?" The charity and love of this, his beloved and dear Spouse, grew with this vision, almost to the point of causing a rapture, and rendering violent her impulse to clasp the Child God in her arms, to no longer be held back by the shackles of her virginal reserve, being frightened by the nakedness of her only and Divine Lover: and thus she said to him, or asked him, "Why haven't you come dressed? Did you lack angels, and your Mother, to cover with precious cloths the loveliness and beauty that the heavenly courts gaze on and enjoy?" He answered her that he wanted it to be she who dressed and adorned him. Catharina replied that she had nothing to clothe him with, nor hands to touch him with, nor even eyes to see him naked, and, succeeding in turning aside her gaze from that God of Purity, her Divine Lover, she would have wished to hide, and sink deep into the center of the earth. . . . But when she was more off her guard, she found herself one day with the same sight, and with manifestations and with the most affectionate expressions of yearning to receive the clothing he had requested from the hands of his beloved. Even though Catharina responded with new, greater, and more ample refusals of his loving purity, that he should leave her alone, go away, disappear; for this nakedness of his humanized divinity frightened and unnerved her, and she could not find the strength to embrace him; seeing him so naked caused her no less embarrassment than divine horror, until such time as she might see him decently clothed to human eyes. This loving dispute between the Divine Love and his beloved spouse went on for more than two years.[24]

A tantalizing image of a woman of such modesty that she refused even to let anyone shake her vile, unworthy hand is eroticized when Catarina is pursued by a God made man and refuses to bow to her beloved's supplications. These gripping tales of aggression and submission, sexual desire and chastity embellish the few documented facts of Catarina's life.

Notably, the third volume (constituting Parts 3 and 4)—published in the final months of 1692, the same year volumes 1 and 2 were put on the Index of Prohibited Books in Spain—shows much more restraint. The third volume comprises about 120 folios and recounts Catarina's virtues and death. Perhaps aware of the Inquisition's censorship and probably in competition with the short biography that was published the same year, volume 3 dramatically diminishes the number and extent of supernatural events recounted. Ramos refers the reader to volumes 1 and 2 to "avoid lengthiness" (*evitar prolijidad*) (vol. 3, 16) and insists on the historical nature of his work, including numerous testimonies from other people.[25]

And yet, Ramos continues to use Catarina as a foil for his own purposes. He highlights his own role as the confessor to such an extraordinary woman and often expounds his own ideas regarding delicate doctrinal points, such as the church's stance about souls that have not received baptism. Using Catarina's concern about the salvation of her brother, Ramos launches into his opinion on the doctrine of salvation, limbo, and hell, but then explains how he is in keeping with the church's teachings:

> Up to here the fact and the historical vision, in which, although extraordinary, on reexamining it with due consideration, I find nothing opposed to it or dissonant with Christian Doctrine and Catholic Theology of Baptism; but because it may have some influence and provoke some discussions when divulged to learned or ignorant men, it has seemed convenient to me to explain it, first stating my own feeling and afterward what one might reflect on when one compares [it with] the whole vision, and its significance with the learning of the Catholic Faith, with the judgment of the Saints and Theologians, who are the interpreters of Christ's Law within His Holy Church.[26]

In some regards, Ramos's third volume anticipates—at least at a rhetorical level, if not in fact—the style used by José Castillo de Graxeda in the third biography written about Catarina de San Juan. Whereas Ramos's work is the coffee table showpiece, Graxeda's *Compendio* (1692), represents the portable paperback, consisting of fewer than 150 cuarto-sized pages (that is, a page one-fourth the size of Ramos's folios). In striking contrast to Ramos's work, Graxeda recounts Catarina's life before arriving in Puebla in only two chapters, each one no more than a handful of pages. We are simply told that Catarina endured many abuses because Domingo had married her without fully understanding her vow to God. The detailed descriptions of Catarina as first and foremost a sexual object who is subject to bloody, abusive, death-threatening encounters with her husband disappear from this new portrait of the China Poblana:

> Since up to then he did not understand her, [Domingo] tried to avail himself now of endearments, now of threats, now of harsh treatment, but she only availed herself of the truth with which she admonished him and availed

herself of the cries she raised to her divine Spouse, and availed herself of many and devout anxieties with which she called out to the Virgin Mary. If, at this resistance from Catarina, annoyance, irascibility, and ill-usage grew in him, in her there grew all the more the steadfastness of her pledge and vow.[27]

In addition, Graxeda never mentions Domingo's mistress and child, but rather focuses on how effectively Catarina wards off her husband's advances with a cross strategically placed between their two beds.

Although Ramos creates a fictional character who overcomes traumatic experiences, Graxeda glosses over the particulars of the suffering and paints a portrait of model behavior, using an understated, condensed narrative style to depict an exotic yet ideal holy woman. Catarina as a conventional model comes forth at particularly crucial points in the narrative. When talking of one of the miracles attributed to her (the case of a cross that sweated blood), Graxeda turns first to a simple, reasoned portrait of her virtuous equanimity: "This venerable and devout woman was always circumspect in her deeds, moderate in her words, sensible in her answers, discreet in her works, prudent without passions, courteous without showiness, quiet without insolence."[28] Catarina emerges as a credible source of divine favor and helps inspire readers to model their own lives on these same behavioral codes.

In addition, Graxeda's narrative terseness when dealing with the supernatural is diametrically opposed to Ramos's extravagance. Graxeda briefly lists a series of revelations Catarina received about Jesuits and the affairs of the Spanish empire, but they are treated matter-of-factly, and the narrative highlights Catarina's visions and discernment of souls closer to home, focusing primarily on New Spain and Puebla. When treating Catarina's colloquies with heavenly figures, Graxeda selects several scenes to describe in more detail, but he opens or closes the passages with a discussion of his sources and method for recording such supernatural occurrences:

> Before continuing, I would like to anticipate with the reader's leave a question which may recur insistently to anyone, to wit, the question of why I report the virtues that Catarina exercised in that youthful period of her life? And how can I give information in such detail about what I never saw at the time? And about more than that, if I never saw it? Therefore when I communicated with her, she reported her virtues to me with the repugnance of a good spirit that only speaks of her faults and not her virtues, leaving those to the understanding of the person who directs her.[29]

Moreover, he cautiously leaves room for his superiors to judge the nature of certain visions. For instance, in the case of Catarina's vision of St. Anne (in which the young Indian girl promised to live a chaste life), Graxeda claims that he cannot determine the category of the vision (corporeal, intellectual, etc.): "I cannot ascertain the manner in which she received this favor, whether she was transported out of her senses and faculties or whether it was an imaginary vision [i.e., seen with the imagination] or whether she saw it visibly [i.e., with her normal physical eyesight], for as I wished to know about the category of thing that happened to her, she was in the habit of telling me."[30] And, as one might have anticipated, no mention is made of a nearly nude Christ.

The Inquisition, Hagiography, and Counter-Reformation Literature

In fact, Graxeda's narrative method responds point by point to the charges the Inquisition made against Ramos's text. The 1692 Spanish edict declared *De los prodigios* to be indecent, unbelievable, and nearly blasphemous. Although we only have an excerpt of the edict,[31] it is clear that the Holy Office viewed the text as falling into grave error regarding doctrinal content and narrative credibility: "Because it contains revelations, visions, and apparitions that are useless and improbable and full of contradictions and improper, indecent, and dangerous comparisions—*que sapiunt blasphemias* [that are almost blasphemous]—that abuse the highest and ineffable Mystery of the Incarnation of the Son of God, and in other places, Holy Scripture and because it contains dangerous doctrines that contradict the understandings of the Doctors and practices of the Universal Catholic Church on no more grounds than the author's vain beliefs."[32] The charge reflects the dual line of inquiry that the Inquisition used for judging texts: Did they contradict or undermine either the holy faith (*la santa fe*) or good taste (*las buenas costumbres*)? In other words, narrative content and style had to uphold Counter-Reformation doctrine and follow acceptable societal and literary norms. Interestingly, the edict also points to Ramos's "vain credulity," a criticism that reflects the church's wish to establish a reputation for its historical rigor in determining evidence of the work of God.

Despite the fact that we have little information surrounding the discussion that led to the Inquisition's decision, the prefatory material to books published in New Spain provides valuable information regarding a book's approbation by secular and sacred institutions. Whereas Graxeda's biography opens with the standard licenses from a *calificador* and another from the bishop's office, Ramos's introductory material in the first volume is overwhelmingly long and complex. More than seventy pages of licenses, approvals, and letters from the highest-ranking ecclesiastics and government leaders arouse the reader's curiosity about the need for such extensive documentation.[33] Is the biography already on trial, and does the ambiguity of the case require extra witnesses? While all the highest authorities over Ramos—the viceroy, bishop, and Jesuit superior—write formulaic statements, the *calificadores* and theologians address in detail the text's ability to pass the Inquisition's test that books contain no material "contra la fe y las buenas costumbres." Likewise, the four extra *pareceres* requested by Bishop Santa Cruz second this opinion, while also emphasizing the significant role that Catarina de San Juan plays in Puebla history.

Key to understanding the tenor and purpose of this outpouring of support is the personal letter that the *calificador* and one-time spiritual director of Catarina de San Juan (who also is widely known as the confessor who was dismissed by Sor Juana Inés de la Cruz), Antonio Núñez de Miranda, writes to his Jesuit brother Ramos. Strategically placed after the prologue and before the massive narrative, this nonstandard letter from one of New Spain's most highly regarded theologians serves an unusual purpose.[34] Elsewhere in the prefatory pages, Núñez grants an official Inquisition license for publication of Ramos's first volume, but the ten-page personal letter reflects a certain anxiety about the text. His letter details seeds of doubt in two areas. First, the "vast ocean" of examples of God's handiwork seen in Catarina's visions, revelations, and prophecies might well make the reader seasick (*marear*) and forget that God's will alone can render one holy. Núñez warns that cases of self-willed visions will bring people into the hands of the Inquisition, as indeed had happened in the infamous case of the Peninsular abbess who had feigned stigmata, Sor María de la Visitación. Second, Núñez advises the reader to avoid the temptation to skip ahead to passages about awe-inspiring, supernatural occurrences and instead to focus on (and imitate) the narrative examples of humility and obedience exemplified by Catarina. With these caveats, Núñez, both as *calificador* and as a Jesuit personally involved with Catarina's story, anticipates the charges that will be made later against the biography. Yet he holds them at bay for a time with his defense, even extending as an example of hope for Ramos the case of Saint Teresa's autobiographical *vida*, which was first withheld from publication by the Inquisition and later approved.

In striking contrast, Ramos's second and third volumes contain far fewer licenses, and the Inquisition's approval is absent. The licenses are from the most powerful figures in New Spain, the Archbishop Aguiar y Seijas and the Viceroy Conde de Galve; two out of the three *pareceres* are from other members of the Jesuit order.[35] Ramos apparently either bypassed the Inquisition or did not need permission for a continuation of a *vida*. Although the absence of a license from the Inquisition might be explained by Ramos's move to Mexico City after the publication of volume 1, it may also be indicative of trouble already brewing, as Núñez himself foresaw earlier.[36]

Although neither Ramos (in the 1692 publication) nor Graxeda reveals any knowledge of the 1692 Spanish edict, the metadiscourse they employ about narrative method points precisely to the problems Ramos's text will have, or was having. Whereas Ramos mentions issues of doctrine, historical rigor, and length, and recaps his third volume with a full recognition of Pope Urban VIII's rules for hagiography,[37] from the first Graxeda diplomatically discusses the merits of Ramos's biography but asserts the value of his shorter *Compendio*. Although the compendium ostensibly aims to make the wonders of Catarina's life available to a wider public, Graxeda does mention several motives for writing, which include concepts of truth and narrative authority. The first motive is that he, too, had served as a spiritual director for the holy woman; for eleven years he heard, up to three times a day, her stammered confession (*su balbuciente pronunción*), which he came to understand as angelic or mystic language. Graxeda reports that in one such rapture Catarina revealed that God wished Graxeda to serve as her confessor, which he then interpreted as divine authorization for his relationship with her and the source of his ability to bear witness to her life. A second motive is implicit in the fact that even as Graxeda writes, death is knocking at his door. No doubt aware of the attempts to beatify Catarina, Graxeda confesses a sense of urgency and need to leave a permanent record of her story. A third, unspoken motive was almost certainly the desire to undo the damage done to the process of Catarina's beatification—not to mention the credibility of her supporters—by Ramos's uncritical and extravagant approach to biography. From the outset Graxeda signals that he takes very seriously his duty to keep to the verifiable facts.

Echoing the humanist historians who had influenced the documentary quality of hagiographic-inspired biography by the turn of the seventeenth century, Graxeda declares: "Let it be known that everything that I report here, I saw, experienced, and verified, proving that all of the material was truthful and reliable. Placing my hand on my heart and making the sign of the cross, *Iuro in verbo Sacerdotis* to tell the truth in everything."[38] Although he assures his readers that he writes with Ramos's blessing, a rivalry or tension with *De los Prodigios* emerges between the lines, as well as a sense that the cause of Catarina's beatification might be in danger because of Ramos's lack of historical rigor. Like his colleagues, Graxeda no doubt felt that Puebla could not afford to lose such a good candidate for sainthood.

Graxeda comments on his historical method throughout the book until he comes to the last two chapters, where he resorts to a hagiographical model by reserving the penultimate chapter to recount Catarina's burial and the last one for identifying miracles that had been wrought through her intercession after death. As mentioned earlier, although the formulas for evidence of sanctity included the working of miracles, along with the demonstration of heroic virtue, the new seventeenth-century norms established for canonization advised clerics to tread carefully in an area that by that time had been reserved for papal interpretation. Graxeda is caught in a bind of needing to provide evidence in order to promote his case but not wanting to overstep boundaries regarding the determination of the sacred. He falls back on his methodological metadiscourse, promising to produce a succinct, truthful narrative based on eyewitness testimony of Catarina's virtue:

> The one miracle that I will here report suffices to substantiate all the rest because it was widely known to many people who witnessed it and who can verify it. I will leave aside the other miracles because there are issues in them that are very difficult to ascertain and are best left to the understanding of those people in the church whose official ministry is in this area. I do not wish stories of other miracles to be an obstacle to seeing the good reputation and virtues in this servant of God, nor do I wish to prolong this story which is intended only to awaken and incite devotion in the faithful.[39]

In one paragraph where he cites an example of Catarina's portrait (before it was banned, of course) aiding in the cure of a sick man, he warns the reader not to interpret the healing as the holy woman's own work, but rather as God working through her.[40]

In the author's conclusion, Graxeda describes yet another dilemma he has had to negotiate: to write a complete history of Catarina's life, he must depend on other eyewitness testimony, which he carefully weighs for reliability before including it in his account.[41] In discussing the trustworthiness of his sources and the authority of his narrative, Graxeda echoes the prologue and at the same time confuses the narrative voice as he reveals in the process that an anonymous woman wrote the last chapters using his own notes. Although readers today may interpret this assertion as calling into question Graxeda's narrative authority, his contemporaries, and in particular church officials, must have read these statements as support for the account's reliability.[42]

Besides painstakingly elucidating his methodology, Graxeda develops a series of stratagems to highlight his unrelenting commitment to historical truth. Like Ramos, he had privileged access to the semicloistered woman in his role as her confessor. But he also shows how, as a learned man, he understood the importance of accurately recording the language and dialect of people's testimony. Curiously, Graxeda never mentions the fact that he was a professor of the Totoneca language, but he employs his expertise as a linguist to decipher and interpret before the reader's eyes Catarina's halting Spanish. He transcribes it—grammatical errors and all—for the reader to "hear." He then "translates" and "interprets" her words by rewriting them, making her speech grammatical, highly rhetorical, and often sermonic:

> [Catarina] In truth my angel, y'worships tell the truth, and so beg God no lose me.
>
> [Graxeda] Which is to say: In truth, your worships tell the truth and sense what I am, that I am a liar and yet for that reason I ask that for the love of God you pray for me, that my soul may not be lost; indeed, I recognize that I am a China [Asian] woman, indeed I see that I am rubbish, that I am a piece of filth and a bitch dog, but for this same circumstance, because of both what you believe and what you say, for this very reason I implore you to make a special entreaty that I end well. (This was Catarina's reply to occasional passers-by who called her *esta perra china embustera*—"that lying China bitch.")[43]

A notable graphic characteristic of the first edition of the *Compendio* is that the italics used for both the transcription and translation of Catarina's speech dominate nearly a third of the text (and such quotes are only ocassional in previous biographies of Catarina). Graxeda thus creates a sense of historical truth—if only as narrative and graphic verisimilitude—that piques the reader's curiosity about the exotic nature of the protagonist and simultaneously indoctrinates by rendering an "Inquisition-safe" conventional Counter-Reformation model of female holiness.

In fact, Graxeda's text reflects church attempts to establish control in several areas. Besides tightening the definition of heresy, as we saw in Rosa's case, the Council of Trent had also stiffened the requirements for sainthood in the spirit of rigor advocated by humanist historians, which, among other things, dictated the need for reliable witnesses and stylistic decorum befitting historical truth. The process began in the thirteenth century when Pope Gregory IX attempted to identify with legalistic precision both saints and heretics. He established the first Inquisition and also created more requirements for canonization. By the seventeenth century, canonization required witnesses, trials, judges, prosecutors, and defenders—all orchestrated from Rome. As a result of the ever-increasing need to define, grade, and limit sainthood, there were only six formal canonizations in the sixteenth century—with a sixty-five-year hiatus between 1523 and 1588—and in the period from 1629 to 1658 there were no canonizations whatsoever.[44]

Even as official sanctity was on the wane, the popular imitation of it was on the rise. The canonization in 1622 of four Spanish saints inspired Spanish Americans for the next century and a half; hundreds of people imitated these saints, while dozens of clergy wrote hagiographic-style *vidas* as supporting evidence sent to Rome to attempt to initiate the process for beatification. Just as Hansen's *Vida* of Rosa had played a crucial role in her canonization, Ramos's and Graxeda's texts were meant to help beatify Catarina de San Juan, but only Graxeda circumscribes his material according to the Vatican's rules, well aware that any definitive claims of miracles or evidence of unapproved cults would count against Catarina's candidacy for sainthood. He uses a notion of decorum proper to the times, employing a style befitting Catarina's pidgin Spanish.[45] Moreover, he has recourse to only reliable witnesses, explicitly defers to papal authority, and always reins in the baroque tales of marvel. Graxeda's text successfully embodies the new historical discourse required by Rome to initiate the beatification procedure.

A third factor comes into play when examining Graxeda's narrative strategies. Given the restrictions placed on fiction in Spanish America, colonial authors frequently employed the rhetoric of historiography, but they created texts that are a hybrid of literary and historical genres. Graxeda's text, like that of his contemporary Carlos de Sigüenza y Góngora's popular chronicle of a shipwrecked man (*Los infortunios de Alonso Ramírez*), is a series of rapid narrative sequences that read almost like an early novel, except that they are framed by a painstaking exposition of how the author came to find the historical record of the adventures and how each adventure illustrates the exemplarity of Catarina's life. This structure clearly reflects Counter-Reformation guidelines for literary production.

Authors were to observe rules set by the Council of Trent that governed almost every aspect of practice of the Catholic faith, highlighting in particular the importance of the spiritual world, salvation as the meaning of existence, and the church's role as mediator between God and his earthly subjects. This ideology was transmitted to the faithful through preaching, frequent confession, insistence on complete obedience to church hierarchy, and control of religious practices, which included new rules for religious orders and oratorical style, as well as guidelines for art and literature. The goals underlying this program were to achieve religious homogeneity and to maintain the political, economic, social, and religious status quo in a period of increasingly rapid change.

The tenets that informed works by learned men like Ramos and Graxeda were drawn from guidelines for doctrinal and devotional literature which emphasized that moral instruction should teach (*enseñar*) and entertain through aesthetic appeal (*deleitar*) in order to persuade by moving (*mover*) the reader or listener to salutary change. To effect change, literature depended on appeal to the emotions rather than to the intellect. Gwendolyn Barnes-Karol explains how one of the most important theologians of Counter-Reformation Spain, Fray Luis de Granada, details this approach in his *Ecclesiasticae rhetoricae* (1567).[46] Creating visual images in the reader's mind, dramatizing events, employing rhetorical devices to astound and provoke awe and linguistic experimention worked to effect a suspense of the ordinary state of understanding (*suspenso*) and thus a state of mind in which the reader or listener might be more easily persuaded to absorb the doctrines being preached. Granada warns, however, that theatricality had to be tempered with a natural style (verisimilitude) in order to be believable and, therefore, emulated. These guidelines for literary practice and indoctrination clearly shape both Graxeda's and Ramos's authorial intentions, narrative style, and content. Both biographies draw on highly charged, exotic material to strike awe in readers and act as springboards for preaching. Graxeda's creation of narrative strategies to underline his adherence to the criteria of brevity and eyewitness testimony, however, saves his text from the hands of the Holy Office, while Ramos's abundant flourishes, theatricality, and lack of verisimilitude eventually caused his works to be banned from bookshelves in both the Old and New Worlds.

Not surprisingly, the literary practices advocated by the Council of Trent are echoed in the Inquisition's rules regarding books. Within a decade of the close of Trent, the first official tribunal of the Holy Office was established on American soil, and, as mentioned earlier, promulgated edicts regarding the ownership of books. By the mid–seventeenth century, the majority of autos-da-fé had already been staged, and the censorship of books was now one of the most vital roles played by the Inquisition. A set of fourteen rules—"Reglas, mandatos y advertencias generales del novissimus librorum et expurgandorum"—drafted at the turn of the eighteenth century, illustrates the determining factors in a book's fate when examined by the Inquisition.[47] Depending on a book's perceived danger to the faith, it could be placed in one of the three categories of censorship: complete prohibition, ownership by designated people such as priests, or censorship of offending passages. Although not condemned on the gravest charge as being heretical or containing witchcraft, Ramos's text received the toughest sentence possible for a book: complete prohibition from being owned or read. The type of censorship depended not only on the gravity of the errors found in the material but also on the frequency with which they appeared in the book.[48]

Assertions about Catarina's holiness and visionary powers were so abundant and extensive in Ramos's three-volume work that the Holy Office could not merely censor certain passages. As judged by the second round of *calificadores*, who lived in Spain and had not known Catarina, *De los prodigios* commits errors outlined in several rules as in rule 6, books that contain "things against holy doctrine" (*cosas contra la buena y santa doctrina*) and rule 7, works that "endanger the good practices of the Holy Catholic Church" (*dañosas a las buenas costumbres de la Iglesia Christiana*), citing love stories, among other types of fiction.

Rule 8, which banned all types of portraits, medals, rings, and crosses bearing a person's image and to which are attributed effects worked only by God, also clarifies why in 1691 the New Spanish Inquisition brought forth an edict prohibiting portraits of Catarina de San Juan (see figure 2.2). The edict states that any images in which Catarina de San Juan appears alone or next to Bishop Juan de Palafox y Mendoza should be limited to private use, and it banned the lighting of candles around them, thus reflecting Pope Urban VIII's restriction of such practices to beatified or canonized holy people.[49] The 1696 New Spanish edict ordering the closure of the oratory dedicated to Catarina de San Juan further demonstrates the church's desire to control popular devotion. While Ramos's record of frequent supernatural occurrences and continual recourse to the technique of suspense (*suspenso*) may have led to the Inquisition's verdict that the text lacked verisimilitude and was nearly blasphemous, the fact that a cult was forming around the holy woman was surely a major factor that could have tipped the judgment against Ramos.[50]

FIGURE 2.2 Portrait of Catharina de San Juan from Alonso Ramos *De los prodigios*
(Courtesy of Manuel Ramos Medina)

Sanctity, Cults, and Church Politics

Why did New Spain lag behind Spain in censoring Ramos's biography, only prohibiting it four years later, in the same year that the oratory was closed? In theory, the New Spanish Holy Office had to observe all edicts promulgated in Spain about censored books, and communication between the metropolis and the colony tended to be efficient. Although our documentation about the debate that surely would have surrounded the 1696 edict is limited,[51] a letter written by Mexico's inquisitor general three years after the Spanish censorship of Ramos's work asks the Spanish office about the status of the text: many people have claimed that it had been prohibited, but he had not been officially informed of its censorship.[52] Certainly the head of the Inquisition could not have been so completely in the dark about the verdict in Spain— there must have been strong forces behind the delay. Quite probably, the simultaneous prohibition of the oratory and biography came only under great pressure. Perhaps the fact that the first prohibition comes from Spain, even as portraits of Catarina are being confiscated in Puebla, points to the possibility that the case was too hot to handle in New Spain. Although the church had to regulate popular cults in order to maintain its authority, local ecclesiastics may have been reluctant to censor the circulation of a book that they themselves had approved earlier, especially one about a local heroine who was the spiritual daughter of the locally powerful Jesuits. Her story exemplified the Jesuit mission to convert and assimilate peoples from Asia into the Catholic faith.

Loath to lose a good candidate for sainthood, the Jesuits undoubtedly would have been reluctant to abandon the case for Catarina de San Juan. Having a saint associated with their order would have enhanced its power and prestige, and as one of the more powerful orders in New Spain by the turn of the eighteenth century, the Jesuits may have lobbied successfully for a time and warded off censorship. Beside being powerful in New Spain, the Jesuits also championed the criollo cause, enhancing a strong, independent identity for colonists under Spanish rule—a posture that would lead to the whole order being expelled from Spanish America nearly a century later. The Inquisition's prohibition of the two Jesuit-authored biographies (Aguilera and Ramos) and the approval of the non-Jesuit Graxeda's text may also indicate a backlash against the order.

Jesuit records about Ramos's sorry ending reveal how the order clearly attempted to protect its image. Ramos was recalled to Puebla to resume his position as rector of the order in 1693 after having moved to Mexico City three years earlier. By 1694, records report a discussion about possibly removing Ramos from office because of his "lack of moderation and excessive drinking" (*destemplanza y exceso de beber*). By 1695, however, another entry details a change in tactic: because news had arrived that the prohibition of Ramos's text was in the works, the Father General approved a decision to keep Ramos on as rector for the time being in order to avoid fueling the scandal that was sure to erupt upon the news of the censorship. Soon after, however, Ramos was confined to a cell where he spent years, escaping once in 1698 with a knife and nearly stabbing to death the man who replaced him as rector.[53]

Repeated assertions of Catarina's popularity among the townspeople of Puebla and the censorship of her portraits and oratory suggest that devotion to her was hard to stamp out.[54] Another as yet unexplained phenomenon in Catarina's case is why her portrait was often circulated with that of Bishop Palafox, the bishop who provoked so much admiration that he was promoted for beatification and who also so angered some Jesuit factions that he was recalled to Spain. On the one hand, we must ask why a prodigy of the Jesuits would be promoted alongside a bishop who fought for increased secularization of the clergy, thus diminishing the power of regular orders like the Jesuits. On the other hand, Palafox was already seen as a saintly man, so that associating Catarina with him could only help promote her orthodoxy and holiness.[55] Although many of the answers lie in uncovering more about the political nuisances of the time, this may simply reflect that, despite Jesuit efforts to claim Catarina as one of their own, her appeal, like Palafox's, cut across all sections of society and the church. In fact, in many ways, the framing of her story in both Jesuit biographies is that she is first and foremost a symbol for Puebla. We have seen how Ramos dedicates his third volume to Puebla and how Aguilera calls Catarina the mother and teacher ("Madre y Maestra") of Puebla. She is less a symbol for the Universal Catholic Church, perhaps, and more a symbol for Puebla's protagonism within that history.

Perhaps even more intriguing is the broader question of why the Jesuits and Puebla itself would fervently promote a non-white, lay holy woman when she deviated from the model female saint promoted by the Counter-Reformation Church. Perhaps it was these very deviations that allowed Catarina to be considered singular enough to be worthy of veneration by local people. In fact, Catarina de San Juan's life story was a far cry from the typical biography of a Counter-Reformation saint. As Peter Burke notes, the typology of a saint canonized between 1588 and 1767 reflected a collective representation of people well-born, of white upper-class parents, living in powerful countries (Italy and Spain dominate), and professed in important religious orders, primarily the Franciscans, Dominicans, and Jesuits.[56] Most saints were founders of religious orders or missionaries, while a significant number were ecclesiastic pastors, mystics, or people devoted to charitable works. The centralization and control of sanctity demanded that candidates conform to Rome's definition of holiness as judged by its examiners, which discouraged individualization and local cults. In the prefatory pages to Ramos's first volume, several licenses discuss how local opinion of a person's sanctity had been considered essential as a reliable collective witness for a case, but unlike earlier cases such local support was now insufficient for establishing sainthood.

From what we have seen, Catarina may have had a strong local appeal not only because she satisfied the popular taste for heroes who embodied the paradoxes of the baroque age but also because she exemplified the racial and cultural mixture that characterized New Spain. The edict about Catarina's portrait and biography may have served as a warning to keep non-white populations in their place.[57] The whole question of Catarina's race perhaps belongs to part of a much larger debate that had been brewing and that would take a more concrete form in Mexico City in the 1720s. From the beginning of the Spanish conquest and colonization of America, Catholic

Church leaders had debated the spiritual capacity of indigenous peoples for taking formal religious vows. Early Franciscans had begun to train indigenous men for the priesthood, but soon the tide turned and in theory they were banned from the elite ranks. Likewise, ideas about native women taking the veil as brides of Christ were being discussed. As Kathryn Burns has shown, in Cuzco, from the earliest decades of colonization elite indigenous women, daughters of *caciques*, were integrated into the new administration and economic system by creating nunneries for them. But in New Spain, native women were not allowed to take the veil as high-ranking nuns until the Convent of Corpus Christi was founded in 1724.[58] Even then, however, a debate raged about the ability of indigenous women to observe religious vows, in particular the vow of chastity. It is during this polemic that the story of the lay Iroquois woman, Catherine Tekakwitha was first translated into Spanish and published in New Spain.[59] When Aguilar holds up the beauty of Catarina's wheat-colored (*trigueña*) skin, he is entering into this debate about race and its relationship to spiritual beauty and capacity. Notably, however, all three biographies highlight the supposed white elite origins of Catarina. Said to have been born blonde and white, Catarina prayed to be turned into a dark, ugly woman in order to keep her chastity. Thus in the eyes of the Spanish church the all-important question of origins and "purity of blood," so carefully examined by the Inquisition, is settled for Catarina—legend changed her race. The backlash against Ramos's biography could have come from all these forces: Catarina's race, the role of the Jesuits in New Spain, and Counter-Reformation rules for literature and sainthood.

Not a simple case of how one life or book was deemed saintly and one deemed heterodox, the story of the representation of Catarina de San Juan's life showcases the issues involved in studies of colonial Mexico, the church, and women. Race, social status, religious status, and the role of male patrons and life stories as mediated by male biographers all need to be taken into consideration when studying women's history and literary works from this period. As we have seen, Catarina was construed by Ramos and others as the essence of holiness, an important symbol of religious identity for New Spanish citizens and ecclesiastics. It is her male biographer's works that are targeted by the Inquisition. Catarina de San Juan's case, like that of Rosa de Lima's for Peru, demonstrates how the lives of holy women became important to the definition of New Spanish society and, accordingly, were targets of mediation and control by church hierarchy.

Catarina as a person gets lost in the shuffle of church politics and didactic ends. Historical facts about religious women and writings by them often faded as official discourse took over to create an ideal portrait—albeit, in this case, a hotly contested one—that might serve the institutional church. The true face and voice of an Asian Indian woman who ended her final days surrounded by revering townspeople and clergy is impossible to recover completely; the facts are eclipsed first by an out-of-control confessor's account that fictionalizes and eroticizes Catarina's life story, and then by a biographer who follows rules so closely that he turns her story into a paradigm of sanctity. Apparently, Catarina's opportunity for sainthood was lost in the cross-fire of rules about holiness, hagiography, and blasphemy.[60] And yet, as the letters, Inquisition edicts, and hagiographic biographies about Catarina de San Juan discussed issues such as blasphemy and inspirational prose, heresy and sanctity, the role of the elite vis-à-vis the lower classes in the church, popular devotion and institutional religion, historical truth and literary verisimilitude, we begin to glimpse more fully the complexity of mid-colonial Mexican society and literature. Perhaps most significantly, unlike Rosa, Catarina never learned to write and, therefore, we are unable to hear her voice directly. Nonetheless, popular support for her was sufficient enough that she lives on today in the popular legendary figure of the China Poblana. Statues and portraits of her can be found in modern-day Puebla.

Chronology of Catarina de San Juan

ca. 1600	Born Mirrha in the Mogul empire of India.
ca. 1610	Captured by Portuguese slave traders.
1619	Converts to Christianity; baptized by the Jesuits in Manila.
ca. 1620	Arrives to New Spain, via the port of Acapulco, and is bought by a couple from Puebla.
ca. 1625	Marries her master's slave, Domingo.
ca. 1640	Becomes a free woman.
1688	Dies in Puebla, Mexico.
1689	Ramos publishes the first volume of his biography of Catarina, *De los prodigios*.
1690	Ramos publishes the second volume.
1692	Ramos publishes the third and final volume.
1692	The Spanish Inquisition bans the first and second volumes of *De los Prodigios*.
1692	Castillo de Graxeda publishes his *Compendio* of Catarina's life.
1696	The Mexican Inquisition bans *De los Prodigios*.

3

The Mystic Nun

Madre María de San José (1656–1719)—

Confession and Autohagiography

"How I longed to be a saint!"
—María de San José, *Vida*, vol. 3

"Your path is very similar to Saint Teresa's."
—God speaking to María de San José, *Vida*, vol. 1

"I have seen these papers. . . . God is apparent in this creature. Hurry her up and ask her to write the rest of what happened to her."
—Letter from Bishop Fernández de Santa Cruz to María's confessor, in
    Santander y Torres, *Vida*

As Rosa's canonization process was being renewed in Rome and Catarina de San Juan was leading a life as a visionary in Puebla, half a day's journey away in New Spain, a girl experienced a vision that changed her life. Juana Palacios Berruecos recalls in her autobiographical *vida* that a vision of the devil, followed by one of the Virgin Mary, led to her decision to follow a religious vocation. Living on a rural hacienda on the outskirts of Tepeaca, she began an extreme ascetic practice and later was associated with the Franciscans as a lay *beata*. But unlike Rosa, who refused to enter the convent, Juana sought the safety of the cloister and the vow of perpetual enclosure. In fact, she struggled for more than two decades to achieve her wish, often encountering family conflict over her decision. At the age of thirty-one, Juana finally entered the Augustinian Convent of Santa Mónica in Puebla, Mexico, and rejoiced at becoming "dead to the world." After professing final vows and changing her name to María de San José, she could no longer leave the walls of the convent or see family and friends without an iron grate between them and a chaperone present. Beginning with these early years on the hacienda and continuing throughout more than three decades of convent life, María strove to be saintlike with all her heart: she exclaims in her confessional journals, "How I longed to be a saint!" (vol. 3).

Significantly, when María de San José wrote years later from the point of view of a high-ranking nun about her twenty years of living on the hacienda as a lay religious woman, she omitted the fact that she had worn the third-order Franciscan habit (vol. 1). Only in her final years would she mention this, and then only once (vol. 11). Moreover, while she had followed an ascetic practice that was closely related to the medieval models established by Catherine of Siena and imitated by Rosa de Lima, María never mentions either saint's names in her more than twelve volumes of writing. And yet, she borrows almost verbatim details from Hansen's life of Rosa in order to describe her own fasting, retirement to a garden hut for prayer and mortification, secret pacts with Indians who helped her with penitential practices, and mystic marriage to Christ. María cites instead works by or about the Spanish ascetic Peter of Alcántara, the popular medieval Italian hermit Anthony of Padua, St. Francis's Rule for the Clarist nuns, and several spiritual exercise books. Perhaps more telling than the list of influences on her secular life are the mentions of models she used once she took the veil (and as she began to write). The authors that figure most prominently are Teresa of Avila; the founder of María de San Jose's order, the Augustian Recollects, Mariana de San Joseph; and, a distant third, another Spanish nun and devotional author, María de la Antigua. Not surprisingly, once María was in the convent and a writer herself most of María's models were other nuns who had authored texts that supported Counter-Reformation teachings about the enclosure of religious women and the careful ecclesial monitoring of the spiritual life.

María was not the only cautious writer, however. The same Dominican friar, Sebastián de Santander y Torres, who inaugurated the Puebla convent dedicated to Rosa with a warning to its members about the dangers of being a lay holy woman, also wrote the official biography of María de San José. He frequently compares María to Rosa—their fast, charity, humility, visions of the host, and prophecies of convent foundings.[1] But he never mentions that both women spent formative years as Franciscan lay holy women. On the one hand, as a Dominican, he surely wanted to claim Rosa for his own order and focused on her later association with them; on the other hand, no doubt he was wary of religious women living outside the convent. Like Hansen before him, Santander y Torres responds to a superior's request (that of the bishop of Oaxaca) for a hagiographical-style biography in order to inspire readers and possibly begin a canonization inquiry. In his prologue, Santander y Torres inscribes María de San José's life story into church convention for holy women and ardently proclaims her as having a "virile heart" (corazón varonil) worthy of Christ and his saints.

The writings of both María and Santander y Torres reveal the continuity of the tradition of hagiography and the centrality of imitation both to the establishment of an individual's spiritual path and to the textual representation of that life journey in confessional autobiographical accounts and didactic biographies written to inspire further emulation. María's life also reveals that the ambiguity and threat of a visionary woman living outside the convent had not changed since Rosa's time; indeed, vigilance had become more stringent. Many of the concerns about sanctity and heresy found in the biographical stories of Rosa and Catarina de San Juan marked the daily lives and confessional accounts of devout girls and women who wished to follow the way of the saints. Questions about doctrinal purity, prayer, and the nature of visionary activity, as well as concerns about how to represent these in oral and written accounts for spiritual directors, became central to many colonial religious women's lives. María de San José, in particular, divulges the interior life of a woman who desperately sought to meet institutional church expectations. For at least twenty-five years she documented her spiritual life for God and her confessors (ca. 1691–1717). The resulting two-thousand-page manuscript journal clearly illustrates how she eagerly, and at times painfully, sought to follow the model of heroic virtue.[2] (See figure 3.1.) Although it was strongly promoted by two bishops, María de San José's case never made it to Rome for formal consideration by the Congregation of Holy Rites. Her cloistered status perhaps accounts for the fact that her visionary writings and hagiographic biography also never fell into the hands of the Holy Office of the Inquisition. Instead, after being used as a primary source for her biography and the popular eighteenth-century publication of her guide to the Stations of the Cross, the journals were returned to the Augustinian convent in Oaxaca where she had died.

Once returned to the convent archives, María's journals remained there until the convent was closed in the nineteenth century.[3] Considered lost by at least one twentieth-century historian,[4] the autograph manuscript is now housed in a collection of colonial documents in the United States. Since my serendipitous find of the

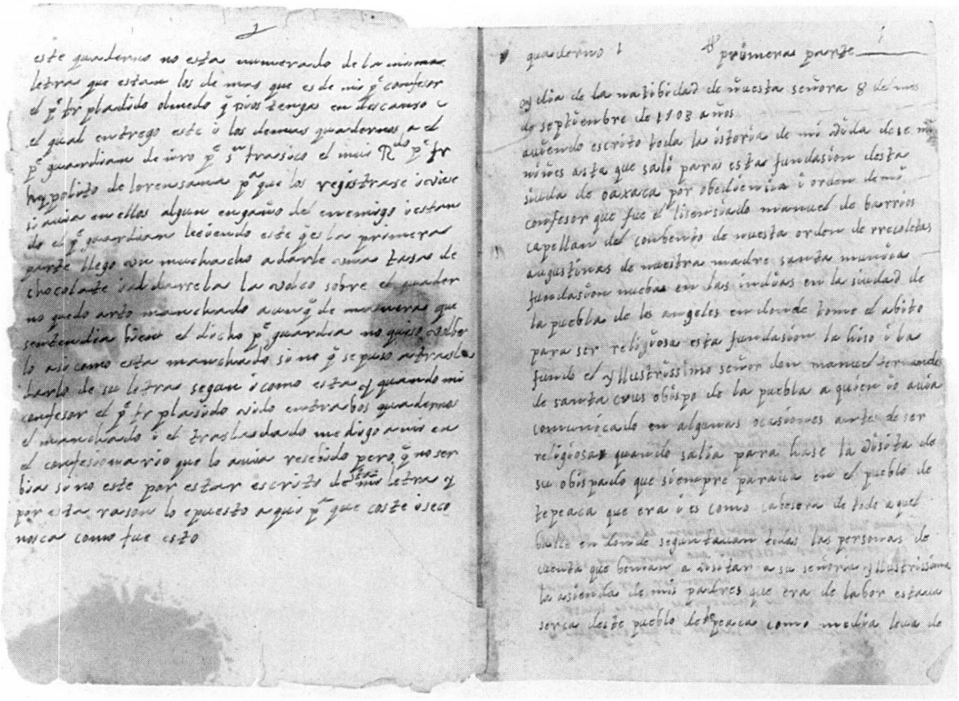

FIGURE 3.1   Opening pages from *Vida*, by María de San José, vol. 1, ca. 1703 (Courtesy of the John Carter Brown Library, Providence, Rhode Island)

manuscript in 1984, we are now able to see the extent to which male biographers altered nuns' words when they quoted them. We also see the extent to which twentieth-century critics have misread these quotes.[5] As I will show in this chapter, María de San José's extensive autobiographical text provides us with a unique opportunity to study the role of religious women in America.

In many ways, María's life and life writings as a religious woman are both unique and paradigmatic. She is the only woman considered in this book who spent as many years outside the convent as in it (about thirty-two years), and thus she offers the dual perspective of a *beata* and a nun. Also, she is the only nun studied who professed her vows in a reformed order, like St. Teresa's. In addition, the contemporary textual corpus by and about María de San José is the most extensive we have to date for any colonial Latin American woman. We have samples of all the most popular period biographical and autobiographical religious narrative genres for one individual: a funerary sermon, a hagiographic biography, and a tract proposing canonization, as well as a formal confessional *vida*, a series of *cuentas de conciencia*, and a first-person devotional guide and chronicle of convent founding.[6] These documents provide an unusual opportunity to compare biographical and autobiographical representation, and to reconstruct the narrative models and purposes for each. Because María de San José earnestly sought the way of the saints in her daily routine and writing, her manuscript also offers a certain transparency for seeing how church rules and texts informed her identity. Her journals illustrate a process that has been called "autohagiography" by several scholars.[7] The church's rescripting of her journals for an official biography and prayerbook further illustrate the complex intertextuality between confessional and hagiographic writings for church ends.

Portrait of a Mystic Nun

María de San Jose's life story is best understood as part of a flourishing spiritual and religious movement in seventeenth-century New Spain. In the two major religious centers, Mexico City and Puebla de los Angeles, people were founding dozens of religious institutions and devoting their lives to the church. Puebla, the site of María's first convent, boasted wealth and a large number of criollos among its inhabitants, as well as two successive bishops, Juan de Palafox y Mendoza and Manuel Fernández de Santa Cruz, who promoted Puebla as a religious center in the New World. By the time María took the veil in 1687, the city maintained the largest number of convents per capita and published the largest number of biographical *vidas* of its local holy people in the Americas.[8] In a search for their own saint, even after the fiasco of Ramos's biography of Catarina de San Juan, Poblanos wrote, published, and sent to Rome dozens of hagiographical biographies. Sisters who had preceded María in Puebla in the first half of the seventeenth century had gained popular and institutional support for their holiness. (María herself cites two of them, Isabel de la Encarnación and Maria de Jesús, in her journals.)[9] Bishop Santa Cruz, in particular, fervently promoted several of these women. But he was also instrumental in blocking María's first attempts to enter the convent, and only later promoted her role as a mystic writer and convent founder.[10] Impressed by her visionary life once she was a nun, he in fact initiated her writing career, asking for a written record of her life story (ca. 1691, bound in vol. 12).

In a revised account of this formal *vida* (vol. 1), written at least a dozen years later (ca. 1703) for a new confessor, Fray Plácido de Olmedo, María states she was born in 1656 on a *hacienda de labor*, a rural agricultural plantation, located about seven leagues from Puebla and a half-league from the important but small Indian town of Tepeaca.[11] Born to a criollo couple from Puebla, the rather well-to-do Luis Palacios y Solórzano and Antonia Berruecos López, María was one of eight daughters and a son, and the sixth daughter in line for a dowry, which was often necessary for marriage or entrance into the convent. The couple had moved from Puebla to the hacienda in order to manage it and raise a family. Unfortunately, luck had not been with them, and large debts were owed on the properties by the time Luis died in 1667.

Following a pattern typical of many lives of the saints, María reports that soon after her father's death, when she was only ten or eleven, she experienced a sudden, dramatic conversion to the spiritual life. As discussed in the introduction to this volume, María had participated in family routine by sewing with her mother and sisters, listening to her father and brother read the lives of saints, and playing with sisters and neighboring girls during free time. One day, however, while playing at grinding flour with her friends and swearing at one of them, María saw a bolt of lightning strike a wall, which then tumbled and killed a horse. After running into the house, she saw a vision of the devil as a nude mulatto man who said, "You are mine. You will not escape my clutches."[12] A subsequent vision of the Virgin Mary offering to wed the girl in mystic marriage to Christ convinced María to take the vows of a bride of Christ: obedience, chastity, and poverty. From that moment forward, María established an ascetic life—imitating the saints and closely following spiritual exercise books and the Rule for Saint Clare. Although her family frequently reined in her practices, María describes a rigorous schedule of prayer, fasting, and labor that was supplemented by sessions of mortification, which included wearing shirts made of animal hair and filled with lice, as well as refraining from unnecessary contact with anyone. Like Catherine of Siena and Rosa de Lima before her, María built a hut in the backyard and spent hours there every day in prayer and spiritual practices. In addition, she informally associated with the Franciscans, who occasionally passed through the area, offered periodic guidance, and stayed with the family. For two decades, María followed the path of a lay *beata*, yet she longed to live in an urban center with access to a confessor, daily mass, and convents. María blamed the long delay in becoming a nun on the isolation of the rural hacienda and the family's financial straits and conflicts.

Much of this description echoes conventions for the trials of the spiritual path, and yet María's account provides striking details about the conflicts that her vocation caused. She describes the painful effects of the often contradictory messages society gave to young girls. Extreme fasting, mortification, and dedication to God were highly exalted practices, but they also created grave concerns within many families. A young woman like María, who spent hours alone in the garden and also had an Indian servant help her perform penitential practices, such as flagellation, in secret, could be suspected by church or society as being dishonorable and feigning holiness (*falsa beata*). Plain old sibling affection and jealousy also played an important part: while one sister feared losing María to perpetual enclosure, another competed with her for a dowry. The hefty two- to four-thousand peso dowry required for entrance into a convent became an obstacle for María and her two other sisters who wanted to become nuns. With the at-times reluctant charity of Bishop Santa Cruz and another patron, however, all three girls finally achieved positions as nuns, but only after a number of false starts. Because of the family's good social standing and the fact that marriage dowries could often consist of the inheritance of property, three other sisters married into prominent local families.[13]

This family dynamic wreaked havoc on María's good intentions and health; she blamed familial tension and severe penitential practices for a five-year illness that began within several years of her conversion. At first diagnosed as a bad heart (*mal de corazón*), after several life-threatening treatments, doctors concluded it was not a natural sickness but one sent by God. The illness left María an invalid, alternately experiencing fits of uncontrollable movement and near paralysis. Her sisters had to feed and dress her. María reports that she was cured only after the departure of the most troublesome sister for the convent (Francisca, ca. 1675) and with the miraculous intercession of María's favorite saint, Anthony of Padua. Once she was about eighteen and of age to take the veil, María returned to her rigorous practices but also began a series of attempts to enter the convent. Years later, in 1687, María's Dominican brother-in-law Fray Gorospe (one of the same friars who had helped Catarina de San Juan) interceded on her behalf and encouraged Bishop Santa Cruz to grant María a place in the newly established convent reserved for women who were "virtuous, poor, and entirely Spanish, with no mulatto, *mestiza*, or any other mixture of race."[14]

Entrance into the Convent of Santa Mónica did not bring release from conflict, however. María's first four years were filled with self-doubt, illness, inability to talk with her confessor, torments by the devil, and reprimands from the convent sisters. Reporting in volume 2, she describes the trials. Upon entrance into the walled-off cloister, María lived with about twenty-five nuns and as many servants and slaves. After years of living as a lay *beata*, largely following her own schedule, she now had to eat at designated times, pray the divine office regularly throughout the day, perform duties assigned by the abbess, and carry out all tasks with complete obedience to superiors. As a novice, María was subjected to extra tests of perseverance and obedience. Upon taking final vows a year later, she agreed to dedicate her life to praying for the Christian community and to observe the four vows required of all nuns. Following the Carmelite order's reformed rule established a century earlier by Teresa of Avila for her nuns, the Augustinian Recollects of María de San José's order strictly observed the vows of perpetual enclosure, complete obedience to their superiors, poverty (not owning anything for themselves), and celibacy. From the day of her profession of vows forward, she lived a communal life, having only a small individual cell with a sleeping mat, stool, table, and crucifix to retire to for her nightly rest. Having her own private space was something that had been hard to come by on the busy hacienda, and she exclaims several times in volume 2, "my cell seemed like a little bit of heaven." Yet, perhaps because of the relative freedom she had enjoyed on the hacienda, a much more regimented and communal life of duties proved hard at first. Later in the same volume, María reports that the prioress whipped her for not wearing her habit correctly and for arriving late to the Divine Office; the convent sisters taunted her about her extreme mortification practices; doctors treated her with more than a dozen blood-lettings (*sangrias*) for bad humors, boils on her feet, and hives; and three demons reportedly tormented María:

> The first of the three demons had a very narrow waist that nipped in at the middle of his body, in the form of a very fierce animal: none other than a black dog. It was very common to see this one, and I always saw him with this shape and form. When he became most enraged was when he tried by some temptation to make me fall into hell, for they only tormented me regarding my faith. By this one temptation alone, I have never been afflicted; I have been greatly pressed by the others, by all other temptations that ever existed. Well, as I was saying, when they wanted to make me fall into some temptation they became fiercely enraged, especially this one with the waist nipped in that I always saw with the face and shape of a black dog. I would see him, just like a dog when it wants to bite, and it opens its mouth all furious and shows its teeth. I saw him exactly like that, for he would raise his head as if he meant to bite me. And then he would do it; he would sink his teeth into my flesh so that I had to cry out. Yet I never did, helped and aided by the strength of the Lord and by holy obedience, so that I scarcely uttered a single word or made even the slightest gesture whatsoever to indicate anything of what was happening, when I had the Mother Superior hanging over me. For she would hush me by whipping me with a belt, and if she could not do so in person she would send another nun to do it.[15]

At one point, María even describes, through the voice of the devil, thoughts of suicide.

These same years, however, were also filled with vivid and consoling visions of God, Christ, the Virgin Mary, and other saints and souls. Moments of prayer and the taking of the sacrament of communion frequently turned into specific visions that often reassured María that she was on a path to God or that expounded some doctrinal point. For example, in her new job as wardrobe keeper, she described seeing (as she sewed) an inner vision of a bed of flowers with Christ in the middle. In another vision, she was embraced by Christ:

> One day when I was at my prayers I saw Our Lord crucified, quite close to me, and I saw how He took out the nails, lowering Himself from the cross, and then came towards me. The cross stayed standing upright and He came to where I was, and He entered inside me and embraced my soul with a very fond and close embrace, and He said to me, "You see, this is the embrace of a husband and of a father, to strengthen you and comfort you so that you can sustain the trials that await you.[16]

In yet another mystical experience her heart became so engorged with love for God (*ensanchamiento*) that the nun in the infirmary later testified that two of María's ribs were raised higher than the rest:

One day while I was feeling this fire of love which inflamed my breast, and my heart did not fit in it, and lacking breath and bodily strength to endure such a blaze, I prayed to His Majesty to douse the flame of His love a little, because I was lacking life itself. And in this, I felt someone come to me and they raised up two ribs right over my heart and stretched my chest larger so that my heart could fit inside it. And with this my heart was eased and released, and those two ribs remained raised up four fingers higher than the rest. I saw and felt this, seeing the two hands. And what I say here, that my two ribs remained higher, I saw with the eyes of my body after seeing all of this with interior vision; and they stayed that way, higher than the rest.[17]

Time and again María records how God even told her that she was a beautiful bride for him. After four years of difficulty confessing, María finally began to reveal this visionary activity to her confessor, the convent chaplain Manuel de Barros. He reported it to Bishop Fernández de Santa Cruz, who, in turn, gave the order that María record the visions and events leading up to them: "I have seen these papers. . . . God is apparent in this creature. Hurry her up and ask her to write the rest of what happened to her."[18] The year was 1691 or 1692.

Five years later, María had made her mark as a model nun. Bishop Santa Cruz chose her to be one of five founders of the Convent of Nuestra Señora de la Soledad in Oaxaca. In addition, she was to be the instructor of novices—training future nuns for the convent—a post she would keep until her death more than twenty years later. As María describes in volumes 4 and 10, after the long journey to Oaxaca and the first days of setting up the convent, she again encountered a myriad of difficulties. The tension between town members and the new convent was high. The nuns were accused first of sending the beloved statue and patron of the city, Nuestra Señora de la Soledad, to Puebla and then of giving convent dowries designated for local Oaxacan women to women from Puebla. The latter conflict lasted for years and reached such a pitch that the city council, the bishop, and even the viceroy were consulted in an attempt to settle the dispute.[19] María's account demonstrates the keen rivalry between Puebla and smaller provinces regarding their religious institutions and monies. In addition to describing external challenges, she narrates recurring bouts of illness, vivid temptations by the devil, problems with novices, and dismissals by confessors who got fed up with her demanding visionary life.

In spite of these struggles (or perhaps as part of the process), the nun's spiritual path progressed from the intense individual visions (generally corporeal and imaginary) that characterized her life at Santa Monica to a more world-serving stage (intellectual or unitive).[20] Later volumes record visionary activity that sped María along the spiritual path, but also describe more powers of prophecy and intercession. She interceded before God on behalf of everyone from Pope Clement XI (during a controversy in Rome, vol. 11); to Bishop Maldonado (the conflict over his proposed election as archbishop, vol. 11); to her birth family and religious family (usually for their souls); to whole towns, such as Puebla (she sees them "without heads" in 1708 because of current controversy, vol. 7), Oaxaca (during earthquakes, droughts, and floods, vol. 6), and San Lorenzo (a town with many people of African descent and who she says were lax in their practice of Christianity, vol. 11). María de San José portrays herself as an "enclosed missionary" who worked closely with God:

> Here I began to speak with God and to show Him my distress and to ask His mercy, not only for me but for everyone. . . . While I was in this, I felt the Lord draw near to me, and with that my fears and frights grew calm. Here I heard His Majesty speaking to me, and among various things He told me . . . that the city of Puebla was in very great travail, because in it many sins were being committed. And to avoid these offenses and so that those souls should not be lost, He was letting fall the lash of His justice; yet not like a severe judge, but rather like a father, for He was sending that city the thorns of many tribulations and griefs, so that by those same blows they might be made to understand and might return to the Lord contrite and sorrowing, praying to Him for mercy so as to offend Him no more. That was what His Majesty told me, without letting me know a single thing more; and when I asked Him, "Lord, and what can I do in matters of such weight, that are told to my lowliness and wretchedness?" He answered me, "Pray to Me for that city."[21]

By following the way of the cross, the *imitatio christi*, and the mystic's path, María de San José became a powerful intercessor, recognized by clergy and the local community.

After a half-century of living a life devoted to God, María died March 19, 1719, having fought high fevers and chills for three months. Upon her death, as her biographer reports in hagiographic tradition, María's face glowed once again with youth and her body gave off a sweet aroma. All the highest-ranking Oaxaca church officials and elite reportedly attended her funerary service, as guards fought off the crowds of people who wanted to enter the church and take a bit of her tunic as a relic. They already saw her as possessing saintly qualities and powers. First, Santander y Torres's panegyric sermon (1719) and then two editions of his hagiographic biography (1723, 1725) documented María's model behavior. These were soon followed by Bishop Maldonado's tract proposing her canonization (ca. 1726). In these same years, María became a published devotional author in her own right with the first two editions of her *Stations of the Cross* (1723), a work that would be republished at least three more times in the eighteenth century. Apparently, however, María de San José's case was too weak to even have been recorded at the Vatican. Indeed, only a handful of New Spanish candidates did enter into the long, costly process of canonization. Of these, only two reached the stage of beatification and none were canonized during the seventeenth and eighteenth centuries.[22] Although she never achieved the highest institutional distinction within the Catholic Church, María de San José played an important role in the development and promotion of the institutional church in central New Spain.

The Mystic Path, Discernment, and Authority

Apparently, María de San José's contemporaries were unanimous in believing that they had witnessed the life of an individual chosen to enjoy mystic union with God and whose life had been beneficial to the community. The preliminary pages to María's biography written by Santander y Torres, much like those in Ramos's life of Catarina de San Juan, published the judgments passed on her life. In an attempt to distinguish *alumbradismo* and religious fakery from mysticism, high-ranking church authorities examined the nature of María de San José's spiritual life and writings and deemed them not only orthodox but worthy of emulation. Needing to cite how they came to their conclusions, the *calificador* for the Inquisition, the canon of the cathedral, a Dominican (the biographer's brother) who had heard María's confessions, and the author himself all address the issues that needed to be taken into consideration when judging a visionary's life. In addition, the preliminary material includes three letters confirming the worth of María's writings, including the one from Bishop Santa Cruz.

Perhaps it is the Holy Office's *Parecer* that best reveals the church's meticulous process of evaluation of a person's spiritual life. The *calificador* Luis de la Peña clears María on three grounds: (1) her visions were numerous and based on a life of virtue; (2) the type of material found in the visions followed the rules of not introducing new doctrine or contradicting previous visionaries and Scripture; and (3) María herself was healthy, silent, virtuous, and not rich, revealing an equanimous person not prone to false visions. In his discussion of each of these areas for examination, references to previous models were essential. Key guidebooks about the visionary life and its discernment included those by St. Francis of Sales, Martin Delrio, and Raphael de la Torre. Women mystics to emulate included the medieval saints Brigit, Catherine of Siena, Gertrud, and Hildegard, as well as the Spanish *beata* Juana de la Cruz. The license of approval by the cathedral's canon adds to the list: Saints Isabel, Clare, Magdalene of Pazzis, and Teresa, as well as two of Puebla's own, Isabel de la Encarnación and María de Jesús Tomelín. On the opposite end of the spectrum, the *calificador* warns against false visionaries, such as Magdalena de la Cruz (in Córdoba) and María de la Anunciación (in Portugal), as well as several unnamed women in Peru and Mexico. All licenses conclude that María de San José followed in the footsteps of sainted mystic women, although one admits to the unusual character of María's writings—nonetheless, even he approved the biography on the basis of the heroic virtue that María demonstrated in the general confession of her life in volume 1.

Santander y Torres's prologue further assures readers that María's visionary life is distinct from the heretical *alumbrados*; hers was a "virile heart" (*corazón varonil*) worthy of Christ, who safely guided her through a spiritual path full of snares. First and foremost, Santander y Torres states that María avoided heresy by frequent confession and consultations with Christ's mediators on earth, her confessors. Second, she was a shining example of heroic virtue, especially the three fundamental theological virtues of faith, hope, and charity. In addition to these, he argues, she had achieved the rare final stage of mystic union, of experiencing moments of complete similitude with God. Just as the Inquisition and later the Congregation of Holy Rites had judged Rosa de Lima to have experienced this rare mystical process of union, New Spanish clergy were now coming to a similar conclusion about María de San José. Whereas in Rosa's case the church based most of their information on testimony taken about Rosa's life, in María's case church officials came to their conclusions through a careful examination of María's writings. Her mystic passages provoked both concern and awe. María's eagerness to partake in the confessional process cleared her of a possible charge of heterodoxy, and her journals were essential later, when the church promoted her as a model of heroic virtue.

As María began to set her life story to paper, she was deeply aware of the extensive process of spiritual discernment and the potential of being cast as a saint or a sinner because of her visions. Her seemingly colloquial—at times, untrained—style, often misunderstood by readers today as spontaneous and unlettered, disguises an encoding of nearly every aspect of her recorded experience. At the heart of María's journals—and especially of those reflecting more formal genres like the *vida* and *stations*—lies a carefully constructed narrative embedded with passages that echo the rules for confession and holiness. Volume 1, María's most formal confessional life story, provides the key for understanding this process, as the Inquisition's censor had noted. Although María de San José followed conventions in stating that God is the "true Book" and that his teachings in her life almost eliminated the need for books to learn the spiritual path, she frequently incorporated passages from devotional texts and sermons into her notebooks.

Hagiography and spiritual guidebooks served as a lens through which María recalled her life and narrated her textual *vida*. The precept of the *imitatio Christi* and the imitation of the lives of saints that had first informed her daily spiritual practice later influenced the written representation of her life. María inscribed already canonized stories and rules into her narrative. Perhaps viewed as plagiaristic from a present-day perspective, in María's time the process of incorporating other texts into one's own was part of finding one's place among the community of saints. Integral to the confessional process, life writing and imitation helped transform the self before God, just as did the living imitation of Christ's earthly sufferings. María's story unfolds within the conventional hagiographic structure of a Christian upbringing, a fall from grace, a conversion experience, a new vocation from God, and the trials of following God's will, while also receiving divine mercies and grace. For women, in particular, this confessional account in a hagiographic narrative structure needed to include statements of humility, obedience, and ignorance—all in keeping with church teachings about the limits on women's attainment of knowledge.

In addition to following standard narrative structure and rhetoric, María de San José carefully includes phrases from other texts and more general echoes from authors in the mystic tradition, scriptural and liturgical texts, and devotional works. A dictum on virtuous silence and poverty ("do not speak with anyone . . . and do not take or give anything—even though small and insignificant"), for example, appears both in María's account and in a sermon delivered at the Convent of Santa Mónica by Joseph Montero (of course, he may not be the original source for it but may have borrowed from elsewhere). And María explicitly mentions the teachings of Bernard of Clairvaux (his rules for novices, vol. 6) and John of the Cross (his advice not to will a vision, vol. 7). Besides these brief references, María included information about her spiritual practice from a wide range of spiritual exercise guides (in particular, the one attributed to Peter of Alcántara), Franciscan hagiographies (Sts. Clare and Anthony of Padua), the Augustinian Rule, and, especially, the writings by other mystic nuns. She refers to her Spanish Convent sisters—Teresa, María de la Antigua, and Mariana de San Joseph—at least five times each and also mentions the *vida* of another Augustinian Recollect sister, Juana de San Agustín. These nuns provided powerful examples—and justifications—for María's own spiritual progress and writings. For instance, in a vision of a sympathetic Teresa, the saint promises to watch over María's notebooks (vol. 7). Choice phrases from Teresa's writings about spiritual practices, experiences, and confessors are also woven through the fabric of María's narrative. María repeats a popular Teresian dictum, "suffering or death" (*padecer o morir*), more than twenty times and also discusses such Teresian topics as the "prayer of quiet and union" (vol. 2). In fact, María's first volume opens with whole phrases from Teresa's own opening chapter to her spiritual autobiography.

As she wrote her *Vida*, María draws most heavily, however, on the life narrative of the order's founder, Mariana de San Joseph, who in turn notes having read and imitated Catherine of Siena, Rosa de Lima, and Teresa of Avila.[23] María interpolates whole sentences and paragraphs nearly verbatim from the founder's *Vida*.[24] Whether María did so at her confessor's prompting, as part of her own efforts to inscribe her story into that of her order, or because of her lack of training in writing, she imitates her model without alerting her reader. Those familiar with period devotional literature and its conventions would have heard distinct echoes, as the author no doubt intended. The long, borrowed passages tend to sound more rhetorical or homiletic than María's otherwise more colloquial style, but some descriptions of her immediate situation and emotional responses are less easily discernable as borrowings. For example, María signals the formal opening of the *Vida* by copying the first page of the founder's story:

> My Lord and God, it is not the least of the mercies that You grant me now and have granted me before in accepting this confession of mine, which gives a written account of my entire life and of the mercies You have granted me; so that if he so wishes, the one who commands me may know and have a record of the ingratitude and wretchedness with which I have responded in the course of my life to the benefits I have received from Your most liberal hands, unworthy as I am of a single one.[25]

The passage emphasizes the author's chosen status: although she is a miserable sinner, God wishes to use his favors in her life as an example for all to see. The formulaic story about her Christian family and upbringing, about ten pages long, also relies heavily on the model account. The Mexican nun borrows Mariana's idealized description of a long-suffering, devout Christian mother:

> Although she was just a girl, her dresses were those of a woman of many years, so that it could be seen that she had great virtue, and that persons without it should not speak to her, nor would she permit conversations that were not of that kind; and in all things she showed her great understanding. She was very devoted to Our Lady and fond of taking the Holy Sacraments very often. For the rest of her life, she went through many very great trials and illnesses.[26]

In addition, María uses the founder's words for potentially controversial assertions, which suggests that the model text may have made self-expression safer from criticism. Employing the founder's words, María comments on the lack of good confessors ("I had no confessor . . . with whom to unburden my heart,") and her first deep spiritual transformation ("a great window had opened in my soul, and through it came a very bright light,").[27] These were recurring themes in the genre by the turn of the eighteenth century. More unusual, however, is the use of the founder's text to describe María's own sister, Francisca: "The two of us had very different natures, and hers was very good indeed. Her disposition was severe, and withdrawn, and somewhat melancholic. Because of this they thought her rude and disagreeable . . . the Lord permitted her to be harsh with me, to my great good."[28] María's anxiety in recounting the "bloody war" she had with Francisca may explain her borrowing: the saintly Mariana de San Joseph before her had encountered a similar conflict of personalities and seen it as God's will to test her.

To further position her *Vida* within accepted church texts and authority, María insists on the role of clergy and the divine in the construction of her account. The opening pages of volume 1 recall the history of her writing career, which includes an impressive list of Puebla's most talented churchmen who ordered the accounts, read them, and officially registered them.[29] While informative, the passage also is a preemptive move: it establishes the authority of previous accounts and, by extension, the current one. Like her mystic counterparts, María also added to this list of authorities God himself:

> The Bishop told me I should obey at once, without the slightest hesitation, by beginning to write; that even though I could not write, nor had I been able to learn how in spite of all the efforts I had made, obedience could work miracles. Besides this, I knew it pleased Our Lord to make manifest the great deeds that His powerful hand had worked in this lowly and wretched creature that I have been; because in one of the favors that His Divine Majesty had granted me, He had told me, among other things, that it was now time to proclaim and make manifest the great deeds that He had worked in me. And thus His infinite power and mercy might be praised and extolled, knowing that all comes from that powerful hand, and that in me there has never been nor is there more than lowliness and wretchedness.[30]

She attributes the ability to write for her confessors to miraculous intervention. Most women who took the veil had at least some ability to read and write, which were essential skills for devout life in the convent, but any notable degree of learnedness found in their texts usually came from training received before they became nuns. In part because of the isolation of her parents' hacienda, María says she learned only the rudiments of reading and writing from her mother, but that these fell into disuse for many years. After her conversion, she relearned the skill of reading within a few days (with a sister's help) in order to study devotional texts.[31] Later, when first commanded by her confessor to write, she records that God suddenly empowered her to do so.

María's transcription of God's speech and will sets up a dynamic that I refer to as the mystic triad. Based on a triangular relationship between God, clerics, and nuns about designated church roles and authority for men and women, the mystic triad characterizes nearly all religious women's autobiographical accounts from Teresa on.

God as divine author of all life (and, therefore, texts) placed clerical mediators on earth to be his intercessors. All types of clergy—whether bishops, priests, or monks—took vows to guide souls toward God and were recognized as being ordained to interpret God's will. Because the sacraments had become paramount to Counter-Reformation Catholic Church practice, confessors had a good deal of authority to judge a person's life.

For their part in this triad, nuns took vows of complete obedience to their superiors and therefore were required to follow confessors' mandates. Yet the very nature of visionary experience meant that God spoke directly to the individual, without an intermediator. Because women were thought to be more prone to visionary experience, the most typical situation to emerge was one in which God spoke directly to a woman like María, who acted as an instrument through which the divine sent messages to others. She was God's visionary scribe: "His Majesty answered me with these words: 'Your name shall not be mentioned, nor shall My name be on anyone's lips without saying I am He who has accomplished it all. You are nothing more than a lowly tool.' It is clear to see that these words are His alone, both good and true, and would be even if they were spoken to me by the enemy himself; yet even this does not keep me from fear."[32] María's confessor, in turn, required written accounts of her experiences and monitored them with the hope of guiding her along a safe spiritual path. In this system, María is a "writer only by obedience" (*escritora por obediencia*) to God and confessor. Depending on her own narrative needs, however, María, like her convent sisters, negotiated her position as scribe by playing off her experience of God and His authority with her confessor's institutional authority. As we see in the following passage, God interrupts the confessor and speaks directly to María: "This happened in the confessional and I could not attend to or respond to what your Lordship was telling me while this was occurring."[33] The dynamic interplay of God as ultimate author, confessor as official intermediary, and María as visionary scribe frames nearly every account in María's journals. Writing becomes a balancing act: a confession and *apologia por vita suya* before God and clerical intercessor, a vehicle for revealing God's handiwork and goodness, and an outlet for the creative construction of a self that weaves together her personal history and the expectations for model behavior.

Within this institutionalized method for gaining interpretative authority, however, María's journals vary widely in tone and content, depending greatly on the nature of her relationship with the confessor who had requested the account. Writing for at least five confessors over a quarter century, the nun describes an often collaborative, rather than adversarial, situation. In some cases, she struggled for control over the interpretation of her spiritual life. In others, María and her confessor worked together in a partnership in which each had a specific and vital role. In still other instances, confessors freely reversed traditional roles, asked María for advice, and heeded her spiritual insights. With her first addressee, Manuel Barros, who had encouraged visionary activity, she confidently records evidence of divine mercy in her life; with Plácido de Olmedo, the addressee of volume 1 and a fairly reserved confessor, the author expresses anxiety and frequently withholds material from him; and with Bishop Angel de Maldonado, María's last addressee and the man who later called

María a mystic chronicler, the nun communicates conviction in her role as a mystic and writer, even assuring the bishop of his good standing with Saint Augustine (through her visionary experience, vol. 10) and describing her prophecies about the pope (vols. 10 and 11).

These were a series of dynamic confessor-penitent relationships from which both parties gained, even though María was the subordinate partner with regard to institutional power. Only one confessor, Juan Dionisio de Cárdenas, appointed for less than a year, significantly abused his authority by variously requiring her to write twenty-three hours a day or not at all.[34] From her confessors, María de San José gained recognition as a mystic, received guidance, and was given the authority to write extensively. They, in turn, at the least had prayers said on their behalf and stood the chance of gaining more direct access to the divine; as she herself says, she tried to "teach them how to speak with God." Some of María de San José's confessors also found spiritual guidance and an indirect chronicler for their own lives. (For example, she wrote short biographies of several of her confessors.) But negative aspects also abounded on both sides. Her confessors surely had their patience tested over the years. They must have felt significant anxiety as well: serious consequences could result if they misjudged the nature of her spirit, as the Inquisition found Fray Luis de Granada to have done with María de la Visitación. Ultimately, the confessor was responsible for his spiritual daughter. María de San José, of course, had to deal with the fact that each confessor in turn determined what, when, and how she confessed and wrote, because she was always under obedience to him. That María often had little control over her writing was part of a larger effort to help her renounce attachment to and ownership of all worldly things, even her own journals. The nun's resolve was tested at times: the first version of the confessional *vida* was withheld from her, and she was told it had been burnt. Later, she was commanded to rewrite it. Similar incidents of writings being withheld (or worse) marked the writings of Teresa of Avila's *Vida* and Madre Agreda's *Mística ciudad*, as well as that of works by John of the Cross and Fray Luis de León.[35]

María's ongoing commentary about her writing clearly demonstrates the degree to which she writes with full awareness of both her role as a woman writing and of writing as an act of obedience to God and the confessor:

> And if I were to tell your Reverence of the violence and opposition I encounter in writing, I would never finish, because every sentence I write is an enormous trial to me, and it causes me anguish and distress. And so I would prefer not to go on, because I still have not set down all that I had to write. And so your Reverence, being my Father, must ask Our Lord that if I please Him by writing under this order of obedience, He should give me some ease to write about the suffering by which the Lord tries me.[36]

As she attempts to find her place before God and the church, she illustrates the impossibility of writing nakedly about one's self, of ignoring culturally defined models or awareness of potential readers. But while these factors could shape her narrative, they could not wholly dominate it: she blends the time-tested model of the *perfecta religiosa* with the multifaceted realities of her world.

Official Biography and Rescripting Life Stories

When the time came for María's biographer to follow the bishop of Oaxaca's command that he write a sacred biography of her, Santander y Torres had a distinct advantage over Hansen when he wrote the life of Rosa de Lima. First, Hansen had to depend on secondhand material; Santander y Torres had access to María's multi-volume set of confessional writings. Perhaps because of this, he is one of the more generous biographers of nuns in this period: he quotes extensively from her journals and grants them validity within church doctrine. Nonetheless, Santander y Torres exemplifies how a male biographer often miscites his source or refocuses the material.[37] At times he slows the narrative tempo to recount María's penances and ecstasies; he quotes her own extensive details about self-mortifications and consolations, demonstrating the essential link of a mystic's body to access to the divine. (See figure 3.2.) From the medieval biographers of mystics such as Catherine of Siena onward, a male preoccupation with extravagant asceticism and suffering at the hands of others often eclipsed the more subtle meanings that women like María attached to their experiences.[38]

Santander y Torres carefully edits the nun's accounts and manipulates his citations of her journals when material did not fit the portrait of a *perfecta religiosa*. In particular, he recasts María's stories about people who hindered her efforts to enter the convent. He completely villainizes María's sister Francisca, while María's own portrait of the difficult sister was more ambivalent. In another passage, Santander y Torres radically alters María's portrait of Bishop Fernández de Santa Cruz, perhaps in order to protect the prelate's image. Although she relates hagiographic stories of severe trials, María's discussion of her dealings with the bishop is strikingly harsh. She forthrightly depicts him as the embodiment of all those whom God put in her path to test her vocation—an angry, stubborn man who publicly humiliated her in the cathedral when she pleaded for a place in the Convent of Santa Mónica:

> Seeing that some women approached as if to confess to his Grace, I too made my way to his feet. And as I was entirely wrapped in my shawl, he did not know me at first until I began to speak to him. As soon as he recognized me, he asked, "Why have you come here?" I told him why I had come, to ask him for a place [in the convent], the place soon to be empty. I had no sooner spoken these words than he pushed me away from his feet, saying, "Leave here at once, and do not bother me! Have I not told you there is no place for you?"—in a very loud voice, as though he had grown angry at my impertinence. All the people there were astonished to see this, and how annoyed the lord Bishop had become with me. For everyone there heard his shouts. My fright and astonishment were so great upon hearing him that I could not raise myself from his feet and did not know where to flee, because the fright robbed me of all my strength. I got up as best I could, so stunned that I neither knew nor saw where I was setting my feet, and as I was going down the steps of the altar, I missed a step or level. I fell headlong, and slid down I don't know how many steps. I landed right by the

Retrato dela. Mᵉ María de S. Joseph. Religiosa de
las Agustinas Recoletas, fundadora de dos conven
tos; murio con el cargo de Maestra de Novisias el dia 8 de Marzo del 719= su edad 63. años.
fundo enla Puebla y en Oaxaca. Sylverio ſM.

FIGURE 3.2   Woodcut of Madre María de San José, 1723, from *Vida* by Santander y
Torres (Courtesy of the Lilly Library, Bloomington, Indiana)

skirts of one of my sisters who had gone with me. There I lay a short while until I had recovered somewhat. I cried a great many tears, and though I suffered this mortification, I had courage and valor to undergo still greater trials to attain what I so desired, which was to become a nun.[39]

Rewriting this dramatic scene almost comically, Santander y Torres first silences María's repetitive use of the strong adjective "entero" (sternly upright) to describe the bishop and then removes the sting from her criticism with an editorial comment about the humor (*gracia*) of her angry words: "And in truth (María says with much humor), if the bishop had kicked me, I would consider it well done in order to attain what I so desired."[40]

As this example demonstrates, Santander y Torres clearly paraphrases her words and yet he makes them appear as her own words from her journal. He conflates his voice as biographer with hers as autobiographer. At times he writes in the third person about María, but uses her exact words from the manuscript. In other instances, he interjects in the first person words for María that are not in the original account. In the biography, "María" speaks about letting go of her earthly father in order to gain knowledge of her heavenly father, but nowhere in her manuscript account about her father's death does she directly relate these two. Her narrative sequence suggests this transition from biological father to spiritual father, but she did not record it as the clearly didactic passage found in Santander y Torres's text. By directly citing "María" and elaborating on her life in the first person, Santander y Torres creates a certain doubling of María's "I": it becomes not just her voice, but that of the official church as well.

In addition, the biographer foregrounds María de San José's lineage as a descendent of noble conquistadors—a fact she herself rarely mentions—and that she was born in the Tepeaca-Tlaxcala region, where indigenous warriors had joined forces with Cortés to defeat Montezuma. In so doing, Santander y Torres complements the conservative messages preached in the church oratory about maintaining the status quo. Much as María's Spanish-born confessor, Bishop of Oaxaca Ángel de Maldonado, had preached in 1707 about St. Teresa's support for a troubled monarchy, the criollo Santander y Torres attempts to use María's spiritual prestige to reinforce New Spain's elite social order and church hierarchy.[41] Through his mediation of her self-representation, the male biographer safely frames the nun's account in orthodoxy and subordination to the ecclesiastical hierarchy, while at the same time promoting her as a new spiritual *conquistadora*. He admits in the prologue that while it is safer to read the *vidas* of saints, a life like María de San José's demonstrates the "honey" that is being produced in "Our rich America" (*nuestra riquissima America*). While María's writings helped the church form a new hagiographic *vida* and exemplar, by changing her words Santander y Torres furthered María's dream of becoming like a saint.

The history of the only work by María to be published before the twentieth century shows the same deep clerical reluctance to permit a woman to speak freely in her own voice, no matter how useful and inspiring her words. Beginning while she was still a nun at the Convent of Santa Mónica (ca. 1693), every year during Holy Week, María de San José had an ecstatic vision of the Virgin Mary, who guided the nun through the *Stations of the Cross*—a multipart evocation of Jesus' final sufferings and death. As María reports in volume II, around 1710, cooperating with the Virgin's instructions to record and to publish the *Stations* for others' benefit, María wrote out her visions and gave them to one of her confessors, Fray Tomás Pérez de la Torre. Ten years later she heard that her *Stations* had been copied and were being circulated in manuscript form in at least one monastery in Oaxaca, without ever having been published. After receiving a second heavenly command, she rewrote the *Stations*, which were finally published posthumously and went into at least five editions during the eighteenth century.[42]

María possessed a strong sense of mission in the dissemination of the *Stations* for others' benefit, and although clergy responded slowly, they cooperated. Yet the published text alters the original in three significant ways. First, the narrative of the apparition is changed from first to third person; second, María's descriptions about her own feelings are completely deleted (for example, "Here I didn't know . . ."); and third, a prayer written in first person is inserted after each station. The church used María's personal experience of the divine to revitalize and stimulate popular devotion to the Stations of the Cross, while curtailing some of María's more personal comments about the experience, perhaps to render the documents more universal and to discourage the formation of a cult.

Nonetheless, upon Madre María's death, clerics recognized her popularity and value as an exemplary model. At the funerary mass celebrated upon her death, Santander y Torres delivered a panegyric sermon about her heroic life that was published twice within the next four years.[43] The church quickly converted her life story and writing into exemplary representations for convent and public consumption: Madre María de San José is depicted in at least three portraits and four books as a mystic nun who had all the makings of a saint (see figure 3.3). What is more, three of the books were popular enough to go into second editions within a decade of the first printing.[44]

Through this hierarchical process of mediating women's writings to turn them into official church texts, María de San José became part of the Christian female visionary tradition. Upon her death, she was compared with other important New World visionaries; not surprisingly, these were some of the same women whose life stories María had imitated throughout her life. By following the rules for her order and emulating the lives of the saints, she was believed to have been granted divine favors; thus she too became a model of Christian virtue for other criollas. Her life story later influenced other biographers, such as those writing about her sister Leonor, who was abbess of a Carmelite convent in Guadalajara, and another founder of the Oaxaca convent, Antonia de la Madre de Dios.[45] These two biographers inscribe their subjects into a tradition that only fifteen or twenty years after her death included Madre María's life story. Even today in the modern Convent of Santa Mónica, the nuns keep the exemplary life of their mystic sister alive by reading Santander y Torres's biography.[46]

Through the highly encoded genre of spiritual autobiography Counter-Reformation visionary women formulated their own life narratives, working with the precept of the *imitatio Christi* and the special role allotted to mystics. Using a narrative mixture that reflects personal and institutional beliefs, María's accounts fill in many gaps in our knowledge about daily life in the home and cloister and tell of a society and a

FIGURE 3.3   Oil portrait of Madre María de San José, ca. 1720, in the Museo del Arte Virenal, Mexico (Courtesy of Josefina Muriel)

person whose identities were built on certain all-pervading convictions and norms. Her voice also expresses the dynamic relationships that were born out of these interactions between individual and institution—between daughter and family, woman and the Catholic Church, mystic and confessor, nun and God, high-ranking director of novices and other nuns, and elite colonized subject and Spanish hegemony.

In the end, María's close adherence to devotional codes kept her within orthodoxy, but it also probably contributed to the weakness of her case in Rome. The Vatican wanted singular cases—of truly extraordinary holy individuals. By living in a convent, safe from the public eye, and creating a conventional autohagiography, María's spiritual path was not innovative or remarkable in the way that Teresa of Avila's or even Rosa de Lima's had been. Nonetheless, in Spanish America, church texts about her spiritual life became popular enough to go into several editions. For our purposes, María's manuscript journals are key. In both Rosa's and Catarina de San Juan's cases, we have little or no evidence of their own writings. But, we hear María's voice directly, providing us with the opportunity to study the process of church mediation in posthumous texts. Her journals reveal the transmission of Teresian elements to America—the narrative ingredients of and the possibilities for a confessional *vida*. María de San José's narrative of religious vocation, mystic experience, and spiritual authority provides a blueprint for understanding the often unspoken models which were futher rewritten by the women studied in the next three chapters.

Chronology of María de San José

1656   Born Juana Palacios Berruecos, near Tepeaca, New Spain.

1687   Enters Convent of Santa Mónica, Order of Augustinian Recollects, in Puebla.

1688   Takes final vows as a black-veiled nun.

1691   Begins confessional accounts for Manuel Barros and Bishop Fernández de Santa Cruz.

1697   Leaves Puebla to found Convent of Nuestra Señora de la Soledad in Oaxaca; serves as novice mistress for the rest of her life there.

1703–4   Writes a formal *Vida* for Plácido de Olmedo (vol. 1).

1710   Drafts her only work published in the colonial period, *Stations of the Cross*.

1717   Rewrites the *Stations*.

1719   Dies and is buried at the Convent of Nuestra Señora de la Soledad, Oaxaca.

1719   Two editions are published of her funerary sermon, *Oración funebre*, by Fray Sebastián de Santander y Torres.

1723   Two editions are published of her biography, *Vida de la venerable madre*, by Fray Sebastián de Santander y Torres; two editions are published of her *Stations*.

1726?   Bishop Angel Maldonado writes and publishes his tract proposing María's beatification, *Patri Excelso*.

1773, 1782   María's *Stations* are republished.

II

Not Quite Sinners

4

The Tenth Muse

Sor Juana Inés de la Cruz (1648–1695)— Letters and Learning in the Church

Am I perchance a heretic? And even if I were, could sheer force make me a saint?
—Sor Juana, *Letter to Father Núñez*

They can leave such things to those who understand them; as for me, I want no trouble with the Holy Office, for I am but ignorant and tremble lest I utter some ill-sounding proposition.
—Sor Juana, *La respuesta*

Between 1690 and 1693 a storm was brewing over a nun's writings in the cultural center of New Spain, Mexico City. The same bishop who had urged María de San José to begin writing and who had signed the license granting the publication of Ramos's biography of Catarina de San Juan had just published Sor Juana Inés de la Cruz's scholastic critique of a theological point. As we saw in Madre María's case, rarely were nuns' works published in their own lifetimes and, in theory, nuns were barred from publicly discussing theological issues. And yet Sor Juana, the most famous nun of the colonial period, had written and published profane and sacred works at the behest of clergy and viceroys. She was one of the first two women published in America and wrote in nearly all the literary genres used by both men and women.[1] For decades after her entrance into the cloister in 1669, Sor Juana had escaped the literary limits imposed on religious women, composing everything from sharply biting lines about men's contradictory demands for women ("Silly, you men—so very adept/at wrongly faulting womankind,/ not seeing you're alone to blame/ for faults you plant in woman's mind") to sublime devotional dramatic pieces ("Tell me where he is whom my soul loves,/ where he feeds his lambs,/ and where he lays him down to rest/ at the noontide hours./ For why should I be one who turns aside/ by the folds where flocks of other swains abide?").[2] By 1690 she had acquired an extensive library and her fame had spread with a collection of her work published in Spain (*Inundación castálida*, 1689). Sor Juana's artistic and intellectual life also extended to frequent gatherings (*tertulias*) that she held in the convent *locutorio*, often attended by Mexico City's leading figures—among them, the noted intellectual, Carlos de Sigüenza y Góngora, two sets of viceregal couples, and Bishop Manuel Fernández de Santa Cruz. Unlike the spiritual gatherings of important Limeños hosted by Rosa de Lima, however, Sor Juana's *tertulias* covered a wide range of secular and sacred topics.

It was perhaps in one such gathering, often forums for artistic and philosophical debate, that Sor Juana first offered a scholastic critique of a theological point in an influential Jesuit's sermon. Her critique began a three-year debate (1690–1693) about both her literary career and the appropriateness of her incursion into theology. In the critique, Sor Juana noted how the sermon's premises were built on illogical reasoning. One of the interlocutors (by some accounts, Bishop Santa Cruz), taken with the brilliance of the rebuttal, asked the nun to write down her arguments. Apparently without Sor Juana's consent, Bishop Santa Cruz then published Sor Juana's thesis, the *Carta atenagórica* [Letter worthy of Athena] (Puebla, 1690). In an outwardly contradictory move, Bishop Santa Cruz made the nun's incursion into the forbidden terrain of theological debate available to a broader public and then admonished Sor Juana in his prologue for her literary and theological pursuits: "It is a pity that so great a mind should stoop to lowly earthbound knowledge and not desire to probe into what transpires in heaven. But since it does lower itself to ground level, may it not descend further still and ponder what goes on in hell!"[3] He encouraged Sor Juana to follow, instead, Teresa of Avila's example as a woman author writing on devotional topics. While the bishop's intentions remain enigmatic, what is clear is that the publication unleashed a flurry of responses from supporters and detractors, as well as from Sor Juana herself. She would later write her most famous autobiographical work, *La Respuesta a Sor Filotea de la Cruz* [the Reply to Sor Filotea] (1691), as a response to the bishop's prologue and an attempt to clarify her position as a lettered nun.

The *Respuesta a Sor Filotea de la Cruz* makes a daring defense of Sor Juana's right as an individual, intellectually gifted by God, to study and write, in spite of church restrictions on women's learning. Sor Juana's boldness continued after these initial letters; with the help of her ally, the ex-vicereine of New Spain, Sor Juana's second volume of works—*Obras*—was published in Spain in 1692.[4] The collection did not exclude love verses or satire, and even republished the *Carta atenagórica*.[5] A much larger polemic over Sor Juana's vocation was building, however, and it would end with one of her defenders being summoned by the Inquisition. She herself may have been entered into a secret trial conducted by the archbishop of Mexico (*proceso arzobispal secreto*).[6] In any case, the events led to the selling of her extensive library and her official rededication to her religious vows in 1693–1694.

Ultimately, Sor Juana's life, although very different from the women studied thus far, also embodied the contradictory attitudes of her times. While for years she wrote for and entertained the most prominent civic, ecclesiastical, and intellectual leaders of New Spain, she was the target of heated debates in both Mexico and Spain. In Sor Juana's case, the controversy over the interpretation of proper behavior for a religious woman did not revolve around the representation of sanctity as it had for Rosa, Catarina de San Juan, and Madre María; now the drama unfolded around her secular accomplishments as author and intellect, over the issue of the propriety of a religious woman's education and writing. Sor Juana avoided for more than two decades the role of the *perfecta religiosa* who imitated Christ's Passion and become known instead as the Phoenix of America and the Tenth Muse, an author worthy of mythical titles during her own lifetime.

What can the debate about Sor Juana's literary and religious vocations and her letters in response to the polemic tell us about the rules for religious women and their roles in the church and in society? How do her letters employ conventional epistolary and *vida* genres for nuns and at the same time undermine the traditional portrait of a nun? As we will see, Sor Juana took advantage of church and society's desires to capitalize on the phenomenon of a bright woman who could serve as a cultural or spiritual icon for the colony. She deftly worked with allies and, when necessary, worked within church limits. In all cases, however, she created a strong individual voice. Indeed, Sor Juana's self-presentation is so strong throughout her work that one critic argues it is the most clear and insistent in colonial Mexican literature.[7] The autobiographical voice, whether in prose, poetry, or drama, consistently presents the idea of the genderless nature of the soul and the intellect, and this, in turn, had strong implications for reinterpreting women's roles.

Feminist studies in recent years have naturally focused on Sor Juana's contribution to a historic redefinition of the "appropriate" role for religious women. Although her work was widely published in the three decades after her death (1695–1725), with the spread of neoclassical culture, many baroque authors like Sor Juana faded from the public eye for several centuries.[8] At first slowly, with the mid–twentieth century commemoration of her birth, and then more dramatically in 1995 with the three-hundred-year anniversary of her death, readers began to rediscover Sor Juana's literary corpus. Perhaps one of the most notable turning points, however, occurred in the 1980s when the larger political-intellectual trends of feminism embraced Sor Juana as a precursor of the women's rights movement. At the same time, Nobel Prize winner Octavio Paz published his landmark "restitution" of Sor Juana, *Sor Juana Inés de la Cruz or The Traps of Faith* (1982), which was soon translated for English readers.[9] A variety of contemporary studies exist regarding the nun's life and works; they tend to revolve around feminist analyses of Sor Juana's work, new theories about church teachings on obedience and free will, contextualizing studies of the major characters in Sor Juana's life, and the study of early editions and related primary documents that have surfaced.[10] The last decade in particular has seen the rediscovery of documents related to Sor Juana's life. Some scholars claim that several documents were actually penned by her.[11] What has not been studied thoroughly, however, is how Sor Juana used the confessor-nun relationship to discuss topics that were typically off-limits for religious women. Building on the work of a handful of scholars who have pointed to the important role of epistolary and *vida* genres, I argue that, in fact, Sor Juana exploits the ideological structure of traditional confessor-nun communiques—and the *vida* genre in particular—in order to accomplish her own reworking of it.[12]

Three letters—the *Carta al Padre Núñez* (ca. 1682), *Carta atenagórica* (1690), and *La Respuesta a Sor Filotea de la Cruz* (1691)—help us understand the limits imposed by the church on women (and religious women writers, in particular), as well as the flexibility in how those restrictions were applied.[13] Whereas hagiographers reworked the life of Rosa de Lima to construct an identity that served a broad range of popular and institutional demands, and María de San José cautiously inserted her voice into the conventions of saints' lives and divine authorship with the hope of becoming a saint herself, Sor Juana drew on the prescriptions for nuns and their writings but created a new script. Using the broad ideological possibilities of the epistolary genre and mixing them with an at-times ironic use of hagiographic and *vida de monja* conventions, Sor Juana carefully rendered a new portrait of a *perfecta religiosa*, one that could include a lettered nun (*religiosa letrada*). In the process, she contributed to the debate about self-determination for women in the Catholic Church.

Portrait of an Author

Sor Juana was a product of her times—in terms of the circumstances of her birth, her move to an urban area and eventually into the convent, and in her tenuous relationships with church hierarchy. Yet, she was a highly unusual woman because of her intellectual drive, her success in reaching the highest echelons of both church and court, and her well-known and extensive publications in her own lifetime. Because of Sor Juana's fame and status as a Spanish American canonical author, we know more about her life than about almost any woman of the period. Recent discoveries of historical documents, however, have revised our knowledge about Sor Juana's date of birth, final years, literary corpus, and interaction with important clergy.

Born in 1648 in a small town a day's travel from Mexico City, Juana Inés de Asbaje y Ramírez, was the daughter of a Spanish captain, Pedro Manuel de Asbaje, and a criolla woman, Isabel Ramírez, who ran her father's farm and gave birth to a total of six children.[14] Like nearly half the women of her time, Juana's mother had her children out of wedlock. As recent studies show, there were several economic advantages for this choice, and Juana came from a long line of independent-minded women who sought such advantage.[15] By her own account in the *Respuesta*, Juana portrays herself as having a certain independence of spirit and precociousness; she claims that by age three she tricked a teacher into letting her attend an *amiga* (a girls' school for rudimentary education held in a private home) with her sister. Later, she reportedly learned Latin in fewer than twenty lessons and asked her mother if she could disguise herself as a man in order to study science at the university in Mexico City. Clearly unable to do so, Juana set about studying the books in her grandfather's library. By about age ten, Juana left home to live with relatives in Mexico City, a not uncommon occurrence in criolla families if a young woman or man wanted to pursue more urban social or vocational outlets.[16]

In this multiracial city of some fifty-thousand inhabitants, the landscape was dominated by the canals surrounding the city and the bridges leading into it. By the mid–seventeenth century, the city center boasted a large main plaza with a cathedral-in-progress on one side, the government offices (*cabildo*) on the other, and the viceregal palace on another. Sor Juana would spend five years in this religious and civil administrative heart of New Spain.

Within a few years after her arrival in Mexico City, Sor Juana's wit, charm, and intellectual curiosity won her a place as a lady-in-waiting in the viceregal court. For nearly five years she attended to the vicereine, the marquise of Mancera (who soon became a friend), and participated actively in ceremonial and social activities at court.

Juana's phenomenal gifts for writing verse and accumulating knowledge became widely known and sought out. The viceroy himself decided to test (and perhaps display) Juana by assembling forty of the most learned secular and religious men in Mexico City. The viceroy described how a variety of theological, scientific, and historical questions were posed. Juana outmaneuvered all her examiners: "The way in which a royal galleon would ward off a few canoes who were assailing it, so did Juana Inés dispatch the questions, arguments, and replies which so many persons, each in his own way, proposed to her."[17]

By 1667, Juana had taken stock of her gifts and desired nothing more than to pursue her intellectual vocation. As she herself reports in the *Respuesta*, she was against the idea of marrying (perhaps because marriage was far too demanding of a woman's time) and, instead, chose the convent, which offered a degree of autonomy for study. In consultation with the Jesuit Antonio Núñez de Miranda, who served as both her own and the viceregal couples' spiritual advisor, Juana first entered the prestigious but strict order of the Discalced Carmelites located just a block from the palace. Within months, however, she left because of illness. In 1669 Juana made a second attempt, this time in a regular order, the Hieronymite Convent of Santa Paula in Mexico City. Given a dowry by her godfather and able to circumvent requirements for legitimate birth because of her talent, Sor Juana took final vows. As in the case of other black-veiled nuns, her duties included praying the Divine Office and helping run the convent, at times in the capacity of accountant and music teacher for the girls' school that was annexed to the convent. Although the nuns at the Convent of Santa Paula observed the Augustinian Rule for nuns, which was also used by María de San José's order, as adapted by Bishop Santa Cruz for the Hieronymites, they did not follow it to the letter.[18] Sor Juana and her convent sisters lived comfortably, received visitors, and in general did not adhere strictly to vows of poverty or total enclosure.

Sor Juana lived in a two-story "cell" (more like a condominium) within the walls of the convent, had her own slave (a gift from her mother), maintained one of the largest libraries in New Spain, held regular conversations with the viceroys and others, and continued to write poetry. Not restricted to literary activity, Sor Juana's mind held an insatiable curiosity for a broad range of knowledge. Period documents reveal that her library had theological, philosophical, scientific, and literary works and that she corresponded with some of the greatest intellectuals in Mexico City.[19] In spite of communal duties and a vow of obedience to church superiors, the convent gave Sor Juana a degree of protection and solitude for her intellectual and artistic vocation.

From within the cloister, Sor Juana continued to have ties with the court. Through her writing she participated fully in the thick of religious, civic, and cultural celebrations in viceregal Mexico. Commissioned to write poetry of etiquette for birthdays and funerals, popular musical religious verse (*villancicos*) for church feasts, courtly love poetry for literary contests, one-act sacramental plays for Corpus Christi celebrations, and prose descriptions of ceremonial arches to be erected for the entrance of a new viceroy, Sor Juana's work covers the gamut of popular and erudite, profane and sacred baroque literature. Beyond these official commissions, Sor Juana

herself delighted in writing about her quest for knowledge and about human relationships. She wrote some of her most touching verse to her close friends the vicereines
(the marquise of Mancera in 1664–1676; the countess of Paredes in 1680–1688). Some
of her most barbed satire focused on relationships between men and women. One of
the most stunning poetic pieces to emerge out of baroque Hispanic letters is Sor
Juana's nine-hundred-line *silva*, *First Dream*, which elaborates in meter the abstract
discursive journey of her soul as it attempted to comprehend the nature of the universe. Simultaneously inscribed within and breaking out of baroque conventions for
popular and erudite verse, Sor Juana's work added an innovative, often rebellious
voice that appealed to her contemporaries.

Her record of intellectual questing and her verses about society's views of women
help set the scene for the controversy that later erupted over her literary career. Up
until the last several years of her life, Sor Juana parodied conventional depictions of
women and created alternate portraits. To underscore the artificiality of artistic
conventions for describing women, Sor Juana rewrote—often with a strong dose of
humor—Petrarchan conventions in which women's exterior beauty was the sole focus
of the male poet's eye and was described in terms of metaphorical equivalents that
had little to do with human qualities.[20] She argues instead for the idea that all human
beings are most essentially beings with a soul, which is sexless: "My body/ disin-
clined to this man or that, serves only to house the soul/ you might call it neuter or
abstract."[21]

During this time, Sor Juana enjoyed the support of the court and the tolerance of
most clergymen, but early in 1682 she broke with her adversarial and influential confessor Antonio Núñez de Miranda. In a letter rediscovered twenty years ago, *Carta al Padre
Núñez*, Sor Juana bitterly complains about his insistence that she follow a narrow interpretation of proper behavior for nuns and that she stop writing verse. She promptly
dismissed him as her confessor. With Núñez's power over her life diminished, Sor Juana
wrote copiously for nearly a decade. She only returned to writing in defense of her
literary pursuits in 1691 with the *Respuesta* to the bishop's publication of the *Carta atenagórica*.
But this time, the letters were made more public and led to her official silencing in
1693–1694. She died a year later in an epidemic that swept the convent.

Letters, *Vidas*, and a New Role for Nuns

The core of the polemic over Sor Juana's religious and literary vocation is clearly
revealed in the 1682 confrontation between the nun and her confessor, Núñez de
Miranda. Núñez was a powerful figure within the Catholic Church: he was a confessor to viceroys, *calificador* for the Inquisition, one-time professor at the Jesuit Colegio
del Espíritu Santo (in Puebla), head of an important brotherhood, and a prolific
devotional author.[22] A spiritual counselor who took his charge seriously, Núñez wrote
several guides for nuns. He took the church's teachings that nuns were "brides of
Christ" one step further: they were "widows of Christ" who should retire completely
from worldly concerns. In addition, he adhered staunchly to the Counter-Reformation
emphasis on obedience to church superiors as the most fundamental vow of monastic life: "For the [vow] of obedience she sacrifices her own volition, free will and

entire soul."[23] In his official position as censor for the Inquisition, as well as one of her spiritual directors, Núñez had approved Catarina de San Juan's virtuous obedience to the Jesuits and, later, he wrote a prologue to Ramos's biography of the *beata.* Likewise, Núñez had helped guide Sor Juana into the religious life, advising her of the danger of staying "in the world" with her beauty and wit. By some accounts, he persuaded a rich gentleman to be her benefactor and pay the large dowry required for entrance into San Jerónimo.[24] Clearly, Sor Juana's continued literary production and interaction with court members flew in the face of his hopes for her religious vocation.

The letter that Sor Juana wrote to Núñez in 1682 to break with him reveals the essence of their dispute, a dispute that Sor Juana would voice formally in the *Respuesta.*[25] Using the personal tone of an informal letter, the nun questioned Núñez's authority to interpret God's will for her: "What direct authority . . . did you have to dispose of my person and my God-given free will?"[26] She argues that only God has the power to make saints: "Only the grace and assistance of God are capable of producing saints."[27] To study was to employ God's gifts and, in so doing, move along the road to salvation. God created many keys to heaven, and Núñez's was not the only one:

> For the God who created and redeemed and bestows so many mercies on me will provide a means whereby my soul . . . will not go astray even if it be without Your Reverence's guidance, for heaven has many keys and is not restricted to one judgment only. . . . Salvation consists more in the desiring than in the knowing and the former depends more on me than on a confessor. . . . What rule dictates that this salvation of mine must be by means of Your Reverence? Cannot it be someone else? Is God's mercy restricted and limited to one man, even if he be as prudent, as learned and as saintly as Your Reverence?[28]

Like María de San José, Sor Juana exercised her right as a nun to choose a compatible confessor (and, therefore, to dismiss one as well). She pointed a finger at Núñez's misinterpretation of God's will and left him so that she could continue on her path toward God without interference.

Sor Juana's two letters, written almost ten years later, reveal that, after years of relative freedom after breaking with Núñez, differences of opinion over religious women's roles had again surfaced. To understand Sor Juana's masterful *Carta atenagórica* and *La Respuesta,* as well as her alternative religious self-portrait, we need to understand Sor Juana's artful molding of the conventions and ideological possibilities of the epistle with the confessional *vida.* Rosa Perelmuter argues that Sor Juana was well aware of the rhetorical possibilities of the letter as a genre. In the *Respuesta* she adeptly blends the Ciceronian forensic model, in which letters were the expository vehicle for proving a case, with the Erasmian personal letter, based on an informal, conversational style of writing. In fact, Sor Juana employed Renaissance epistolary conventions in all the letters discussed in this chapter and drew on the genre's ideological purposes to strengthen her arguments.

By Sor Juana's time, the epistle had a long history and a varied use. A well-defined, broadly used genre that dated from antiquity, the letter was used for both personal and official purposes. As Jamile Trueba Lawand's study of the Renaissance epistolary tradition reveals, Greco-Roman authors such as Demetrios and Cicero characterized the letter as half of a dialogue aimed at an absent person and generally written in a simple yet elegant style (chap. 1). Personal letters in particular were to be written "as a portrait of one's soul."[29] The official letter, discussed in particular by Cicero and Quintilian, could serve as the expository vehicle both for information and for treatises of a poetic or philosophical nature (chap. 4). Early church fathers of Christianity used letters to accentuate the personal experience of religion on the one hand and to expound theological points in a clear format on the other.[30]

By the medieval period, the precept of the *ars dictamen* greatly influenced the development of the genre, and the formal aspects of the letter were highlighted over its possibilities for personal correspondence. With the early modern rediscovery of literary forms from antiquity, the genre gained new life and became a varied expository vehicle. Besides its use for personal correspondence, the letter became part of the *studis humanitatis* curriculum and also was widely used for literary and philosophical treatises. Lorenzo Valla, Erasmus of Rotterdam, and Juan Luis de Vives were among the many humanists who wrote treatises defining the genre.[31] In addition, collections of letters were widely published for popular reading. For our purposes, it is interesting to note that Teresa of Avila's *Epistolario* was published in two volumes in 1658, including both official letters (which reflected a high style and rhetorical use of repetition) and personal letters (written in a familiar, low style). Teresa herself was no stranger to treatises that had used the form, as she had read St. Francis of Borja's and Fray Luis de Granada's works.[32]

As studies of Sor Juana's library reveal, she was familiar with authors who had written in or about the epistolary genre. She cites many, such as Cicero, Quintilian, early church fathers (especially Paul and Jerome), and Teresa of Avila. In addition, Sor Juana had read several of the letters addressed to nuns written by Núñez de Miranda and Bishop Santa Cruz.[33] Drawing on the epistolary genre's possibilities, in the *Carta atenagórica* Sor Juana employs a familiar yet legalistic tone and structure. In the *Respuesta* she continues to combine the familiarity of a personal letter with the formal, rhetorical defense of a case. But she also adds to it the pedagogical purpose of an epistolary treatise.

As mentioned, Bishop Santa Cruz was the probable catalyst and addressee for Sor Juana's *Carta atenagórica*. Addressed rather generically to "Muy Señor mío," the *Carta* was a brilliant refutation of a sermon delivered about fifty years before by a well-known Portuguese Jesuit, Antonio Vieira. Using scholastic argumentation within the context of a letter, Sor Juana highlighted the errors in Vieira's sermon—itself a refutation of three church fathers' arguments about Christ's greatest *fineza*, or gift to mankind. She cleverly dismantled the sermon, restored the church fathers' theses, and added her own theological interpretation. As a woman who defended her right to pursue god-given talents, she presented Christ's greatest gift as that of the *beneficios negativos*—that is, despite being all-powerful, God allows individuals to use free will and thus to grow in virtue. The theology of free will and God's gifts to each individual would become one of Sor Juana's champion causes.[34] While taking on serious theological polemics, Sor Juana masked the letter's contents with a conversational, at times jovial, tone and drove home her logical development of a case within the main body of the letter, which is organized around a series of "proofs" ("prueba más," "más," "probado pues," "apoyar más," "pruébalo por razón," "el mayor aprieto del precepto," etc.) and blocks of oratorical exclamations and rhetorical questions.[35] Nonetheless, Sor Juana did not fail to close the refutation with a brief bow to superiors and a recognition of her own obedient role: "I place all I have said under the *censure* of our Holy Mother Catholic Church, as her most obedient daughter."[36] The multifaceted roles of the epistolary genre served Sor Juana well: she blurred the line between a conversational, humble letter befitting her status as a woman addressing a superior and a more formal philosophical argument.

When Bishop Santa Cruz published the refutation with his ambiguous prologue about Sor Juana's learned and literary pursuits and gave it the laudatory title *Carta atenagórica*—emphasizing its nature as an erudite letter, one worthy of the Goddess of Wisdom, Athena—the bishop firmly placed Sor Juana's work in a narrative genre that was permissible for a nun; she had written a letter, not a sermon or a theological treatise.[37] As we saw in María de San José's case, Bishop Santa Cruz was a powerful, sometimes mercurial bishop who was devoted to building charitable institutions for women, and he wrote numerous letters and convent rules for his beloved nuns. He delighted in God's prodigious hand at work in an exceptional woman and yet endeavored to ensure that the world did not "rob God of His own."[38] Ultimately, however, Sor Juana's incursion into theology went beyond Bishop Santa Cruz's control; the publication reached other readers who strongly objected to Sor Juana's literary and public roles.

To many readers today, the storm unleashed by a debate about a nearly fifty-year-old sermon is perhaps puzzling. Sor Juana's love poetry seems much more daring. But it is important to recall that sermons could be published—and Vieira's had been republished several times after 1650—and they often dealt with sensitive church doctrine. Thus they could be influential church documents for many years. In addition, recent studies underscore that Sor Juana's text may have served to deepen the rift between her ex-confessor Padre Núñez and herself. Elías Trabulse in particular argues that the real target of Sor Juana's *Carta atenagórica* was not Vieira, but her ex-confessor Núñez: both were Jesuits who strongly advocated the role of the Eucharist in the church.[39] The differences of opinion extended to clergy at the highest echelons in New Spain, including the misogynistic, ascetic archbishop of Mexico, Francisco Aguiar y Seijas. Although there are several hypotheses about the motives behind Santa Cruz's publication and the archbishop's role, it seems that Sor Juana was caught in a dispute over the church's enforcement of proper behavior among religious women. And, because she was such a highly visible nun, the stakes were high.[40]

In response to the polemic caused by her own literary vocation, Sor Juana drafted *La Respuesta a Sor Filotea de la Cruz* and returned to the arguments she had used against Núñez.[41] This time, however, her remarks are directed to Bishop Santa Cruz and written in a more formal statement that ultimately was made public through the circulation of manuscript copies and a posthumous publication.[42] Referring to her own previous letters and Bishop Santa Cruz's prologue, Sor Juana builds her *Respuesta* on the foundation of the central theology of free will, as expressed in the *Carta atenagórica*.

She applies this theology in personal terms, within the spiritual director-daughter relationship, as seen in the *Carta al Padre Núñez*; and she refers to Santa Cruz's invocation of Sts. Paul and Teresa in his discussion of model behavior for women in the Catholic Church.

La Respuesta a Sor Filotea de la Cruz is a carefully crafted rhetorical piece that defies strict generic categorization; the letter is variously called a self-defense and autobiography.[43] Sor Juana includes in the *Respuesta* a long narrative of her life story and her vocation for letters. Studying the epistolary structure of the *Respuesta*, Rosa Perelmuter observes that Sor Juana purposely highlights the narrative section, rather than the proof. Sor Juana opens with statements of humility (the *exordio*, lines 1–215), continues with the story of her call to a life of study (the narration, lines 216–844), and then culminates with a list of antecedents: a catalogue of learned women, church fathers' views of women and poetry (the proof, lines 845–1418). The *Respuesta* then closes by repeating statements of humility (the *peroración*, lines 1419–38).[44] Perelmuter proposes that the familiar tone and the lengthy narrative section reflect a move away from the Ciceronian juridical style and toward the Erasmian personal letter. Notably, these familiar elements also coincide with the extended nun-confessor communiqué, the *vida espiritual*. The letter, used in the early church to express personal religious experience, had developed over the centuries into a frequent expository vehicle for religious women writing to their male superiors. As we saw with María de San José, what often began as a series of *cuentas de conciencia* or *relaciones de espíritu* (in which a nun detailed her intimate spiritual experiences at the behest of her confessor) could later develop into a request for a formal *vida*. While continuing to reflect the confessor-penitent, reader-writer dynamic found in letters, the *vida* genre was much more highly structured and influenced by hagiographic conventions.

Sor Juana creates a tight rhetorical parallel between her self-presentation and the narrative posture, structure, themes, and topics that characterized the *vida* genre. She builds her argument by cleverly reworking the very beliefs and traditions about religious women that she seeks to undermine. But how exactly does Sor Juana employ the rhetoric and structure of the *vida* to alter its ideology? Taking Bishop Santa Cruz's suggestion to follow in Teresa's footsteps, Sor Juana models her *Respuesta* on Teresian conventions from the *Libro de su vida* to justify her life path and to critique percepts about women's religious lives. As we will see, Sor Juana begins her *vida* at essentially the same point as her sisters—the moment of the divine call (*vos me coegistis*)—and follows much the same process: the *imitatio Christi*. But she deliberately chooses a nonconventional way to justify her path: she shuns the culturally acceptable (though still dangerous) practice of following the mystic's path. Instead, Sor Juana suggests that a woman who has been given a good intellect should use it to fashion her self-image, just as the woman who has been given visionary gifts should use them to define herself. After all, she argues, all things issue from God. By employing the conventions of the *vida* for an alternate life story, Sor Juana validates the use of the genre for religious women's self-representation, but she changes the typical portrait of a nun.

From the first, Sor Juana's *Respuesta* moves well beyond conventional epistolary humility in the *exordio* (paragraphs 1–5), which suggests that she is not drawing on

Cicero or Erasmus but rather on church expectations for nuns in their writing to confessors. In a hyperbolic style, Sor Juana emphasizes her humility, ignorance, and obedience to superiors, echoing the *vida*. As a nun she is an *escritora por obedienca*. Sor Juana confesses to being tearful and speechless upon learning that "Sor Filotea" (Bishop Santa Cruz's alias) had published the *Carta atenagórica*. As a "humble" nun, Sor Juana argues, tongue-in-cheek, that her writings are not hers to control. She asks: "By chance, am I something more than a poor nun, the slightest creature on earth and the least worthy of drawing your attention?"[45] And yet, Sor Juana claims a likeness to Moses, who was chosen by God in spite of his "stammering": she is unable to articulate her confused thoughts about writing and publishing under obedience to others. She further evokes the triangular relationship between a nun, her clerical superior, and God by repeatedly using the word "confess" (*confesar*) and reminding Bishop Santa Cruz that God is the ultimate author and judge of her life: "Blessed are you my Lord God, for not only did you forbear to give another creature the power to judge me, nor have you placed that power in my hands. Rather, you have kept that power for yourself."[46] In addition, Sor Juana ironically portrays herself as ignorant and bowing to the Inquisition: "They can leave such things to those who understand them; as for me, I want no trouble with the Holy Office, for I am but ignorant."[47] Sor Juana's ironic tone is yet more apparent when she uses a string of hyperbolic adjectives to describe the bishop's own letter: "your immensely learned, prudent, devout, and loving letter."[48]

Vos Me Coegistis

Having parodied the framing device and rhetorics of the *vida*, Sor Juana moves into the core element of the genre, the narration of a vocation, which coincides with the narrative section of the letter. An essential element of every *vida* was an *apologia por vita sua*, which presented the author's life as one that mirrored the lives of Christian saints and martyrs. As we saw in Madre María de San José's narrative, the *vida* typically sketched a Christian upbringing, a call to the religious life, and proof of following a life devoted to God's will, often depicted as a mixture of suffering (*imitatio Christi*) and the manifestation of God's goodness (*misericordias*) in her life. If the *vida* deviated from this pattern, the author was obligated to reveal the cause for this lapse.

In Sor Juana's hands, the conventional narration of a Christian upbringing and religious vocation takes on a new twist. She announces that God called her to the life of letters:

> My writing has never proceeded from any dictate of my own, but a force beyond me; I can in truth say, *"vos me coegistis"* [You have compelled me]. One thing, however, is true, so that I shall not deny it (first because it is already well known to all, and second because God has shown me His favor in giving me the greatest possible love of truth, even when it might count against me). For ever since the light of reason first dawned in me, my inclination to letters was marked by such passion and vehemence that neither the reprimands of others (for I have received many) nor reflections of my own (there have been more than a few) have sufficed to make me abandon

my pursuit of this native impulse that God Himself bestowed on me. His
Majesty knows why and to what end He did so.[49]

According to church teachings, spiritual vocations and powers were divine gifts,
and nuns spent much time in demonstrating God's grace at work in their spiritual
paths. They needed to tame their own wills in order to passively receive his mercies,
but they also had to work actively at prayer, good deeds, and penance in order to
make themselves worthy of such blessings. Sor Juana clearly frames her narration
within this context of *vos me coegistis*.[50] The call, as in her convent sisters' experiences,
led Sor Juana to take the veil as a bride of Christ, to become "dead to the world,"
and to leave the development of her vocation in God's hands: "Your Majesty knows
too that, not achieving this, I have attempted to entomb my intellect together with
my name and to sacrifice it to the One who gave it to me; and that no other motive
brought me to the life of Religion."[51]

The call to God required work and sacrifice. Sor Juana uses conventional vo-
cabulary and stories to report her own experience in following the road to Christ.
She echoes *vida* phrases, such as "To go on with the narration of this inclination of
mine, of which I wish to give you a full account,"[52] formally linking the *Respuesta*
with autobiographical genres. And she recalls the feeling of urgency toward her vocation, which she experienced at an early age. Rather than describe a burning love
for Christ and reading about his saints like other nuns, Sor Juana talks of a burning
love for reading. Rather than speak of disobeying parents in order to fight the Moors
as Teresa had wanted to do, Juana records sneaking off at age three to learn to read
at a local girls' school. Rather than practice severe self-mortification to remain in
prayer as Rosa had, Juana cut her hair to punish herself for not learning enough. All
the same, Sor Juana's "inclination" also led her to the convent. Notably, however
the *Respuesta* says nothing about the nearly five years between leaving her family and
entering the convent, a time spent as a lady-in-waiting at the viceregal court. Perhaps this seemed an unbecoming element in an ideal portrait of a studious, solitary
bride of Christ removed from the world.

In recounting her years as a bookish nun, Sor Juana continues to draw on the
key spiritual precept of the *vida*: everything comes from God. As in the account of
her secular life, Sor Juana transforms the burning love for Christ and knowledge of
the divine universe through spiritual experience seen in Teresa and Madre María into
an insatiable love of learning in order to understand the Queen of Knowledge, theology: "In sum, we see how this Book contains all books, and this Science includes
all sciences, all of which serve that She may be understood. And once each science is
mastered (which we see is not easy, or even possible), She demands still another
condition beyond all I have yet said, which is continual prayer and purity of life, to
entreat God for that cleansing of spirit and illumination of the mind required for an
understanding of such high things. And if this be lacking, all the rest is useless."[53]
Much as a mystic who pursues divine knowledge through the three *vias*, Sor Juana
argues that she must pray, go through the active process of purgation of the will, and
seek illumination. Notably absent is a direct reference to the rare, final stage of union
in which the mystic is submerged in the Godhead. Sor Juana proposes that simply

studying the multitude of disciplines and the world around her leads to God, who is the center and author of all things: "All things proceed from God, who is at once the center and circumference, whence all lines are begotten and where they have their end."[54] Most religious women who wrote *vidas* describe visionary and at times mystical experiences of knowing God. Sor Juana is content to know God through the study of his creation.

Imitatio Christi

To follow the path to God, however, was to experience suffering, as Christ had suffered in his Passion in order to save humankind. Taking Christ's life as an example, the precept of the *imitatio Christi* in Spanish America centered on the Teresian dictate "padecer o morir." Suffering—and the acceptance of it as God's will—was the essence of the *imitatio Christi* and the one path to salvation. Sor Juana begins with themes common to her sisters' accounts: the difficulty of following a calling without direction from a confessor (for Sor Juana, a teacher: "What a hardship it is to learn from those lifeless letters, deprived of the sound of a teacher's voice and explanation; yet I suffered all these trials most gladly for the love of learning")[55] and without the solitude necessary for cultivating a religious vocation (for Sor Juana the duties of communal life in the convent). To remind the reader that she is writing a confessional *vida*, Sor Juana repeats such words as "confieso" and "inclinasión," before going on to describe her willingness to endure hardships and even to seek them out for the sake of her vocation. For weeks at a time she refrained from contact with her beloved convent sisters—risking their rebuff—in order to devote herself to her studies. Yet more difficult was enduring the outright envy of others who condemned her.

After noting Athenian and Machiavellian thought on the nature of envy, Sor Juana draws a more extended parallel between her "strange martyrdom" and Christ's own Passion. While most of her Mexican contemporaries focused on mirroring the physical suffering of Christ—with bodily mortification, fasts, and prayers concentrated on his cruxifiction—Sor Juana shifts the focus to two symbolic moments in the Passion: the condemnation of Christ by the Pharisees and his crown of thorns. Christ's Passion becomes a vehicle to discuss the interconnected nature of knowledge, wisdom, and love, and humankind's contradictory responses to them. Echoing the debates between the *experimentados* and *letrados* that Teresa struggled with, Sor Juana discusses the conflict in a new context. While the learned Pharisees condemned Christ, Teresa responded to him with love. Envy and arrogance blind human beings, especially some men, argues Sor Juana.

At this point in the narrative, Sor Juana audaciously identifies her path with Christ's suffering and the apostle Peter: she has been persecuted not because she is wise, but rather because she pursued wisdom in the name of God, who is knowledge: "My Lady, I do not wish (nor would I be capable of such foolishness) to claim that I have been persecuted because of my knowledge, but rather only because of my love for learning and letters, and not because I had attained either one or the other."[56] Certainly many *vida* authors at the climax of the account of their suffering claim a special relationship with or resemblance to a saint. In most cases, however, the parallel is not made directly by the author but through a supernatural appearance of the saint speaking on behalf of the autobiographer: the author declares that she is merely recording the incident in the narrative. The saint, and in some cases God himself, acts as an intermediary through which the author can assert the value of her life, without overstepping the limits of humility. Sor Juana, however, chooses to present the parallel using her God-given capacity to argue a logical, convincing case.[57]

Continuing the "full report about her inclination," Sor Juana recounts specific anecdotes about suffering at the hands of others, only to see God's gifts shine more brightly in her. When prohibited for a period of time from reading because the prioress thought it might lead to monitoring by the Inquisition, Sor Juana could not help but study the marvels of the natural world of geometrical lines, patterns of spinning tops, and chemical characteristics of eggs when cooking. All lead to the same underlying argument: the lack of individual will in the manifestation of her talent, a key indication of its divine origins ("without my having control over it").[58] And yet, Sor Juana mixes humor with her portrait as an ideal nun. She concludes: "Had Aristotle cooked, he would have written a great deal more."[59]

Sometiéndome Luego a lo que Sentenciare

Sor Juana closes the "simple account of my inclination to letters" and suggests that her reader can now judge her life: "And so I entrust the decision to your supreme skill and straightway submit to whatever sentence you may pass, posing no objection or reluctance."[60] The use of juridical language, as noted by Perelmuter, serves as a transition to the "proof" section of the letter. The case history has concluded, and the arguments for the case will be presented: a defense of Sor Juana's right to write poetry and to study, and, by extension, a proposal to allow all individuals with the proper aptitude to do the same (suggesting, in turn, that this could include religious women and exclude dull-witted men). Acting as her own attorney, Sor Juana draws on historical precedent, the authority of the Bible, and patriarchal church texts as she logically examines the polemical issue of women's learning and roles in the Catholic Church. Elaborating on arguments first presented years earlier in her letter to Padre Núñez, she catalogs learned women from antiquity to the seventeenth century, reinterprets St. Jerome's and St. Paul's teachings about women, particularly the latter's "Let women keep silence in the churches" (Mulieres in Ecclesia taceant), and creates a new authority by citing contemporary Mexican theologian Juan Arce's work, which advocated the pursuit of learning by women. Sor Juana's catalog of learned women who played important roles in history adds more credence to her argument.

And yet, as we saw in the narrative section of the letter, this "proof" section, which is characteristic of legalistic epistles and treastises, also employs the conventions of a woman religious writing about her life. Each element in the proof corresponds to a strategy used by her convent sisters. Sor Juana first compares her life's pursuits to the genealogy of saints, within the catalog of learned women: "I see the Egyptian Catherine, lecturing and refuting all the learning of the most learned men of Egypt. I see a Gertrude read, write, and teach."[61] Next, Sor Juana argues that her calling follows contemporary published guides by clerics. Just as Teresa carefully delineated the type of spiritual vision she experienced, by using specific church guidelines published on the topic, Sor Juana demonstrates how she followed Arce's counsel about women's need for education. Boldly ignoring her own ex-confessor's guides, Sor Juana suggests that Arce's argument elucidates how Paul's and Jerome's writings about women in the church have often been misinterpreted. Historical precedent itself shows that paradigms of feminine saintliness in the seventeenth century contradicted contemporary interpretations: "How is it that we see the Church has allowed a Gertrude, a Teresa, a Brigid, the nun of Agreda, and many other women to write? . . . . And now in our own time we see that the Church permits writing by women saints and those who are not saints alike; for the nun of Agreda and María de la Antigua are not canonized, yet their writings go from hand to hand. Nor when Sts. Teresa and others were writing, had they yet been canonized."[62] Sor Juana shows how church history itself contradicts Paul's dictum that women should be silent in the church.

In fact, Sor Juana proposes, much like Teresa and María de San José in their *vidas*, that men often were poor spokesmen for God. Whereas her sisters subtly instruct confessors through examples of good versus bad spiritual directors—a sort of alternative to the popular manuals for confessors—Sor Juana lists men who have harmed the Catholic Church with their use of knowledge, among them, Martin Luther himself and his reform: "This is what the Divine Letters became in the hands of that wicked . . . Luther, and all other heretics. . . . Learning harmed them."[63] Sor Juana asserts that the dilemmas women encounter with the church are often caused by men and, by implication, suggests that if women could share equally in the pursuit of understanding and truth, such difficulties would be diminished.

Drawing on the didactic potential of the *vida*, Sor Juana creates a new role for women in the Catholic Church. She exclaims: "Oh, how many abuses would be avoided in our land if the older women were as well instructed as Leta and knew how to teach as is commanded by St. Paul and my father St. Jerome!"[64] Moreover, she calls for change, suggesting that people be examined for their talent before beginning to study. The lesson is clear: inept individuals of any sex can cause great harm, and girls need to have access to female teachers to avoid being uneducated. Mixing the didacticism of the *vida* with the pedagogical and ideological possibilities of the epistle, Sor Juana adds to the well-established *querelles des femme* debate and literary tradition, which date at least from the fifteenth century and the work of Christine de Pizan.[65]

As Sor Juana closes the section on the proof, she both reiterates her thesis and rhetorically apologizes for it. She alternates between didactic statements and self-defense, between authoritative church texts and proclamations of obedience. After arguing that most heretics were men, for example, Sor Juana retreats: "Yet I protest that I do so only to obey you; and with such misgiving that you owe me more for taking up my pen with all this fear. . . . But withal, it is well that this goes to meet with your correction: erase it, tear it up, and chastise me."[66] In another instance, she makes the most clear, direct defense of her particular case: "If my crime lies in the 'Letter Worthy of Athena,' was that anything more than a simple report of my opinion? . . . If it is heretical, as the critic says, why does he not denounce it? Thus he would find revenge and I contentment . . . for just as I was free to disagree with Vieira, any person shall be free to disagree with my judgment."[67] But she then makes a dramatic rhetorical retreat: "But where am I bound, my Lady? For none of this is pertinent here, nor meant for your ears; instead, as I was speaking of my detractors, I recalled the phrases of one such who has recently appeared, and all unwittingly my pen strayed."[68] Nonetheless, this "slip of the pen" makes way for a clear petition: "The study of sacred letters is not only permissible but most useful and necessary for women, and all the more so for nuns."[69] The *perfecta religiosa*, she argues, can also be a *perfecta letrada*. She closes by arguing that the Bible's poetry proves that verse form coexists with the sacred. Not surprisingly, this strong statement is quickly followed by a conventional phrase about her humility.

No Me He Atrevido a Exceder de los Límites de Vuestro Estilo

These final paragraphs, the *peroración*, return full force to the rhetorical posture of the *escritora por obediencia* found in the *exordio*. As Sor Juana approaches the end of her defense, she comes full circle—back to the problematic situation of the woman writer who has taken a vow of obedience. Sor Juana concisely repeats, probably for the reader's sake, her own adherence to the virtues of the model nun, including humility ("I confess straightway my rough and uncouth nature"), writing at the behest of others ("I have never written a single thing of my own volition, but rather only in response to the pleadings and commands of others"), ignorance, and suffering.[70] She parallels the opening allusion to Moses again: her writings were abandoned like the orphaned prophet, but the comparison itself suggests a chosen status.

The final passage provides the key to reading the *Respuesta* in a confessional genre. Like her convent sisters, Sor Juana will have to give "strict accounting" (*estrechísima cuenta*) on judgment day, accounting for the use of her God-given talent, which her version of the *vida* has attempted to justify. Sor Juana used the form of the *vida* not only as a mask to cover her assertive response to cultural expectations for women but also to make clear the dilemma of the seventeenth-century woman writer through the use of the only culturally acceptable form for writing about the self that was then available to religious women. In a baroque layering of forms and meanings, Sor Juana simultaneously employs the genre and rejects it as inadequate, displaying the faulty teachings about women that led to its conventions. She exposes the flaws of church practices toward women and undermines the church's precepts. No longer simply a personal defense to a confessor found in her *Carta al Padre Nuñez*, the *Respuesta* lays claim to a much broader agenda: the justification of education for all who are so gifted. Religious women could be *experimentadas* (mystics and visionaries) or *letradas*. Hidden in the rhetoric of the *vida* form, Sor Juana has carved out a unique role for herself in the church.

The Replies to the *Reply*: Sor Juana's Final Years and Hagiography

How did the church deal with its famous, rebellious daughter upon her death, four years after writing the *Respuesta*? Recent work by several historians about Sor Juana's supporters and detractors in her final years of life enrich the familiar story of how the church struggled to control the representation of its elite women.

For years, competing versions of the end of Sor Juana's life have circulated. Irving Leonard and Octavio Paz, for example, talk of the fury of some church fathers—Núñez and Archbishop of Mexico Aguiar y Seijas, in particular—who exercised their power over Sor Juana and forced her "conversion," a renunciation of her literary career and a renewal of her vow to be a *perfecta religiosa*. More recent studies have radically revised this dramatic story. Marie-Cécile Bénassy-Berling, for example, demonstrates that even after writing the *Respuesta*, Sor Juana continued to have Bishop Santa Cruz's support. For example, he approved Juana's carols about the learned martyr Catherine of Alexandria, an alternate canonized model for women. The female saint's wisdom conquered her male oppressors:

> Catherine bears the victory!
> For with knowledge pure and holy
> she's convinced the learned men
> and has emerged victorious
> —with her knowledge glorious—
> . . . .
> Never by a famous man
> have we been shown such victory,
> and this, because God wished through her
> to honor womankind.
> Victory! Victory!
> . . . .
> Sacred tutor, patroness,
> she shelters all our learning
> that she who made of Sages, Saints,
> new Sages may illumine.
> Victory! Victory![71]

Through the devotional vehicle of sacred carols, Sor Juana again took one of Núñez's pet projects, his own prologue to a book about Catherine, and reconfigured its meaning.[72] Other scholars have revealed how supporters worked from across the Atlantic on Sor Juana's behalf. As mentioned, in 1692 Sor Juana's close friend the ex-vicereine, Condesa of Paredes, published in Seville the nun's second collection of works. The volume opened with a new edition of the *Carta atenagórica* and included hundreds of changes, many of which emphasized further the most polemical aspects of the original letter.[73] Meanwhile, Sor Juana also wrote a satirical defense of her literary pursuits, *Enigmas ofrecidos a la Casa del Placer*.[74] In fact, this work was commissioned by a group of Portuguese nuns who knew the Condesa of Paredes.

While it seems that Sor Juana and her supporters worked actively in the years following the *Respuesta*, according to Elías Trabulse the initial storm caused by the *Carta atenagórica* died down after several months. But early in 1693, the hiatus was broken by the arrival from Spain of Sor Juana's second volume of collected works in Mexico City. It seems that Núñez and the archbishop may have been at work trying to contain their rebellious daughter and her supporters. One of Sor Juana's advocates, Francisco Javier

Palavicino, had preached a sermon in Sor Juana's convent about the wisdom of the "monja teóloga." When he tried to publish the sermon, he landed in the hands of the Inquisition—perhaps because Núñez was still a censor for the Inquisition and signed licenses for publication.[75] (It is important to note, however, that the power of the Inquisition extended to Núñez himself: a recent study shows that several of his works were censored as well.[76]) The documents based on this case reveal that Sor Juana's name was mentioned before the Inquisition.[77] Elías Trabulse argues that in these same years, Archbishop Aguiar y Seijas initiated and pursued a secret case against Sor Juana herself, the *proceso espicopal secreto*, which culminated in the 1694 sentencing of Sor Juana; she was to "abjure all her errors, confess to being guilty, to make amends to the [Congregation] of the Most Holy Conception, not publish any further, and give over her library and worldly goods to the archbishop."[78] The five documents of Sor Juana's so-called conversion, several supposedly signed in blood, emerged out of these efforts to silence her. On paper, Sor Juana had renewed her vows, accepting the role of the *perfecta religiosa*, and returned to Núñez as her spiritual director. While nothing else was published in the remaining year or so of Sor Juana's life, and her library and scientific instruments were sold, these measures taken by the church did not effect a total renunciation of her literary and intellectual career as the archbishop and Núñez had hoped. A recent archival find, a copy of an inventory of Sor Juana's cell taken upon her death (which is still in the process of being authenticated), reveals that she may have had several manuscripts with writings and had begun to acquire another library.[79] This would support what we already know of Sor Juana's continued literary activity with her composition of the *villancicos, romances,* and *Los enigmas.*

Clearly, the traditional portrait of Sor Juana as submitting to clerical pressure or undergoing a radical religious conversion is in question. As we might imagine from studying other cases about religious women and the church's rescripting of their lives, this hagiographic version of her story began with clerical control of information and posthumous publications about Sor Juana's life. Immediately upon Sor Juana's death in 1695, Archbishop Aguiar y Seijas began to manipulate the release of information about Mexico's famous nun. Just as biographers selected, edited, and interpreted the lives of Rosa, María de San José, and Catarina de San Juan for official church ends, the archbishop began the hagiographic process for Sor Juana. First, as Elías Trabulse notes, Aguiar y Seijas silenced the sentencing of Sor Juana and halted the Inquisition proceedings against her supporters.[80] Next, he began the all-important textual representation and dissemination of Sor Juana's life story. Within months of Sor Juana's death, the archbishop published the *Protesta de la fe* that Sor Juana had signed while other testimonies were sent to Spain to be published in the third volume of Sor Juana's collected works—*Fama y obras póstumas.*

Outwardly promoting this literary nun, *Fama* actually distorts Sor Juana's life and works. According to Trabulse, only 14 of 356 pages contain secular verse, and neither the *Enigmas* nor anything from the manuscript writings found in her cell were included.[81] The opening portrait of *Fama* graphically illustrates the reconfiguration of an independent woman who loved to study into an icon of a holy nun who symbolized America's contribution to culture (see figures 4.1 and 4.2). Unlike the popular eighteenth-century portrait by Cabrera, which portrays Sor Juana as an author in

FIGURE 4.1   Oil portrait of Sor Juana Inés de la Cruz by Miguel Cabrera, 1750 (Courtesy of the Instituto Nacional de Antropología e Historia, Mexico)

her book-filled study, the *Fama* engraving displays a bust of Sor Juana as a generic nun with a pen in hand. The bust is framed by a European conqueror on the one side and a Native American on the other. Underneath are the iconographic symbols of her knowledge—medicine, music, philosophy—aimed at boasting of America's cultural parity with Europe. The inclusion of the royal coat of arms clearly claims Sor Juana as part of the Spanish Empire.

FIGURE 4.2 Woodcut of Sor Juana Inés de la Cruz, in the edition of her *Fama y obras*, 1700 (Courtesy of the Lilly Library, Bloomington, Indiana)

The extensive prefatory pages, licenses, laudatory poems, and first *vida* of Sor Juana by the Jesuit Diego de Calleja bespeak the official nature of the *Fama*. The hagiographic *vida*, as we have seen in previous chapters, was perhaps the most important vehicle for promoting a "canonized" version of an influential person's life. After describing his subject as "the life of that rare woman, born into this world in order to justify the vanities of prodigy to nature,"[82] Calleja refocuses the story of Sor Juana's life. He misrepresents Sor Juana's birth status, depicting her as the daughter of a married couple. He repeats Sor Juana's own myth-making process and says her first writings were devotional pieces. Later, he echoes Sor Juana's own language, the "inclination to study books." Significantly, however, Calleja retells the story, deliberately leaving aside the "contradictions" caused by the *Carta Atenagórica*, although he mentions that it is a brilliant scholastic critique. Indeed, Calleja neutralizes the influence of Sor Juana's *Carta atenagórica* and *Respuesta* by emphasizing her humility:

> See in this admirable woman a humility of such circumspect simplicity that Whoever would see a full reply to the objections of those who take mere apprehension for fully rendered judgment . . . herein will see that Madre Juana Inez did not intend this piece of writing to be widely known . . . herein will see that the response the poetess gave to Padre Vieira rendered him more illustrious than did the defense of one who paints the snow [i.e., to try to improve on its beauty] . . . and herein, finally, she did not fail to make amends for her own offense.[83]

Calleja creates an obedient nun by highlighting the fact that even as Sor Juana was a *rara muger* of stunning intelligence, she still is one of the church's own humble *perfectas religiosas*. He transforms Sor Juana's vexed interactions with clergy into a life story that is not so different in tone and ideology from other *vidas*.

Another contemporary biographical account of Sor Juana was embedded into the biography of Núñez by Juan Oviedo. Not surprisingly, he applies his own hagiographic style to Sor Juana's life.[84] He paints the portrait of a nun whose only desire was to flee from her intellect:

> So far was this lady from wanting or desiring these extraordinary favors from God that she would tremble and be horrified by their mere recollection, and did so judging herself unworthy and incapable of them all, as though she feared the risk and danger they entailed, of which so many Icaruses have been the frightening example. . . . She immediately pleaded with God to free her from this way [and] lead her only on the sure path of suffering, aided by the most living faith, firmest hope and burning love.[85]

The very words that Sor Juana used with ironic intent, to critique church prescriptions for women, were later used by Oviedo at face value, in order to portray her as a model nun. Whereas Sor Juana deliberately marginalized the role of the confessor in her writings and defended her right to use her God-given talent to write and to interpret God's will, the New Spanish Church resumed its role as mediator by reinterpreting her life using hagiographic conventions and by publishing works that echoed official discourse. Sor Juana's most published works in eighteenth-century New Spain were her devotional exercises.

In the archbishop's hands, Sor Juana's life became a vehicle for promoting his reforms of religious life for women in Mexico City. His manipulation of the *Fama* and Calleja's *vida* demonstrate how hagiographic and devotional works were often used to settle questions of power. In 1692, as Antonio Rubial notes, Aguiar y Seijas had signed an edict to enforce the vow of enclosure for nuns by limiting contact of any kind with the outside world. Perhaps Sor Juana was to be a scapegoat and exemplary lesson. A nun who had written secular drama and entertained court members and professors at the convent grate was now a repentant obedient spiritual daughter, signing in blood her religious vows to withdraw from the world. As with Rosa de Lima and Catarina de San Juan, Sor Juana's life story highlights how the interpretation of church rules could change and, therefore, affect the destiny of individual lives and the representation of those life stories. Once again, we see that the church's response to questions of sanctity, heresy, or behavior of nonmystics was not unilateral or unidirectional (i.e., controlled by Spain). Court and church members in Spain supported Sor Juana's literary production, while some members of the New Spanish clergy sought to limit it. A famous bride of Christ, like Sor Juana, fueled the debate over the role of the church's most gifted individuals. Hagiographic rescripting and publishing were part of a larger political process of reinforcing ideal behavior.

Besides the church's redefinition of Sor Juana's life, the hyperbolic titles bestowed on the nun during her own lifetime solidified soon after her death and became part of the broader colonizing process of America. Just as the hagiography of Rosa de Lima had elevated her to patron of America, Sor Juana became known as America's Tenth Muse (reference to Plato's title for Sappho of Lesbos) and a *rara avis*, a Phoenix and an Icarus-like figure. As Margo Glantz reveals in her study, Sor Juana's own self-portrait as an insatiable intellect was maintained by her friend and fellow intellectual, Carlos de Sigüenza y Góngora who called her "learned" (*docta*), but others claimed her for purposes linked to the process of building criollo identity in the mid-colonial period.[86] Sor Juana helped put America on the map, as an equal power to Europe. One poet of the period explains how, like Christopher Columbus, Sor Juana became an icon for America, a genius-nun who represented America.[87] Even a late-eighteenth-century convent history written by nuns eulogizes Sor Juana in this manner: "This southern America, so famous for its rich minerals, can take pride in having been the homeland of such a heroic woman that we may give her the epithet of the strong woman."[88]

When compared to the religious women studied in part I of this volume, Sor Juana symbolized for her contemporaries an expanded role for religious women, a role that went beyond aiding in the redemption of America. In spite of church efforts to make Sor Juana a *perfecta religiosa*, she represented the possibility of a more multivalent role for women and individuals. Besides writing about the role of women in colonial society, Sor Juana also briefly touched on indigenous beliefs in a *Loa* and imitated popular African-Hispanic dialects in some popular poetic pieces.[89] Because of the range of voices in Sor Juana's writings, she was used to champion many causes. No doubt this fact helps account for Sor Juana's immense popularity in recent years in Mexico; she has moved symbolically out of her ex-cloister (now a center for higher education) into the national press, movies, and plays, and she has increased in value from being portrayed on the old 1 peso coin to the 200 peso bill. Like Rosa de Lima in the Andes and Catarina de San Juan in Puebla, Sor Juana has become a contemporary symbol for Mexico's identity.

In the traditional story of Sor Juana's dramatic end, official church politics won out over a more authentic representation of a religious woman and poet. The numbers and ranks of officials involved in Sor Juana's final years and the years immediately following her death show the critical importance of controlling access to and reinterpreting the lives of the church's brides. The effectiveness of this official revision of Sor Juana's final years is clear from the hundreds of years that it endured. But the clarity and startling freshness of Sor Juana's own voice in her verse, drama, and letters rings out in her published texts and ensures that her voice is not lost. Remarkably unmuddled and free of the ambiguity that often characterized nuns' writing as they walked the tenuous line between self, cleric, and God—and the institutionalization of the meaning of that relationship—Sor Juana's letters wittily exploit the full range of arguments, texts, and genres available to her.

Chronology of Sor Juana Inés de la Cruz

1648/1651	Born Juana Inés Ramírez y Asbaje in Nepantla, Mexico.
1654	Attends an *amiga* school.
1658	Composes her first known poem (a religious *loa*).
1661	Moves to Mexico City to live with relatives.
1664	Becomes a lady-in-waiting to the vicereine, the marquise de Mancera.
1666	Enters and leaves the Carmelite Convent.
1669	Enters the Hieronymite Convent of Santa Paula, Mexico City.
ca. 1682	Writes letter to Padre Antonio Núñez de Miranda, breaking with him as her confessor.
1689	*Inundación castálida*, Sor Juana's first collected works, published in Madrid.
1690	*Carta atenagórica* published in Puebla by Bishop Fernández de Santa Cruz.
1691	Drafts *La Respuesta a Sor Filotea de la Cruz*.
1692	*Obras*, the second collection of Sor Juana's works, published in Seville.
1693	Possible *proceso arzobispal secreto* against Sor Juana.
1693	Signs her general confession.
1694	Signs a declaration of faith and gives away her library.
1695	Dies in an epidemic.
1700	*Fama y obras pósthumas*, a third collection of Sor Juana's works, published in Madrid. The edition includes Diego Calleja's *Vida* of Sor Juana in the prefatory material.

5

The Happy Saint
Ursula Suárez (1666–1749)—Rogues and New Saintly Roles

I haven't yet had a comedienne saint, and as there are all manner of things in palaces, you are to be the comedienne.
—God speaking to Ursula, *Relación*, 230

I put St. Paul's words in you because I want you to preach as he did.
—God speaking to Ursula, *Relación*, 202

Don't talk to me in Latin, don't mention St. Paul to me, and don't quote the Bible to me.
—Bishop Romero talking to Ursula, *Relación*, 262

The voice of Ursula Suárez, a Chilean colonial nun, rings out with startling freshness in her autobiographical account. Whereas Sor Juana describes the inequality of male-female relationships, Ursula records in her *Relación autobiográfica* how she wittily pushed the limits of women's roles—often at men's expense. In a famous scene from one of Sor Juana's plays, a male comic servant (*gracioso*) cross-dresses and makes fun of men's attitudes toward women.[1] Ursula did this in real life by dressing a young mulatto slave as a woman in order to dupe male patrons of the convent:

> I dressed the convent mulatto as a nun, taking him to the turn and the locutory where the men were, so that he should enter behind me and captivate a few of them; and he did this with such flair that I died laughing, all the more so when they asked for his little hand and the mulatto brought it out, all covered with calluses; and they were so smitten that they never noticed how rough and large it was. Anyway, they would give him their coins and powder boxes and the mulatto was so wild that once he had grabbed the money he would scratch their hands, having been talking in falsetto with a thousand breaks in his voice, me at his side, just like the devil. The convent *provisora* [Ursula] would spend her time in these activities; would that she did not have this office, was she to be so perverse.[2]

With behavior hardly befitting a nun, Ursula often used tricks and ruses to bring economic benefit to the convent. The nun boasts that she was to be a different sort of saint, one who brings in money to the community: "I will work miracles, and they are to pay for them. Have you ever seen male or female saints out for a profit? I will be one of the latter, for if I heal the sick or restore sight to the blind, they will have to come and serve the convent and you [the other nuns] will reap the benefits while I do the work: they will be tormenting me, and I must be a happy saint."[3] Clearly, Ursula had a different interpretation of God's plan than Rosa de Lima or María de San José. Although her text draws on canonized *vida* authors, such as Augustine, Teresa, and the Clarist nun of her own order, María de la Antigua, the tone and purpose are significantly altered. Ursula's dialogues with God and confessor reveal her nonconformist path. As we see in the opening quote to this chapter, God spoke directly to Ursula: "you are to be the comedienne."[4] Her role, as God reminds her more than once, was to be a happy saint (*santa alegre*) and to use her voice to preach like St. Paul.[5] Finances, laughter, and preaching all mix together in the nun's unusual *vida*.

Ursula's confessional narrative structure parallels those of her convent sisters while also introducing more secular concerns. From an early age the girl felt a special calling, and she fought family obstacles to pursue it, until finally she entered the convent. To this point, hers is a traditional story of religious vocation. Ursula employs the conventional language and narrative voice of a nun writing under obedience to her confessor. But the Clarist nun also records unexpected reactions to the religious life: she is horrified that nuns often practiced mortification even while sleeping, laughs at the "inward light" of God's presence, and flirts with male suitors and clergy. Rather than tell a typical tale of true religious conversion, of turning toward God and demonstrating increased humility and charity, Ursula delights in recalling her pranks at home and in the convent. Later, a profound experience of God's presence helps Ursula leave behind her pranks and embrace the difficulties of living in a religious community. Yet her transformation remains firmly grounded in the world around her. Her later notebooks talk of suffering conflict and illness and hearing divine locutions, but instead of responding with prayer and increased humility (the *camino de perfección*), Ursula often insists on a playful verbal response.

In a lively style of writing Ursula incorporates ballad and verse forms, folkloric elements, and extensive dramatic dialogue into her prose to recount her journey to become God's first "comedienne saint" (*santa comedianta*). Borrowing elements from popular period theatre and the picaresque novel, she expands the parts nuns could literally and figuratively play in God's and the church's production of female saints. By intertwining elements from secular literary genres with the confessional didactic possibilities of the *vida*, Ursula expands the form and ideology of confessional literature. Through these literary genre crossovers, she critiques secular and religious women's economic dependence on men and the church's models for female sanctity. In the process she creates an alternate "autohagiographical" narrative.

How did a nun who resisted traditional roles for women come to write a confessional account with so many secular overtones? How did the Catholic Church respond to it? Although there are still many gaps in what we know of Ursula's life and writings, the scholars who published her account for the first time in 1984 provide some guideposts. In 1708, Ursula was commanded by her confessor to rewrite her *vida* because, as in the cases of Teresa and María de San José, the first draft reportedly had been burned. This second version consists of at least the first eight notebooks of the *Relación autobiográfica*.[6] (See figure 5.1.) Written about 1708–1710 as a single narrative unit, these notebooks recount Ursula's call to the religious life and the first decades in the convent, leading up to the narration of her spiritual experience (1666 to ca. 1694).[7] The remaining six notebooks (9–14), are *cuentas de conciencia*, discrete narrative units that relate specific events, most often, conflicts, illness and dialogues with God.[8] These notebooks were composed at various times and addressed to several different readers between 1708 and 1730–1732. (Some may be revisions of earlier notebooks.) We do not know how this group of writings came to be bound with the *vida*, but in general they relate incidents from 1694 to 1715.[9]

No hagiographic biography or funeral sermon was published upon Ursula's death. Although she had risen to the rank of abbess and had powerful contacts with Jesuit confessors and several bishops during her seven decades in the cloister, Ursula was not posthumously promoted by the Catholic Church—unlike Rosa de Lima, Catarina de San Juan, and María de San José. Even Sor Juana, the rebellious intellectual who was forced to sell her library in her final years, was promoted as one of the church's model daughters. Clearly, Ursula's life was unusual enough to require a confessional *vida*, but was it too unconventional to become the subject of a biography?

In the small but growing scholarship on Ursula's account are references to its tone of roguishness and the seeming rejection of the model nun. Rodrigo Cánovas notes the influence on Ursula's account of a mercantile society caught between writing as sacred and writing as profane; Sonia Montecinos also notes a shift between the transcendental and the quotidian. In more feminist studies, Andriana Valdés describes the "double authority" of confessor and God, and María Inés Lagos argues that the text shuttles between Ursula's narcissism and the symbolic order, represented by the confessor. Both Kristin Routt and Kristine Ibsen link Ursula's use of humor with her definition of sanctity: Routt describes the inversion of mystic desire and language in order to create a model nun who entertained God, and Ibsen highlights Ursula's borrowing of two character types from period theatre (*comedia*), the manly woman (*mujer varonil*) who defies society's conventions for women and the clown (*graciosa*), a point we will return to later.[10] I will build on this scholarship but redirect its focus to examine the fundamental role of literary genres and ideologies in Ursula's critique of church and society and how these structure her self-portrait as a roguish saint. Before delving into literary types and portraits, it is useful to know more about Ursula's life in colonial Chile.

Ursula Suárez and Chilean Society

Ursula was well-positioned in the elite *criollo* society of colonial Santiago de Chile. She was born in 1666 to Francisco Suárez del Campo and María de Escobar Lillo; while the maternal side of her family still enjoyed social prestige as direct descendants of conquistadors, her paternal relatives were well-off merchants and bureaucrats.[11] Both sides of the family, however, were experiencing a relative decline by the latter half of the seventeenth century, as the initial spoils of conquests and colonization decreased significantly. This economic and social decline strongly influenced

Ursula's upbringing. Although Ursula's mother brought a prestigious name to the marriage, her lack of economic resources led to a tense relationship with her mother-in-law. Wedded without a dowry, and therefore with no belongings of her own, María used Ursula as a go-between to obtain household items from her husband's rich mother.[12] Living in a household with four adults, one sister, and many servants and slaves, Ursula talks of endless domestic conflict over financial concerns.[13]

Like many *criolla* girls of good birth, Ursula was trained from an early age to marry well and run a large household. In her *Relación*, the nun reveals some details of her training and education. At age six, Ursula moved temporarily to an aunt's house, where she received lessons in reading, accounting, and needlework. Skilled at reading and memorizing books, Ursula spent hours impressing her relatives by reciting passages from memory. Later, like Sor Juana, she received more education at her grandfather's house. Although it is difficult to reconstruct the depth of Ursula's learning, she learned some African dialect, kept financial records for the convent, and taught her convent sisters Latin.[14] The *Relación* itself reflects a good ear for language and story-telling, and has some Latin phrases (although words are often misspelled).

While Ursula's mother fought hard to prepare the girl for a good marriage that might benefit the family, Ursula herself rebelled and countered her mother's efforts at every turn. Ursula had decided to become a nun. She recounts in an almost parodic style her first attraction to the convent: after suffering an illness, a servant carried Ursula to a convent. Upon nearing the building, the girl's skin tingled and a sweet aroma overwhelmed her. While the servant scolded Ursula for her nonsense, the nuns "praised her wit." Perhaps a literal reference to the sweets that convents often made, the passage also echoes hagiographic tradition, which equates "a sweet scent" emanating from convents and corpses as a sign of holiness.[15] This call to the religious life and complete antipathy toward marriage led to years of domestic struggle, a struggle reminiscent of the one between Rosa de Lima and her mother. Ursula worked hard to convert her mother to her cause, and one uncle helped Ursula, despite her often mischievous behavior.

These years at home were not filled with devotional practices, however. Instead of reading devotional works as Rosa and María de San José had, Ursula confesses to reading secular material voraciously, especially entertaining stories, novels, and plays. She admits to reading only the dramatic, tragic saints' lives: "If I picked up a book it was for entertainment and not for benefitting from it; and I looked for ones on history or tales, novels or comedies. . . . Back then during my novitiate I also read a little Scripture and also saints' lives, though if they were not tragic, I left them."[16] Rather than begin a rigorous schedule of prayer and penitential acts, the girl began to deceive men: "I formulated the intention of never letting an opportunity go by in which I would not attempt to deceive as many [men] as my ability would allow, and this with due payment as though God in this present state were rendering a very good service."[17] She was horrified at the treatment of women, particularly the way some men lied to women and considered them objects of economic exchange.

Finally, in 1678 at age twelve, Ursula overcame her mother's opposition and entered the newly opened Clarist Convent de la Plaza, which her paternal grandfather had founded by leaving dowries for thirty women.[18] She lived there until her

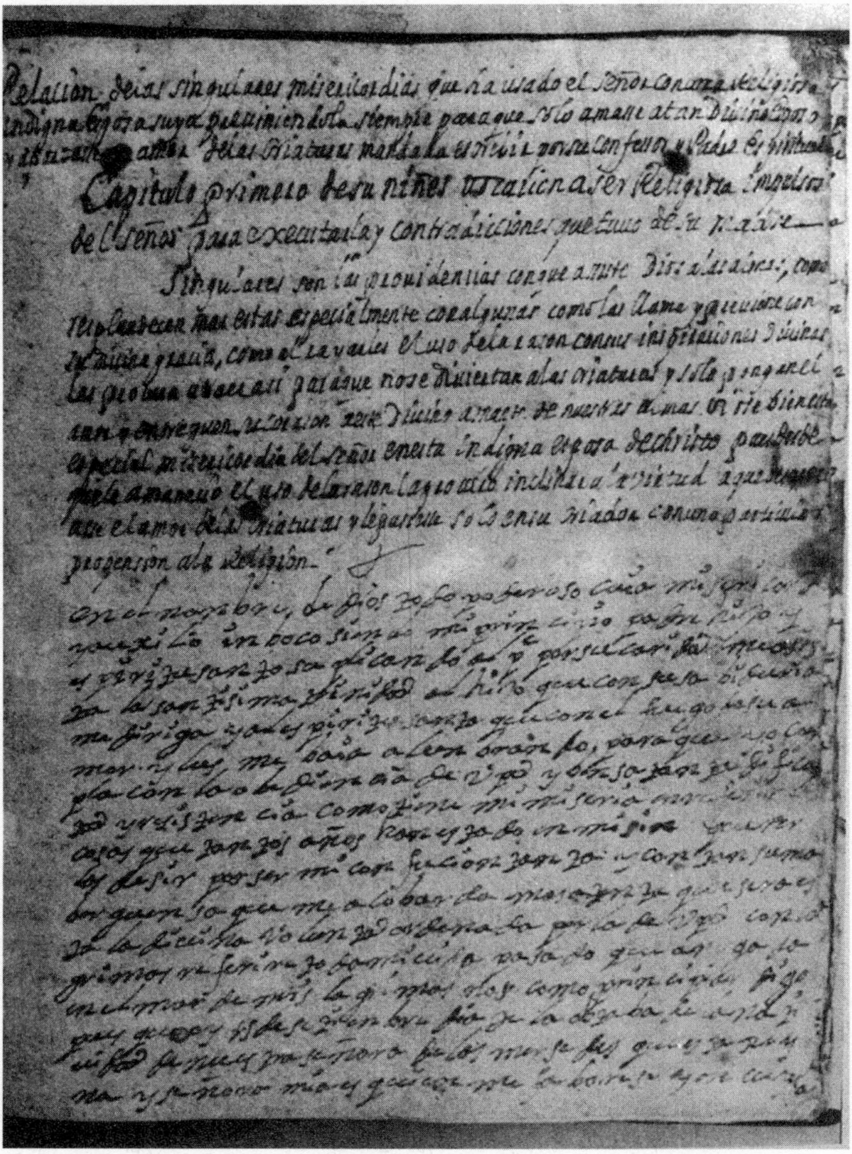

FIGURE 5.1 Opening page, *Relación autobiográfica,* by Ursula Suárez (Courtesy of Mario Ferreccio Podestá)

death at age 83. The third convent to be established in Santiago (but soon followed by one more), the Clarist Convent was integral to Santiago society. Located on the central plaza where festivals and civil ceremonies took place, the convent had little in common with small, reformed orders like María de San José's. More in keeping with Sor Juana's convent, nuns were allowed to own their own "cells," which actually were more like small houses. By 1738, the convent itself owned and rented out some twenty-six stores (*tiendas*) and four years later was building twelve more.[19] At one point the convent housed about five hundred women (only about sixty were professed nuns). In some respects it resembled a small walled town within the relatively provincial city of Santiago, which had a total population of twelve to fifteen thousand inhabitants.[20]

In theory Ursula became dead to the world upon entering the cloister, but in practice she brought much of her life with her. Ursula did not have to part completely with family: seven other relatives, including cousins and an aunt, entered the convent with her.[21] Because Ursula was not of age to take the veil yet, she spent five years in the noviciate, of which she complained: "There was never a stricter novitiate, as we had a teacher who was very upright and of a severe temperament, who had us locked up all day long in a small cell into which thirty novices could barely fit, as this cell had neither a yard nor a garden."[22] Within twelve years of her entrance, Ursula owned a house (*celda*) and garden within the convent compound. In some years it housed as many as eleven women, ranging from a small toddler to servants and several women who lived with Ursula nearly thirty years.[23] Although she had taken a vow of poverty, the interpretation of it was obviously quite lax since she talks of amassing luxury items through the generosity of her *devotos*. These were men who visited nuns and, in return for the nun's attentions, donated money to the convent. They bought her silver platformed shoes, dresses, and even helped pay for remodeling her cell.[24] According to period accounts, the vow of enclosure was not strictly enforced until the early eighteenth century. Although nuns could not leave the convent, they had a good deal of contact with the world outside the convent through the comings and goings of family members, priests, servants, and *devotos*.[25] Along with an active life and a high economic status within the convent, Ursula also had powerful ties to influential clerics outside the convent, including several bishops and a host of Jesuit priests.[26]

Ursula's privileged status is particularly clear from the positions she held in the convent and the conflicts over power. Some time during her years as a novice (1678–1684), she became a teacher. When she was old enough to profess her vows six years later at age 18, Ursula took on roles with more responsibility: first, she controlled the inventory of supplies and access to the convent as *provisora;* later, in 1687, she helped the abbess control the dissemination of information to and from the convent as *definadora*.[27] Ambitious in her goals, Ursula attempted to become abbess several decades later, in 1710, but failed to gain the bishop's support and was appointed second-in-command as *vicaria*, in spite of having won the convent vote.[28] One of her confessor's sisters, in fact, had been named instead (María de Gamboa).[29] For more than a decade the convent split into two camps over issues of governance.

Directly connected to the conflict between the new abbess, the bishop, and herself—and after a second defeat in her bid to become abbess—in 1715 Ursula was sentenced to a severe punishment. The Ecclesiastical Tribunal of Santiago and Bishop Juan Francisco de Romero, at one time Ursula's close ally, confirmed the abbess' and her supporters' accusations that Ursula had been an instigator of upheaval in the convent. Like the archbishop's case against Sor Juana, the punishment was aimed at breaking Ursula's spirit: the sentence called for public humiliation by imposing corporeal punishment, solitary confinement for nine days, and the severest punishment of all—the suspension of the privilege of receiving the sacrament of holy communion for months. Ursula herself summarizes the sentence:

> This was the drift of the sentence [meted out] to doña Ursula Suárez: because she incited the convent and was disrespectful and disobedient to the abbesses, causing disturbances and enraging the nuns, not allowing them to speak because they had not elected her abbess and prelate, and for so many offenses and rebellions His Illustrious Lordship ordered that I be whipped in turn; of the assembled community each one was to whip me, and later I was to kiss the feet of all the nuns, and eat on the ground, and be shut in my cell without leaving it; and this was to be done for nine days, that His Lordship had decided and ordered it in the presence of his notary, and had signed it thus.[30]

Ursula's *Relación* closes with this story of being punished and developing an illness in which she began to bleed at the mouth (notebook 14). The account's final note emphasizes how she humbled herself to clergy. When Ursula recounted a dream about a bloody serpent to her confessor, he argued with her about the interpretation of the dream. Ursula reacted by choosing to remain silent: "I was silent and fought it no more."[31] Although the account ends on this note, Ursula refers to her promotion to abbess some six years later. With the help of a new bishop, she served as abbess from 1721 to 1725. Only one passage briefly points to the fact that Ursula ended up as abbess five years later with the full support of a new bishop. In the eleventh notebook, as she talks of the time the convent election was undermined when Bishop Romero appointed a different abbess, Ursula states: "Eleven years before I was elected abbess, His Majesty told me: "I will favor your convent if you will govern it."[32] Ursula goes on to state how she had held all the major governing positions in the convent, except teacher of novices, which she turned down on three separate occasions.

Ursula highlights the role of divine will in her administrative roles, but she simultaneously demonstrates a willfulness in her choice of convent duties. According to Ursula's twentieth-century editor, these last notebooks correspond to the final two periods in which Ursula wrote, 1726 and circa 1730–1732—both after her tenure as abbess. Indeed, a remark at one point in the manuscript dates Ursula's final revisions to her account as having been made about 1730, but there is little mention of the years in between the bishop's sentence and finishing her account (1715 to 1730–1732).[33] Even less is known about the last two decades of Ursula's life. A period chronicle states: "Mother Ursula Suárez died on October 5 of the year 1749. Upon her death several particular items were found, such as a paper on which she took notes, which has been left in this."[34] But no other records found to date tell us much about Ursula's final years.

No doubt this is another case in which more clues may still lie in archives.[35] As a full-fledged nun for six decades, and particularly as an abbess, Ursula surely wrote many letters. As a high-spirited daughter of several Jesuit confessors—the order that promoted self-examination through confessional accounts—Ursula probably wrote more autobiographical notebooks than the ones published in the *Relación*. For now, however, we can only examine the shaping of a self-portrait within what I refer to as the formal *vida* (notebooks 1–8) and the extant *cuentas de conciencia* (notebooks 9–14), and ask why these notebooks were put together and saved.

New Scripts: *Nun, Pícara,* and *Comedianta*

The formal *vida* of the *pecadora* (sinner) turned *predicadora* (preacher) and *santa alegre* begins in the initial eight notebooks written for Ursula's Jesuit confessor Tomás de Gamboa (1649–1729).[36] Recounting her childhood call to the religious life and its culmination with a religious experience as a nun (ca. 1694), which took place fourteen years before the moment of writing, Ursula frames the information within the *vida* conventions. But a clear counternarrative to the traditional *vida*—a story of transgression akin to that of the *pícara*, the roguish central character found in popular picaresque novels of the period—dominates the first four notebooks. She delights in telling the mostly not-so-holy stories about her upbringing and novitiate.

By the fifth notebook, which corresponds to the period after Ursula confesses as a full-fledged nun, recognizable elements of a conversion experience begin to come through the narrative, albeit unevenly. While expressing remorse for her ruses and a desire to follow St. Teresa ("It seems from that day forward, I was to be like St. Teresa"), in a path of prayer, confessional writing, and visions, Ursula reveals a portrait that flies in the face of Teresian sanctity.[37] She flees from supernatural visions and tries to ignore God's words. And her inability to remain in prayer provoked laughter when she announced it to her convent sisters:

> I said to the others: "How can you have a long prayer when I run out?"
> They all laughed, saying, "How does it run out?" and I told them "I don't
> understand this very well: I have it in my memory, but I can't do a thing
> with it;" they said: "You'll get enjoyment out of other things;" I told them:
> "That isn't it; I'm trying to explain the point"; and they laughed at that,
> too. But at times my prayer was full of anger.[38]

At a narrative level, when about to describe her deep spiritual experience, Ursula abruptly returns to telling roguish stories about getting money from *devotos* (most of notebook 6).

Ursula had both a family of good social standing and, later, a place in the convent as a professed nun. Yet, ironically, she plays up the fact that, whether with her family or her convent sisters, she had to rely on her natural cleverness to help those around her obtain food, shelter, or clothing. Even as a bride of Christ, she used her feminine wiles with *devotos de monjas* and an occasional bishop to help maintain the convent. In a picaresque reworking of the hagiographic stories of saints who ignored threats from husbands or fathers in order to distribute food to the poor, Ursula secured food for her family and sisters and, at least until notebook 8, delighted in the verbal games she had to play to accomplish her task. Without ever using the word *pícara*—but employing most of its possible synonyms: *embustera* (liar), *callejera* (roamer), *bellaca* (rogue), *traviesa* (mischevious), etc.—the Clarist nun depicts herself as a proud "saintly rogue," who retaliates against men and as a *santa comedianta*, a holy actress who plays the comic part of a new type of saint, often in order to criticize society.[39]

A closer look at the popularity of period theatre, the picaresque novel, and the character types of both of them helps reveal Ursula's careful blending of literary and dramatic elements to create a new type of nun. Theatre was a popular vehicle for telling the dramatic lives of the saints, and unreformed convents (like Ursula's) often had performances of plays within the cloister.[40] The most compelling evidence of the influence of theatre in Ursula's account is, as mentioned, her announcement that God wanted an actress among his saints. In terms of theatrical role playing per se, there are only two incidents in Ursula's narrative: at age six she dresses up as a grown woman in order to dupe a suitor, and later she cross-dresses a slave whom she uses in order to deceive a *devoto*. Nonetheless, Kristine Ibsen suggests that Ursula rejects the paradigm of the penitential female saint and creates a role reminiscent of two theatrical character types, the manly woman (*mujer varonil*) and the comic (*graciosa*). Ibsen sees the *mujer varonil* as central to Ursula's narrative because the nun rebels against society, but Ibsen does not account for the nun's relentless use of her femininity to achieve her ends.[41] The *graciosa*, the comic foil, in contrast, was from the servant class and often carried out deceptions that reflect a street-wise manipulator, often motivated by economic concern. Notably, the *graciosa*'s role often blends with that of the *pícara*: both tend to use their feminine wiles for economic gain. While Ursula's narrative presents suggestive parallels with character types from theatre, the fundamental narrative structure and ideology of the first eight notebooks draw heavily on elements from the rogue's tale.

In this regard, the classical picaresque genre is more fundamental to the study of Ursula's account than is period theatre. The picaresque novel incorporated many components of literary and folk traditions to create a countergenre to popular idealized literature of the early modern period. Critics have pointed to an occasional anecdotal roguish element in other nuns' *vidas*, but rarely to any fundamental structuring or linguistic modeling on the picaresque form.[42] The connection between the picaresque tale and the *vida*, however, is closely linked: both may have emerged as a response to Inquisition testimony and its use of confessional and juridical narratives, as Carmen Rabell suggests in her study of the first known picaresque novel, *Lazarillo de Tormes* (1554).[43] Written a decade before Teresa's *Vida*, the anonymous author of *Lazarillo de Tormes* casts the prologue as a confession by the rogue-protagonist to a superior in order to justify his life. Likewise Mateo Alemán's *Guzmán de Alfarache* (1599) tells the story of a repentant rogue who reports his delinquent adventures and intersperses them with didactic passages about conversion and confession.[44] And the blending of literary genre is obvious in the *Libro de entretenimiento de la pícara Justina* (1605), in which the protagonist laments that very few people read *vidas* and talks about having been a holy woman for a short while; still she ends up delighting in her ruses and marrying the *pícaro* Guzmán de Alfarache.[45] No moral is put forth (as the title demonstrates), and the conversion she promises never materializes. Thus, the picaresque narrative uses confessional literature as a formal model, but deviates from its exhortation to virtue.[46] The generic overlap implicitly or explicitly calls into question the purpose of the confessional *vida* by using a fictional first person narrator who often delights in the transgressive aspects of the tale.

But what is the effect of a literary crossover that comes from the other direction—that is, a life story that inscribes itself into confessional literature with elements of picaresque narrative? And why would a woman who was economically and socially advantaged—both in her secular and convent life—choose to borrow the rhetoric and themes of a genre that is traditionally associated with characters from the lower classes?[47] A closer look at Ursula's use of the genre provides some clues.

At the base of both the *vida* and the picaresque narrative is the question of origins and, often, the reality of financial problems (a dowry for nuns and making a living for rogues). Appropriately enough, Ursula begins her story with her own origins and role within the household economy. Rather than inscribing her birth and upbringing within the traditional portrait of the ideal Christian family in which both mother and father are exemplars of virtue, Ursula, in a more picaresque fashion, suggests a certain illegitimacy in her upbringing and recounts her mother's attempts to use her as a go-between. Metaphorically orphaned as an infant because Ursula's mother was unable to breast-feed her daughter (and, therefore, instill her with the virtue that only a mother's pure milk could transmit), the autobiographer notes how she was passed from one nurse (*ama*) to another. In all, she had ten *amas* and concludes that was the reason, "I turned out so bad."[48] Despite being spoiled by her paternal grandmother, Ursula did not have a childhood; her family treated her "as though I were a grownup" and early on she recognized the power of language: "I was careful with what I said."[49]

Cleverly manipulating her grandmother, the young girl acquired food and clothes for her mother, who had married with no dowry and was completely dependent on her in-law's rare generosity for foodstuffs and clothing. When she saw her daughter's ability to extract things from the matriarch, she turned the young girl into a go-between to better their economic situation:

> On one occasion my mother began to complain that she had nothing on which to subsist, and that my grandmother, who had so much wheat, would not give her a bushel, and told me, "Tell her that, little one, so that your grandmother will say that I grumble about her and that I am a daughter-in-law." I waited for an occasion to tell this to my grandmother, because although I was very young—not even five years old—I was careful with what I said. One day, when she had me in bed with her, I said, "Grandmother, my poor mother has nothing on which to live, so why doesn't Your Grace give her something?" She replied, "Doesn't she have three black slave women? Why doesn't she make them work? Why does she rent them out? For I have told her that renting them out will make them sick, and your mother won't listen." This is how she talked to me, as though I were a

grownup. I said to her, "Give her wheat, and with that she will make her bread." "Did she tell you to say that?" "My mother talks to me," I replied. "Give her wheat." I began to cry and complain to her, saying, "You see how you don't love me, Grandmother? Is this your kindness, refusing to give me the keys to the pantry?" On I prattled, until she said, "Take the key, miss; give her two bushels." I went to my mother very content and told her, "Let's go to the pantry, for my grandmother will give you some wheat now." "Didn't I tell you not to tell her? What shameless behavior! Why did you tell your grandmother about it? No one can say a word with you around." I began to tremble, judging that she was going to whip me. Then my aunt said to her: "Don't be like that with your daughter, Marucha: besides trying to save your life and provide you with something on which to subsist, you are making this angel tremble, when you should be praising her. Don't be foolish with her, who is so generous and discreet."[50]

The Clarist nun portrays her mother as a *pícaro's* master: the mother used Ursula to get the basic necessities in life and repaid her daughter with threats ("I am going to kill you"). Making contact with the confessional mode in which she is inscribing her story, the autobiographer concludes that God had chosen her to be her mother's "instrument."[51]

Some years after the grandmother died, Ursula's mother began preparing her daughter for marriage into a well-to-do family, hoping to assure the financial security of the whole family; ideally, Ursula would have access to her husband's wealth and would thus be the solution to the family's problems. With this proposed marriage, the conflict between mother and daughter escalated because the young girl was already set on being a nun, not a nun in a reformed, discalced order but a wealthy nun with, as her grandmother had promised, riches from all over the viceroyalty of Peru in her cell and slaves:

> You will be a nun in all comfort if God sees fit to preserve me until you are of age; no nun will be better installed than you, with your richly furnished cell, very well hung display cabinets and tooled silver, brought from Peru, paintings from Cuzco, and I will send to Lima to have made anything you might need. You will have one female slave for inside and another outside, and four thousand pesos income; this is on top of your inheritance, which you will of course be given.[52]

Describing her mother as a "angry lioness," Ursula says she became the "dog of the house" once the grandmother died. Even though her father and uncle supported her choice to be a nun, she had to fight tooth and nail with her mother to avoid becoming "dead" through marriage and sexual union with a man: "It occurred to me that all women who married were dead."[53] Ursula draws on the a topic in nuns' *vidas*, of becoming "dead" to the secular world (and thus to her body as a source of sexuality) and is ready to marytr herself rather than be taken by a man: "Well, should I consent to be bedded with a man? I would as soon hang myself, or take a dagger and slit my throat or run it through my breast."[54]

In contrast to her self-portrait as being marginalized by her mother and vowing to remain chaste, Ursula reveals her concurrent interests in roaming the streets of Santiago to watch illicit sexual acts. Reworking a tale from folklore, the nun recounts searching for a magic wand (*varilla*) but ending up at the scene of a crime: the young girl had stumbled across a house of prostitution, but in her childish innocence took it to be weddings:[55]

> I had heard tell of a magic wand, that by means of it you could work miracles. I believed it and set out eagerly to look for this wand: I left home and followed a little irrigation stream that comes out from the Augustine convent, and went very far down where the canal flowed swiftly and ran off into the country. . . . There were some empty rooms there with no doors where so many shameless acts were committed that it was scandalous, as it was broad day, and there were not just two people involved in these bad things, but eight or ten; it was not a sight to be seen except by innocent eyes, who knew not that they were committing a sin. I thought they were weddings, and so I went daily to see them.[56]

When she reported the incident to her mother, Ursula was scolded for talking about these "weddings," so the girl deduced that there was no harm in watching them as long as she did not talk about them. A far cry from saintly women's narratives of repugnance to sexuality, Ursula's story talks of repeated interest in male-female relationships of all sorts.

Such a reworking of stories from folkloric tradition and the ironies produced by the literal interpretation of her mother's rules are reminiscent of elements found in picaresque stories beginning with the *Lazarillo de Tormes*. Like Lazarillo, Ursula learns at an early age the power of language—when to use it, and when to withhold it. Moreover, there is a latent sense of sexual awakening in her self-portrait of a young girl wanting to become a nun but being innocently curious about sexuality.

Ursula reveals that according to family lore, as a toddler she was stark naked in the bath and playing at ringing convent bells when she announced she would become a nun:

> I said to [my aunt]: "When I am big I will be the rose among thorns, for I will be a nun." She said to me: "You, a nun? So wicked and of such bad blood, opponents of becoming nuns," and I replied, "I, Aunt, will be the crown of my generation." Said she, "Quiet, imp, for your liveliness is not for the likes of a nun, though when you were very little one day I was giving you a bath in the middle of the patio and you frightened me, for, holding you quite naked, [there you were] clutching my braids and you began to ring them back and forth with great tempo, and imitated the sound of the bells with your mouth. Frightened, I called your mother and said, "Kitty, come and see your daughter who's going to be a nun, look how she peals." My mother and all the other women came out to applaud your charm: I don't know what it was, because you are a great rascal." I told her: "Aunt, Your Grace will see that I will become a nun."[57]

Using the innocence of a child's perspective and the words of others, Ursula unites the good/bad woman dichotomy ("nun," "naked") so often found in period manuals for women and creates a symbolic moment for her own identity.[58] Nuns, as Ursula herself later explains to a suitor, were meant to be asexual, nothing more than "hands and faces," their bodies being made of pure, cold, hard marble.[59] And they were to practice long hours of virtuous silence. *Pícaras*, on the other hand, acknowledged their bodies, their sexuality, and the use of language; their survival depended upon their verbal wit and sexual desirability.[60] For much of Ursula's life she was keenly aware of her sexuality and wit, but innocently depicts it as an integral part of her religious vocation.

Calling herself a roamer (*callejera*) and mischievous (*traviesa*), the Clarist nun goes on to relate children's pranks and other deceptions that she practiced at home—the origin of a vice she continued in the convent. Overhearing a conversation between her aunt and mother about a woman deceived by a man, the six-year-old vowed to avenge dishonored women. Perhaps playing with the common literary theme of honor, Ursula used her femininity to avenge women's honor in general. But by invoking God's blessing in the narrative, she depicts herself as a saintly rogue (*pícara a lo divino*) who rights wrongs: "In conclusion, I formulated the intention of never letting an opportunity go by in which I would not attempt to deceive as many [men] as my ability would allow, and this with due payment as though God in this present state were rendering a very good service; not four days went by that I did not comply with my intention."[61]

At age six Ursula begins to execute her vow to take revenge on men and takes on her first victim. She begins her play-acting by making herself up to dupe a man:

> After compline, it seemed to me a good opportunity to begin to deceive. I went to my aunt's box; like a monkey I began enthusiastically to dress myself up, and said, "When [the women] show themselves in the window they are all dressed up." I got out the makeup and began to plaster it on without a mirror and with very good color; I don't know if I turned out a hideous mask or not, because I paid no attention to that, but to the makeup I had seen women use. . . . I got out a mantilla . . . which would veil my face; I arranged it very well so that one could see that I was white without knowing that I was a child. I thus went to the window. . . . When I was already seated I saw a man come from the direction of the plaza and said: "Thank God, now I'll deceive you." This is what happened: the man came up to the window and began to talk to me. I had no idea what he was saying nor how to reply. . . . He asked for my hand; I realized that if he saw it he would know thereby that I was a child. He got out a handful of silver and was going to give it to me, and I got intimidated about his seeing my hand, not by the money. Finally I said to him, "If you give me the money, put your hand in the window"; I did that to make sure of it and be able to snatch it from him; the handful of silver appeared as I had requested, and I gave his hand a great slap and simultaneously dropped down from the window, with one silver dollar which was the only thing I was able to snatch from him.

As soon as I was down I began to taunt him, telling him: "I have deceived you, fool; such a great booby that you let yourself be deceived by me." . . . I closed the window quickly and went inside to clean up and wash my face so that my aunt would not see me with the makeup.[62]

When the smitten man returned the next day, her disguise was revealed. Upon seeing the young girl without makeup or a mantilla, the man exclaimed: "She must be a saint or a very bad girl" ("ha de ser santa o gran mala"). Accordingly, the reader is given two reactions: as in the story about getting wheat for her mother, the aunt laughed and the mother wanted to whip Ursula as though she were a grownup. She walks the fine line between saint and sinner, between nun and *pícara*. Even the uncle who convinced the mother to let her daughter enter the convent at a young age argues that people are amused by her remarks and, more important, she would be "weighed down by children and perhaps bored if she married."[63]

As a nun, Ursula continues this duality as sinner-saint first established through the words of others—the aunt and mother, the deceived man, and the uncle. When other nuns saw the novice's dismay at the relative poverty of the convent, "They looked on my charm with pleasure, and said that I must be a great rascal and extremely clever."[64] Shocked that walls were not painted and meals were served in clay pottery rather than silver, she confessed: "At first I was displeased in the convent as I missed the neatness of my home and not being able to eat from tooled silver [plates]."[65] The silver from Potosí and the paintings from Cuzco that her grandmother had predicted for her granddaughter's life in the convent did not materialize. Ursula's desire for finery clearly was unfit behavior for a model nun, who would have disdained all worldly possessions and taken a vow of poverty—although as we saw in Sor Juana's case, the interpretation of this vow varied widely. While openly questioning for the first time her reasons to become a nun, she refused to return home and, like a model nun, took to heart the examples in Scripture of the prophets' difficulties in leaving home.

This focus on the financial concerns of convent life ultimately provides one of the richest areas of Ursula's critique of women's economic dependence on men, as well as a newfound justification for carrying on her deceptions of them. In unreformed convents, nuns relied heavily on special male patrons, *devotos de monjas*, who financed many of the operating costs and individual needs of nuns in return for a particular nun's prayers and attention through visits to the locutory. Notably, the last notebook (6) before the story of her religious experience, is essentially a series of entertaining anecdotes about these liaisons with *devotos de monjas*. Many nuns decried the evils of the *devoto* system, while many male literary authors found it a rich area for satire.[66] Elsewhere, Ursula mentions how another nun's life story, the *Vida* by María de la Antigua, exposed the defects of the *devoto* system and implies that no action had been taken to better the situation (230). In Ursula's hands, she mixes a confessional mode with accounts about her deceits and games to describe the crucial yet problematic system of patronage. She relates in detail duping her *devotos*: promising to marry one, getting another to buy her a house, playing off two men's simultaneous visits, telling another man of high social rank to kneel before her, and reprimanding yet another who wanted to hold her hand. She argues that the financial proceeds of these encounters through the grille helped the convent: the *devotos* were the nuns' "stewards" (*mayordomos*, 181). Once again employing words of others to note playfully the direct relationship between economic gain for all and being proclaimed a saint, Ursula recalls that when one thankful old nun called Ursula a saint, she retorted: "I say that, as she saw it, she foretold that not only would I be a great religious but a saint, for this opinion was as good as canonization."[67] She combines the worldly need (and in her case, desire) for material goods with the virtue of charity in her self-portrait. Although she borrows aspects of the *pícara's* character, she attempts to make herself—through the words of others—into an unconventional saint who uses her ruses to benefit others.

But rather than highlight her charity, Ursula delights in telling the transgressive aspects of her tales, which undermines the confessional purpose of the account. Ursula flaunts her manipulation of the *devotos*. In some cases she switches to a confessional mode after telling about an incident ("The time came for confession and I made an examination of so many bad deeds"),[68] but in others there is no remorse for her deceit. After lying to one of her victims saying that she was planning to leave the convent, she describes his gullibility: "This man, well, was he not a fool to give credit to such nonsense? For, seeing as how I was leaving the convent, should I have gone with a married man, and all the more so as he knew my family and who I was? More fool he to believe me, when he said that I seemed exceedingly perverse, that I showed signs of the devil for having deceived him; they themselves say it and it falls upon them; I now believe that they who have been deceived are devils to women."[69] Like the *pícara* Justina, Ursula inverted men's own tricks, and like Sor Juana, she points the guilty finger at men's own folly.

These highly picaresque scenes nearly disappear from the narrative after notebook 8, after Ursula's religious experience. In fact, notebooks 7 and 8 include all the elements of a conversion experience found in other nuns' *vidas*. Preparing for a general confession, Ursula says she experienced a series of *vuelos* and interior light, followed by feeling such deep remorse for her sins and recognition of her unworthiness that she cried for three days. Deciding to begin a new life, the nun wanted to avoid unnecessary contact with other people and to strive to "exceed the most holy." She started praying four hours daily, until her confessor reigned in her practice. At this moment of desire to transform her ways, God appeared and provided direction. Although Ursula says she was fearful and like a slave ready to be beaten, God insisted she listen to his message: she was to preach like St. Paul after his conversion. God explains: "I put St. Paul's words in you, because I want you to preach as he did."[70] Although there is never any further clarification of this divine command, of what it meant to preach like St. Paul, it is a directive that echoes throughout the other notebooks, in spite of her confessor's command that Ursula follow the Virgin Mary's submissive role rather than St. Paul's active one.

At this key moment in the account of her spiritual life, Ursula justifies herself by invoking divine will. When her confessor Padre Viñas questioned Ursula's new role and suggested a more subservient one, God corrects the confessor:

Father Viñas told me not to tell him what St. Paul said, but rather Samuel, and the words of the Most Holy Virgin: *Behold the handmaid*; I, as I didn't know, said whatever came to mind . . . and it seemed that it came not from my soul, but was only spoken by my mouth; I said it because the priest had ordered it, but not with the efficacy with which I had said St. Paul's words, because the latter were dictated by my heart. On another occasion . . . this inner voice said to me: "I want to manifest the strength of My power in you."[71]

By quoting God directly, Ursula undermines her confessor's authority over her life. Ursula then decides to turn a new leaf: she leaves a *devoto*, reads devotional works on the Incarnation and Passion of Christ, and prays for the souls of her parents. Rather than advertise her spiritual transformation, however, Ursula swore Padre Viñas to secrecy and begs her current confessor Padre Gamboa to keep the secret as well.[72]

In Ursula's case, these changes do not lead to a desire to follow the mystic's path, but rather to create a new life that leaves behind the rogue's deceit while maintaining a sense of humor and wit when facing hardships. After relating her defining spiritual experience, Ursula's subsequent *cuentas de conciencia* focus more on conflict within the convent after 1694, with abbesses, confessors, and the bishop of Santiago. These individual narrative units, like those written by María de San José (vols. 3–12), follow a general chronological order but often describe unrelated incidents. With the exception of the last two notebooks that appear to be written as a single piece (vols. 13–14), the others were clearly written as discrete units (9, 10, 11, and 12).[73] Some were written after the death of the nun's first addressee, Tomás de Gamboa, and may have been written for an unnamed confessor who came upon the scene later, as discussed later in this chapter. With the exception of the incomplete notebook 12, notebooks 9, 10, 11, and 13–14 recount a series of trials and illnesses.[74] Struggles with the vicress over convent rules (notebook 9), with her confessor Padre Alemán, whom she dismisses (notebooks 10 and 13), with the abbess about Ursula's close contact with the bishop (notebook 10), and with the bishop himself and the convent over the vote for abbess fill the pages (notebooks 10, 13–14). Convent politics and schisms apparently dominated Ursula's life during the first decades of the eighteenth century. Not surprisingly, it is in the final two notebooks, which recount the most intense years of power struggles dealing with the controversial vote for abbess (1710–1715), that Ursula pauses to question bitterly the church's determination of model behavior for women and of its canonization and Inquisitorial procedures in particular. In nearly every notebook, however, God's wish that she be a happy saint who uses her speech to spread God's Word comes through the anecdotes about conflict, even in the darkest moments after the bishop's punishment of her actions.

Both the nun and the *pícara* lack complete discursive freedom because of their positions in the church or in society, and the telling of their respective life stories is often difficult.[75] In the case of Ursula's narrative, the tension between her desire to construct her own self-portrait and her need to bow in obedience to her confessor becomes apparent after she leaves her roguish ways behind. Subsequent notebooks talk increasingly of rifts with the abbess, bishop, and confessors, but these often provide a springboard for Ursula to follow her belief that God wanted her to use her voice both to preach and to offer laughter.

If before Ursula turned the tables on suitors and *devotos*, now she uses her link to the divine to gain a degree of control over her confessors. Like María de San José, Ursula exploits the possibilities of the mystic triad, the tripartite struggle for authority so typical of nuns' *vidas*. In the scene where God tells Ursula to preach like St. Paul, she feels empowered to sermonize, which was a task strictly reserved for clergy. Padre Viñas, in contrast, is portrayed as a spiritual director who fails to respect the Word of God. This pattern characterizes all of her anecdotes regarding preaching. Upon telling her confessor about her mystical transport to India to evangelize, he concludes that she fabricated the story because her description of the inhabitants corresponded to Chinese peoples.[76] Although she decides to refrain from telling him anything else, soon she boasts of more mystical transports to "Arab lands" and of converting a group of African workers in the convent: "I asked them why they had not been baptized before; they said they hadn't known how to pray. 'You,' they said, 'taught us how.' I laughed at their foolishness in saying that they had been unable to learn from the priests, but did so from me."[77] Ursula highlights her role as an evangelist, but at the same time downplays her own importance by putting the words into another's mouth and making light of the situation. Through the use of dramatic technique, of dialogue and humor, Ursula objectifies her personal conflicts with the church and creates an almost theatrical role for herself as a woman evangelist.

In addition to preaching, Ursula exalts her use of voice as a story-teller in the convent. Among her convent sisters she was known as storyteller, for weaving entertaining tales: "I am such a chatterbox that the nuns sought me out to amuse them, and called me the storyteller."[78] Men and bishops sought her out for her humorous stories and, in turn, donated money for new buildings. Before imposing the sentence on Ursula, for example, Bishop Romero fondly called Ursula "the philosopher"; she explains, "the bishop suffered from hypochondria; I, to amuse him, told him jokes and made him laugh. . . . He enjoyed my silly jests."[79]

In fact, remnants of the former *pícara* who delights in her ruses come through the narrative, but now the accounts are often "authored" by God himself. Although there was talk in the convent of an affair between Ursula and Bishop Romero, for example, God instructed her to accept the church father's gifts because she had to put up with his ill humor. Ursula reports that on another occasion God playfully interjected a retort for her when the bishop stepped out of line. When discussing the burdens of wearing religious clothing, the bishop asked her to touch his foot, to witness the number of socks he wore. At that point, as Ursula records it, God piped in saying a bishop should give her his hand, not his foot: "Tell the bishop that to have offered you his foot was not by chance, but he should have given you his hand, for many times [his feet] have trod on you. . . . Let him give you his hand and have him remember that if indeed he has given his foot to a woman, in your case he should put it away as for that reason I consecrated him."[80] Just as other nuns invoke God's words in their accounts about interactions with confessors, Ursula plays with church hierarchy through the use of humor and dialogue with the divine. This incident, in particular, is acoustically highlighted through the use of internal rhyme in the origi-

nal Spanish. Even God becomes a character that plays into these somewhat tantalizing scenes. In another instance, Ursula records how God pleaded with her to remove
her nun's wimple because he wanted to see her better (notebook 12). In Ursula's eyes,
God is often playful.

As we saw in the opening of this chapter, when Ursula laments not being more
like her Clarist models, the mystic nun and author María de la Antigua and Mariana
de Escobar, God explains to Ursula the reason for this deviation: "My Lord and
Most Loving Father said to me: 'I haven't yet had a comedienne saint, and as there
are all manner of things in palaces, you are to be the comedienne.' I said to Him:
'My Lord and Father, I am grateful for all your benefits and mercies, and as you
wish to make me a saint, let it not be a saint without wit.' He replied: 'You will no
longer envy Doña Marina and [María de] la Antigua.'"[81] As she explains later to her
convent sisters: "You are to know that I am going to be a saint, and not just any
saint, for the Church will have no other saint as madcap as I."[82] She will be the saint
that breaks the rules for sainthood, but will have God's blessings for it. In fact, she
tells her reader(s), God had already granted her a divine mercy by assigning Maria
de la Antigua's own guardian angel to Ursula, in addition to her original one. A nun
striving to be a *perfecta religiosa* like the popular Maria de la Antigua, whose mystic
Stations and exemplary biography were in nearly every Spanish American convent library, now had an alternate path, the holy comedienne, who would be a character
who spoke God's script for her and the mad cap saint (*santa disparatada*) who could
use humor for saintly ends.

Clearly, the balance of confession and the exhortation to virtue found in a model
nun's *vida*, such as María de San José, is challenged in Ursula Suárez's *Relación*. Whereas
María's *vida* details penances and trials in following the road to perfection and is
offered as both a confession and an example to her readers, Ursula's stories from the
time she was three years old focus on the evils of the system of *devotos de monjas* and
argue that both secular and religious women should have more economic independence and freedom to speak. She is a storyteller who details the flaws in men, the
injustices done to women, and her own playful revenge.[83] Men were permitted to
deceive women outside the convent and misjudge them in the cloister. In contrast,
society was harsh in its treatment of women who played with language in the same
way; they were called liars and heretics (*embusteras* and *herejes*).

Just as Sor Juana's *Respuesta* weaves a multitude of genres into a new *vida* form in
order to highlight the shortcomings of the script for religious women, Ursula Suárez's
literary borrowings help critique a patriarchal system that encouraged women to be
silent and financially dependent on men.[84] As we have seen, both the *vida* and the
picaresque novel share an autobiographical form. But the *vida* tells the story of a
spiritual conversion bestowed by divine grace upon an undeserving sinner, while the
picaresque novel tells of a sinner on the margins of society who attempts to better
her economic circumstances. The "model nun" uses church-approved rhetoric to
establish the authority of her story as the will of God and exhorts others to follow
her example; in doing so, she secures a place for herself within society. The *pícara*, in
contrast, masters a language of wit and cunning—often based on her sexual desirability—in order to take advantage of men and invert society's hierarchies. Unfortu-

nately for the *pícara*, by sacrificing her integrity, she becomes the butt of her own jokes and is held firmly in place by a comic distance established between character and reader, one that reflects the impossibility of class ascent.[85] As for the female characters in the *comedia*, even if they rebel against conventions, generally in the end order is restored—usually through marriage. In the hands of a female dramatist such as Sor Juana or María de Zayas, however, the portrayal of these characters implies a more far-reaching critique of society's norms. Such divergent outcomes in the three genres help readers recognize each genre and respond in different manners. The *vida* provokes admiration of a real person well-connected to God; the *comedia* explores society's boundaries for male-female relationship and conventions; and the picaresque novel serves as both entertainment and negative example.

Manuscripts, Compilers, and Meaning

But in the end, what effect does this inscription of Ursula's story into the confessional form—with borrowings from other literary genres—have on our understanding of her story? Is she a *pícara a lo divino*, with the Catholic Church's blessing for her ruses? Or, as Kristine Ibsen suggests, does the moving story at the end of Ursula's *Relación*, about the severe punishment she received from a bishop—the only man who seems to break her spirit—undo her self-portrait as a happy saint?

Upon first reading of the final notebook, it seems Ursula may have capitulated to the demands of male church hierarchy. After several difficult encounters with nuns who humiliate her, Ursula describes her tears and desire to be more saintlike and to suffer. Then, in spite of her verbal mastery and partial success at portraying herself as chosen by God, she recounts the alienation and illness that followed the bishop's sentence. In this moment, Ursula compares her public suffering at the hands of others with Christ's Passion. The pain of this account only seems to be heightened in the closing pages of the narrative. As mentioned earlier, she tells Padre Viñas about a dream in which she killed a serpent by crushing it in her mouth, which turned bloody.[86] The dream might have originally been a rewriting of the association of woman with Eve and the serpent with deceptive language and sin, but Ursula's confessor dismisses it. He insists that snakes don't have bones, and Ursula decides to drop the topic:[87] "When I told Padre Viñas about this, he told me: 'It has no bones.' I replied: 'But I heard them crunch.' 'It has no bones,' he repeated. I remained silent and fought him no longer."[88] But even in the darkest moments after her sentencing by the bishop, Ursula thanks God and jokes with him after a vision: "His Majesty [God] told me: 'There will be repercussions,' and I told Him: 'Thunder as well, so that we will have a good party.'"[89] It is a touching portrait of a nun who believes in a God as a friend with a sense of humor.

On the other hand, Bishop Romero and Padre Viñas are portrayed as blocking divine will. While Viñas argues with her in the confessional, the bishop follows a pattern Ursula has criticized throughout her text: she criticizes men who support nuns physically, but not intellectually or spiritually. She records in the final notebook that he sent her money and food after the sentence. But he also sent a warning: "Don't talk to me in Latin, don't mention St. Paul to me, and don't quote the Bible to me.''[90] In addition, Ursula urges her current, unnamed addressee and confessor to keep her secret, something Bishop Romero failed to do.

Why did Ursula's account end with these episodes with Padre Viñas and Bishop Romero in 1715? Why, when some of the writings were probably composed as late as 1730 or 1732 and one of the manuscripts we have was Ursula's own copy of her original notebooks, is her rise to abbess mentioned in the context of the 1710 election fraud but never described once she was in power in 1721? As in the case of Catarina de San Juan, only more archival research will give us definitive answers—just as recent finds for Sor Juana's life have clarified some of the enigmas of her last years. Nonetheless, we can conjecture that perhaps Ursula, as an *escritora por obediencia*, was asked to copy certain notebooks, ones that recounted an engaging life story, but also offered a moral in the end. In other words, as in the picaresque tradition, there probably is a didactic message in Ursula's story: too much roguishness and irreverent laughter lead to the need to undergo penance, experience remorse, and learn to be silent. Perhaps this is the effect that she foreshadows in notebook 10 when she records the following:

> Considering so many mercies received from [God's] infinite goodness, I said to Him: "Lord and Master of all that I am, my only love and entire goodness, it seems that You wish to make my folly truth." He responded: "You were prophesying about yourself." I said to Him "I, a prophet in my land?" He said "In your case all is pardoned." I said to Him: "And when do I get to be a saint?" to which He responded: "When you are silent." I said to Him: "I have a long way to go, for I cannot be silent."[91]

What is more, if Ursula's notebooks had traveled a path like those of Teresa and María de San José, the writings would have been turned over to confessors and later carefully reordered, and at times recopied.[92] Perhaps Ursula's own confessors reordered the notebooks, using the first eight as the basic *vida* narrative unit, and then added on miscellaneous notebooks as they saw fit to fill in the years leading to the 1715 sentencing in order to create a final ending more in keeping with the model nun. If this scenario is true, Ursula's story ultimately follows the pattern we have seen in Rosa, María, Catarina, and Sor Juana: the Clarist nun's own life story and self-representation is once again mediated—in this case, by selection or omission of certain notebooks—so as to inscribe her story, however unusual, into a conventional tale that ends on a note of submission. Readers of this version of the *Relación* are left to think that Ursula's talkative, witty ways were quashed permanently in 1715. What a story might Ursula's other letters and confessional notebooks written during her years as abbess and her last quarter century tell (if they exist at all)?[93]

In fact, we might conjecture that her case could have been like that of Sor Juana's—an independent spirit that the church ultimately could not silence. In a previous reading, I suggested that in the end Ursula is marginalized much like the picaresque figure from the literary world. Other critics have also taken this final portrait at face value.[94] A number of half-answered enigmas and a closer look at the narrative tone, however, point to a plausible and very different conclusion. Piecing together period church politics, confessors, and addressees, a completely different scenario and interpretation could be argued—one in which Ursula is not humbled but, rather, encouraged by a new confessor to reveal the details of a severe conflict and schism in the convent and the turbulent times that male clergy were experiencing with their own superiors, the Inquisition, and the king.

Although the final notebook depicts a humbled Ursula, for the most part the tone and extensive detail belie the portrait of a truly submissive nun bowing to church superiors. In the notebooks that appear to be written for a new addressee (notebooks 11 and 13–14), Ursula reveals full names and details for the events that took place during a decade of intense church politics (ca. 1710–1720).[95] Ursula describes unjust treatment with no restraint, and records through direct quotes the often uncharitable words of others; she writes a script of the events. She names her confessors, Padres Viñas and Gamboa, though infrequently, but portrays Padre Alemán, the confessor she dismissed, as a primary source of conflict. Likewise, she assigns the role of the jealous antagonist to the abbess who won out over Ursula (who was Gamboa's own sister). But she reserves her harshest words for Bishop Romero. After chatting frequently with Ursula, he turns on her: he revokes the convent vote, sentences her to punishment, fails to keep his sacramental vow of secrecy, and blocks God's will that she follow in St. Paul's footsteps. Mostly, it is the direct discourse of other characters who condemn the bishop, as when the abbess cautions Ursula about some bishops' immoral conduct: "She said to me: 'Haven't you read of cases where bishops have had children?'"[96] Ursula's final portraits of Padre Alemán and Bishop Romero read more like a vendetta than the words of an obedient nun.

Who was the new addressee of these notebooks? Why did Ursula write these accounts for him? And why were they included in the *Relación*? As we have seen in María de San José's case, the role of the reader had everything to do with the material, as well as the tone of an account. For example, María's first account of a convent schism was full of ambiguity. But later, under the protection of a new addressee, the bishop of Oaxaca, a second account clearly describes the cause of the schism.[97] Ursula may have been encouraged by a new regime of clerics to describe the tumultuous Santiago church politics in the 1710s. Writing at least a decade after the events, and having been vindicated by being chosen as abbess by the new bishop Alejo Fernández Rojas, Ursula was now in power.[98] Moreover, most of her antagonists had died by the time the last changes were made to these accounts (ca. 1730–1732).[99] Viñas and Alemán died within a year of each other (1718 and 1719, respectively), and Gamboa and Romero both died in 1729. Perhaps it was then safe to reveal the difficult change in confessors and the politics of a controversial convent vote. Romero's death, combined with that of her first addressee for the *vida*, Gamboa, may have served as a catalyst for these final notebooks, binding them with the first eight.

A look at the difficulties Ursula's antagonists had with their own superiors may further support the theory that these accounts were written to shed light on several controversial situations from 1710 to 1720 in Santiago. Kristine Ibsen notes that Antonio Alemán served as confessor to one of the accused in the polemical Inquisition trial of the Jesuit Juan Francisco Ulloa. Ulloa was posthumously tried for heresy. Because he had been a spiritual director for several religious women, the repercussions of the trial affected female religious communities like Ursula's where many nuns worked with

Jesuit confessors. Begun in 1715, the same year as Ursula's sentence, the trial did not come to a complete close until nearly fifteen years later (about the time she finished her notebooks).[100] At one point, the bishop removed a Clarist nun from her administrative post as a result of the trial, and this may explain why Ursula mentions the infamous Inquisition trial in Peru against Angela Carranza and the case in Spain in which the well-known Fray Luis de Granada was implicated in promoting a "false holy woman." Ursula questions God: "My Lord, why, when you are merciful to women, does the Inquisition make inquiries about them?"[101] These situations that Ursula mentions may have served as a foil for the circumstances in Ursula's own convent.[102]

Another historical fact may come into play in Ursula's portrait of Bishop Romero. In 1710 he took a hard reformist stand by ordering new prayer routines and banning the *devoto* system—the important, if highly criticized, source for income—and enforced complete enclosure of the convent.[103] Despite Ursula's constant critique of the system, she records the bishop's lack of discretion in his public announcement of the new rule. In fact, Juan de Guernica's history of the convent reveals the constant financial straits of the convent and its need for funds. In some ways, the *devoto* system, may have been simply a practical mechanism to address the convent's economic situation. A probably all-important part of this historical puzzle is that in 1718 Bishop Romero himself was accused of disloyalty to the Crown and was stripped of his position in Santiago and sent to Quito.[104] His death in 1729 may have provoked more inquiry into his life from other clergy asking Ursula for a record of her interactions with him. Ursula's criticism may have been solicited by clergy bent on further discrediting the bishop. In addition, other historical events, such as the 1730 earthquake that devastated large parts of the Clarist convent and another controversy over the position of abbess, certainly would have contributed to a change in convent administration and power.[105]

While more questions than answers surround the role of readers and church politics, and their effect on Ursula's life writings, the questions themselves point once again to the crucial interaction between church institutions and individuals. Like the nuns themselves, confessors and bishops were often asked for an accounting of their actions, but they usually did not write life stories about the turmoil and controversy. Moreover, the hierarchical system among women religious within the convent often caused as much strife as the spiritual father-daughter relationship, as seen in the conflict over elections of the abbess.

In the end, Ursula's own self-portrait offers an alternative to the saint or sinner models codified by the official church for religious women. Her account mentions examples of both extremes—the holy mystic Sor Maria de la Antigua and the heretical Angela Carranza—but her life follows neither completely. She fashioned a life path in which she avoided the Inquisition, but she did not escape being punished by a bishop and did not become the subject of a hagiographic biography. Ursula successfully deviated from strict interpretation of church mandates for women because she was willing to risk censure in order to create an alternate path to the divine, and because for years she was well connected to influential clergy. The one case on record that Ursula was punished can be explained by a change in church politics and her personal relationship with a bishop.

Ursula's story may not have been promoted for many other reasons as well. Like the Colombian mystic Madre Castillo (1671–1742), whose life was not posthumously promoted by the church, Ursula lived in a large convent for seven decades.[106] Being enclosed for so many years and living in one of the nonprestigious orders surely limited her exposure to a wider circle of society. Other factors, such as chronology and geography, may have also been important. By the time Ursula died in the mid–eighteenth century, the most prolific period of *vida* writing and publication was ending. And there is some evidence that the norms for nuns' writing had become more lax. Kristin Routt argues this point in the case of Madre Maria Ana Agueda de San Ignacio, whose mystical works were published in her own lifetime, in mid-eighteenth-century New Spain. Electa Arenal and Stacey Schlau argue in the case of another late eighteenth-century nun that the language of mysticism had become so heavily codified that it lost the fresh individual expression of the writings by earlier nuns (Sor Marcela in particular).[107] Parodies of a literary genre often seem to emerge when the form becomes weighed down with stylistic conventions. Ursula was also isolated geographically. Although Santiago had convents and a bishop, it was nonetheless on the periphery of the Spanish empire. More than a thousand miles from the center of the viceroyalty in Lima—where the major institutional church decisions were made, executed, and published—Santiago had the same provincial flavor as Madre Castillo's Tunja in Colombia. As we will see in the next chapter, with the Lieutenant Nun, norms were often more relaxed as one traveled farther from the ruling centers of colonial institutions. Ursula's colloquial register may have been tolerated because the system of official surveillance was weak at such a distance from the seat of power.

Within several decades of Ursula's death, broadly based convent reforms were initiated by the Bourbon monarchy. Large convents that followed regular rule (versus reformed orders, such as Teresa's and Madre María's orders) were particularly targeted. In the end, while neither Ursula nor her text were sent to the Inquisition, her voice and life were forgotten for many years because no rescripting of her life occurred and her manuscript was buried in the archive. But since its publication at the end of the twentieth century we are now able to appreciate how a text like Ursula's adds to our store of life stories. The *Relación* reveals Ursula's creative response when confronting prescriptions for women's roles and stories. More than any woman discussed in this book, Ursula comments directly on the daily life of upper-class women. Through a hybrid self-narrative, she critiques marriage and the financial workings of a household, as well as the politics, spirituality, and economics of convent life.

Chronology of Ursula Suárez

1666	Born Ursula Suárez de Escobar in Santiago de Chile.
1678	Enters the newly founded Clarist Convent located on the Plaza de las Armas.
1684	Professes as a full-fledged black-veiled nun.
1684–1710	Holds various roles in the convent as *dispensora, definadora, provisora, escucha.*

1708	Begins the *Relación* for her confessor Tomás de Gamboa.
1710	Loses bid for position as convent abbess; is appointed as *vicaria* by Bishop Romero.
1715	Defeated a second time in convent elections for abbess.
1715	Ecclesiastical sentence imposed on Ursula by Bishop Romero.
1718	Padre Viñas dies.
1719	Padre Alemán dies.
1721–1724	Serves as convent abbess.
1725	Serves as convent president (a one-year extension as abbess).
1729	Bishop Romero and Padre Gamboa die.
1730	Earthquake partially destroys convent.
1730–1732	Probably wrote/revised some of the final notebooks in the *Relación* (in particular, notebook 10).
1749	Dies.
ca. 1850	Don José Ignacio Víctor Eyzaguirre, presbítero, copies the manuscript held by the original convent.
1914	Transcription of the *Relación* made.
1984	First published edition of the manuscript (done by Mario Ferreccio Podestá).

6

The Lieutenant Nun

Catalina de Eruaso (1592?–1650)—Soldiers' Tales and Virginity

"I kissed the foot of His Holiness Urban VIII and told him succinctly, and as best I could all about my life, adventures, gender, and virginity. His Holiness appeared to be astonished thereby, and graciously gave me permission to continue to lead my life dressed as a man, urging me to lead an honest life from now on."
—*Vida*, chap. 25

"News of this event spread everywhere very quickly, and people who had seen me before, and people, both before and after, who heard my story all over the Indies were amazed."
—*Vida*, chap. 20

Only a few years after the streets of Lima had filled upon news of Rosa de Lima's death, they filled again with onlookers as the now infamous Lieutenant Catalina de Erauso arrived in a litter escorted by ten men of cloth and six swordsmen.[1] After having disguised herself as a man for nearly twenty years and earned a reputation as a brave soldier and rogue on the frontiers of the Spanish empire in Chile, Catalina had been ordered to take the veil as a nun.[2] She had killed a man in a duel over a card game, and in order to protect herself from the law, she had confessed to a bishop and revealed her true identity as a woman who had once lived in a convent in Spain. The bishop spared her life under the condition that she return to her previous profession as a bride of Christ.

In her account to the bishop, Catalina reported having been born to a well-to-do family in the Basque country, entering her aunt's convent at the age of four. She escaped before professing her vows at age fifteen, donned male garb to serve as a page, and finally embarked for America, where she worked at various occupations, including those of merchant and soldier. Catalina also confessed to having maimed and killed many men. Thus, after years of battles against fierce indigenous tribes, duels over gambling and ladies, and quick escapes, the Lieutenant Nun (*La Monja Alférez*)—as she came to be known—entered a convent for several years. There she awaited official confirmation from Spain that she had been a novice but had escaped the convent before taking final and irrevocable vows, which carried with them mandatory enclosure for life. After letters crisscrossed the Atlantic and proof of her secular status finally arrived, Catalina again rejected the nun's veil and put on trousers. Rather than take up her previous life on the frontier, she embarked for her homeland. She spent the next six years settling her share of the family estate, initiating a series of petitions, and dictating or writing her memoirs.[3] During these years she also sat for a portrait done by the well-known Spanish painter, Francisco Pacheco (see figure 6.1). In 1630 Catalina again set sail for America—this time to base herself in New Spain as a muleteer and small merchant, under the alias of Antonio de Erauso—and appears to have lived in relative obscurity.[4]

The admiration and astonishment expressed by the crowds that had gathered to witness Catalina's entrance into Lima and the religious authorities who heard her confession were mere preludes to the sensation her story caused in Europe. Although both canon and civil law prohibited cross-dressing, the highest ranking officials of the Catholic Church and the Spanish Empire granted Catalina's petition to remain dressed as a man.[5] The Monja Alférez's petition to the Crown, in fact, builds a case upon a dual argument: the merits of her deeds as a soldier and the singularity of her position as a woman fighting in the army.[6] The reactions of King Philip IV and Pope Urban VIII upon hearing Catalina recount her story, as recorded later in the first-person memoirs *Vida i sucesos de la Monja Alférez* (ca. 1625), confirm that it was indeed the uniqueness of her position as a valiant woman soldier—and, more important, an "intact virgin"—that brought her such acceptance.[7] Catalina de Erauso slipped through the cracks of Spanish society's roles for women and reemerged as a cultural phenomenon, due in large part to her successful negotiation of institutionalized codes for behavior and the remoteness of the American frontier.

Perhaps more than any woman discussed in this volume, Catalina's story highlights the contradictions between period rules and actual practices. In the very years that Rosa de Lima's case for sainthood was being questioned in Lima, Seville, Madrid, and Rome, Catalina's rebellion against being enclosed in the convent was given the seal of approval from church and Crown in these same cities. Although one woman came to represent the saint and the other the pardoned sinner, both were incorporated into the institutionalized aspects of the Spanish empire and Counter-Reformation Catholic Church. The lapses in Rosa's and Catalina's behavior—in particular, their refusal to be enclosed in a convent—were overlooked because their life stories demonstrated heroic virtue and astounding singular feats for their sex. In spite of her lapses in following Counter-Reformation guidelines, Rosa came to represent the universal qualities of saintly virtue. By rejecting the life of a woman, Catalina created an alternate identity—one that was both notorious and officially accepted because of its valor and singularity.

Key to both women's success was their manipulation of the rules governing the female body. Following medieval models, Rosa's hallmark for sanctity was her extreme penances, which highlighted the role of women's bodies as the vehicle for virtue and fame. Through suffering it was thought women erased female characteristics of sexuality and become virile, manly women.[8] Biographic and hagiographic tradition further promoted the idea that women needed to transcend their nature to achieve great virtue. Sacred biographies narrated the lives of transvestite women, including such popular sainted women as Margaret of Antioch, Eugenia of Alexandria, and

FIGURE 6.1   Portrait of Catalina de Erauso by Francisco Pacheco, ca. 1625 (From *The Nun Ensign* by James Fitzmaurice-Kelly, London, 1907)

Joan of Arc. A brief look at these life stories, recorded in the popular *Flos Sanctorum*, reveals that male garb helped women follow a virtuous Christian path. In another tradition, women were compared to the mythic Amazon warrior women. Since at least Teresa of Avila's time, biographers had employed the metaphor of the Amazon woman to signal the level of heroic virtue religious women achieved; they were warrior women for Christianity.

Catalina de Erauso's life drew on the central role of women's bodies for determining their life paths, but she inverted the tradition of the saintly transvestite and the manly warrior religious woman. Through cross-dressing, Catalina's life truly became like a man's, but her virtue was dubious at best. Catalina played the roles of a conquistador (for gold rather than souls) and lawless adventurer. A closer examination of the ways in which Catalina (and others) could "re-present" her life in legal petitions, first-person memoirs, and biographies exemplifies the flux found in seventeenth-century rules and society. Whereas Ursula Suárez and Sor Juana worked closely with the model of the *perfecta religiosa* in order to modify it and included roles for humorous saints and lettered women, Catalina de Erauso lived out a life that blatantly defied rules. Gender roles, narrative genre conventions, and geographical settings all contributed to the success of this alternate life story.

The Life and Adventures of a Wanderer

Catalina was born in 1592 to a well-established Basque family in northern Spain, one of nine children.[9] The first dozen years of her life do not differ significantly from other upper-class women of her time. Her earliest years were spent with her mother and father, Doña María Pérez de Galarraga y Arce and Captain Miguel de Erauso, both natives of San Sebastián.[10] At the young age of four, Catalina went to live with an aunt and several sisters in a Dominican convent in the same city. In this large, unreformed convent, she had access to a fairly lively life and a good education. Nonetheless, according to the account in her memoirs, as an adolescent she had a conflict with one nun, so she escaped the cloister and set out to see the world disguised as a boy. For about three years she stayed in Spain, despite several close encounters with family members. It is clear that Catalina received a fairly good education in the convent because she continually landed posts that required good writing and accounting skills; more than once she was entrusted with managing a shop. In another post, she served as a page to a high-ranking official in the king's court in Vallodolid. Another master, a university professor, recognized Catalina's facility for Latin and vehemently urged her to follow a university education. An offer that might have been snatched up by Sor Juana, was flatly refused by Catalina, who confesses to having an urge (*inclinasión*) to travel: "I had a taste for roving and seeing the world."[11] She soon embarked on a Spanish galleon headed for America. Following the paths of several brothers, Catalina set out to seek her fortune.[12]

Part of a well-connected, adventurous Basque clan, Catalina coincidentally landed on her uncle's ship; unbeknownst to him, he had hired his own niece. The ship was part of the Spanish enterprise in the Indies: the crew encountered enemies, and many Spaniards died before the vessel was loaded with silver and headed for Spain again.

But Catalina jumped ship to stay in America, where she would spend nearly two decades (ca. 1603–1623) moving from the center of the Spanish American shipping industry in the Caribbean to the more remote areas of the viceroyalty of Peru. Even in the New World, Catalina seemed to be well connected. Her memoirs describe how she was given a letter of presentation to the chief consul of Lima for a post (chap. 5). She served as a shop clerk until having a run-in with her employer—over a woman. At this point, Catalina decided to join the *entradas*, the mercenary soldiers hired in Lima to travel south 540 leagues to Concepción and Valdivia, Chile, to fight the rebellious Mapuche (known in colonial times as the Araucanians). There fate once again would bring Catalina close to family: she served as a soldier for her brother Miguel de Erauso, the secretary of war. He never recognized her in disguise, perhaps because he had left home when she was two years old. Another altercation over a woman—this time her brother's own mistress—would change the course of her life again. Catalina was banished to fight on the front line in Paicabí for three years. Enduring frequent invasions by the enemy, Catalina made her mark in Paicabí as a hero by recapturing the Spanish flag and being wounded. With this heroic act, she would receive the title of "ensign" (*alférez*). Soon afterward, she accidently killed her own brother in a duel and began years of wandering from city to city.

A period chronicle by an anonymous writer gives us a sense of the social flux in which Catalina lived in early seventeenth-century Peru. Many men lived as vagabonds or became soldiers as a way to make a living. According to the chronicle, the most ambitious went off to become soldiers in Chile, as Catalina had. The most lazy lived off of others and gambling. This is the life Catalina would live after her years as a soldier:

> There are other poor proud [men], who, as they are unable to bite, bark, and always go around with their head down looking for an opportunity; they neither wish to be controlled, nor is there any reasoning with them. This type of people are called soldiers, not because they are, but because they wander freely from one place to another, always with cards in their hands so as not to miss any opportunity of playing with whomever they may meet, and if by chance they encounter a greenhorn or a newly-arrived Spaniard who is not skilled and well disciplined in his own malice, or whose malice does not go so far [as to include] false cards, they best them and take away their money and their property. . . . They are boundless cheats, whose only concern is mastering the art of deception. There are many of this ilk who are wandering around Peru. And for the most part they are enemies of the rich, and live only for news and quarrels and trouble-making in the Kingdom, for thieving and getting their hands on goods they can only get by means of wars and strife. They are people who do not wish to serve. They are all well dressed, as they are never in want of a negress or an Indian woman and some Spanish women, and not necessarily of the poorest kind. . . . They are the greatest vagabonds in Peru . . . and they seek their living as best they can. Another type of people of lesser importance, who are less skilled and not as free in the art of flattery, and who lack the means to vagabond about from one place to another, and also because they are

more willing to work and bear arms and eat the King's bread, these enlist as soldiers, as every year people in Lima are recruited for the kingdom of Chile. And they take them down there under their banners to fight the Araucanians. In Lima they give them two hundred pesos, with which to get a uniform. By these means the land is rid of them and people are sent against the indomitable Araucanians. Few of these soldiers return to Peru.[13]

As recorded in her memoirs and frequently confirmed by other petitions, Catalina's adventures took her across great distances, much of what today is Peru and Bolivia, from the desert Pacific coast across the Andes into the center of the Inca empire in Cuzco, to the mining town of Potosí and back again to Lima (chaps. 4–20). In the memoirs, these years are characterized by short stays in towns and occupations interrupted by the need to flee because of conflict over ladies or gambling. At one point, Catalina even toyed with a marriage proposal to a woman (chap. 7). At another, she faced the death penalty but escaped (chap. 17). The duel and resulting death of one opponent, however, finally led to her flight to Guamanga, where she was detained by authorities (chap. 20). A period letter describes how Catalina appeared armed and dressed as a man when she met with the bishop of Guamanga Fray Augustin de Carvajal.[14]

At this moment, Catalina's fate as a fairly anonymous adventurer changed forever; her disguise was uncovered, and news of her life spread to secular and ecceliastical authorities. As with all the women studied in this book, the moment in which a one-time nun or religious woman had to deal with a bishop's authority to judge her life and either authorize it as valid—and then promote it as exemplary—or censure it, was a pivotal one. If approved by the bishop, the woman's life was frequently institutionalized through autobiographical and biographical accounts. If censured, the woman could have her field of action severely limited, if only temporarily, as we saw in Sor Juana's and Ursula's cases. In Catalina's memoirs, the bishop is characterized as a saintly man who helped her. After questioning Catalina, he marveled at the singularity of her life story, saved her from being prosecuted by secular authorities, decided to place her in a local convent until her ex-convent in Spain could confirm her lay or religious status, and promised to protect her personally as long as he lived.[15] Upon handing Catalina over to the nuns in Guamanga, he required that they sign a statement agreeing to obey his orders when dealing with her. He died five months later, however, and Catalina went to a Lima convent under the supervision of the archbishop. But her fame had spread widely already: the viceroy requested that she dine with him first before entering the convent (chap. 20).

As mentioned, upon her release from the convent, Catalina embarked for Spain to begin a series of petitions. Beginning with the Consejo de Indias in Seville, moving on to the court of King Philip IV, and, finally, traveling overland—and being captured and accused of being a spy en route—to the Vatican, Catalina succeeded in obtaining the monies and licenses she sought. Soon after, she returned to life on the road, but this time as a muleteer transporting goods inland from the port of Veracruz, New Spain. Known as Antonio de Erauso, she apparently did not return to her lawless life. For the final two decades of her life (ca. 1630–1650) she obeyed the pope's request "to lead an honest life from now on, and to refrain from offending my fellow man, reminding me of God's justice with reference to His commandment 'Thou shalt not kill.'"[16]

Although we have few details about these final years of her life, Catalina's notoriety was still intact enough that in 1653 a New Spanish publishing house reprinted a 1625 broadside about her life, as well as a new anonymous account about her life and death. Both publications highlight the sensational aspects of Catalina's life as someone who combined gender expectations. More significantly, the latter broadside claims the Monja Alférez as an officially recognized hero for New Spain. According to this apocryphal account, Bishop Palafox y Mendoza—the same bishop whose portrait circulated with Catarina de San Juan's—wanted to exhume Catalina's remains and rebury them in Puebla, Mexico, in order to honor her memory and to bring fame to his city. Bishop Palafox had left New Spain before Catalina's death (1649), but like other hagiographic works of the period, the account recognizes the power of invoking—even if falsely—a bishop's authority to promote local heroes for the colony.[17] Catalina's notoriety continued for at least the rest of the century in Spanish America; enough so that a satirist compared Sor Juana with the Monja Alférez.[18]

The Writing of a Hybrid Life

During Catalina's life and in subsequent decades, historical and literary works, as well as folk tales, flourished about the unusual Monja Alférez. Theatre, poetry, historical chronicles, and biographical broadsides proliferated in manuscript and published forms, and several were translated into Italian.[19] The most notable contemporary literary work, Juan Pérez de Montalbán's play, La Monja Alférez, comedia famosa (1626), highlights Catalina's cross-dressing and ends with her confessing her true identity as a woman. But while the woman Catalina had courted ends up marrying a man, following Golden Age theatrical plot convention, Catalina does not marry, and the play's final words report her actual whereabouts in 1626: "Where the play ends, so do the actual events, since today the Lieutenant Nun is in Rome."[20] Perhaps the most significant seventeenth-century historical texts that document Catalina's life are the aforementioned broadsides, written in installments and published in both Spain and Mexico (1625, 1653) and a chapter in a history by Diego de Rosales about the conquest of the kingdom of Chile (written ca. 1660).[21] As Stephanie Merrim and Rima Vallbona have shown, the history inscribes the Monja Alférez's story into hagiographic tradition, emphasizing the penitential nature of Catalina's deeds. In contrast, the broadsides, a genre often used to incite interest in noteworthy current events—anticipating the birth of modern journalism—highlight the sensational aspects of Catalina's life. In some regards, they follow the first-person memoirs of Catalina's life, Vida i sucesos de la Monja Alférez, a manuscript which was purportedly deposited in 1625 in the same publishing house where the broadsides were printed. But these memoirs, the mostly lengthy account of her life and attributed at least in part to Catalina, were not published until centuries later.[22] Because the Vida i sucesos is structured like an autobiographical vida, it is the central literary focus of this chapter.

Analysis of the textual representation in the *Vida i sucesos* of Catalina's life story, however, poses the perhaps unanswerable question. To what degree are these first-person memoirs historical fact or legendary fiction? After examining a number of manuscript variants—none of which are the autograph manuscript by Catalina—and secondary documents, mo|t scholars agree on one point: Catalina at least had a hand in her memoirs.[23] Joaquín María de Ferrer's early twentieth-century edition, Rima de Vallbona's recent masterful edition, and Pedro Rubio Merino's edition of new archival versions take great pains to examine the authenticity of texts about a historical figure who so easily lent herself to legend. While Ferrer and Vallbona include a variety of related legal documents, such as the 1625–1626 petitions and sworn statements from character witnesses, these editions focus on the central literary-historical text of Catalina's *Vida i sucesos*. Most critics, and Vallbona in particular, provide a convincing case for Catalina having had a hand in composing the text, which may have been rewritten as she dictated it or was later elaborated on by another author. One of the points often made in the literary ghost writer theory, however, has been that Catalina did not have sufficient training to write such an accomplished piece on her own.[24] Recent studies about the nature of convent life reveal that Catalina probably was well trained, a fact supported by the reports about the posts she filled as clerk and about knowing Latin (*Vida*, chap. 1). In addition, conclusions that adduce that her lack of a formal education proves that her account was composed by a ghost writer do not take into account the power of oral storytelling, so common among soldiers and tavern-goers of the period. The quick, lively scenes of conflict and resolution with a precarious escape found in the *Vida i sucesos* are characteristic of popular storytelling. Vallbona herself points to the need to explore these oral genres in order to better analyze the memoirs and concludes that the issue of the authorship of the *Vida* will continue to be unresolved until the original manuscript is found.[25]

Although this uncertainty about the nature of the authorship of the *Vida i sucesos* limits the claims we can make, it functions to inscribe the memoirs firmly into colonial discourse which is frequently characterized by issues of historical truth and mediation.[26] As we have seen in previous chapters, colonial narratives are often a mixture of legal forms, literary topoi, historiography, and personal testimony, which typically reflect a high degree of mediation as judges, confessors, scribes, and editors altered accounts for political and religious ends. While the *Vida i sucesos* might undermine the notion of a single authoritative author, it reveals a dynamic discursive reconstruction of a life story, one based as much on "the historical record" as on religious, political, and literary codes as they were established in Spain and modified in America. Catalina's official petitions highlight her various roles as brave soldier on the frontier, loyal vassal to the king, pilgrim to Rome, and virgin: "She told the scribe 'she has spent 15 years in the service of Your Majesty in the wars of the kingdom of Chile . . . in defense of the Catholic faith in the service of Your Majesty.'"[27] Her unofficial memoirs, however, tell a story of transgressive deeds that entertain the reader and draw on the full range of narrative possibilities for a man or woman writing a full-length autobiographical life story. The basic facts found in the *Vida* and petitions generally coincide, yet the tone and focus diverge dramatically. The page-long petitions follow the forensic style and formulas of the reports of services and merits (*memorial de servicios y méritos*) in which the "I" petitions a superior—usually the king—for reward after years as a loyal vassal who risked life and limb for the monarch's interest, although Catalina alters the conventions to include the uniqueness of her feats as a woman. Lengthier *relaciones* and *vidas* were often composed as a prolonged petition to place the service rendered in the context of an individual's life story, but in Catalina's case, the *Vida* shifts from tales of heroic courage to anecdotes of doubtful exemplarity.

In fact, most recent critics who study Catalina's case (Marjorie Garber, E. Juárez, Stephanie Merrim, Mary Elizabeth Perry, Sherry Velasco, Rima Vallbona, among others)[28] elucidate seventeenth-century legal, religious, and literary practices, and suggest that the Monja Alférez's life and texts capitalized on loopholes in what has largely been perceived by twentieth-century scholars as a rigid gender and moral code. Perry convincingly argues that Catalina's case slipped through the legal system because civic law reflected society's assumption that people would be prosecuted according to his or her biological sex, either as a man or a woman.[29] Both ecclesiastic and secular frameworks only allowed for two categories for adult whites' sexual identity. Catalina could not be prosecuted as a man for her misdeeds because she had been a nun; but neither could they process her as a woman because she had lived as a loyal soldier. In one of the few literary studies of Catalina's life and texts, Stephanie Merrim astutely argues that the baroque aesthetic, which prized singularity, marvel, and the unveiling of a reality that is not what it seems, serves as a key to understanding Catalina's success; her life had intrinsic literary and cultural value as an anomaly that mitigated the consequences of her transgressive acts. Catalina became a cultural icon through the manipulation of seventeenth-century concepts of gender and fame.

In a later rewriting of this study, Merrim convincingly argues that, in addition to the baroque aesthetic, Catalina's case demonstrates contemporary medical theories about the body. From at least the time of Galen and Augustine, the idea existed of women as incomplete men; women's bodies had lacked the heat needed to complete the process of turning the genitals outside of the body. As a result of this single-sex biological model, there was more slippage for women to become like men than vice-versa.[30] Augmenting this argument, Sherry Velasco analyzes the cultural representations of transgenderism in the Lieutenant Nun across four centuries. Of particular interest are her findings about the possibilities for hybrid identities in the designation of sexual characteristics in the early modern period (chap. 1). In one case I found in the Madrid archives, a contemporary account reports how a nun in a convent in Ubeda, Spain, had undergone a spontaneous bodily transformation and become a man.[31] The account is recorded by the priest in charge of the convent. The popularity of period accounts about transgenderism reveals people's fascination with the topic. Interest in linking these transsexual and transvestite stories with religious women is clear in a famous painting found in a Mexican Carmelite convent of St. Esofrina, who was said to have lived as a man in a convent for more than three decades; one of New Spain's most venerated Carmelites is depicted alongside the saint.[32]

With regard to the most enticing document about Catalina's life, the memoirs, all critics point to the unusual blending of a broad range of literary genres, including confessional literature, picaresque tales, soldiers' accounts, chronicles, and cloak and dagger theatre.[33] And yet, little has been said of the relationship this generic mixture may have to do with the gender-blending life of Catalina. Critics tend to emphasize the transgressive tone of Catalina's *Vida i sucesos* and link it with the soldier's and male picaro's story, or period drama, but they overlook the role of the most prescribed genre for women's self-writing, the spiritual *vida*, and the fictional role of the female rogue. An analysis of the narrative construction of the *Vida i sucesos* helps us better understand how Catalina's life reflected Spain's encounter with the Americas—how the ad hoc nature of life in a new colony or on the frontier often pushed literary, historical, and societal conventions to new limits.

To unravel the intrinsic relationship between the sexual/textual, gender/genre cross-over in the Monja Alférez's narrative, it is important to recall that early modern self-narratives usually were written by men and women to justify their actions as in keeping with societal norms.[34] Whether recorded as an act of obedience to a confessor (as in the case of most spiritual autobiography), as a soldier's petition for remuneration for services rendered, or as a rogue's fictionalization and parody of the need to justify one's actions, the "I" reconstructed through these written forms inevitably engaged in dialogue with society's models for behavior and created its subjectivity by adjusting its image to the "community's gaze."[35] In this adjustment, historical subject became literary artifact. The dialogic dynamic between individual self-representation and institutional norms produced texts that were fraught with tension as authors acknowledged the centrality of real or inferred readers who in some manner judged the accounts according to recognized standards. The text thus inherently carries a petition—tangible or spiritual—and an *apologia pro vita sua*. As we have seen in other chapters in this book, the posturing often vacillates between the exemplarity of the self represented and the manipulation of the reader; the author attempts to implicate the reader in the process of the apology and to locate the conception of truth in her own reconstruction of self and world.

Just as important as the public nature of autobiographical accounts, period autobiographical and pseudo-autobiographical forms depended on whether the subject was a man or a woman; writing about the self was a highly gendered practice. The emerging awareness of the individual and his or her subjectivity, new definitions of gender roles based in part on Counter-Reformation teachings, and innovative narrative forms made possible the literary construction of new identities. Three main autobiographical modes inform the structure of Catalina's self-representation: the (male) soldier/conquistador's memoirs; the picaresque novel, which, as we saw in the last chapter, could have male or female fictional characters but was usually penned by a man; and the spiritual autobiography, which was a predominantly feminine mode of writing but men also wrote in this form.[36] A study of the inherent petition at the core of most autobiographical writing from the period and of the ideological impulse and gender-bound prescriptions that accompany each subgenre, reveals how Catalina's tale uses first-person narrative genres to fashion an identity that was particularly suited to her own lack of religious vocation and urge to see the world beyond the cloister. The reader witnesses a hybrid gender and genre as Catalina undergoes a transformation from a traditional Basque girl educated in the convent to a New World soldier and outlaw, and, finally, to a celebrated European hero. (In fact, the *Vida i sucesos* ends with her successful petitions to king and pope.)

Gender and Genre in the *Vida i sucesos*

As the account opens, Catalina's story is firmly inscribed into the literary form of the soldier's tale. Although *vidas de soldados* rarely were published in their own time, surely Catalina would have been familiar, after so many years in the army, with the form of the petition of merits and services and with the *relación*, which proliferated during the first century and a half of the Hapsburg Empire.[37] Like her comrades, the one-time *alférez* simply states the year and place of her birth, and her parents' names.[38] And yet, Catalina quickly departs from this explicitly male genre: she must deal with her biological sex in order to live and write a soldier's life story. Altering the conventional narrative sequence that moved from humble origins to a vagabond's existence before finding a military vocation, the author slows the narrative tempo and describes her escape from the female environment of the cloister, along with her process of gender reconstruction through a three-day sewing project in which she makes herself a set of man's clothing (chap. 1).[39]

Once outwardly transformed, Catalina returns to the conventional narrative structure, content, and tone for the soldier's tale. Generally boasting a streamlined anecdotal focus on the narrator, rather than the larger historical context, these narratives are structured according to episodic stories with a clear ending (*historias cerradas*), as the protagonist moves from place to place.[40] The style reflects oral paradigms first designed for telling the story to others in the tavern or camp, and later adding the type of information needed to make a petition, such as names, titles, monetary sums, and distances traveled. Control of information and a listing of life accomplishments dominate many accounts. Content generally echoes social and military codes for soldiers: tales of heroic deeds, short descriptions of places, and accounts of defending personal honor and status—often dealing with women, dress, and titles.[41] Critiques of church and society are frequently interpolated into these documents, but the biting satire and pessimism characteristic of period picaresque novels do not dominate.

Catalina recounts with notable economy several years of wanderings in Spain before embarking for America. Once there, leagues traveled, cities visited, posts held, and money received (and lost), as well as occasional ruses and vicissitudes, dominate the account. Movement is rapid—in both actual travel and narrative tempo—while description is slight. After several misfortunes as a clerk, Catalina admitted her wanderlust, and joins six hundred men to fight on the Chilean frontier against the Mapuche (chap. 5). There she was banished to the trenches for interfering with her brother's love life and, later, received the title of ensign for her heroism in one battle (chap. 6). In one of the few purely epic accounts in the narrative, Catalina describes:

> We all joined forces with him, and five thousand men camped on the open plains of Valdivia with a great deal of discomfort. The Indians captured and attacked said Valdivia. . . . Seeing them make off with it [the standard/flag], I and two other mounted soldiers went after it through a great multitude, charging and killing and being wounded in turn. Soon one of the three fell dead. The two of us kept on, and we got to the standard but a

lance thrust felled my companion. I, with a bad wound in the leg, killed the cacique who had it in his possession, took the standard away and spurred my horse, charging, killing and wounding indiscriminately; badly injured, pierced by three arrows and with a very painful lance wound in the left shoulder, I finally reached our men and then fell from my horse. . . . I became the ensign of Alonso Moreno's company, the first captain I had known, and I was very pleased.[42]

In an epic-like rendering of the incident, Catalina became a heroic conquistador, demonstrating valor and loyalty to the Crown by risking life and limb for the flag.

After more than five years in Chile, Catalina left the battlefield, because she accidentally killed her brother in a duel. She headed for El Dorado, La Plata, Potosí, and Cuzco to make her fortune. Catalina recalls a near-death experience when crossing the Andes (chap. 7), working in transporting goods (chaps. 9 and 11), aiding sheriffs with law and order (chaps. 8 and 14), and defending Lima in a naval battle against the Dutch (chap. 17). Such heroic deeds, however, soon lead into stories about Catalina being forced out of towns, often after killing a man in a duel over a woman or a gambling dispute. As an outlaw, Catalina often took refuge in churches. Yet the narrator mocks church practices: She talks of it "raining priests" when at one point she is condemned to the gallows (chap. 12). Later she praises the Franciscans who taught her to hide the consecrated host (believed to be the actual body of Christ) in her hand in order to be moved from a jail to a church, where she could take sanctuary from the law.[43] Like other conquistadors, Catalina recounts her merits, but she does so with sketchy—and often dubious—detail and more than a touch of irony. She clearly shuns the colonization and evangelization projects of the Crown: "The governor wanted crops to be planted there in order to make up for the lack of supplies we had with us, but the infantry refused to do this, saying that we were not there to plant crops but to conquer and get gold."[44]

While maintaining the often lively, action-orientation of the soldier's *vida*, not yet a quarter of the way into her story, Catalina undermines the soldier's petition. Whereas many recount vicissitudes and failings, often criticizing certain aspects of society in the process, rarely is a soldier's tale so blatantly transgressive.[45] Randolph Pope argues that soldiers' stories evolved over time from the early modern didactic portraits of exemplary knights (*caballeros*) to the somewhat contradictory self-portraits by soldiers from the Thirty Years' War who variously embody characteristics of a loyal vassal and an unrepentant rogue.[46] In the opening pages of his memoirs, for example, Catalina's contemporary Domingo Toral y Valdés proclaims that he was "traveling through Spain like another Lazarillo de Tormes."[47] By Pope's calculation, twenty years after the completion of Catalina's *Vida i sucesos*, the first soldier's account written for pure entertainment was published. Estebanillo González's *Relación de vida* (1646) proposes to simply "give pleasure to the reader" and depicts a soldier as a buffoon who fills his account with satire.[48] The reader who sought entertainment increasingly replaced the superior who might have rewarded the narrator for exemplary service.[49]

Written in the midst of this paradigm shift from an account of services rendered to a collection of roguish stories, Catalina's *Vida i sucesos* may focus on the epic and transgressive aspects of her life story for the reader's delight. Her formal petition had been submitted, and perhaps granted, by the time this lively account was drafted.[50] This might further explain why Catalina's *Vida* has no clear petition or specific addressee and shares a good deal with her Madrid counterpart, the Thirty Years' War soldier, Alonso de Contreras, who wrote a story of his years as *alférez* and rogue.[51] Like Catalina, Contreras first presented his *relación de méritos* and then wrote his *Vida* within years of hers (ca. 1630), and there is no direct petition or addressee.[52] The ideology of exemplarity gave way to less didactic storytelling in these two soldiers, who, coincidently, may both have been in Madrid in 1624 and heard of each other. The effect of gender on the genre, however, changed the outcome of the protagonists' lives. Whereas Contreras was knighted into the military Order of Malta, Catalina no longer could follow a military career, in spite of demonstrating her capacity for it and being granted a license to live dressed as a man.

Like Contreras's brawling story, Catalina's describes a society in flux and a moral practice that did not match the one being promulgated by the Council of Trent. Indeed, in Catalina's case, the source of many anecdotes is the patriarchal formation of a society in which men all too quickly drew their swords because of pride and boasting, and women were seen as objects to be married off or to be kept safely enclosed from other men. As Michele Stepto points out, a substratum permeates the text, one that parodies masculine culture, especially men who make great claims without corresponding actions.[53]

In fact, the inherent petition for monetary reward or recognition in many soldiers' accounts is all but absent in Catalina's life as the language and content of the picaresque tale are intertwined with the story.[54] The narrator seems to ask for recognition of her cleverness in extracting herself from compromising situations. Writing when the picaresque was already a well-established genre, Catalina's *Vida* shares with it an emphasis on an unrepentant rogue. Although, as in Ursula Suárez's case, Catalina does not share the pícaro's story of illegitimate birth and life on the margins of society, the text echoes the genre's lexicon ("pícaro cernudo," chap. 12), ideology (the mockery of hard work in favor of "industria," or cleverness, chap. 10), and plot (the protagonist moves from master to master living by her wits). Much of the narrative plays with Catalina's hunger for adventure and sexual desirability that led to the need for a quick wit, sword, and escape, as well as the resulting hand-to-mouth existence. For example, Catalina's first master in the New World asked her to marry his mistress (chap. 3). Although reminiscent of the situation that the popular fictional rogue Lazarillo de Tormes found himself in at the end of his tale, the *Vida i sucesos* rewrites the model (perhaps because nature dictated it); Catalina rejected the offer and moved on to a new post and master: "One should know that this Doña Beatriz de Cárdenas was my master's particular lady, and he wanted to be sure of both of us: me to serve him, and she for his pleasure. . . . One night she locked me in [her room] and declared that in spite of the devil I had to bed her. . . . Later I told my master that there was no way I would marry her; not for all the world would I do it. He persisted in this matter and promised me mountains of gold."[55] Indeed, the author seems to purposely inscribe the action into the picaresque genre with two key elements: the discourse of poverty and the discourse of sexuality.[56]

Catalina's ambiguous gender role pushes literary conventions to new limits. As we studied in the last chapter, a male pícaro generally lived by his wits and actions. If he had rights to a woman, he often used her sexual desirability to better his economic situation, but rarely is his own sexuality directly at stake.[57] A pícara, on the other hand, lived by her wits and her sexual attractiveness in order to dupe men and advance her own situation. Drawing on both pícaro and pícara prototypes, the protagonist of the *Vida i sucesos* blends the female protagonist's use of sexual innuendo with the male's tendency to use women and fall back on quick action to escape a tight spot. Catalina became the object of sexual desire, like her female counterparts, but took action to remedy the situation, like her male counterparts. The ambiguity of her gender categorization and the genre's possibility for either a male or female central character allow Catalina, who in some aspects is both a male and female protagonist, to create a humorous tension in standard narrative genres.

Catalina's story fits surprisingly neatly into the rogue's tale, while also in some ways subverting the typical outcome. Avoiding the fate of most pícaros, who become the butt of their own jokes through the comic distance created in the narrative and, thus, remain firmly marginalized by society, Catalina became famous throughout secular and ecclesial society. Her story reached the archbishop and viceroy of Lima in the New World, as well as the Crown and the Vatican in the Old. In addition, she received her share of the family estate, an honorable title, and remuneration for military service.[58] And yet, in the end, Catalina chose to return to the road—a choice the pícaro rarely had. Catalina's trajectory was unique: her story began with enclosure in a well-to-do family and convent in the Basque region; it moved into the public arena of the tavern and military life in the periphery of the Spanish Empire; it jumped into the centers of power for the viceroyality of Peru and, after a brief hiatus in a Lima convent, the elite arena of the courts of Madrid and Rome. Ultimately, it returned to a relatively anonymous itinerant life in the Indies, when she chose to travel the roads between Veracruz and Mexico City as a muleteer. Was it only in the vast uncolonized areas between New Spanish city centers that Catalina could live easily?

Notably, Catalina in many ways can only borrow the pícaro/a's story to employ her transgressive acts because she lacks the essential keen sense of marginalization and pessimism that are key to the genre. Undermining the inherently conservative ideology of the genre, which was to maintain the status quo, Catalina de Erauso overcame financial straits and triumphed in her gender choice. Although several critics have read Catalina's success as completely dependent on her masculinist/macho rhetoric and her recapitulation of patriarchal society, one epitomized by the soldier's and rogue's tales, such readings overlook the reworking of these literary forms and, thus, their accompanying ideologies.[59] The author capitalizes on the ambiguity of truth that characterizes picaresque plot and discourse. Essentially an ironic mode, things are not what they seem, and multiple readings are possible in most situations. Language boasts its own unreliability in revealing any inherent, transcendent truth. As

we saw with Ursula Suárez, taking its form and structure from confessional literature, the picaresque turns convention on its head, secularizing the narrative, and creates a protagonist who repeats offenses rather than repents.[60] Catalina's tale suggests
that the geography and politics of the Spanish colonies were fertile terrain for creating a hybrid gender and tale.

The final chapters of the *Vida i sucesos* flaunt a different type of gender-genre
blurring, one based on the most popular feminine life writing form. With the exception of a few short stints in jail, Catalina escaped serious consequences for her illegal
acts. But by about 1619, she came face to face with the bishop of Guamanga after
killing "El Nuevo Cid."[61] (The name of the opponent itself suggests an honorable,
heroic prototype that the Monja Alférez symbolically undermines.) Hard-pressed
to seek sanctuary, Catalina began to confess—even after swearing off confession in
a previous situation. The bishop had rescued her from the hands of the *corregidor,* and
she now had to account for her actions. In a double movement of unmasking her
true identity as a woman who had spent about ten years in the convent and a rhetorical echoing of the confessional *vida de monjas,* the Monja Alférez saves her hide. Interestingly, the narrative tempo slows dramatically in this account of transformation
from outlaw to nun, underscoring the importance of the event. Whether from the
pícara's appreciation of a newfound comfort or the nun's experience of an enclosed
but well-cared-for life, Catalina describes meals, rest times, and comfort as time passes
between visits to the bishop.

Catalina borrows elements from a nun's self-representation by capitalizing on
its inherent tension for control over the interpretation of the story told. The account
is at once apologetic and didactic, a petition for absolution of sins and an illustra-
tion of God's presence in her life. To understand Catalina's use of the genre, it is
useful to recall from our discussion of María de San José that this popular autobiographical genre for women revolved around the dynamic of a triangular relationship
between confessor as judge, nun as visionary scribe, and God as divine author on the
one hand, and a somewhat linear structure of spiritual conversion, transformation,
and progress on the other. Moreover, there is a clear focus on the role of the body in
nuns' autobiographical writings. The account of epic struggles found in the male
conquistador's writings transform into women's heroic battles against individual and
community sins in the pursuit of divine union and salvation. Action and evangelization become renunciation of the body's passions in order to receive divine gifts and
take on suffering for the good of the church as a whole. Spiritual conversion required
a vow of chastity which, in turn, could lead to a religious life and great change. Written
accounts of this transformation tended to emerge only upon request of the confessor who witnessed—albeit secondhand—evidence of possible divine gifts or demonic
illusion. This spiritual focus and the very real mediation of the confessor set this
genre apart from the previous two we have examined in this chapter. Moreover, since
women were considered both more prone to being instruments for direct manifestation of the divine and more in need of supervision of these gifts, this is the only
narrative genre dominated by women.

In the hands of a male author, spiritual autobiography could recount the wide
range of roles men played in society, and, therefore, much of the focus is on exterior

transformation and individual autonomy.[62] The most famous male author of a Spanish spiritual *vida*, of course, is Teresa of Avila's contemporary, St. Ignatius of Loyola. In fact, both Spanish saints helped found or reform a religious order, both wrote spiritual accounts of their lives, and both were canonized in 1622. And yet, while Teresa's spiritual *Vida* was published and widely imitated in the years after her death, Ignatius's was only published in the nineteenth century and seems to have had few imitators. While women religious wrote frequently about their interior lives, few of their male religious corollaries wrote. When they did write, the accounts differ dramatically from women's. Ignatius, for example, brings together the *vida de soldado* with the spiritual *vida*. Ignatius's account begins with a fast-pace recounting of his military life and travels and his lack of compliance with local authorities. On more than one occasion, Ignatius refused to confess and was banished from a town or prohibited from confessing others until he had completed a series of studies at the university. Even when he was recounting his conversion and decision to transform his life, in order to create a religious order of "soldiers" for the pope (the Company of the Society of Jesus, also known as the Jesuits), Ignatius's narrative lacks the introspection found in nuns' accounts. Moreover, the fundamental structure of the *vida de monja*, of the woman as *escritora por obediencia*, is absent: Ignatius of Loyola dictates his stories to a scribe, and he does so at his own leisure.[63] As a result, the account lacks the immediacy of the first person; it is narrated in third person.

Most of Catalina's account follows the more masculine rendering of a life story in terms of its focus on outward action. Like Ignatius, she recounts in a lively fashion the movement from one town to another and her differences with local clergy; moreover, there is no direct clerical addressee. Like some of her military and roguish counterparts, Catalina plays with confession as a necessary life account before God's intercessor in order to achieve salvation. On three separate occasions she confronts confession for her misdeeds. In the first, she refuses, even as she is taken to the gallows (chap. 12). The next time, she reveals her identity as a woman to a priest who gives her sanctuary from the law and safeguards her secret as he nurses her back to health. But her account moves toward a more feminine rendering of a life story when she must finally reveal her true identity, make a sincere confession, and change her way of life.

A complex scene that mixes a true sense of recognition of the transformative power of confessing in the presence of God, vis-à-vis a holy bishop, with a highly condensed, parodic literary representation of an hours-long life confession (*confesión general*) leaves the reader both laughing and perplexed at the meaning of this central scene:[64]

> Sir . . . The truth is this: I am a woman, I was born in such-and-such a place, the daughter of so-and-so, and at a certain age was placed in a certain convent with my aunt so-and-so. There I grew up, put on the habit, and was a novice. When I was about to profess, for such-and-such a reason I left. I went to such-and-such a place, took off my habit, put on other clothes, cut my hair, went hither and thither; went aboard ship, put into port, went to and fro, killed, wounded, cheated, ran around, and finally landed here, at the feet of Your Most Illustrious Lordship.[65]

Catalina's account of her confession to the bishop borrows rhetorical elements from a nun's *vida* and capitalizes on its inherent tension for control over the interpretation of the story told. The prototypical protagonist of a nun's account—a repentant sinner overcome with cleansing tears and witnessing the manifestation of God's grace—is absent from this account. In fact, the usual formula is inverted; after listening to the Monja Alférez's three-hour account, the bishop's face streams with hot tears, and he encourages her to review her life and make a good confession: "The saintly man was all ears: he listened to me without speaking or batting an eyelash, and when I finished he said not a word, but wept bitterly. . . . He exhorted me to go back over my past and to make a proper confession."[66] Some of the elements of confession as a first step toward recognition and the need to write are present, but no true spiritual transformation or conversion is recorded.

The next scene further undermines the ideology and narrative conventions of a woman's spiritual autobiography. Knowing proof of her virginity will be her trump card, Catalina capitalizes on the bishop's marvel upon hearing her life, and she encourages him to have matrons examine her. They report her status as "intact a virgin as the day I was born." This proof of virginity clinches Catalina's fate. The bishop proclaims his full support of her: "I respect you as one of the amazing people of this world, and promise to help you in any way I can, to take care of your needs, and to do that to serve God."[67] In short, he protects her henceforth from the law. After she makes a sacramental confession with him, he absolves her and exhorts her to lead a virtuous life. Catalina's paradoxical situation as a sexually pure outlaw, however, mocks the church's insistence that sexual purity begets and reflects spiritual wholeness and virtue. The textual rendition of Catalina's confession meets the genre's requirement that transformation occur, but it subverts both its purpose and the outcome. Although Catalina states she was inspired by this saintly man and apparently ceased her life of brawls and stealing, much of the internal spiritual process of transformation is externalized and secularized in this confessional account. No longer strictly portraying a written record of reconciliation between individual and God, the narrative form becomes Catalina's safety net for her gender change. By echoing and yet radically altering the genre's central passage, the moment of conversion and confession that led to a return to the community's norms, Catalina's spiritual transformation becomes her gender (re)transformation. The confession to and absolution by the confessor-bishop is in many ways the narrative center of Catalina's life story. Confession both saved her from prison and, after a temporary reinstatement of the nun's habit, served as the springboard for legitimizing her gender choice. She records how this unmasking of her identity was the beginning of her fame: "News of this event spread everywhere very quickly, and people who had seen me before, and people, both before and after, who heard my story all over the Indies, were amazed."[68]

To emphasize further her inherent critique and manipulation of church and society's sexual and moral codes, several chapters later the author records the pope's own marvel and approval of her life and travels, gender, and virginity. According to a broadside about Catalina's life, which might be highly fictionalized, the pope even defended Catalina against a cardinal's criticism, saying: "Give me another Monja Alférez and I will give her the same [permission]."[69] The pope's only request was that she observe the commandment "Thou shall not kill." The final chapter of the *Vida i sucesos* also mentions the rich and famous who wanted to catch a glimpse of the Monja Alférez; now more than just the plebeian crowds in the streets of Lima gathered round to witness the phenomenon of the manly woman. Whereas the conventional nun's account bore witness to how a lowly woman's life overcame the limitations of her sex and revealed the role of the divine in it for a confessor, the Monja Alférez's life rewrote that formula to bear witness to how a woman could undo "natural," God-given gender categories with approval by the pope himself. Recording circumstances like those in which her religious sisters confessed and wrote (the confession to the bishop), but having the written version be noncompulsory (the *Vida i sucesos*), Catalina is free to echo the genre's format and change its outcome. Her story—both in real life and in the text—is neither marginalized by society nor mediated by ecclesial superiors; through a creative use of her notoriety, the Lieutenant Nun slipped through established categories and constructed her own identity.[70]

As we have seen in previous chapters, nuns in Spanish America frequently manipulated the form of spiritual autobiography to redefine within the genre's limits a role for themselves in the church. Madre María de San José's fight for spiritual authority, Sor Juana Inés de la Cruz's argument for women's learning, and Ursula Suárez's presentation of a *santa comediante* reveal women who studied the genre and pushed its limits in order to critique the often straight and narrow path that Catholic Church hierarchy prescribed for religious women. All three nuns talk of God-given vocations (*inclinaciones*) and the Divine as the omnipotent author of lives (and, by extension, their texts). Catalina completely undoes these generic underpinnings: first by stating a purely secular "inclination" to adventure that required cross-dressing, and then by authorizing her life with human personages. While convent sisters remain cloistered, traveling only occasionally by mystic transport to evangelize or prophesize, Catalina exploits the power accorded to virgins, rewrites central elements of the conversion narrative, and returns to the Americas as Antonio de Erauso.[71] Some years later, a friar who met Erauso in Veracruz, Mexico, describes her: "In male garb, with sword and dagger, the sword guard of silver, a few limp hairs for a beard, and she was the boldest of the bold. She had a great mule train and blacks with whom she brought clothing to Mexico."[72]

In destabilizing the transcendent meaning of confessional literature, altering the male soldier's tale, and employing ruses common to both the *pícaro* and *pícara*, the *Vida i sucesos* goes beyond the simple blurring of literary and gender conventions and creates a complex, at times ambiguous, text. Competing motives undermine traditional paradigms with their narrow embodiment (both literal and figurative) of self-representation and identity. Although all autobiographical writing of the period tends to be a hybrid genre that moves between petition and authority, author and addressee, historical person and literary construct, the *Vida i sucesos* manipulates genres and their inherent gender-related rules to create a truly unique text, one that even has a first-person narrator who fluctuates between using feminine and masculine adjectives to describe herself or himself.[73] In the same years that the soldier-poet Alonso de Ercilla revised the epic tradition when talking about battles on the Chilean frontier and the ex-soldier Miguel de Cervantes parodied idealized literature by mixing it with more realistic elements to create a new narrative genre, Catalina de Erauso's life story worked with European legal codes and literary genres to create a new identity and narrative type for the cross-dressed woman living on the American frontier.

Hagiographic Rewritings?

Upon her death in 1650, Catalina's story both continued in the same titillating vein as the *Vida i sucesos* and took a more didactic turn. As we saw in the publications of the 1620s, the popular contemporary literary response to Catalina's life was the retelling of the singular acts of her story in two broadsides while Montalbán's theatrical rendition of it focused on her cross-dressing and love triangles. In the mid–seventeenth century, a posthumous third and final broadside maintained yet reframed the transgressive focus of Catalina's tale, while a chapter that formally incorporated her biography into the historiography of Chile completely changed the facts.

This 1653 broadside is one of the few documents that recounts the final twenty years of Catalina's life. Whereas the first two broadsides unabashedly recount the first thirty-some years of her life and her singular acts as a cross-dressed woman, the third both borrows conventions for hagiographic biographies of religious women and centers on Catalina's audacity. The titles are telling of this shift: the first, *Relación prodigiosa de las grandes hazañas, y valerosos hechos que vna muger hizo en quarenta años que sirvió a Su Majestad...* [The prodigious relation of the great deeds and brave acts which a woman did in forty years of service to His Majesty], changes to *Ultima y tercera relación en que se haze verdadera del resto de la vida de la Monja Alférez, sus memorables virtudes, y exemplar muerte en estos Reynos de la Nueva España* [Third and last relation in which is truly told the rest of the life of the Ensign Nun, her memorable virtues and exemplary death in this kingdom of New Spain].[74] After announcing its hagiographic intentions—the telling of virtue and a good death—the narrative launches into the details of a pro-hibited love affair: Catalina purportedly fell in love with a woman, offered to pay her dowry and to enter the convent with her, and challenged the woman's other suit-ors to duels. While the text even documents the case by quoting a letter referring to the matter, next to nothing is said about other events during the nearly twenty-year period it covers; the broadside's central piece is a story of unrequited, prohibited love. The narrative ends with a single formulaic hagiographic statement about the Monja Alférez's fasts, penances, observance of sacraments, and virtue, and another about the bishop's recognition of her status as "marvelous woman."[75]

The title and brief conclusion contradict the substance of the story, revealing on the one hand a continued interest in telling an engaging tale so evident in the *Vida i sucesos* and on the other a clear attempt to frame it within conventional, posthu-mous biographical accounts of women. Perhaps times had changed, or, more likely, since the first *Relación* was republished in 1653 as well, the death of the biographical subject required a certain idealization or reincorporation of the individual into Catho-lic norms, to better institutionalize her story. In fact, as mentioned earlier, the broad-side says Bishop Palafox y Mendoza tried to obtain the Monja Alférez's remains in order to bury them in Puebla. By the time Catalina died, however, Bishop Palafox had been recalled to Spain. This apocryphal account, then, further illustrates how women would often be associated with an already institutionalized figure in order to promote their acceptance into the ranks of outstanding individuals whom could be promoted as symbols of identity.[76]

The Jesuit Diego de Rosales's *Historia general del reino de Chile* (chap. 37), leaves no ambiguity about the reinterpretation of Catalina's life; he rewrites nearly every event, casting her in the role of a *perfecta religiosa*, one with a true vocation but who goes astray before ultimately returning to the cloister and rejoicing.[77] Echoing conventional language used to describe the mystic brides of Christ that we saw with Santander y Torres's descriptions of Madre María de San José, Rosales transforms the woman soldier into the wounded lover found in *The Song of Songs*. She goes to the mountains to suffer monthly periods, wear hair shirts, and observe fasts and long for confession and renewal. Catalina is the wounded deer (*sierva herida*), wounded by the arrow of divine love, taken quite literally to be the near mortal wounds she suffered in battle. Unable to bear separation from her Divine Spouse after her sinful deeds, Catalina searches out confession, "like another Mary Magdalene." Inscribed into the traditional conversion narrative, this account contrasts sharply with the tone of this same scene in the *Vida i sucesos*: "Bathed in tears like another Magdalene, she departed, determined to pay no attention to the Pharisee's and the world's slander, to prostrate herself at the feet of Christ to wash them with tears from her eyes and dry them with her hair; she fell at the learned man's feet . . . and begged him with many tears to hear her confession; recounting the events of her entire life, weeping all the while, she resolved not to leave there until she was on her way to the convent."[78] After throwing herself at the bishop's feet, confessing her sins, and professing her faith, the Monja Alférez ends her days in the cloister observing a "holy life."

Why such a drastic rewriting of Catalina's life? Once again the ideology of the genre may have influenced the story's outcome. Montalbán's theatre piece, for example, follows dramatic conventions of the period: the love triangle in the *comedia de enredo* ends with a marriage that at least partially restores the status quo. Rosales's formal history adheres to church historiographical conventions and restores Catalina to prescribed behavioral models for women. As Stephanie Merrim notes, Catalina is remade into an exemplary figure; moreover, as a Jesuit who was writing about a woman that confessed first to a fellow Jesuit, Catalina's "marvelous" (*prodigiosa*) story is coopted for the history of the order's role in colonizing Chile.[79] Rosales follows the same pattern we observed in the Jesuit-authored hagiographic biographies of Catarina de San Juan and Sor Juana: their stories help establish the order's role in developing a strong Christian identity in the New World.

The Spanish American Frontier and Social Mobility

Studying the literary context and construction of Catalina's *Vida* and its rescripting in other sources reveals the encoding of life stories according to narrative purpose, addressees, and gender. But given the questionable authorship of the autobiography, it is debatable whether one can make claims beyond the literary realm—especially since new versions of the *Vida* have surfaced and more may appear in the future as scholars cull the Spanish archives. Previous texts examined in this book illustrate how thousands of religious women lived and worked within church roles. Does Catalina's life story reflect a larger reality and response by women or society as a whole? Focusing on the outcome of Catalina's petitions, Mary Elizabeth Perry concludes that Catalina's life "can be analyzed more effectively as a symbol than as a person." Catalina's transformation from outlaw to hero was possible because her life embodied the values of patriarchal society that condoned a man's right to defend his honor.[80] But what of Catalina's initial decision to reject the options of marriage or the veil— options that were open to her as a well-born Spaniard, options her four sisters chose— and her subsequent choice to cross-dress and follow in the footsteps of her four brothers who left for America and held good military and administrative positions there?[81] And, how did the reality of establishing rule in a land thousands of miles from the Crown affect the roles of women? Surely, just as the reality of the Spanish soldier-poet, Alonso de Ercilla's years fighting the Mapuche influenced his epic tale, the reality of life on the frontier of the viceroyality of Peru influenced Catalina's story. No doubt it is significant that the majority of Catalina's tale as a secretly cross-dressed woman took place in nonurban areas of Peru, and that even after receiving papal permission to remain in male garb, she chose to return to America and, what is more, to a new viceroyalty and to a career that did not require permanent residency in a city.

In their searches to answer some of these questions, Perry and Merrim have turned up few cases of cross-dressing in Spanish historical records and see most of the cases in literary sources as a means to an end for women to regain honor or lovers.[82] Merrim also discusses how Spanish tradition and moral codes seem to have severely restricted cases of manly women, even as they flourished in England, particularly in the form of the female soldier.[83] In Spain, as Encarnación Juárez notes, Moorish women took up arms in the rebellion in the Alpujarras. Helen Nader's new work on the fifteenth-century Mendoza noble-women also is highly suggestive; it brings to light the variety of roles played by some Spanish women: she notes that women in this family held positions in the court, managed estates, and traveled to England in order to evangelize. Looking at the radically different context of the Americas, Susan Midgden Socolow gives a general background of a range of activities colonial Spanish American women participated in, while Carmen Pumar Martínez sketches portraits of women of Spanish descent who made their mark in the New World as colonizers, governors, explorers, and soldiers.[84]

Establishing rule in a land thousands of miles from the mother country created conditions that often allowed women to take over for husbands who died, as in the case of the *adelantada*, Isabel de Barreto, or to work alongside their lovers as nurses and soldiers (since wives were often absent), as in the cases of Inés Suárez and María Estrada who accompanied the conquerors of Mexico and Chile, respectively. However, Pumar Martínez only mentions one case of a woman living for years in complete disguise as a man: Catalina de Erauso.[85]

Other period accounts talk of temporary cross-dressing in Spanish America. Nuns in one of the large convents in Lima dressed as men for theatrical performances, despite the bishop's prohibition of such events.[86] The *Historia de la Villa Imperial de Potosí*, tells stories of women in the silver-mining frontier lands of Peru who exchanged skirts for trousers and left home, although many were forced to return.[87] Perhaps as Julia Wheelright demonstrates in her study of women in the military, we don't have more accounts of women leading nontraditional lives because women often were erased from the historical record or portrayed as amusing freaks of nature. This is especially important to consider in conjunction with Diane Dugaw's observation that female warrior types flourished in England when the military was not centralized; with the more organized Victorian army, women began to disappear from the ranks.[88] On the frontiers of the Spanish Empire, the military was anything but centralized. Catalina's *Vida i sucesos* itself hints at the often ad hoc nature of conquest, defense, and rebellion quashing. At the turn of the seventeenth century, companies were raised and *entradas* (expeditions of volunteers paid around 200 pesos to set out and conquer or control new lands) were sporadically formed (chap. 5). Furthermore, the memoirs note how few people actually lived on the frontier, and, therefore, the welcome the soldiers received: "Because of the scarcity of people in Chile we were well received." Indeed, the Jesuit historian Rosales who rescripted Catalina's role in Chilean history complained bitterly in the text about the difficulty of controlling the large number of women who moved from camp to camp with the soldiers in Chile; soldiers brought along servants and lovers.[89]

Beyond the lax military organization and the sparse population in some areas, Spanish America also broke every rule set by Madrid regarding marriage, dress, caste systems, and other customs. For example, although canon law required a couple to be married before a priest, historians believe that almost 40 percent of Spanish American couples living together in the seventeenth century were not officially married. Recall, for example, that despite Sor Juana's illegitimate birth, she became part of the viceregal court and, later, the convent, although the latter in theory required nuns to be born to a married Christian couple. Likewise, according to the Spanish Inquisition, Catarina de San Juan's biography was to be banned immediately, but it took four years to go into effect in Mexico. As the final stages of conquest came to an end and Spanish Americans and native Americans set about organizing life in new racial, geographical, political, and religious contexts, much of society was in flux. Colonization and redistribution of power and resources often created a fluid society that contradicted period documents and edicts written by elite Spaniards who spoke of control and rigid legal and moral codes. Historians note the at times dramatic socioeconomic transformation of seventeenth-century Spain. And the further one lived from the centers of power, often the more fluid the social mobility and interpretation of the law.

Catalina, who for many years lived hundreds of leagues from the center of the viceroyality of Peru, which itself was not within easy reach of Madrid, may have found it more easy to pass undetected as a man, and may possibly have had female comrades who never made it to Madrid to tell their own stories and publicize them. Catalina's accomplishments as *alférez* and renowned outlaw, and her skill at manipulating the system, may have catapulted her into a position of telling her story and gaining fame, while other military women's lives may have never been documented. It took nearly twenty years for Catalina's true identity to be revealed to the authorities who would help publicize it. As the narrator of the *Vida i sucesos* boasts ironically after a close call with the law: "Miracles like this often happen in these types of conflict, and more so in the Indies, thanks to refined cleverness."[90] Her account outdoes the roguish tales of many combatants in the Thirty Years' War; after nearly twenty years in America, Catalina's life reflected the lawlessness, rebellions, mobility, and search for riches that characterized early-seventeenth-century Peru.

Such social, religious, and political upheaval and flux lent itself to itinerant lives, changes in positions, and, perhaps, identity. In the end, given this fluidity, was Catalina's cross-dressing less of an anomaly in her times than we have believed until now? Only more archival research will help answer this question. The work done in the last fifteen years to restore the most famous colonial woman, Sor Juana Inés de la Cruz, to the context of New Spanish culture—in particular, illuminating her participation in a widespread convent culture—provides an encouraging precedent. By studying documents by many religious women writers, we have been able to appreciate Sor Juana's role in an active feminine textual context. If more stories of cross-dressed military women in the New World are found, they may reveal that Catalina opted for a path that other women followed out of necessity or ambition; we may also see that, like Sor Juana, her story stands out because of the circumstances that aided its sensationalization: a bishop's request, strong political ties through Basque comrades, combined with her own ambition, creativity, and adequate training to petition both king and pope.

While the actual number of female comrades in the military is pure conjecture at this point, we do know that in the first Chilean literature from the colony, Ercilla talks of guerrillas and Amazonian archetypes on the Araucano frontiers. And the popular sixteenth-century romances of chivalry often included cross-dressed women who temporarily donned men's clothing to restore their honor. In Europe, Queen Isabel La Católica dressed in armor to enter Granada upon its surrender and Christine of Sweden abdicated her throne to live as a Catholic in Rome, often dressed as a man. For its part, the church had sainted several women soldiers, such as Joan of Arc, who demonstrated patriotic Christian behavior.[91] Catalina's petition to the king for reward states that she fought for him and for the Catholic faith, against infidels.[92] In fact, as Stephanie Merrim notes, Catalina took quite literally Teresa of Avila's advice to her nuns to be "more manly" in their behavior.[93]

While legend credits Rosa de Lima with invoking divine intercession to defeat the Dutch fleet that laid siege to Lima's port in the first decades of the seventeenth century, Catalina's *Vida i sucesos* describes a cross-dressed woman soldier fighting on a flagship that was sunk in one of these naval battles. One with hands folded in prayer, the other with musket in hand, Rosa and Catalina soon received popular and institutional approval for their roles in defending the king's empire and aiding the Catholic faith—Rosa because of her holiness, Catalina because of her bravery and creative rebellion. In the end, Rosa had many followers—although most had to be enclosed in the cloister to gain recognition—while Catalina seems to have had few that have been documented. In the final analysis, Catalina de Erauso's life and text may raise more questions than it answers. Examined in all its nuisance and contradiction, it parades before us ambiguities about gender and genre and about legal and ecclesial codes. It suggests a relatively unstudied fluidity in Spanish American society and institutions. The *Vida i sucesos* urges us to reexamine our assumptions that women had to follow the narrow dictates of moral and religious treatises on proper feminine behavior in the seventeenth-century Hispanic world.

Chronology of Catalina de Erauso

Note: There are many discrepancies between the dates given in the *Vida i sucesos* and other documents. The *Vida* states that Catalina was born in 1585 and embarked for America in 1602, but a baptismal certificate puts her birth around 1592, and another document states she sailed for America in 1605. See Rima de Vallbona's extensive footnotes in her edition of the *Vida*, which are based on her own extensive research and Ferrer's work.

1585/1592	Baptized Catalina de Erauso in San Sebastián, Spain.
Age 4	Enters the Dominican convent in San Sebastián where her aunt was prioress.
Age 15?	Escapes convent.
1602/1605	Embarks for America.
ca. 1605	In Lima enlists as a soldier to fight on the frontiers of Chile.
1608	Awarded title of Ensign (Alférez) after the Battle of Puren.
1615	Fights in the battle against Joris van Spilbergen in Lima's Port of Callao.
ca. 1619	Confession to Bishop of Guamanga, Augustín de Carvajal.
ca. 1620	Enters the Convent of the Santísima Trinidad in Lima.
1624	Returns to Spain.
1624 and 1625	*Relación verdadera*, published in Madrid and Seville.
1625	*Petition* to the Spanish Crown for reward; *Vida i sucesos* reportedly completed and given to an editor in Madrid.
1626	Pérez de Montalbán's play, *La Monja Alférez*, written and performed in Madrid.
1626	Goes to Rome and receives permission from Pope Urban VIII to remain dressed as a man.
1630	Returns to America and lives in New Spain as the mulateer Alonso de Erauso.
1650	Dies in New Spain.
1650 and 1653	Broadsides published in Mexico.
166?	Fray Diego de Rosales writes his *History* of Chile and includes a chapter on Catalina (chap. 37).
1784	Manuscript copy of the *Vida i sucesos* made by Juan Bautista Múñoz.
1829	First edition of *Vida i sucesos* published in Paris by Joaquín María Ferrer.

Conclusions

Two key periods in time and two geographical centers frame the lives of the women discussed in this book. The first place and time was Lima, Peru, in the early 1620s. It was there that America's most lauded saint, Rosa de Lima, and one of America's most officially approved sinners, Catalina de Erauso, came to significant turning points in their respective paths to sanctity or notoriety. The two women had lived within the same viceroyalty, but Rosa lived under the vigilant eyes of confessors in the capital, Lima, while Catalina roamed on the periphery of the empire, in the Andes and on the frontiers of Chile. By the early 1620s, however, Rosa had died and her canonization process had been halted because her followers were being interrogated by the Inquisition. Meanwhile, the Lieutenant Nun was ordered to enter a convent in Lima. Within years, the tables turned again—returning Rosa to the good graces of the Catholic Church and Catalina to life on the road dressed as a man. In both cases, bishops, the Crown, and finally the pope himself played important roles in determining the often fine line between saints and sinners. Through these examples of the two extremes of official saint and pardoned sinner, we gain a perspective on the other four women's lives.

The setting for the lives of Catarina de San Juan, María de San José, and Sor Juana Inés de la Cruz was Spanish America's other viceroyality, New Spain, in the last years of 1680 and early 1690, under the energetic pastorship of the Bishop of Puebla, Manuel Fernández de Santa Cruz. Their lives illustrate the overlapping, often contradictory relationships between institutions and individuals. While Madre María eagerly sought to live like a saint, she was at first blocked from entering the convent. Sor Juana, in contrast, was encouraged to enter the convent, even though she admits her own motives were to pursue a life of letters in the cloister. And Catarina de San Juan, barred from becoming a nun because of her Asian origins, was promoted by local clergy as a symbol of holiness in Puebla. Like Rosa and Catalina in the viceroyality of Peru, Maria's, Juana's and Catarina's stories became heavily institutionalized, coopted by Church authorities who either refashioned official images for posterity or limited access to the women's original self-portraits by controlling publications, portraits, and cults. Even so, the stories of their lives still made the transatlantic crossing to the Consejo de Indias in Seville and the Court or Inquisition in Madrid. Extraordinary cases were even taken to Rome for the pope and his advisors to cast the definitive vote.

Perhaps the only exception to this pattern of individual lives used by authorities to establish a colonial identity is the story of Ursula Suárez. She wrote from the far reaches of the colony, from Chile, the southern-most part of the Viceroyality of Peru, and died when the *vida* genre was in decline in the second half of the eighteenth century. And yet she was still subject to the local bishop for the successful fashioning of her spiritual path. Ursula drafted a confessional account that challenges the validity of the sinner-saint dichotomy. Easily the most playful of all the autobiographical life accounts written, Ursula's *vida* foreshadows the demise of the standard model for religious women. The fact that there is no trace of a subsequent biographical rescripting of her life further supports this argument.

Geographically, then, these life stories move from colonial frontiers, to colonial centers, and on to European civic and church centers. Chronologically, they are written during the mid-colonial period, the high point of feminine confessional and hagiographical *vida* production, the seventeenth century. But they have strong antecedents in sixteenth-century Spain and overlap into the first half of the eighteenth century. The key figures are largely the elite: Spanish and criollo male clergy and criolla women. And yet, a cross-dressed Basque woman and an Asian house servant also became exemplars for all society—indeed, at least temporarily, they were promoted as symbols of colonial Spanish American Christian identity.

The Lieutenant Nun's story, in particular, showcases the way in which the authorities integrated deviants into the system and even celebrated them as heroes. In spite of secular and ecclesiastic mechanisms put into place to monitor behavior, tolerance for deviance could be high if the circumstances were right. The viceroy's well-established practice of "I obey, but do not fulfill" (*obedezco pero no cumplo*) was practiced in kind at many levels in the colonies. Upon receiving an edict (*cedula*) from the king, the viceroy could put it on his head, then kiss it, and say "I obey, but do not fulfill." In this way, he did not commit the crime of refusing to obey the king (*lesse majeste*); he obeyed, but did not put the law into practice. Because many laws were enacted in Spain without a real knowledge of their consequences in America, this allowed the viceroy to respond to the king with his own advice. No rebellion: simply precautionary advice to His Majesty.[1] In the case of religious women, the distance between official church rules and doctrines and actual practice could be great. In every case discussed in this book, we see that the two extreme designations of saint or sinner set by the Catholic Church were contested and altered—at least for a time. There were dramatic reversals in judgment of the lives and works of religious women, as well as of those of their clerical superiors; recall that Sor Juana's confessor Núñez was a censor who had himself been censored; Catarina de San Juan's biographer was censored; and Ursula's Suárez's bishop was removed from office on the grounds of disloyalty to the Crown.

Within this flux of judgments, there was an urgency among criollo inhabitants of Spanish America to create their own stories and identity. Rather than repress individual expression, close monitoring and extensive codification of religious behavior appears to have encouraged self-examination and the articulation of identity in colonial Spanish America. Individuals, often encouraged by church officials, compared themselves to authorized models. Colonial communities used these individual stories to claim a collective identity and to assert their parity with and even superiority to Europe.

In addition to seeing the influence of political and church agendas on these stories, we have seen the effect that life-writing genres in the early modern period had on this dynamic. Each genre had its own set of conventions and ideologies. Whether confessional and hagiographic *vidas*, Inquisition and canonization testimonies, epistles and soldiers' stories, or new literary genres like the picaresque novel, these forms provided a framework and heavily influenced the portrayal and goals of the life story told.

But what happened to the use of life writings to construct religious identity after 1750, after our last protagonist, Ursula Suárez, died? Historians often identify this period as the end of an extended religious baroque period—the "long seventeenth century"—and the beginning of a more secular society that reflected the ideas of the Enlightenment and the reforms initiated by the new Bourbon monarchy in Spain. Additional reforms came from Rome: Pope Benedict XIV, a specialist in the Congregation of Holy Rites before becoming pope, made significant changes to the canonization process in 1734 and 1738 and signed an important treaty (*concordato*) with the Bourbons in 1753. These eighteenth-century reforms reveal attempts both to facilitate the process of canonization and to politicize it.[2]

By the mid–eighteenth century in Spanish America, the number of hagiographic *vidas* published dropped dramatically, and scientific and artistic texts became the ascendent form.[3] By the nineteenth century and the post-independence years of nation building in Latin America, this secularization of society resulted in nations like Mexico turning popular colonial saints' feast days into secular national holidays. The government coopted Mexico's only canonized saint's feast day (Felipe de Jesús, February 5) for a patriotic national holiday to celebrate the 1857 constitution.[4] Secular liberals frequently initiated strong anticlerical movements, which led to extensive church reforms, including the closing of many convents and monasteries, and this, in turn, contributed further to the decline of the *vida*.[5]

The close examination of religious women's lives was deemphasized in other arenas as well. As Emma Rivas notes, after 1750 the Mexican Inquisition turned its focus to the new threats of the Enlightenment and the French Revolution, and by 1850 it had performed its last *auto-da-fé*.[6] Nonetheless, while relatively few new canonization cases were initiated after 1750, cases of local holy people already entered into the canonization process in the seventeenth and early eighteenth centuries continued to move forward, promoted by devotees in America and approved in Rome. Since Independence, five seventeenth-century Spanish American candidates have been beatified and four have been canonized.[7]

The memory of the lives of the women studied here did not die. We saw how their lives were reinterpreted yet again in the late nineteenth and twentieth centuries. After Independence, Rosa became a symbol of Peruvian national identity and Catarina de San Juan was refashioned into a popular local heroine known as the "La China Poblana." By the middle of the twentieth century, María de San José's two convents became artifacts of colonial Mexican cultural heritage when they were converted into museums. Late in the twentieth century, Sor Juana once again became an icon of Mexico's artistic achievements, while in the United States she has been discovered as an early supporter of women's rights. For her part, Catalina de Erauso has become a popular figure in Latin America, Spain, and the United States: she is heralded as a bold sexual rebel. The only exception to this rewriting of meaning and identity has been Ursula Suárez. Her story only reappeared in the 1980s, so the time may yet come for her promotion as a symbol of Chilean identity. In the meantime, Ursula's case points to the most recent phenomenon occurring with all these women's stories: the rediscovery and reinterpretation of many religious women's lives by students and scholars in the Hispanic and Anglo-American world. Their life stories offer us the opportunity to broaden our knowledge of the past and of the stories that have emerged out of it. The women and their clerical counterparts demonstrate how a single spiritual model, the *perfecta religiosa*, could produce a multiplicity of lives, life stories, symbols, and identities. A simple spiritual model, framed within conventional religious and literary genres, created the grounds upon which a richness of voice and experience could be expressed in the New World.

Appendixes
Selections of Life Writings in Translation

Appendix A

Rosa de Lima: Selections from Testimony for the Canonization Process

From *Colonial Spanish America: A Documentary History*, ed. Kenneth Mills and William B. Taylor (Wilmington, DE: Scholarly Resources, 1998), pp. 197–202.

[*We join the testimony of Don Gonzalo de la Maza at his answer to the fourth question.*]

Answering the fourth question, this witness explained that he had known the said Rosa de Sancta María for about five years, and he told of the personal contact he had with her. Although this witness had wanted to make her acquaintance years before, knowing the considerable virtue she possessed, he had not done so out of respect for her rigorous seclusion. His first direct experience came on the occasion when the said Rosa de Sancta María wrote to this witness asking him to assist her in a charitable deed, which greatly delighted him. However, he was afraid to disturb her tranquility, until one day soon thereafter this witness chanced to see her enter his house with her mother, the said María de Oliva, and his wife, Doña María de Usátegui. As strangers, they [the three women] had met and spoken in the Jesuit church, for she [Doña María], too, wanted to meet the said Rosa. And for much of the time between that day and the one on which she passed from this life, he saw a lot of the said Rosa de Sancta María in his house with his wife and daughters due to the special affection they all had for one another. Rosa's taking of a room in this witness's house was favored both by her natural parents and by her spiritual fathers [her confessors], with whom she communicated. Sometimes, it was even by their orders, as this witness learned from her confessors, Padre Maestro Lorenzana of the Order of Saint Dominic and Padre Diego Martinez of the Society of Jesus. Through her stay and his personal exchanges with her, this witness learned of the beginnings of her calling.

Rosa told this witness of an incident that occurred when she was about five years old, while she was playing with one of her brothers, Hernando, who was two years older. Rosa [then Isabel] had grown beautiful blonde hair and [on this occasion] it had been handled roughly and soiled by her said brother. Once she saw the state of it, she started to cry. Her brother asked why she cried. Did she not know that on account of [worrying over] their hair many souls were in Hell? Knowing this, she should not be crying over her hair. [Rosa said] that this retort had so imprinted itself in her heart that in thinking about it she was seized by so great a fear in her soul that from that moment on she did not do a thing, not one thing, which she understood to be a sin and an offense to God Our Father. From this fear Rosa gained some knowledge of the divine goodness, which helped her [understand things about] her grandmother [who had died] and a sister, a little older than her, who died at the age of fourteen. [Rosa was now able to see them] as souls that, in her opinion, had been very pleasing to Our Lord, [and] whose deaths had been a great consolation to her because the things she had seen in them and been given to understand by His Divine Majesty convinced her that they had certainly gone to Heaven.

Thus, the said Rosa de Sancta María said to this witness that at that tender age she had dedicated to God Our Lord the gift of her virginity, with a vow [of chastity], and that, to this witness's understanding, the great outward modesty and purity of life attained by the said Rosa suggested she honored the said promise not only in her deeds but also in her thoughts, as one of her spiritual fathers expressed it to this witness. And her introspection was such that the said Rosa also revealed to the witness that in her life she had neither seen nor longed for a feast day or worldly celebration, not even a common procession, and that during the time that he knew her he clearly perceived this [to be a true account of] her way of withdrawal [from the world] and devotion. She withdrew not only from direct communication but also from seeing people and [worldly] things in order that they might neither impede nor delay the serenity of her soul, the power of which this witness saw at that time to be so focused that he beheld it with great admiration.

And as much [was true] in other senses, because this witness never saw her tongue move to utter an unnecessary thing. [This was true] in her answers or advice to others, in her praise of the Lord and in her encouragement of others to give praise. Her words were so careful and serious that they demonstrated very well that it was God who moved her. She was so chaste in her speech that if she said something that might be understood in more than one sense, she added, "What I am saying" or "I wish to say." She wanted everyone to do the same, as was demonstrated on the occasions when other people recounted something she had said or done. If [the relation of her words or acts] was not undertaken with absolute precision, she pointed out whatever was wanting with complete courtesy, [noting] that she had said or done this [or that]. And this witness noticed this perfection of the truth in her speech until she died. [In fact, this was] so much the case that on the very day she died, a devoted friar had come and asked one of the people who were attending Rosa in her illness if it would be acceptable for Father So-and-So, for whom Rosa had asked, to enter, at which point the said Rosa, though in very great anguish and pain, spoke up, saying "I said I wished to see him before I die."

The downward cast of her eyes was notable, so much so that this witness said that, in communicating with her so familiarly and with such openness that he called her his mother, it was amazing how few times he saw her lift her gaze. She was so chaste and pure in her sensibilities that in no manner would she attend conversations that were not spiritual and directed toward the good souls and the service of Our Lord. And if it happened otherwise, or if some person began to speak on secular themes, with very great modesty she attempted to divert them or absent herself from the conversation, as this witness saw in his house on many occasions. Thus, in the time they knew one another, it was very rare for her to go out [or be among] people from outside the house, not counting the times in which some spiritual fathers visited, because the whole of her interest was in retreat and solitude. . . .

The day of her birth is recorded in her father's book and the certificate of baptism. Concerning the day of her death [in order to establish her age at death], it occurred in this witness's house on Thursday, August 24, Saint Bartholomew's Day, one half hour after midnight. And after the said beginning of her calling, the said Rosa de Sancta María told this witness that she scorned the things of this mortal life, such as trying to impress people and be their object of curiosity. To manage this, for some time she had worn the habit of Saint Francis until, at the age of twenty or twenty-one years, she dressed in that of Saint Dominic and Saint Catherine of Siena, her mother, whom she had wanted to imitate since the beginning of her life, and become a nun of her order. And this witness has never heard, understood, or seen anything which contradicts what he has said, nor anything against the virtue, honesty, spiritual absorption, and virginal purity of the said Rosa de Sancta María. This is his answer to the question. . . .

To the sixth question. . . . Although they kept secret her mortifications of the flesh and penances until she died, this witness and his family knew of her way of life. This witness said that from a young age she was given to mortify herself with fasts, scourges, and other [self-inflicted] sufferings, and that from early on she had subsisted on bread and water for many days [at a time]. And, from the age of ten or eleven years she kept to her fasts of bread and water, especially on the days that her mother would excuse it, that is, on the Wednesdays, Fridays, and Saturdays of each week. At the age of fifteen and sixteen years she had made a conditional vow to forego meat and to fast on bread and water for the rest of her life. . . .

This witness observed her abstinence when she lived in his house, during which time even when she had a fever and her doctors and confessors ordered her to eat meat, she would not do it. Her fasts on bread and water were continuous. . . . [In fact,] this witness saw that she would go a day or two or more without eating or drinking anything, particularly on the days when she took Holy Communion, because at certain times of the year confessors granted permission for one to take Communion every time one went to church, and this is what she did with much modesty and without drawing attention to herself. During these fasts and abstinences, [when] she left the church or her secluded room in his house, she had such color [in her face] and showed such health [that it seemed] as if she was fortifying herself with plenty of nutritious dishes. Worrying over her stomach pains and all that she suffered, one would ask her why she did not eat anything, to which she ordinarily responded that Holy Communion made her feel full to bursting and that it was impossible for her to eat [even] a bite. . . . (It often happened that in ill health Rosa would be made to eat meat and other food, especially by her well-meaning mother, but also by doctors and her worried confessors. In this witness's experience, these feedings had the effect of worsening Rosa's condition.) During one of her dangerous illnesses three years ago, the doctors forced her to eat meat, which left her weary and so short of breath that she could walk no more than a few steps for many days. She said that it [her worsened condition] had resulted from her distress at having eaten meat, and she began getting better when she resumed her abstinence. . . . During the time that the said witness knew her, the said Rosa's manner of abstinence was such that the amounts she ate even when she was not observing it [her fast of bread and water] did not, to him, seem enough to sustain the life of a human body, especially one so young. . . .

To the seventh question this witness answered that he knew for a fact that since the beginning of her life the said Rosa de Sancta María performed continuous and rigorous mortifications of the flesh, usually with iron chains. And this witness knew [about these mortifications] from what he had heard from her, her mother, some of her confessors, his wife the said Doña María de Usátegui, and his two young daughters, from whom even given their tender ages and the love and concern he had for them, he did not deny exposure to [Rosa's] virtuous example.

With the same certainty, this witness learned that for a long time she [Rosa] had worn an iron chain wrapped two or three times around her waist and fastened with a padlock for which she had no key. [At one point when] she was in her mother's house, she developed a very severe pain in her abdomen, and the chain had to be removed in order for her to be helped. She suffered much as the lock was broken because her skin and, at some parts, her flesh had become stuck to the said chain, as this witness saw after Rosa's death.

Because all of this information was communicated to his wife, the said Doña María de Usátegui, on the understanding that it might be told to this witness, he also understood with the same certainty that she [Rosa] had employed different hairshirts from her shoulders down to her knees. For a long time she had worn tunics with sackcloth on the inside until, after two years, her confessors noticed her health so diminished that they took them away. This witness had seen them on the occasions when she changed them and hung them out in the sun. By order of her confessors, from that time [when the rough tunics were forbidden] until the point of the illness from which she died, her simple outfits were brought to her, on which occasions this witness also saw that she changed them.

The said Rosa de Sancta María sometimes told this witness and his wife and daughters that from an early age she had greatly detested putting on a good appearance for people and the care taken by her mother in arranging her hair, face, and clothes. Seeing that she was not getting very far [toward the realization of her ascetic designs] with her mother, at the age of twelve years she cut off her very blonde head of hair, at the sight of which her mother scolded her harshly. [But her quests continued.] Feeling that her fasts and mortifications were not sufficient to drain the color from her cheeks, she poured pitchers of cold water over her chest and back even when she was dressed. Because of this, or because of divine will and providence, she contracted an illness at the age of thirteen years and became crippled and [had to be] clamped to a bed by her hands and feet for a long time. [She suffered] a great pain over her entire body that could not be explained, but in bearing it, a very great relief and comfort came to her, in [knowing] that on account of Heaven her patience and compliance with the divine will had never faltered. She told this witness that on this occasion, as on others, Our Lord had rewarded her with so much pain, of a kind she had not believed a human body could withstand. [It was] nothing like the kind [of pain] He Himself had suffered, [she had said,] yet she was bewildered at having enjoyed so much forgiveness from God's hand, [considering] it was not possible that this [reward] would be bestowed on so wretched a creature as herself.

This witness also understands it to be a certain thing [based on what he had learned] from his wife the said Doña María de Usátegui, and from other people, that the bed in which Rosa slept from the age of one and a half or two years in her partents' house, [eventually] taken by her confessors, was a barbacoa, a small platform of rather coarse canes, like those used for threshing wheat in Spain. [It was] bound together by leather cords, with sharp, two- or three-cornered shards of an earthenware jug scattered over it and between the said canes. . . .

And after the said bed was taken away, and put on a shelf so that the said shards would not fall away, this witness knows that the said Rosa de Sancta María normally slept either on a plank of wood with a blanket, or seated in a small chair, as she did the whole time she lived in this witness's house. This witness also knew that from the beginning of her life the said Rosa de Sancta María had endeavored to punish her body by depriving herself of sleep, and there came a time when in a day and night she slept no more than two hours, and sometimes less. . . .

And, on the matter of her ways and mortifications, from one of Rosa de Sancta María's spiritual fathers this witness has heard [of one of her methods] to be able to keep praying when she was overcome by drowsiness. She set about tying together a number of the hairs at the front [of her head], [hair's] which concealed a crown of thorns that she wore [underneath], [and then attaching these knots] to a nail she had driven into the wall of her refuge. [Thus] she would be virtually hanging [there], only able to reach the floor with difficulty. And in this way she conquered weariness and continued her prayers. . . .

To the twenty-ninth question he answered that he has heard said that there have been many, and very exceptional, miracles performed by Our Lord God for the greater glory of His name and in demonstration of the virtue and sanctity of the blessed Rosa. [By these miracles] many people with different maladies, [who] entrust themselves to her intercession [by] touching some traces of her clothing and the earth from around her tomb, have been restored to health. This witness defers to the testimonies and proof of the said miracles.

Since the day on which the body of the said blessed Rosa was buried in the chapter room of the said convent of Saint Dominic, every time this witness entered [the chapter room] he has found a great gathering of people of all orders, stations, and sexes, and at the tomb this witness has seen many of the sick, crippled, and maimed.

And in the same way he has observed what is [equally] well known, [namely] the veneration and devotion which the notables of this city, like the rest of the general population, have for the blessed Rosa de Sancta María and for the things that were hers [and that were associated with her life]. [This is demonstrated] by the number of people of all stations who have gathered at this witness's house to visit the rooms in which the blessed Rosa stayed and died. In particular, there have been very few, if any, distinguished women who have failed to turn up in this witness's house to ask for relics from the clothing and other things that belonged to the blessed Rosa. And the same [close attention] has been paid by important men; indeed, the first one whom this witness saw request relics was Dr. Francisco Verdugo, the inquisitor of this realm, and this witness sent them to him. And [then] there was the judge from the royal Audiencia who has come twice to ask for them.

The demand has been such that if the tunics and habits which she left were many, they [still] would not have been enough to share in very tiny parts among the people who have come with such great affection and devotion. [One notes] particularly the monks from the five religious orders and the nuns in the convents of this city, whose request [for relics] have not been small.

The flow of people who have visited the house of Rosa's parents in which she grew up and lived has been of no less magnitude. [They visit] the little cell that was her room, taking from it what they have been able to prize away and remove, even the little latch from the door, as this witness has seen, and [even] the threshold and planks are cut out from the room and its door. There was one time when this witness wanted to do the same, and he visited her parents only to find so many people and coaches and horses outside the door and in the street that he returned [home, having been] unable to enter. . . .

What this witness had most noticed were the tears shed by many people [while] talking about the life and things of the blessed Rosa. Some friar-confessors told him of the exceptional conversions of souls and arduous transformations of [people's] lives that had occurred among those who commended themselves to the blessed Rosa after her death. Other people, especially devout women, have told this witness they wanted to receive the habit that the blessed Rosa had worn and to found the convent of Saint Catherine of Siena that she [Rosa] so much desired. A prelate of a religious order, and not even the Dominicans, has told him the same thing. And this witness knew a maiden whom he took to be very virtuous, who now was attempting to imitate the life of the blessed Rosa. And [there are] spiritual people, very devout, among them some friars, who have said to this witness that since the death of the blessed Rosa de Sancta María they have received from Our Lord remarkable favors and rewards, much better than those which they had received before. And this he knows and is his response to this question.

Appendix B

Catarina de San Juan: Selections from *Compendio de la vida*

From José Castillo de Graxeda

Translated by Nina M. Scott

Chapter 1. *Of the homeland, parents, and birth of Catarina*

Catarina was a native of the Mogul kingdom; the place where she was born is unknown, nor did she herself know it because she was so young when she left there. Her mother was named Borta; neither was she able to tell me the name of her father with any certainty, but rather doubtfully, and in cases of doubt, as they are not radically certain, it is best to omit them. God gave her parents clear knowledge of His boundless omnipotence, and as he was Creator of heaven and earth, His great power sent them great mercies even within the heathen state in which they lived, which in my opinion were like omens: one was to give them enlightenment and understanding by means of prodigious acts that He wished them to be saved, and after they died the Lord informed their fortunate daughter of this; in my opinion they achieved this joy because of their desire for baptism. (According to what has been said and to what our Holy Mother Church teaches us, it is baptism which is called *Flaminis*, or by another way which Divine Providence mysteriously possesses. . . .) The other omen was by means of the miracles that God rendered unto them, foretelling that they would have a daughter whom He favored even before she was born, and bestowing repeated favors upon the parents as though in celebration of such a birth.

An example of the many which they received is the one when, Catarina having already been conceived in Borta's womb, the Virgin Mary appeared and told her (according to what Catarina told me) that she would deliver a most lovely girl who would be her daughter whom, once born, she was to raise with great care. Of this mercy shown her mother and of many others I was told by this servant of the Lord herself: "Look, Yr. Grace, Father, this mercies and much other things when I was little, persons who knew and witnessed everything about me and things to do with my parents would tell of them whenever they saw me, weeping tenderly: great people is this girl, royal blood she has. Other things as well when I received understanding, which Divine Majesty gave me very soon, so I knew this and am telling to Yr. Grace."

As though she were saying: "Everything that happened to my parents at my birth, during my upbringing, and the marvelous events which occurred when I came into the world, I was told by persons who saw them, and though perhaps it is difficult for you to understand how I came to know all this and a great deal more before I was even born, or even when I was born and was so very young, and furthermore how can I give you an account thereof? And for this reason I reply to you that when I came to have the use of reason and understanding—His Majesty bestowed light and clarity onto my faculties at a very early age—many completely trustworthy persons told me thereof, and these same persons, when they regarded me carefully [when I was] away from my homeland, never ceased looking at me for long periods of time and would burst out while weeping tenderly: I know this little girl, who is of royal blood. So that, Father, all I have told you of what happened is exactly how I have told it."

Thus any doubt anyone might have must be satisfied, as she herself has answered it.

As I said, Our Lady the Virgin Mary favored Borta with the news of her fortunate pregnancy, and, as Catalina used to tell me, the Queen of Heaven was there to help when the birth came: "When I was come to be born or my mother to have me, the Most Holy Virgin helped her very much, and said to her: 'Borta, arise from your bed and in the grass there, under the big earthen jug, go dig a hole, and you will find riches there to bring up your little girl very well, as I am choosing her for my daughter.' This, Father Castillo, the people told me; if it's true, praise, triumph and victory, and if it's not, curses, damnation, and to hell you will go."

As though she meant to say: "When I was born, the Most Holy Virgin assisted and aided my mother, and then, after I had been born, told her: Borta, as soon as you get out of bed go to a place in your garden, and in the part where there is an earthen jug, take it away and dig down, and you will find treasure which I am giving you so that you take very good care of this girl for me, for I am choosing her as my daughter. This, Father Castillo, was told me when my judgment was more mature; if it is true, I give thanks for this event to the triumphant and militant Church, but if it is of the devil, then of course I renounce it all."

Borta arose from her bed after the fortuitous birth of Mirra [which means *bitterness*], which was the first name she was given; she complied with what the Queen of Heaven had ordered her to do by going to the appointed place, and hardly had she begun to dig when she found the treasure hidden in the earth, the carats of whose worth were the gift of Mary's hand. What I mean to say is that this gift represented the treasure trove of virtues which Mirra was destined to have, with Borta's womb being the center of this happy world, for she brought forth this treasure to the world.

Chapter 3. *About her captivity and her baptism, and the voyages in which she was brought to the port of Acapulco*

Under the guise of traders, some pirates came to Mirra's homeland and lay in wait to capture some slaves; they were successful in their intentions, because in their first encounters they found Mirra, who had gone to the seashore, either in search of solitude or because God had ordained it to happen so that she would leave that heathen land, even at the cost of much suffering and misfortune which she would undergo during the voyage on which she was taken. They finally reached a port or place called Cochin with her, where, as soon as she spied several fathers of the Society of Jesus, she felt a little better about the troubles she had had in such a terrible calamity; she used to tell me: "Look, Father, when they captured me and made me slave, much worry, much cares; only Divine Majesty know what I went through, but when we got to Cochin, other place now very far from my country, I saw Fathers from Society, got to know them and felt bit better, because when I saw them I remembered when I was little girl on one occasion Divine Majesty show me many Fathers and said: 'They teach you.' That's how it was, Father, because before they got water to put on me for baptizing, they taught me very fine, and then a priest, with a collar like your collar, baptized me and during baptism Most Holy Virgin, Saint Joaquín, Saint Anne very happy in their eyes and looked at me glad and kind and I looked at them. Name they put on me at baptismal font was Catarina de San Juan."

As though she meant to say: "When I was the pirates' prisoner, who made me their slave, I had many troubles at the outset of the voyage, and God alone knows this; but when they took me to Cochin, a port far from my own country, where I saw Fathers of the Society of Jesus, I calmed down a bit, for as soon as I saw them I knew who they were, for when I was still a small girl His Divine Majesty showed them to me and said, 'These men are to be your instructors and will guide your soul; they will teach you before baptizing you,' and that is how it was, my Father, because their Reverences instructed me in all I needed to know before receiving holy baptism, which a churchman in holy garb administered; at said baptism I had the presence of the Most Holy Virgin, Saint Anne and Saint Joaquín, who with indications of their sovereign countenances showed great gladness, and I, with the greatest humility and modesty I could show, gazed upon them reverently, giving thanks to the God of Heaven and earth for everything, and for the name which they bestowed upon me at the baptismal font, which was Catarina de San Juan."

When Catarina had received in Cochin the baptism she so ardently desired because of the things foretold her by Christ Our Lord and by His Holy Mother when she was still living in a heathen state, the master in whose charge she was decided to sail to several ports until he reached Manila; during this voyage it appears that all the furies of hell were unleashed against Catarina, causing her new afflictions and causing her to suffer bloody strife in the mistreatment she endured in all the places where she was taken by her master. At last she and the other slaves reached the port of Manila; the ship's captain took her to a house to be carefully guarded, where she spent several days. At that time the Marquis of Galves, then viceroy of this land of New Spain, had put in an order for several handsome, pleasing women slaves for his palace staff, and one of the chosen ones to fill this order was Catarina, who thus was sent to the port of Acapulco for His Excellency. But at that time there was a great disturbance in Mexico and with it had come a change of government (as change there was), and also in the conveyance of Catarina; the ones who had the good fortune to receive her were Captain Miguel de Sosa and his wife Doña Margarita de Chaves, who had ordered a correspondent of theirs to find a *chinita* [Asian girl] to raise as their daughter, as their marriage had borne no fruit; thus she was sent to the aforementioned couple as their slave, having been born free. But all of these were divine intentions so that this city [of Puebla] would have an ornament of such glorious deeds as Catarina.

Chapter 4. *Of the life she led in the home of Captain Miguel de Sosa and Doña Margarita de Chaves*

As soon as Captain Miguel de Sosa and Doña Margarita de Chaves welcomed Catarina into their home, her fine natural gifts and heroic virtues in themselves recommended her [to them], not as a slave but as a daughter, becoming in effect more an adopted child, for, as soon as she came into their hands, within a few days of her arrival she received the Holy Sacrament of Confirmation from the hand of the Most Illustrious Doctor Don Alonso de Mota, Bishop of this City of the Angels, with her owners acting as godparents.

At that time, when she must have been twelve or thirteen, Catarina showed a sense of judgment that stemmed not from the fresh exuberance of youth but from judicious maturity. With this, and with many other similar actions, she made her godparents regard her carefully, all the more so when they saw in her great assiduousness for housekeeping, applying herself very quickly to this work . . . and being extremely meticulous in everything.

Having convinced themselves of her faithfulness, her godparents had her manage the expenses of the household; without being wasteful she yet gave liberally, and without stinginess helped those who were in her care with what she had. Her godfather many times had proof of her loyalty and disinterestedness in material things, as often he would intentionally let some coins fall from his desk onto the floor of his office just to see what Catarina, who would come in to clean, would do; what she did was to look on the coins as so much trash, for she swept up both with the same indifference, as she held both to be worthless. Her godfather would then say to her, "Catarina, when you were sweeping, didn't you see the money in the trash?" And she would reply: "Me, I did not look well, didn't remember and if I see it, have forgotten."

As though she were saying, "I am oblivious to everything, as I am ever mindful that I am dust, and since that thought moves me, I pay no attention to money."

The little store that Catarina put by money and the simplicity with which she dealt with this matter gave her godfather much pleasure; on a daily basis, he and his wife felt greater admiration which such examples offered.

Who would not assume that in a house of such wealth Catarina would be the one who would come out best, as every material comfort was under her command? And who would not think that she would lead a life of ease and leisure? But no, because in the first case she always so subdued her flesh and was so abstemious in what she ate that she fasted continually, eating mainly bread and water, that since her childhood she had scorned those foods which are held to be delicious in taste, tending always to the humblest sustenance, eating only what was necessary and with no condiment; she preferred foods of little substance, such as vegetables and herbs, to dainty dishes and sweet delicacies. And if on some occasion Nature led her to feel a slight longing for something sweet, Our Lord Christ would say to her: "Catarina, what is this? My mouth is tasting gall and vinegar and yours wants something sweet?" And she, to such delightful words, would answer Him: "No, my dearest, that is long years gone."

As though she meant to say: "No, my Lord and my love, I will not taste it, I will not enjoy it, and will only enjoy that which you wish me to taste; for you I abandon everything and only want to taste bitterness and sorrows, which is what you taste and give to those who are your friends, and I, though unworthy, am one of those who wants to be your slave. Sweeten me only with bitterness, taste me only with sorrows."

And thus she refrained from eating it, and if she did eat it, it would be when she was ill or unwilling to eat, and then only with the express command of her superiors, not of her own will or desire.

Speaking of the latter I could expand on this at length, but the story does not warrant it, for I have promised to tell this life as succinctly as I can. When she had finished her domestic duties it was Catarina's consolation to seek out the most secret corners and the most secluded places, and, once there, on her knees and arms extended wide, she tenderly uttered that which a heart, melted in the fire of divine flames, might be wont to say. Sometimes it was with Christ Our Lord, another time with His Most Holy Mother, another with other heavenly host, so that, ever more kindled with this divine ardor and burning with divine love that gently consumed or delicately completed her, she gave herself up to such terrible flagellations that often times it was necessary for the angels to temper the number of strokes with which she mortified her flesh, saying to her, "Hey, Catarina, enough."

For this she used small iron chains, as well as hair shirts of pig's bristles and other various instruments with which she so imprisoned and confined her flesh and her body that everything was a scourge of terrible self-mortification. Even though she appeared to have a narrow bed on which she slept, the cold stone floor was her place of rest, and when she realized that people might find out that she was not sleeping in the bed, she used a judicious ruse to make it appear that she had actually gone to bed, but little by little she shook off the warming covers, so that her delicate skin made use of the hard wooden planks for softness, and the stinging splinters for respite. These, and others like it, were Catarina's ways of consolation, and she executed them with such tenacity that I understood that at the end of her life she had accustomed herself to such a degree of discomfort and multiplicity of acts of penitence that only divine grace could keep her on her feet, strengthening her to such a degree that no human effort without this divine assistance could have borne the rigor with which Catarina punished her body. . . .

Chapter 32. *About an event which this servant of God, after her death and with God's help, effected*

On this point of the miracles which God, with Catarina's intercession after her death, has wrought, many things might be told and I am omitting many of them, because the sole example I will relate is sufficient to prove them all, above all since it was known to many people who saw it, and can give witness of it; I will omit all others, for in the matter of miracles, as they are in and of themselves so difficult to ascertain, and the preserve of the knowledge of the Church, which has this ministry by profession, that I do not want them to become an obstacle to the credit of the virtues of this servant of the Lord, nor do I wish to extend this story, whose purpose is but to awaken and touch the devotion of the faithful.

Before the Holy Office of the Faith, as in all matters with its holy zeal and vigilant concern, removed and forbade the likenesses which popular devotion had made of Catarina, it so happened that the learned Francisco de Ayala, assistant in this city to the parish of the renowned and illustrious martyr Saint Sebastian, came down with a serious, painful, and acute illness, which was so severe and life-threatening that he had reached the final stages thereof, with paroxysms and death throes. While in this dangerous and painful state, a portrait of Catarina was placed on his chest, and when he had had it with him but a short while, he began to vomit what he had in his stomach, spitting up a kind of bag of thick skin. Witnesses hereof were the doctor who was attending him, as well as his helpers and numerous other companions, and the said learned Francisco de Ayala was left well, in good health, and free of the affliction because of the contact with Catarina's portrait. I do not relate this as a miracle done by Catarina, but as a marvelous work of God, who has the power and the knowledge when He wishes to bestow health or illness, life or death, and, having reached the end of Catarina's life, the author hereby concludes this brief relation.

Appendix C

María de San José: Selections from *Vida*, vol. 1

From Kathleen Myers and Amanda Powell, *A Wild Country out in the Garden* (Bloomington, Indiana: Indiana University Press, 1999), pp. 3–19.

[*Written in Oaxaca, in 1703–04, to María's confessor Fray Plácido de Olmedo, addressed as "your Paternity"* (vuestra paternidad)].

Today, the feast of the Nativity of the Blessed Virgin Mary, the eighth of September of the year 1703: I had already written the entire story of my life, from my childhood until I set out for this foundation in this city of Oaxaca, under order of obedience from my Confessor who was the licentiate Manuel de Barros, Chaplain of the convent of our Order of Augustinian Recollect nuns of our Mother Saint Monica, which was a new foundation in the Indies, in the city of Puebla de los Angeles, where I took the veil to be a nun.

This foundation was established and founded by his most Illustrious Grace Don Manuel Fernández de Santa Cruz, the Bishop of Puebla. I had spoken with him on a few occasions before becoming a nun, when he would go out on the visitation of his diocese; for he always made a stop in the town of Tepeaca, which served then as it does still as the principal place in all that valley, where all the important people would gather who had come to see the Illustrious Lord Bishop. My parents' hacienda, which was a farming hacienda, was near the town of Tepeaca, about a half a league away. On these occasions, I would do everything in my power to be able to speak with him, and though very hastily, I would give him an account of the extraordinary path—which put me at such risk of being deceived by the enemy—by which God was leading me, and of my great desire to become a nun. And though this was but every now and then and very hasty, being such a great spiritual Father, he perceived and understood my path at once. And so, after I had become a nun, he would come from time to time to the confessional and hear my account of my soul and what was happening in it. When he heard my confession, he commanded me to write my life story.

On this occasion his Illustrious Grace came to the convent and, as would be expected, he already knew the order my Father Confessor had given me, because my Confessor communicated all my affairs to him. I had not carried it out, because I did not know how to write. The Bishop told me I should obey at once, without the slightest hesitation, by beginning to write; that even though I could not write, nor had I been able to learn how in spite of all the efforts I had made, obedience could work miracles. Besides this, I knew it pleased Our Lord to make manifest the great deeds that His powerful hand had worked in this lowly and wretched creature that I have been; because in one of the favors that His Divine Majesty had granted me,

He had told me, among other things, that it was now time to proclaim and make manifest the great deeds that He had worked in me. And thus His infinite power and mercy might be praised and extolled, knowing that all comes from that powerful hand, and that in me there has never been nor is there more than lowliness and wretchedness.

All these things occurred before I ever began to write. I began and I went on writing, which clearly showed the miracle of obedience. But the travail that writing has caused me and causes me still is something for God alone, Who is the only one Who can know it, for I can find no terms to explain the extreme travail it gives me. When I had filled one notebook I sent it at once to my Confessor, who as I have already said was the Chaplain of the convent. As soon as he had read it, he carried them [sic] in person to the Bishop, Santa Cruz, who being the prelate had made this arrangement with him. He would leave them in [the Bishop's] hands so that as soon as he might have time, he could read them and inspect them. His most Illustrious Grace would then do so, and after having read them he would consult with his Confessor, a gentleman canon who was Confessor to some of the nuns of the convent. With this canon, who was his own Confessor, [the Bishop] would soon return the papers and deliver them to my Confessor. Little by little they all came into his hands. . . . [María continues to discuss who read her notebooks and where they are.]

My conversion is late and lacking in response to Your loving voice, which has called me so many times. Do not permit me, sweetest Lord and Father of my soul, to turn back and go down the dark paths of my faults; but give me Your hand that I may not turn from the path of following Your sweetest Son, Our Lord Christ, since with the love You have for us, You were pleased to give Him to us as the ransom and remedy for our souls. Grant that mine, united with His infinite merits, may reach the dear harbor of Your eternal and loving company; nor may my enemies dare to enter this inheritance, which You have guarded so carefully and taken from their hands so many times. May the angelic spirits praise You, and give You thanks on my behalf, my Lord and God! And may they give me memory and light, that I may succeed in telling my entire life with the clarity that has been commanded of me and that You have given me to know. May all be for Your glory and service, and my annihilation and abasement. Amen.

Among the great mercies that Our Lord God has shown me, and indeed one of the very greatest, is to have made me the granddaughter and daughter of very Christian parents. Although I was among the last of the daughters of the family, I do recall that all four of my grandparents were gachupines from Spain, and that they took part in the conquest of these lands, the kingdom of the Indies. I never knew them. My father's name was Luis de Palacios y Solozano, and my mother was Antonia Berruecos. Both were very rich in worldly goods, though as time passed their fortunes diminished, as is the way with all earthly things in life. My mother was born and raised in the city of Puebla de los Angeles, where her parents lived all their lives. And as her parents were very rich (for they had a great fortune, even more than my father, though he too was rich), a large portion fell to her.

My mother was married at the age of fifteen. When the wedding and festivities of those days were finished, my father took her to one of the two farming haciendas that he owned in the valley of Tepeaca. God had endowed her with lovely gifts, besides her very pleasing appearance. Although she was just a girl, her dresses were those of a woman of many years, so that it could be seen that she had great virtue, and that persons without it should not speak to her, nor would she permit conversations that were not of that kind; and in all things she showed her great understanding. She was very devoted to Our Lady and fond of taking the Holy Sacraments very often. For the rest of her life, she went through many great trials and illnesses. She bore it all with the greatest patience; for patience was the virtue in which she shone the brightest. For all of us she stood as a great example and edification. From the day my father brought her to the hacienda, when as I said she was just fifteen years old, he never again took her from the house.

The hacienda had very good buildings and a nicely adorned chapel. They had a license so that Mass could be said in it. The first daughter my mother had, as soon as she was born, my father sent word to the lord Bishop of Puebla at that time, asking license that the child might be baptized in his chapel. The Bishop granted it right away, and she was baptized to my father's great delight. And so it went with all the children born to my mother, for we were eleven in all; two of her children died as babies. She was left with eight daughters and one son, which makes nine. They were named Tomás, who was the oldest, Agustina, Ana, Leonor, Francisca, María, Juana— that was I, for when I entered the convent I changed my name from Juana to María. After me, my mother had two more girls, Isabel and Catalina. All were baptized in the chapel of the hacienda.

All of the daughters grew up without any of us being confirmed until God took my father. Some time after my father had died, it happened that a Bishop passed through that valley on the way to his diocese. He made a stop in the town of Tepeaca, where he made confirmations. My mother, wanting us to be confirmed, set out on the road and took all her daughters to the town, which was near the hacienda. There we were all confirmed, thanks be to God, except for Tomás who already was. And as far as I recall, I was already more than twelve years old. We confessed and received Communion that same day, as we were now able to receive that most Blessed Sacrament.

By the mercy of Our Lord God, all the girls resembled their parents in being virtuous, except for me; for I turned out quite different from them, although I had greater obligation to be so, and the inclinations the Lord had given me were good. I lost them all, letting myself be carried away by my passions, which grew pitiably with age. Blessed be God, Who waited so long for me.

My mother raised her eight daughters and one son with great internal quiet, and my father helped her teach them to be good Christians, as I have said. Both were fond of virtue and of good books, which they made them read. God had given my mother great skill in doing clever and neat handiwork and everything that a mother should know in order to teach her children. She taught us all to read and, in short, no schoolmaster or mistress was needed to teach us anything, save for my brother Tomás who, when he came of age, was sent by my father to the city of Puebla to live with one of my father's relatives so that he could study. My father kept Tomás at his studies until he was a grown man. When he saw that Tomás had no inclination to enter the religious life or any other profession, my father brought his son home to help him with the hacienda.

And this was ordained from on high, for God saw fit to take my father, and he left all his eight daughters with no position or support whatsoever, and my mother burdened with the responsibilities of such a large family. My brother Tomás was and is so good that he has been both father and protector to my mother and to all of us; for he has given us all some position and support. And besides all this, he has kept the two haciendas going that my father left him at his death—may the Lord reward my brother in the same measure as Tomás has trusted in His great mercy. My father died a most Christian death on Saturday, the Feast of the Nativity of Our Lady, 1667. My mother was left with much sorrow and loneliness, though in great conformity to the will of Our Lord God. When my father died, I was at the end of my tenth year, just turning eleven. . . . [*María goes on and talks of her father*]

I was born on the feast of Saint Mark the Evangelist, the twenty-fifth of April, 1654, and because my godfather's name was Juan, they called me Juana. And when I took the veil, they called me Juana de San Diego. Then, when it came time for the profession of vows, I asked them to change my name from Juana de San Diego to María de San José; for so great was my longing and desire to strip myself entirely of all the things of this world, that it seemed better to leave behind even the name that was mine and take another, as I did.

Right after my birth my mother said that she wished to nurse me herself, without help from any other woman such as she had with all the other daughters she raised. And she did as she said; for I never took a drop of milk from any woman other than my mother. I remember quite well that when I had reached the age of five, my mother still nursed me at her breast. She did all this to avoid yet another childbirth. As soon as I was born, she began to entreat the Lord not to give her another child, because she was quite worn out with all the ones she already had. But the Lord, Who knows full well what is best for us, did not grant her this. And to test her patience, when I was five, He gave her two more births. As soon as she knew that she was pregnant, she felt grief and pain, though she always conformed to the will of God. Right away she turned from me and sent me away from her side to be cared for by my older sisters and especially by a maid who had been raised in the house and was a girl of great virtue.

As I recall from that time when I was five years old, I already knew the four prayers, which my mother had taught me, and she had set me to learn to read in Christian doctrine; for she took more pains with my upbringing than with any of her other daughters. It seems to me I can say in all truth that even before I could speak at all clearly, the Lord gave me an indifference to all earthly things of this life, and I was well known for feeling uneasy in any state but solitude, with nothing that I could call my own. Only here could I find repose.

As soon as I was left without my mother's care, I began to lose all the good I had received from the upbringing she gave me. Heavens bless me, what could I not find to say in these pages to the parents of children! How important it is to keep them always in your sight and not let them go with bad companions! The family at home was very large, for there were many servants, and so there were girls to play with and make mischief; for they were all very close to my own age, but none of them did me the harm that was done to me by an orphan girl, who was raised by a lady that was our neighbor in those parts, and who most days came to our house with the others to make mischief. As I have said, I had then turned five years of age. This neighbor girl was older than I; she must have been about seven. My sisters had learned common sense because they were bigger. The two who came after me were still so little they were not old enough for anything. In this group of girls I began to lose all my good inclinations and let them go to waste, for I learned to curse and swear and use some words that were not very decent. In our games and pranks, which were all the kind played by young girls with no capacity for reason or understanding, I lost all that I had and let myself be carried away by my passions, which increased as I grew older. Sad to say, I reached ten years of age and was so absorbed and distracted by these games and pranks—which, as I say, went no further than that; but it was all time wasted and very poorly spent. And I had tied God's hands, so that He could not favor me and give me light and the use of reason to recognize it, and to recognize the wretched life that I had chosen to my utter ruin and perdition. . . . [*María describes the games she played with neighboring girls and her vanity*]

One afternoon I left my mother's sitting room and went out to the patio, where I set about grinding flour. There I was joined by other girls my age, for we usually amused ourselves, most afternoons, by grinding flour. I was the one doing the grinding. We were all leaning against the wall that surrounded the patio. One of the girls near me did some sort of a bad turn. As I was a girl of bad habits, I cursed her, and before the word was out of my mouth, God permitted a lightning bolt to strike. And although it appeared to be only an ordinary bolt of lightning, for me it was nothing less than a bolt of light that the Lord Himself aimed at my very heart. The lightning struck in the midst of those of us gathered there, and although it threw all of us to the ground, it did no one any harm. But it broke through the corner of the wall, and through the opening it made, it leapt out and killed an animal that was standing in the field near the same wall.

May God bless my soul, how clearly and plainly did His Majesty show me that as He took the life of that animal, He could with much greater cause have taken my own! For I served Him in no other way than to offend Him and to bury myself in the abyss of hell. May His vast goodness and mercy be given infinite thanks, for working such good with such a one as I, who deserve to be cast into a thousand hells for my great sins and evils.

Once we had recovered from this terror and fright, which were dreadful, we arose from where we had fallen all stunned and bewildered by the lightning. Without tending to any of the girls or speaking a word, I walked back towards the parlor where my mother and sisters were. And as I passed the staircase, I encountered the devil, who was seated on the bottom step in human form, like a naked mulatto. He was gnawing at one of his hands. Just as I saw him, he raised a finger as if to threaten me, and he said to me: "You are mine. You will not escape my clutches." I saw this more with my soul's interior vision than with the eyes of my body. The words he said to me sounded in my ears; I heard them spoken. But, comforted and aided by He Who can do everything, Who is God, I managed to enter the sitting room where my mother was.

This second fright was no less than that caused by the bolt of lightning. I concealed what had happened to me, saying not a word to my mother or to a single soul of how I had seen the enemy in such a dreadful form, nor of the words he had spoken to me, once I recovered and returned to my senses. I found myself so altered that even I did not know myself. I was no longer what I had been. For it was as though a great window had opened in my soul, and through it came a very bright light, by which I could see and understand with great clarity and light all that the Lord had done and suffered and undertaken to ransom me at the expense of His most precious blood. And at the same time I became aware of all that I had said and done in the course of eleven years, which was then my age; I am not sure whether I had entered my twelfth year when this happened to me. I clearly saw and understood the many and grave faults into which I had fallen, giving offense to His Divine Majesty with my rude ingratitude. I felt great sorrow for having offended my God and Lord, Who was favoring me with such a liberal hand. I was all sighs and tears, as I begged the Lord that He might furnish me with a Confessor to whom I could confess all my sins; for each one I held up to view was a spear that ran through my heart and my soul, and all of them together were the very sharpest sword-points that pierced my heart and soul and set them to rout. For I longed rather to have lost my life a thousand and one times, than to have displeased His Divine Majesty in even the slightest way.

I spent all that night doubting and plotting out what mode of life I might choose to repudiate and cast from me all the things of this world. Being in the condition I was in, I rose terribly upset the next day, with no hope of finding any means or remedy for my longing to make confession—while each moment and instant seemed centuries to me—nor of finding any means or resolution as to what way of life I should lead. As soon as I saw that my mother's bedroom was empty, with no one in it—for by now I was fleeing everyone so that they would not see me in the condition I was in—on the morning of that same day, I went into the bedroom and shut the door, staying there alone to unburden myself and give free rein to my sobs and tears and sighs, praying for mercy from Divine Wisdom, Who knew well how I had offended Him.

I was walking about the room as I did this; and when I grew tired of walking, I sat down on a footstool that was there next to my mother's bed. And on the head of the bed was an image of Our Lady. This was an image holding the Baby Jesus in her arms. While I was there as I said, sitting on the footstool, with my chin in my hand and deep in thought, unable to resolve anything, I heard this Lady of whom I have been speaking tell me: "Juana, come to me." (I have already said that my name was Juana, and in religious life María.) As soon as I heard these words, it seemed I was restored from death to life, recovering my strength and receiving great consolation in my soul. I rose with all haste and got down on my knees, with my hands clasped in front of this image of Our Lady, and turned into a sea of tears; for as I have understood and experienced since that day, the Lord granted me the favor of the gift of tears. . . . [*María describes her vision of the Virgin Mary*]

Here the Most Blessed Virgin continued, and she told me: "My daughter, you have given your consent to be the bride of my Most Blessed Son. Now you must take vows, just as the nuns do who renounce the world and all its effects, entering into the religious life and enclosure." I answered and said, "My Lady and Mother, I do not know what vows these are or what religious life is like. You know my great ignorance and small understanding, and how I was born and raised here in the countryside without ever seeing nor speaking with a single person save my parents and our household. I do not even know how to read. What do I know that could give me any light as to what you tell me I must do?" Here the Most Blessed Lady answered me, and she said: "My daughter, do not be troubled by what you do not know. Draw near to me, and I shall teach you what you must do. Place your hands upon mine."

I did as she said, and this Lady set about telling me just how and in what way I must take them, each vow in its turn. I did nothing but follow along pronouncing the same words the Virgin was telling me—that I should say them as soon as she had finished making the four vows, in the same way and form that they are taken in religious life by the nuns when they profess. I found myself, without knowing how it could possibly be, with the ring placed on one finger of my hand, the same ring I had seen before that the Child had on a tiny finger of His little hand. I have already said that this was the Baby Jesus this image of Our Lady was holding in her arms. I felt great wonder and confusion to find myself wearing the ring.

Here the Most Blessed Virgin went on speaking to me, and she said: "My daughter, I have now fulfilled the promise I made you, that my Most Blessed Son would give you His ring, as a token of His love. Now, I want to explain and show you how you must fulfill and observe the vows you have made. The first you made was obedience to the Lord God Most High, and in His place and name, to your superiors and prelates. And for as long as you live in your mother's company, you must obey her in all that she may order and command you to do, save when it might be anything that you know to be against the commandments and precepts of Our Lord God. In such a case, you should not obey her. With regard to poverty, you should have no private thing you call your own, in even the smallest amount; rather, leave all to the Lord's providence, and take care only to love Him and serve Him, giving over to Him a heart disengaged and unattached to any earthly things of this mortal life. For I assure you, daughter, that if you truly give yourself over and leave yourself to His providence, He will not fall short or fail to help you in all your needs with His accustomed mercy. With regard to chastity, you must guard not only that of the body, but of the heart, living on this earth like an angel of the Lord. With regard to enclosure, you must live and keep to your retreat in solitude, speaking only with God, withdrawn from all things of this world, without speaking or communicating with a single person who is not someone you know. All must be to set you on your way and guide you entirely toward God, and always subject to your mother; you may do all this without displeasing His Divine Majesty. Your clothing and dress must be entirely of wool, and your life just like a nun's, very strict and proper. I shall be a help to you so that you may fulfill everything that you have promised His Majesty and me in these four vows."

With these words, the Most Blessed Virgin finished and brought to an end everything that I have told here. At once, everything disappeared. I have never seen the ring again. The image of Our Lady, which as I have said had the Child in her arms, went back to the way it was before. I stayed kneeling just where I had been while all this was happening, as I have told it here. My eyes were fountains of tears. I did not know how to thank His Divine Majesty for the great deeds He had worked in my wretchedness and misery. I found myself so changed that even I did not know myself, nor was I what I had been before.

O my Lord and God! Of the mercies You have shown me, oh what a great conversion this was! I cannot perform my duty, Lord and Father of my soul, by being anything less than holy and rendering You great service and working great things for Your love, to give thanks and return in some part the great gifts I have received in this conversion of mine. When I was most removed and forgetful of You, Your merciful heart was moved to halt my unruly steps toward my perdition. I offer infinite thanks to You for what You have worked in me, an unworthy sinner.

Appendix D

Sor Juana Inés de la Cruz: Selections from
La Respuesta a Sor Filotea

From *The Answer/La Respuesta*, ed. and trans., Electa Arenal and Amanda Powell (New York: Feminist Press, 1994), pp. 39–53, 61–63.

It has not been my will, but my scant health and a rightful fear that have delayed my reply for so many days. Is it to be wondered that, at the very first step, I should meet with two obstacles that sent my dull pen stumbling? The first (and to me the most insuperable) is the question of how to respond to your immensely learned, prudent, devout, and loving letter. For when I consider how the Angelic Doctor, St. Thomas Aquinas, on being asked of his silence before his teacher Albertist Magnus, responded that he kept quiet because he could say nothing worthy of Albertist, then how much more fitting it is that I should keep quiet—not like the Saint from modesty, but rather because, in truth, I am unable to say anything worthy of you. The second obstacle is the question of how to render my thanks for the favor, as excessive as it was unexpected, of giving my drafts and scratches to the press: a favor so far beyond all measure as to surpass the most ambitious hopes or the most fantastic desires, so that as a rational being I simply could not house it in my thoughts. In short, this was a favor of such magnitude that it cannot be bounded by the confines of speech and indeed exceeds all powers of gratitude, as much because it was so large as because it was so unexpected. In the words of Quintilian: "They produce less glory through hopes, more glory through benefits conferred." And so much so, that the recipient is struck dumb.

When the mother of [John] the Baptist—felicitously barren, so as to become miraculously fertile—saw under her roof so exceedingly great a guest as the Mother of the Word, her powers of mind were dulled and her speech was halted; and thus, instead of thanks, she burst out with doubts and questions: "And whence is this to me . . . ?" The same occurred with Saul when he was chosen and anointed King of Israel: "Am not I a son of Jemini of the least tribe of Israel, and my kindred the last among all the families of the tribe of Benjamin? Why then hast thou spoken this word to me?" Just so, I too must say: Whence, O venerable Lady, whence comes such a favor to me? By chance, am I something more than a poor nun, the slightest creature on earth and the least worthy of drawing your attention? Well, why then hast thou spoken this word to me? And whence is this to me?

I can answer nothing more to the first obstacle than that I am entirely unworthy of your gaze. To the second, I can offer nothing more than amazement, instead of thanks, declaring that I am unable to thank you for the slightest part of what I owe you. It is not false humility, my Lady, but the candid truth of my very soul, to say that when the printed letter reached my hands—that letter you were pleased to dub "Worthy of Athena"—I burst into tears (a thing that does not come easily to me), tears of confusion. For it seemed to me that your great favor was nothing other than God's reproof aimed at my failure to return His favors, and while He corrects others with punishments, He wished to chide me through benefits. A special favor, this, for which I acknowledge myself His debtor, as I am indebted for infinitely many favors given by His immense goodness; but this is also a special way of shaming and confounding me. For it is the choicest form of punishment to cause me to serve, knowingly, as the judge who condemns and sentences my own ingratitude. And so when I consider this fully, here in solitude, it is my custom to say: Blessed are you my Lord God, for not only did you forbear to give another creature the power to judge me, nor have you placed that power in my hands. Rather you have kept that power for yourself and have freed me of myself and of the sentence I would pass on myself, which, forced by my own conscience, could be no less than condemnation. Instead you have reserved that sentence for your great mercy to declare, because you love me more than I can love myself.

My Lady, forgive the digression wrested from me by the power of truth; yet if I must make a full confession of it, this digression is at the same time a way of seeking evasions so as to flee the difficulty of making my answer. And therefore I had nearly resolved to leave the matter in silence; yet although silence explains much by the emphasis of leaving all unexplained, because it is a negative thing, one must name the silence, so that what it signifies may be understood. Failing that, silence will say nothing, for that is its proper function: to say nothing. The holy Chosen Vessel was carried off to the third Heaven and, having seen the arcane secrets of God, he says: "That he was caught up into paradise, and heard secret words, which it is not granted to man to utter." He does not say what he saw, but he says that he cannot say it. In this way, of those things that cannot be spoken, it must be said that they cannot be spoken, so that it may be known that silence is kept not for lack of things to say, but because the many things there are to say cannot be contained in mere words. St. John says that if he were to write all of the wonders wrought by Our Redeemer, the whole world could not contain all the books. Vieira says of this passage that in this one phrase the Evangelist says more than in all his other writings; and indeed how well the Lusitanian Phoenix speaks (but when is he not well-spoken, even when he speaks ill?), for herein St. John says all that he failed to say and expresses all that he failed to express. And so I, my Lady, shall answer only that I know not how to answer; I shall thank you only by saying that I know not how to give thanks; and I shall go say, by way of the brief label placed on what I leave to silence, that only with the confidence of one so favored and with the advantages granted one so honored, do I dare speak to your magnificence. If this be folly, please forgive it; for folly sparkles in good fortune's crown, and through it I shall supply further occasion for your goodwill, and you shall better arrange the expression of my gratitude.

Moses, because he was a stutterer, thought himself unworthy to speak to Pharaoh. Yet later, finding himself greatly favored by God, he was so imbued with courage that not only did he speak to God Himself, but he dared to ask of Him the impossible: "Shew me thy face." And so it is with me, my Lady, for in view of the favor you show me, the obstacles I described at the outset no longer seem entirely insuperable. For one who had the letter printed, unbeknownst to me, who titled it and underwrote its cost, and who thus honored it (unworthy as it was of all this, on its own account and on account of its author), what will such a one not do? What not forgive? Or what fail to do or fail to forgive? Thus, sheltered by the assumption that I speak with the safe-conduct granted by your favors and with the warrant bestowed by your goodwill, and by the fact that, like a second Ahasuerus, you have allowed me to kiss the top of the golden scepter of your affection as a sign that you grant me kind license to speak and to plead my case in your venerable presence, I declare that I receive in my very soul your most holy admonition to apply my study to Holy Scripture; for although it arrives in the guise of counsel, it shall have for me the weight of law. And I take no small consolation from the fact that it seems my obedience, as if at your direction, anticipated your pastoral insinuation, as may be inferred from the subject matter and arguments of that very Letter. I recognize full well that your most prudent warning touches not on the letter, but on the many writings of mine on humane matters that you have seen. And thus, all that I have said can do no more than offer that letter to you in recompense for the failure to apply myself which you must have inferred (and reasonably so) from my other writings. And to speak more specifically, I confess, with all the candor due to you and with the truth and frankness that are always at once natural and customary for me, that my having written little on sacred matters has sprung from no dislike, nor from lack of application, but rather from a surfeit of awe and reverence toward those sacred letters, which I know myself to be so incapable of understanding and which I am so unworthy of handling. For there always resounds in my ears the Lord's warning and prohibition to sinners like me, bringing with it no small terror: "Why dost thou declare my justices, and take my covenant in thy mouth?" With this question comes the reflection that even learned men were forbidden to read the Song of Songs, and indeed Genesis, before they reached the age of thirty: the latter text because of its difficulty, and the former so that with the sweetness of those epithalamiums, imprudent youth might not be stirred to carnal feelings. My great father St. Jerome confirms this, ordering the Song of Songs to be the last text studied, for the same reason: "Then at last she may safely read the Song of Songs: if she were to read it at the beginning, she might be harmed by not perceiving that it was the song of a spiritual bridal expressed in fleshly language." And Seneca says, "In early years, faith is not yet manifest." Then how should I dare take these up in my unworthy hands, when sex, and age, and above all our customs oppose it? And thus I confess that often this very fear has snatched the pen from my hand and have made the subject matter retreat back toward that intellect from which it wished to flow; an impediment I did not stumble across with profane subjects, for a heresy against art is not punished by the Holy Office but rather by wits with their laughter and critics with their censure. And this, "just or unjust, is not to be feared," for one is still permitted to take Communion and hear Mass, so that it troubles me little if at all. For in such matters, according to the judgment of the very ones who slander me, I have no obligation to know how nor the skill to hit the mark, and thus if I miss it is neither sin nor discredit. No sin, because I had no obligation; no discredit, because I had no possibility of hitting the mark, and "no one is obliged to do the impossible." And truth to tell, I have never written save when pressed and forced and solely to give pleasure to others, not only without taking satisfaction but with downright aversion, because I have never judged myself to possess the rich trove of learning and wit that is perforce the obligation of one who writes. This, then, is my usual reply to those who urge me to write, and the more so in the case of a sacred subject: What understanding do I possess, what studies, what subject matter, or what instruction, save four profundities of a superficial scholar? They can leave such things to those who understand them; as for me, I want no trouble with the Holy Office, for I am but ignorant and tremble lest I utter some ill-sounding proposition or twist the true meaning of some passage. I do not study in order to write, nor far less in order to teach (which would be boundless arrogance in me), but simply to see whether by studying I may become less ignorant. This is my answer, and these are my feelings.

My writing has never proceeded from any dictate of my own, but a force beyond me; I can in truth say, "You have compelled me." One thing, however, is true, so that I shall not deny it (first because it is already well known to all, and second because God has shown me His favor in giving me the greatest possible love of truth, even when it might count against me). For ever since the light of reason first dawned in me, my inclination to letters was marked by such passion and vehemence that neither the reprimands of others (for I have received many) nor reflections of my own (there have been more than a few) have sufficed to make me abandon my pursuit of this native impulse that God Himself bestowed on me. His Majesty knows why and to what end He did so, and He knows that I have prayed that He snuff out the fight of my intellect, leaving only enough to keep His Law. For more than that is too much, some would say, in a woman; and there are even those who say that it is harmful. His Majesty knows too that, not achieving this, I have attempted to entomb my intellect together with my name and to sacrifice it to the One who gave it to me; and that no other motive brought me to the life of Religion, despite the fact that the exercises and companionship of a community were quite opposed to the tranquillity and freedom from disturbance required by my studious bent. And once in the community, the Lord knows—and in this world only he who needs must know it, does—what I did to try to conceal my name and renown from the public; he did not, however, allow me to do this, telling me it was temptation, and so it would have been. If I could repay any part of my debt to you, my Lady, I believe I might do so merely by informing you of this, for these words have never left my mouth save to that one to whom they must be said. But having thrown wide the doors of my heart and revealed to you what is there under seal of secrecy, I want you to know that this confidence does not gainsay the respect I owe to your venerable person and excessive favors.

To go on with the narration of this inclination of mine, of which I wish to give you a full account: I declare I was not yet three years old when my mother sent off one of my sisters, older than I, to learn to read in one of those girls' schools that they call Amigas. Affection and mischief carried me after her; and when I saw that they were giving her lessons, I so caught fire with the desire to learn that, deceiving the teacher (or so I thought), I told her that my mother wanted her to teach me also. She did not believe this, for it was not to be believed; but to humor my whim she gave me lessons. I continued to go and she continued to teach me, though no longer in make-believe, for the experience undeceived her. I learned to read in such a short time that I already knew how by the time my mother heard of it. My teacher had kept it from my mother to give delight with a thing all done and to receive a prize for a thing done well. And I had kept still, thinking I would be whipped for having done this without permission. The woman who taught me (may God keep her) is still living, and she can vouch for what I say.

I remember that in those days, though I was as greedy for treats as children usually are at that age, I would abstain from eating cheese, because I heard tell that it made people stupid, and the desire to learn was stronger for me than the desire to eat—powerful as this is in children. Later, when I was six or seven years old and already knew how to read and write, along with all the other skills like embroidery and sewing that women learn, I heard that in Mexico City there were a University and Schools where they studied the sciences. As soon as I heard this I began to slay my poor mother with insistent and annoying pleas, begging her to dress me in men's clothes and send me to the capital, to the home of some relatives she had there, so that I could enter the University and study. She refused, and was right in doing so; but I quenched my desire by reading a great variety of books that belonged to my grandfather, and neither punishments nor scoldings could prevent me. And so when I did go to Mexico City, people marveled not so much at my intelligence as at my memory and the facts I knew at an age when it seemed I had scarcely had time to learn to speak.

I began to study Latin, in which I believe I took fewer than twenty lessons. And my interest was so intense, that although in women (and especially in the very bloom of youth) the natural adornment of the hair is so esteemed, I would cut off four to six fingerlengths of my hair, measuring how long it had been before. And I made myself a rule that if by the time it had grown back to the same length I did not know such and such a thing that I intended to study, then I would cut my hair off again to punish my dull-wittedness. And so my hair grew, but I did not yet know what I had resolved to learn, for it grew quickly and I learned slowly. Then I cut my hair right off to punish my dull-wittedness, for I did not think it reasonable that hair should cover a head that was so bare of facts—the more desirable adornment. I took the veil because, although I knew I would find in religious life many things that would be quite opposed to my character (I speak of accessory rather than essential matters), it would, given my absolute unwillingness to enter into marriage, be the least unfitting and the most decent state I could choose, with regard to the assurance I desired of my salvation. For before this first concern (which is, at the last, the most important), all the impertinent little follies of my character gave way and bowed to the yoke. These were wanting to live alone and not wanting to have either obligations that would disturb my freedom to study or the noise of a community that would interrupt the tranquil silence of my books. These things made me waver somewhat in my decision until, being enlightened by learned people as to my temptation, I vanquished it with divine favor and took the state I so unworthily hold. I thought I was fleeing myself, but—woe is me!—I brought myself with me, and brought my greatest enemy in my inclination to study, which I know not whether to take as a

Heaven-sent favor or as a punishment. For when snuffed out or hindered with every [spiritual] exercise known to Religion, it exploded like gun powder; and in my case the saying "privation gives rise to appetite" was proven true.

I went back (no, I spoke incorrectly, for I never stopped)—I went on, I mean, with my studious task (which to me was peace and rest in every moment left over when my duties were done) of reading and still more reading, study and still more study, with no teacher besides my books themselves. What a hardship it is to learn from those lifeless letters, deprived of the sound of a teacher's voice and explanations; yet I suffered all these trials most gladly for the love of learning. Oh, if only this had been done for the love of God, as was rightful, think what I should have merited! Nevertheless I did my best to elevate these studies and direct them to His service, for the goal to which I aspired was the study of Theology. Being a Catholic, I thought it an abject failing not to know everything that can in this life be achieved, through earthly methods, concerning the divine mysteries. And being a nun and not a laywoman, I thought I should, because I was in religious life, profess the study of letters—the more so as the daughter of such as St. Jerome and St. Paula: for it would be a degeneracy for an idiot daughter to proceed from such learned parents. I argued in this way to myself, and I thought my own argument quite reasonable. However, the fact may have been (and this seems most likely) that I was merely flattering and encouraging my own inclination, by arguing that its own pleasure was an obligation.

I went on in this way, always directing each step of my studies, as I have said, toward the summit of Holy Theology; but it seemed to me necessary to ascend by the ladder of the humane arts and sciences in order to reach it; for who could fathom the style of the Queen of Sciences without knowing that of her handmaidens? Without Logic, how should I know the general and specific methods by which Holy Scripture is written? Without Rhetoric, how should I understand its figures, tropes, and locutions? Or how, without Physics or Natural Science, understand all the questions that naturally arise concerning the varied natures of those animals offered in sacrifice, in which a great many things already made manifest are symbolized, and many more besides? How should I know whether Saul's cure at the sound of David's harp was owing to a virtue and power that is natural in Music or owing, instead, to a supernatural power that God saw fit to bestow on David? How without Arithmetic might one understand all those mysterious reckonings of years and days and months and hours and weeks that are found in Daniel and elsewhere, which can be comprehended only by knowing the natures, concordances, and properties of numbers? Without Geometry, how could we take the measure of the Holy Ark of the Covenant or the Holy City of Jerusalem, each of whose mysterious measurements forms a perfect cube uniting their dimensions, and each displaying that most marvelous distribution of the proportions of every part? . . . .

In this respect, I do confess that the trial I have undergone has been beyond all telling; and thus I cannot confirm what I have, with envy, heard others say: that learning has cost them no drudgery. How lucky they are! For me, it has not been knowledge (for I still know nothing) but the desire to know that has cost me so dear that I might truly say, like my good Father St. Jerome (though not with the benefit he offers): "What efforts I spent on that task, what difficulties I had to face, how often I despaired, how often I gave up and then in my eagerness to learn began again, my own knowledge can witness from personal experience and those can testify who were then living with me." Save for the mention of companions and witnesses (for I have lacked even this mitigation), I can in all truth affirm the rest of his words. And to think that this, my wicked inclination, should be such, that it has vanquished all before it!

It has often befallen me—for among other favors I owe to God a nature that is mild and affable; and the nuns, good creatures that they are, love me very much on this account and take no note of my failings, and so they delight in my company. Knowing this, and moved by the great love I bear them with more cause than theirs for me, I take even greater delight in their company.—And so, as I say, in the times they and I have not been occupied, I have often gone to offer them comfort and to find recreation in their conversation. I began to notice that I was stealing this time away from my studies, and I made a vow not to step into another nun's cell unless I were thus obliged by obedience or charity to do so; for unless I reined myself in this harshly, love would burst the restraint exerted by my intent alone. Thus, knowing my own weakness, I would hold to this vow for a month or a fortnight; and when it was done, I gave myself a truce of a day or two before I renewed it. That day would serve not so much to give me rest (for to desist from study has never been restful for me), but so that I might not be thought gruff, withdrawn, and ungrateful in the face of the undeserved affection of my most beloved sisters.

This shows all too well just how great is the strength of my inclination. May God be praised that He inclined me to letters and not some other vice, which would have been, in my case, nearly insurmountable. And from this, too, it may well be inferred just how my poor studies have found their way (or, to be more exact, have foundered) in steering against the current. For I have yet to tell the most strenuous of my difficulties. Those accounted for to this point have been no more than hindrances caused by my obligations or by chance, posed indirectly; they are not purposeful obstacles directly aimed at impeding and prohibiting my training. Who would not think, upon hearing such widespread applause, that I had sailed before the wind with a sea smooth as glass, upon the cheers of universal acclaim? Yet God Himself knows it has not quite been so, because among the blossoms of that very acclaim there have roused themselves and reared up the asps of rivalry and persecution, more than I could possibly count. And the most venomous and hurtful to me have not been those who with explicit hatred and ill-will have persecuted me, but those persons, loving me and desiring my good (and, therefore, greatly deserving before God for their good intentions), who have mortified and tormented me more than any others, with these words: "All this study is not fitting, for holy ignorance is your duty, she shall go to perdition, she shall surely be cast down from such heights by that same wit and cleverness." How was I to bear up against this? A strange martyrdom indeed, where I must be both martyr and my own executioner!

Well, as for this aptitude at composing verses—which is doubly unfortunate, in my case, even should they be sacred verses—what unpleasantness have they not caused me, and indeed do they not still cause? Truly, my Lady, at times I ponder how it is that a person who achieves high significance—or rather, who is granted significance by God, for He alone can do this—is received as the common enemy.

For that person seems to others to usurp the applause they deserve or to draw off and dam up the admiration to which they had aspired, and so they persecute that person.

That politically barbarous law of Athens remains in effect, whereby anyone possessing significant qualities and virtues was expelled from the republic to prevent his using them for the subjugation of public liberty; it is still observed in our own times, though no longer for the same reason the Athenians held. But now there is another motive, no less potent though less well founded, for it resembles a maxim of that impious Machiavelli: to abhor the person who becomes significant because that one tarnishes the fame of others.

What else but this could cause that furious hatred of the Pharisees against Christ, when there were so many reasons to feel the opposite? . . .

Appendix E

Ursula Suárez: Selections from *Relación autobiográfica*

Translated by Nina M. Scott

As Your Paternity already knows, last Saturday—the eighth of this month and the day of the Nativity—when I came to speak with you, and the following Wednesday, when you brought me paper so that I should write, I was so wicked that I did not comply punctually with your order, for which disobedience I implore you to pardon me and to impose a penance so that by means of it I will mend my ways. My Father, I know not what to put down with respect to what you want me to write about my young years, because in my infancy and my youth I was extremely wicked. As Your Paternity will see, I was the sum total of evil, for the light of reason had barely shone on me, when I was swept away by bad inclinations, and if Divine Providence had not seen fit to keep me in check with severe illnesses, my life would have been a disaster.

My mother used to say that she barely had a life [of her own] when she was raising me on account of the travails occasioned by so many illnesses which I had. I began to get sick when I was eleven months old, and my mother attributed it to the fact that I had a wet nurse who was pregnant, and she lamented this calamity and hired another wet nurse, and after her eight more, so that I had ten wet nurses: this is the reason I have turned out so bad. Once well paid, all of them left me; my mother said that she dressed them in serge and Castilina flannel, and on top of this advanced them their salary, and then they would still depart. I was constantly more sickly, as was my mother, with an abscessed breast, for this was the reason to be hiring [wet nurses], as my first wet nurse, who was her slave, she suspected of being pregnant.

I will give an account to Your Paternity of my childhood as I was told it. . . . As far as my birth is concerned, [my mother] said that I was born in my paternal grandparents' home: Secretary Martín Suares Madrigal and Doña María del Campo Lantadilla, who, along with my maternal grandfather, Don Antonio de las Cuevas y Escobar, lifted me from the baptismal font with great rejoicing and gladness, for I was the first daughter to whom my mother had given birth, as she had aborted another daughter at eight months, who did not receive the water of baptism, but God made me; may He, the author of this favor, be praised and blessed, as for so long he has shown me his mercies.

I knew nothing more about this [occasion], except that many of my relatives came to my baptism, it being the *provisor* Gaspar Días who baptized me. My aunt Doña Maríana de Escobar, who is still alive, told me that when I was about to be born she pinned on a rose of Jericho [a plant believed to aid in childbirth]. I said to her, "When I am big I will be the rose among thorns, for I will be a nun."

She said to me, "You, a nun? So wicked and of such bad blood, opponents of becoming nuns."

And I replied, "I, Aunt, will be the crown of my generation."

Said she, "Quiet, imp, for your liveliness is not for the likes of a nun, though when you were very little, one day I was giving you a bath in the middle of the patio and you frightened me, for, holding you quite naked, [there you were] clutching my braids and you began to ring them back and forth with great tempo, and imitated the sound of the bells with your mouth. I, frightened, called your mother and said, 'Kitty, come and see your daughter who's going to be a nun, look how she peals.' My mother and all the other women came out to applaud your charm: I don't know what it was, because you are a great rascal."

I told her, "Aunt, Your Grace will see that I will become a nun."

Going back to my upbringing and the trouble my mother told me she had with respect to this, she used to say, "Daughter of so many tears and prayers, why does God protect you, whose life caused me so much anguish, for there is not a saint to whom I have not appealed to make you whole, and you are so bad." My mother would tell me this when I was little and would have gotten into trouble, for I was an extremely mischievous and lively child, the counterbalance being my eternally sickly body, for not a day went by that it was not ill. My mother lugged me from convent to convent, paying for novenas and masses and giving alms at the altar for my life, for on three occasions she said, I had been [completely] emaciated, with such terrible fevers that I neither ate nor drank; she kept me alive by giving me drops of milk, which I could not swallow. As it seemed that she could find no cure for my illness in the city's churches, she went out to Our Lady of Renca, that she should be our intercessor, bringing her wax and silver; but as the Mother of God is not out for profit, I came back in the same shape as I had been brought there. My mother, bathed in tears because she had no other daughter and could see that I was dying, for I was not even opening my eyes, went again the next day, sad and afflicted, and it is well said that persistence carries the day: she went to St. Nicholas's altar and flung me upon it, and said to him: "Blessed saint, she is gone and you must raise her from the dead; I will dress her in your blessed habit, and if she gets well, she will wear it for two years." She had a mass chanted for the saint, and asked that the last rites be administered to me; with that I began to revive.

Appendix F

Catalina de Erauso: Selections from *Vida i sucesos*

From *Madres del verbo/Mothers of the Word: Early Spanish American Women Writers*, ed. and trans. Nina M. Scott (Alburquerque: University of New Mexico Press, 1999), pp. 35–49.

Chapter 1. *Her homeland, parents, birth, education, flight, and journeys throughout various parts of Spain*

I, Doña Catalina de Erauso, was born in the town of San Sebastián, in Guipúzcoa, in the year 1585, the daughter of Captain Don Miguel de Erauso and of Doña María Pérez de Galarraga y Arce, natives and residents of that town. My parents brought me up at home with my other siblings until I was four years old. In 1589 they put me in the convent of San Sebastián el Antiguo, in said town, which belongs to Dominican nuns, with my aunt Doña Ursula de Unzá y Sarasti, my mother's cousin and the abbess of that convent; there I was raised until I was fifteen, when the matter of my profession came up.

When I was almost at the end of my year of the novitiate, I had a quarrel with a professed nun named Doña Catalina de Aliri who, being a widow, had professed and entered the convent. She was strong and I but a girl; she slapped me, and I resented it. On the night of March 18, 1600, the eve of St. Joseph, the convent arose at midnight for Matins. I went into the choir and found my aunt kneeling there; she called me over, gave me the key to her cell, and told me to bring her prayer book. I went to get it. I unlocked [the cell] and took it, and, seeing all the keys to the convent hanging from a nail, I left the cell open and gave my aunt her key and the prayer book. The nuns were already in the choir and had solemnly begun Matins; at the first lesson I went up to my aunt and asked her permission to withdraw, as I was feeling ill. My aunt put her hand to my forehead and said, "Go lie down." I left the choir, took a lamp, and went to my aunt's cell; there I took a pair of scissors, thread, and a needle; I took some coins (*reales de a ocho*) that were lying there and took the convent keys and left. I went along opening doors and shutting them behind me, and at the final one left my scapulary and went out into the street, which I had never seen, with no idea which way to turn or where to go. I don't remember where I went, but I came on a stand of chestnut trees that was outside [of town] but close behind the convent. There I hid, and spent three days designing, fitting, and cutting out clothes. I made myself a pair of breeches from a blue cloth petticoat I was wearing, and from an underskirt of coarse green wool, a sleeved doublet and leggings; I left the habit there because I didn't know what to do with it. I cut off my hair, which I threw away, and on the third night, since I wanted to get away from there, I left for parts unknown, slogging over roads and skirting villages until I came to Vitoria, which is about twenty leagues from San Sebastián, on foot, weary and without having eaten anything but plants I found along the way.

I entered Vitoria with no idea where to stay. A few days later I met Dr. Don Francisco de Cerralta, a professor there, who, without knowing me, took me in with no difficulty and gave me some clothes. He was married to a cousin of my mother's, as I found out later, but I did not reveal who I was. I was with him for about three months, during which time, as he saw that I read Latin well, he liked me more and wanted to educate me, but when I refused he insisted and even laid hands on me. When that happened I made up my mind to leave him, and did so. I took some of his money, agreed to pay twelve *reales* to a muleteer who was leaving for Valladolid, forty-five leagues away, and departed with the latter.

When I got to Valladolid, where the Court was at that time, I soon got a position as a page to Don Juan de Idiáquez, the king's secretary, who clothed me well. There I called myself Francisco Loyola, and was very comfortable for seven months. At the end of that time, while I was standing in the doorway one evening with a fellow page, my father arrived and asked us if Señor Don Juan was at home.

My comrade said he was. My father said to let him know that he was there, and the page went upstairs while I stayed with my father; we said nothing to each other, and he did not recognize me. The page came back and said that he should go upstairs, so up he went and I behind him. Don Juan came out on the staircase and, embracing him, said, "Señor Captain, what a welcome visit!" My father spoke in such a way that the Señor knew he was annoyed, so Don Juan sent away another visitor, then came back and they sat down. He asked what was the matter. My father told how that girl of his had left the convent and the search for her had brought him to that region. . . .

I, when I heard my father's conversation and feelings, withdrew and went to my room. I took my clothes and left, taking with me some eight doubloons which I happened to have, and went to a tavern; I slept there that night, and heard a muleteer say that he was leaving for Bilbao in the morning. I came to terms with him and we left the next day; with no idea as to what to do or where to go, I simply let myself be borne by the wind like a feather. . . .

After I got out, I went to Estella, in Navarre, which I think is about twenty leagues away. I reached Estella, where I became the page of Don Carlos de Arellano, who belonged to the order of Santiago, in whose house and service I remained for two years, well treated and well attired. Afterward, for no other reason than my fancy, I left that comfortable position and went to my native San Sebastián, where I, a well-dressed dandy, spent some time without anyone recognizing me. One day I went to mass at my convent, the same service my mother attended, and saw that she looked at me without recognizing me; when mass was over, some nuns called me over to the choir, but I pretended not to understand, paid them many compliments and left. This was well into the year 1603.

From there I went to . . . Sanlúcar. There I found Captain Miguel de Echarreta, another Basque, who commanded a tender to the galleons under General Don Luis Fernández de Córdoba, part of Don Luis Fajardo's armada, which was sailing for Punta de Araya. I signed on as a cabin boy in Captain Esteban Eguiño's galleon. He was my uncle, my mother's cousin, and today lives in San Sebastián. I went aboard, and we left Sanlúcar on Holy Monday in the year 1603.

Chapter 2. *She leaves Sanlúcar for Punta Araya, Cartagena, Nombre de Dios, and Panama*

As I was new to the job, I had some difficulties on the voyage. Without knowing who I was, my uncle was kind to me and thought very highly of me; when he heard where I was from, and my parents' fictitious name, I had in him a great protector. When we got to Punta Araya, we came upon a small enemy force entrenched on the shore, and our fleet drove it away. We finally reached Cartagena de las Indias, and were there eight days.

I had my name taken off the list as cabin boy, and went into the service of the said Captain Eguiño, my uncle. From there we went to Nombre de Dios, where we stayed for nine days; many of our men died, which made us leave there very quickly.

When the silver was already aboard and everything was ready for our return voyage to Spain, I played a major trick on my uncle, making off with five hundred of his pesos. At ten at night, when he was asleep, I went on deck and told the sentries that the captain was sending me ashore on an errand. As they knew me, they let me pass with no trouble and I jumped ashore, but they never saw me again. An hour later they fired the departure gun and weighed anchor, ready to sail.

When the fleet had left, I took employment with Captain Juan de Ibarra, the agent for the Panama treasury, who is still alive today. Four to six days later we left for Panama, where he lived and where I stayed with him for about three months. He did not treat me well, for he was miserly, and I had to spend all the money I had lifted from my uncle until I had not a penny left; thereupon I departed in order to look for better employment elsewhere.

When I looked around I found Juan de Urquiza there, a merchant from Trujillo, and reached an agreement with him; things went well for me with him, and we were in Panama three months.

Chapter 5. *She leaves Trujillo for Lima*

Having left Trujillo for Lima and having gone more than eighty leagues, I entered the city of Lima, capital of the prosperous realm of Peru. . . .

I gave my letter to Diego de Solarte, a very wealthy merchant who is now chief consul of Lima and to whom Juan de Urquiza had recommended me; he immediately took me into his home with great courtesy and kindness, and a few days later entrusted his shop to me, assigning me a salary of six hundred pesos a year, and there I did my job much to his satisfaction and pleasure.

At the end of nine months he told me that it was time to make my living else-where, and the reason for this was that there were two young girls in his house, his wife's sisters, with whom I used to play and romp about, especially with one who showed a decided liking for me. And one day, while I was in the drawing room with my head in her lap and caressing her legs, while she was combing my hair, he hap-pened to look in through the grille and see us, and heard her say to me that I should go to Potosí to get some money and we would be married. He withdrew, soon after that summoned me, asked me to explain myself, discharged me, and I left.

I found myself unemployed and very out of favor. At that time six companies of men were being assembled to go to Chile; I went to one of them and enlisted as a soldier, for which I immediately received eighty pesos in wages. My employer Diego de Lasarte, who found out about it, was very sorry, for it seemed that he had not wanted it to come to this. He offered to intercede with the officers so that they would take me off the muster roll and return the money I had been given, but I refused, telling him that I had a taste for roving and seeing the world. Finally, having been assigned to the company of Captain Gonzalo Rodriguez, whose camp-master was Diego Bravo de Sarabia, I left Lima in a detachment of sixteen hundred men for the city of Concepción, which is five hundred forty leagues from Lima.

Chapter 6. *She arrives in Concepción, Chile, and finds her brother. She goes to Paicabí and, while participating in the battle of Valdivia, captures a standard. She returns to Concepción and kills two men and her own brother.*

It took us twenty days traveling time to get to the port of Concepción. It's a fair-sized city, with the title of noble and loyal, and has a bishop. Because of the scarcity of people in Chile, we were well received. Soon an order came from the governor, Alonso de Ribera, that we should disembark, and it was brought by his secretary, Captain Miguel de Erauso. As soon as I heard his name I was delighted and saw that he was my brother; even though I didn't know him, nor had seen him—because he left San Sebastián for these parts when I was two years old—I had had news of him, but not of his whereabouts. He took the list of soldiers, read it off, and asked each one his name and place of origin; when he got to me and heard my name and place of birth, he threw down the pen, embraced me, and asked many questions about his father and mother and siblings, and about his beloved Catalina, the nun. I answered everything as best I could, without betraying my identity, nor he guessing it. He went through the list, and when he finished he took me to his home for dinner and I sat down to eat. He told me that the garrison at Paicabí to which I was assigned was a terrible place for soldiers and that he would speak to the governor to have me trans-ferred. During the meal he went over to see the governor, taking me along. He re-ported on the recent arrivals, and asked as a favor that a young lad from his part of the country be transferred to his company, for since his departure he had come across no others from there. The governor had me come in, and when he saw me, I don't know for what reason, he said that he could not transfer me. My brother was upset and left, but a short while later the governor called my brother back again and told him that things could be the way he wanted them.

And so, when the troops left, I stayed with my brother as his soldier, eating at his table for almost three years without having him guess a thing. A few times I accompanied him to his mistress's house; afterward I went a few other times without him, and he found out and took offense and told me not to go back. He spied on me, and caught me at it again; he waited for me when I came out, and whipped me with a belt, injuring my hand. I was forced to defend myself. When he heard the altercation Captain Francisco de Aillón showed up and made peace, but I had to slip into [the church of] San Francisco because I feared the governor, [known to be] a severe man, as he proved to be in this instance, although my brother interceded. Ultimately he banished me to Paicabí; there was no recourse but to go, and I stayed there for three years.

Chapter 20. *She goes to Guamanga, and what happened to her there, until she reveals her identity to the bishop*

I got to Guamanga and went to an inn. . . . I went to look at the city, and liked it, as it had handsome buildings, the best I had seen in Peru. I found three monasteries (Franciscan, Mercedarian, and Dominican), a convent and a hospital, many Indian and Spanish residents, [and] a wonderful climate for settling this plain, neither hot nor cold. There are great harvests of wheat, wine, fruits, and grain; a fine church with three prebendaries, two canons, and a saintly bishop: an Augustinian friar [named] Don Agustín de Carvajal, who people said had been there since 1612, and who was my salvation, though he was taken from me by his sudden death in 1620.

I was there for a few days, and my ill luck would have it that I sometimes visited a gaming house. One day when I was there, the magistrate, Don Baltasar de Quiñones, entered; he looked at me, and as he did not recognize me, asked me where I was from. I said I was Basque. He said, "Where have you come from just now?" I answered, "Cuzco." He hesitated a moment while observing me, and said, "You're under arrest." I said, "Fine with me," drew my sword and retreated toward the door. He shouted for help in the king's name, and I found the door so blocked that I was unable to leave. I drew a three-barreled pistol, got away and disappeared, finding refuge in the house of a friend I had made there. The magistrate thereupon seized my mule and some other trifles I had left in the inn. I spent a few days hiding, having discovered that my friend was a Basque. Meanwhile there was no word of the matter, nor did I feel that the authorities were doing anything about it, but it still seemed a good idea to us for me to move to another place, for I had the same problem there as I did everywhere.

Determined to do this, I left one day at nightfall and, my misfortune would have it, immediately ran into two constables. They asked me, "Who goes there?" I replied, "A friend." They demanded my name, and I answered, "The devil," which I shouldn't have said. They began to lay hands on me, and I took out my sword, causing a great commotion. They cried out, "Help us in the name of the Law!" and people gathered. The magistrate came out of the bishop's house where he had been, more constables came. I found myself in a desperate situation, fired my pistol, and one went down. The brawl got bigger, and I found my Basque friend and some of his compatriots at my side. The magistrate shouted that I should be killed, and shots were exchanged on both sides, until the Bishop came out with four torchbearers, and stepped into the middle of the fray, directing his secretary Juan Bautista de Arteaga my way.

This man stepped up to me and said, "Ensign, give me your weapons."

I said, "Sir, there are many enemies here."

He said "Hand them over, for you are safe with me, and I give you my word that I will get you out of this, cost me what it may."

I said, "Exalted Sir, when I get into the church I will kiss your illustrious feet."

As I was saying this, four of the magistrate's slaves fell upon me and put me into a tight spot, pulling at me ferociously with no regard for His Lordship's presence, so that I had to defend myself and knock one of them down. The Bishop's secretary, with sword and shield, along with others of his retinue, came to my aid, shouting loudly and denouncing the disrespect shown the Bishop, after which the brawling abated somewhat. His Lordship seized my arm, took away my weapons, and, placing me at his side, took me with him into his house. He had a slight wound of mine dressed, and ordered some dinner brought to me; thereupon he told me to go to bed, locked me in, and took the key with him. The magistrate subsequently arrived, and, as I later heard, had a long conversation and high words with His Lordship concerning this matter.

In the morning about ten, His Lordship summoned me into his presence and asked me who I was and from where, who my parents were, and the whole course of my life: the hows and the whys of how I came to be there. I embellished my tale considerably, mixing in good advice, the perils of life, my fear of death and the consequences thereof, and how terrified I was lest the afterlife catch me unawares; I tried to calm and humble myself and to kneel before God, which made me feel very small. And when I saw what a saintly man he was, it seemed that I was already in the presence of God, so I took off my hat and said to him: "Sir, all I have just told Your Lordship is false. The truth is this: I am a woman, I was born in such-and-such a place, the daughter of so-and-so, and at a certain age was placed in a certain convent with my aunt so-and-so. There I grew up, put on the habit and was a novice. When I was about to profess, for such-and-such a reason I left. I went to such-and-such a place, took off my habit, put on other clothes, cut my hair, went hither and thither; went aboard ship, put into port, went to and fro, killed, wounded, cheated, ran around, and finally landed here, at the feet of Your Most Illustrious Lordship."

During the time it took to tell this story, which took until one o'clock, the saintly man was all ears: he listened to me without speaking or batting an eyelash, and when I finished he said not a word, but wept bitterly. Afterward he sent me off to rest and to eat something. He rang a bell, bid an old chaplain come, and sent me to his oratory where they put a table and a mattress for me, and locked me in, I lay down and slept. In the afternoon about four, the Bishop called me to him again, and spoke to me with great kindness of spirit, beseeching me to give thanks to God for the great favor He had shown me by making me see the path of perdition, which leads one straight to everlasting torment. He exhorted me to go back over my past and to make a proper confession, for I had already come a long way, and it would be easy for me.

After this God would lend His help so that we could figure out what to do next. In these and other matters the afternoon drew to a close. I withdrew, was given a good meal, and went to bed.

The next morning the Lord Bishop said Mass, which I attended, and afterward he gave thanks. He withdrew to have breakfast, and took me with him. He expounded on his sermon, and told me that mine was the most curious case of this sort he had heard in his life, and finally said, "But is it really true?"

I said, "Yes, Sir."

He replied, "Don't be affronted if its peculiar nature strains the imagination."

"Sir," I said, "it really is true and if Your Lordship wants to make sure by having me examined by some women, I am willing to do it."

He said, "I'm glad to hear you say that, and I agree."

I withdrew because it was his reception time. At noon I ate, then rested a bit, and in the afternoon about four, two matrons came in, examined me, and were convinced; later they swore before the Bishop that they had examined me to a sufficient degree to be sure and had found me as intact a virgin as the day I was born. His Lordship was touched, dismissed the women and had me sent for; in the presence of the chaplain, who had come with me, he stood up and tenderly embraced me, saying, "My daughter, now I believe what you told with no doubts whatsoever, and will henceforth believe anything you tell me. I respect you as one of the amazing people of this world, and promise to help you in any way I can, to take care of your needs, and to do that to serve God,"

He ordered me put in a suitable room, where I was comfortable and prepared my confession, which I made as soon as possible, and afterward His Lordship gave me communion. Apparently my story got around, and the number of people that came was huge; we were unable to keep them out, as much as I minded it, and His Lordship as well.

Finally, six days later, His Illustrious Lordship ordered me to go into the convent of the Poor Clares of Guamanga, as there was no other, and to put on the habit. His Lordship left his house with me at his side, surrounded by such a mob of people that I don't think there was anyone in the city who didn't come, and for that reason it took a long to get there. We finally got to the porter's lodge, because going to the church, as His Lordship had initially intended, was out of the question for it was completely full. The whole convent was there, bearing lit candles, and the abbess and senior nuns signed a document in which the convent promised to hand me over to the Bishop or a prelate who might succeed him, any time they gave the word. His Lordship embraced and blessed me, and I went in [to the convent]. I was escorted in procession to the choir, and prayed there. I kissed the lady abbess's hand, was embraced by and in turn embraced the other nuns; they then took me to a locutory where His Lordship awaited me. There he gave me good advice, and exhorted me to be a good Christian woman, to give thanks to Our Lord God and to make frequent use of the sacraments; His Lordship offered to come and administer them personally, as he indeed did many times, and generously offered me anything at all I might need. News of this event spread everywhere very quickly, and people who had seen me before, and people, both before and after, who heard my story all over the Indies, were amazed. In 1620, within five months, my saintly bishop suddenly died, and I felt his loss keenly. . . .

[*Catalina de Erauso goes to Lima and spends the next two years in a convent there, until word arrives from Spain that she was never a professed nun, and can therefore leave the convent and take off her nun's habit. She goes to Spain and presents herself before King Philip IV, who grants her a life pension of 800 escudos; she sees him again in Barcelona, having been robbed along the way, and he gives her another gift of money. She subsequently travels to Italy to see the pope.*]

Chapter 25. *She goes from Barcelona to Genoa and thence to Rome*

. . . I left Genoa for Rome. I kissed the foot of His Holiness Urban VIII and told him succinctly, and as best I could all about my life, adventures, gender, and virginity. His Holiness appeared to be astonished thereby, and graciously gave me permission to continue to lead my life dressed as a man, urging me to lead an honest life from now on, and to refrain from offending my fellow man, reminding me of God's justice with reference to His commandment "Thou shalt not kill." My case became well known there, and I was constantly surrounded by a throng of illustrious persons: princes, bishops, and cardinals. Every door was open to me, so that in the month and a half that I was in Rome, rarely a day went by that I was not invited and made much of by princes. One Friday in particular, on specific request by the Roman Senate, I was invited and entertained by some gentlemen who entered my name in a book as a Roman citizen. On St. Peter's Day, June 29, 1626, I was taken to St. Peter's chapel, where I saw the cardinals and the usual ceremonies they hold on that day. All or most of them were extremely courteous and kind, and many spoke to me. In the afternoon, while three cardinals stood around me, one of them, Cardinal Magalón, told me that I had no other flaw than being a Spaniard, to which I replied, "It seems to me, Sir, keeping in mind the deference one owes your illustrious person, that it is the only good thing I have."

Notes

Introduction

1. One account states that of the 6,000 men of Spanish descent living in Lima, 2,500 had taken religious vows, and one in four women lived in the convent. See Galve, "Santa Rosa de Lima," 55, and Martin, *Daughters of the Conquistadores*, 176–180.

2. For a detailed study of these works, see Destefano, "Miracles and Monasticism," and Rubial, *La santidad controvertida*. Rivas, "Gran cosa es el buen ejemplo," and Ragon, "Libros de devoción," also examine publications records of saintly biographies.

3. "Desde que la Sierva de Dios entró en esta Cuidad tuvo a pares las armas, las del Emperador, que la ennoblecen, y las de Catharina, que la defienden; fue la Venerable Sierva de Dios, las armas mas eficaces de la Puebla pues tantas veces la defendio de los enemigos" (Ramos, "Dedicatoria," *De los prodigios*, Vol. 3).

4. "La Nueva España es una época en la que el arrobo de una monja, la milagrosa curación de un agonizante, el arrepentimiento de un penitenciado o los vaticinios de una beata, son más noticia que el alza en el precio de los oficios o la imposición de una alcabala; una época en que son de más momento los viajes al interior del alma que las expediciones a las Californias o a Filipinas. . . . El historiador que ignore esa jerarquía en los valores vitales de la época, podrá ofrecernos un relato documentado y exhaustivo, si se quiere, de los sucesos que la llenan, pero no penetrará en la cámara secreta de su acontecer más significativo" (quoted in dela Maza, *Catharina de San Juan*, introduction).

5. See Rivas's study, "Gran cosa es el buen ejemplo."

6. Santander y Torres, *Vida de María de S. Joseph*.

7. Ibid., unnumbered preliminary pages.

8. For more on the history of the Catholic saints, see Kieckhefer, "Imitators of Christ."

9. Teresa de Jesús, *Libro de la vida*, ch. 26.

10. For excellent studies of the history of confession in the Catholic Church, see Tambling, *Confession*; Tentler, *Sin and Confession*; and Zimmerman, "Confession and Autobiography."

11. For more on the new rules established, see Zimmerman, "Confession and Autobiography," 125–126, and Tentler, *Sin and Confession*, 99.

12. Zimmerman, in fact, studies the relationship between early modern autobiography and Catholic confession in "Confession," 124.

13. Slade, *St. Teresa of Avila*.

14. Greenspan, "Autohagiographical Tradition."

15. Alberro, *Inquisición y sociedad*, 168.

16. These are listed and described in "Nos los inquisidores," Edict of the Mexican Inquisition, 1621.

17. Burke, "Counter-Reformation Saint."

18. In the fourteenth and fifteenth centuries, nearly one in four saints were women, and most were mystics. See Bell and Weinstein, *Saints and Society*, 220.

19. Lerner, *Feminist Consciousness*; McNamara, *Sisters in Arms*; Petroff, *Visionary Literature*; Walker, *Vida de María de S. Joseph*.

20. Santander y Torres, "Prológo," *Vida de María de S. Joseph*.

21. Montero, *Sermón*, 21.

22. "Cuando se quitaron muchos libros de romance, que no se leyesen, yo sentí mucho, porque algunos me daban recreación leerlos, y yo no podía ya, por dejarlos en latin, me dijo el Señor: 'No tengas pena, que Yo te daré libro vivo'" (Teresa de Jesús, *Libro de landa*, ch. 26).

23. There are a few other well-known religious women, whom for reasons of space I have excluded from this study: the Colombian mystic Madre Castillo; the mystic Mexican author Maria Ana Agueda; America's other female saint, Mariana de Quito; and Puebla's beloved nun María de Jesús. I mention these women in passing when they relate to the women studied here.

Chapter 1

My thanks to Jodi Bilinkoff, Mary Giles, and Carla Pestana for their valuable suggestions on this chapter, and to Frank Graziano who helped me locate key bibliographical items. Translations were provided by Jodi Bilinkoff.

1. See Meléndez, *Festiva Pompa*, 20r–31r. For a twentieth-century narrative description of the event, see Wuffarden and Pérez, "Esplendor," 29.

2. Loayza, *Vida de Santa Rosa*, chaps. 27–29.

3. See Meléndez (*Festiva Pompa*) for more information on the brotherhoods, 29r; Mujica Pinilla describes the popularity of her portrait in "El ancla de Santa Rosa," 156.

4. Getino, *La patrona de América*. Also of note are Vargas Urgarte's *La flor de Lima*, a compendium of other biographies, and Angulo's *Santa Rosa*, an extensive bibliography of published sources.

5. While Graziano ("Una verdad ficticia") focuses on the role and significance of her "sacrificial body," Galve's "Santa Rosa de Lima," and Iwasaki's "Mujeres" argue that as a mature colonial city, Lima needed both a saint (Rosa) and scapegoats (Rosa's friends tried for *alumbradismo*) to establish its Christian identity. For his part, Millones (*Una partecita*) sees Rosa as being transformed into a symbol for Andean populations. See also Martínez Hampe, *Santidad*, and Mujica Pinilla, "El ancla." Others, such as Brading (*The First America*, 369), suggest that Rosa's popularity and success stemmed from people associating her with the Virgen del Rosario, who had miraculously appeared during one of Pizarro's battles.

6. See the commemorative work edited by Araoz et al., *Santa Rosa de Lima y su tiempo.*

7. For more information, see the essay by Wuffarden and Pérez, "Esplendor."

8. Mujica Pinilla, *Santa Rosa*, 54.

9. Toribio de Mogrovejo (1535–1606) and Francisco Solano (1549–1602) were beatified in the 1670s and canonized in 1726. Two other Dominicans, Juan de Macías (1585–1645) and Martín de Porres (1579–1639) were beatified in the nineteenth century. Martín de Porres was canonized in 1962. Galve lists other aspirants and venerables; more than sixty hagiographies were published during the period. (Galve, "Santa Rosa," 62–63).

10. My portrait of Rosa is based on the two *procesos*, and the biographies by González de Acuña (*Rosa mística*), Leonard Hansen (*Vida admirable*), Pedro Loayza (*Vida de Santa Rosa*), and Luis Millones (*Una partecita*).

11. Loayza (*Vida*, chap. 7) says that Rosa memorized the saint's life story and that Catherine became Rosa's teacher in a spiritual path centered around imitating Christ's suffering. Another biographer also describes Rosa's close modeling of Catherine's life; See Acuña, *Rosa mística*, 158. Mujica Pinilla ("El ancla," 43, 74) suggests that Rosa probably read Fray Fernando del Castillo's edition of Catherine's *Vida* (Valdecebro, 1669). Hansen (*Vida*, 100v) also notes that Rosa read and imitated the life of the New Spanish hermit, Gregorio López (1542–1596).

12. Millones studies this influential period of Rosa life in "Los Sueños" in *Una partecita*.

13. Accounts disagree on whether Rosa wanted to become a nun. She had three opportunities to enter a convent. While Loayza (*Vida*, 23), maintains that Rosa wanted to enter the Convent of Santa Clara, other accounts say she refused to do so because of a vision in which Catherine of Siena prophesied the founding of a Dominican convent in Lima. See Mujica Pinilla, "El ancla," 64.

14. *Proceso ordinario*, fols. 138–139.

15. "Desde sus tiernos años usó camas penitentes. La primera que tuvo fue de tres maderos gruesos, uno más que otro, y el que le servía de cabecera tenía un hueco donde encajaba la cabeza, de suerte que está el cuerpo quebrantado o como un burro y cuando se levantaba ponía estos maderos debajo de la cama. Otra hizo la misma santa con siete palos, entretejidos en forma de barbacoas, con unos cuernos de vaca, los cuales ponía sobre una tabla, y entre las junturas tenía muchos tiestos de botija puntiagudos, sobre los cuales se acostaba, no para dormir, sino para padecer. La tabla servía para que los tiestecillos estuvieran en pie y no se cayeran hacia abajo y los palos, para que con el cuerpo no se ladeasen. En esta cama durmió quince o diez y seis años" (Loayza, *Vida*, 14–15).

16. "Todas las noches se ensangrentava las espaldas tan dura y cruelmente que corría la sangre por las paredes, suelo, y vestido, creia la inocente doncella que todos estos castigos merecia por sus pecados. Demas destos conpadecida de las calmidades publicas procurava con estas penitencias a imitacion a su Maestra [Catherine], aplaca la ira de Dios, y mitigar su justicia, por lo qual unas vezes por los trabajos de toda la Sancta Madre Iglesia, otras por las angustias y peligros que padecia la republica, heria a su cuerpo, haciendo de si propia un sacrificio cruento sin alguna clemencia, para alcanzar de este modo la clemencia del Cielo, y curar las llagas comunes con las propias" (Hansen, *Vida*, 37).

17. "'Oh, quién fuese hombre, sólo para ocuparme en la conversión de las almas,' y así exhortaba a todos los predicadores con quien tenía conocimiento, que convirtiesen muchas almas, y que fuesen a reducir a Dios a los idólatras de esta tierra. Y que pusiesen en esto el blanco de sus estudios" (Loayza, *Vida*, 93).

18. "Ya la salud de la dicha benidita Rosa estava tan gastada y su natural con tantos achaques y dolores que no podía travajar en sus lavores cosa considerable ni ayudar a sus padres por aquella via como avia hecho en el discurso de su vida" (*Proceso ordinario*). For a transcription of Maza's lengthy testimony about Rosa's life in the *Proceso ordinario* and *Proceso apostólico*, see Millones, *Una partecita*, 147–209. A selection of this testimony has been translated into English, see Mills and Taylor, *Colonial Spanish America*, 194–202; a portion of this is reproduced here in Appendix A.

19. For example, María Luisa Melgarejo (*Proceso ordinario*, 28v.) testifies to having flown in an ecstatic state.

20. Testimony was recorded in 1670; see Martínez Hampe, *Santidad*, 70–71.

21. For an excellent chronology of the canonization process, see ibid., chaps. 3–4.

22. *Proceso ordinario*. The 1617 *proceso* was begun by the prelates of Lima. The original is at the Convento de Santa Rosa in Lima. I consulted the copies at the Lilly Library, Indiana University–Bloomington (a nineteenth-century copy) and the Secret Archives of the Vatican (a contemporary, notarial copy). All citations are from the Lilly Library copy. For more information on the *proceso*, see Martínez Hampe, *Santidad*, chap. 2.

23. A list of the witnesses is contained in the *proceso* itself. See Martínez Hampe's transcription of the list and his study in *Santidad*, chap. 2. Loayza's *Vida* was not published until much later. I use the 1965 Lima edition by the Dominican Fray Carlos Aníbal Álvarez, which Frank Graziano graciously lent to me.

24. See Mujica Pinilla, "El ancla," 177, and Martínez Hampe, *Santidad*, chap. 3. La Valle (*Las promesas ambiguas*, 180–185) explains that two of Rosa's biographers, Bilbao and Meléndez, played important roles in the Dominican schism. In addition, while the order presented five Dominican candidates for sainthood, they were only allowed to promote one; Martínez Hampe (*Santidad*, chap. 2) also cites the astronomical costs of the canonization process as another reason for it being tabled. See also Iwasaki, "Mujeres," 581n1.

25. For more on the role of the Inquisitor General, see Mujica Pinilla, "El ancla," 63.

26. The *alumbrados* of sixteenth-century Spain were mystics who sought direct connection to God without the aid of the institutional church; they were accused of rejecting the sacraments of the church and were condemned by the Inquisition as heretics.

27. The 1617 *Proceso ordinario* was invalid because it had not been initiated by Rome. The original copies of the 1630 *Proceso apostólico* are at the Archbishop's Archives in Lima, Peru, and at the Secret Archive of the Vatican. See Martínez Hampe (1998), chap. 2, for a complete list of the witnesses and their biographical information. Twelve of the 147 witnesses also testified in the 1617 *proceso*.

28. It was translated into Italian, English, French, and Spanish; Domingo Angulo (*Santa Rosa*) lists many of these editions. The *procurador* for Rosa's canonization, Antonio González de Acuña, wrote a compendium (*Rosa mística*) based on Hansen's work, but it was not published until 1671. In a lively narrative, he frequently quotes Rosa and other mystic saints.

29. Medina's *Biblioteca extranjera de Santos* reveals Rosa's popularity as the subject of hagiographic biographies. There are more than forty pages of *vidas* about her; Saint Mariana de Quito has only twelve pages of material; Bishop Juan Palafox y Mendoza has only fifteen.

30. For a full discussion of Rosa's image and icongraphic tradition, see Mujica Pinilla, "El ancla," 54–214. Others have studied Rosa's influence on Andean populations. Ross ("Santa Rosa," 187) argues that Rosa became associated early on with "fuerzas telúricas, cósmicas, astrales." Millones (*Una partecita*, chap. 4) traces her role in Andean traditions that still take place in August every year.

31. Meléndez, *Festiva*, 40r.

32. La Valle (*Las promesas*) discusses the important role of Dominicans in the criollo movement, with Rosa as perhaps their greatest symbolic success. For a history of this process with respect to Rosa, see Mujica Pinilla, "El ancla," 158–171.

33. See especially, Oviedo y Herrera, Cantos I and III, *Vida*.

34. "Fragancias de buenos exemplos. . . han convertido en parayso de delicias santas esta selva antes inculta de nuestra Meridional America" (quoted in Ribero Leal, *Oración*).

35. Meléndez, "Al lector," *Festiva pompa*.

36. See Kieckhefer, "Imitators of Christ."

37. In 1568, Pope Pius V had purged the breviary of many legendary saints and instituted other measures to reevaluate sainthood. Pope Urban VIII added to these changes with his 1625 and 1634 rulings. See Burke, "How to Be a Counter Reformation Saint," 46.

38. For a more thorough discussion, see Kieckhefer, "Imitators of Christ," 24.

39. In the first *proceso* there are between twenty-seven and thirty-two questions asked of witnesses. Questions 1 to 7 deal with Rosa's secular life: her birth, family, and early call to God before becoming a third-order Dominican. Questions 8 to 22 examine Rosa's life as a religious woman: her virtues, asceticism, prayer, and special communication with God. Most of these questions bear directly on the theological and cardinal virtues, as well as the vows of a third-order Dominican. Questions 23 to 26 treat her last illness, death, and the

beginning of her cult and miracles. Question 27 certifies that all testimony is true and freely given. The second *proceso* generally asked twenty-four to twenty-seven questions. Another twelve were asked of some witnesses and dealt with miracles and intercessions and the reliability of the witness. For a more thorough study of these *procesos*, see Martínez Hampe, *Santidad*, chap. 2. For a transcription of the questions, names of witnesses, and selected testimony, see López, "The Roots of the Rose," appendixes.

40. "No fue sacada su historia de Relaciones apocrifas faltas de peso, y autoridad, sino de los procesos, que por mandato de la sede Apostólica se hicieron en Lima; para ponerla en el Catalogo de los santos" (Juan de Paz, "Presentación," in Hansen *Vida*, unnumbered preliminary pages).

41. Rosa's first biographer, Loayza (*Vida*, 30–31), simply introduces the questioning thusly: "Dios abrió el entendimiento a un singular varón seglar, doctor en medicina, excelente filósofo y buen teólogo, y en su teología mística admirable por tener esta ciencia no sólo con estudio, sino también de experiencia... Como se verá del examen que se sigue. Preguntóle el dicho Doctor: '¿Y de qué tiempo a esta parte se había dado a la oración?' Respondió, que de edad de cinco años." Nothing is said about it being conducted with an inquisitor present.

42. *Proceso ordinario*, first witness, Juan del Castillo.

43. For more on this examination and its representation in hagiographies, see Mujica Pinilla, "El ancla," 108–13.

44. "...para que por su sanctidad conste" (Hansen, *Vida*, 91).

45. "Se espantó con las respuestas de una niña sencilla y sin letras, quando preguntada del secreto Mysterio de la Sanctissima Trinidad... que tantas cosas escondidas de los sabios, y prudentes, revelaba y descubria a los humildes, pequeñuelos, y sin letras... parecia a Lorenzana que via no a una muger, sino a un antiguo professor de una y otra theologia" (ibid., 99–100).

46. "Se obrava con espiritu de Dios, que estava llena del don de sabiduria, que se governaba con ciencia infusa del Cielo" (ibid., 100v).

47. For a full study of Castillo's brush with the Inquisition, see Mujica Pinilla, "El ancla," 119–136. Quotation is from p. 117.

48. "Pues es mero seglar y no theólogo"; "por aturdido y es el zensor de todas las cosas de espíritu, con que quieren engañar a muchas mujercillas viendo que en otras es mercanzía segura ha escrito un libro de revelaciones propias y quatro quadernos sobre el compendio y rebelaciones de la madre Theresa" (quoted in ibid).

49. The sentence is as follows: "Habiendo visto todos los escritos, libro y quadernos del Doctor Juan del Castillo médico en esta ciudad de los Reyes, familiar del Santo Oficio-nos parece que contienen mui grandes disparates en rigor theológico y místico, y algunas contradicciones manifiestas en materia grave, y modo de hablar duro escabrosso fuera del rigor de la theología escholástica y mística-y contienen algunas proposiciones temerarias y... muchas rebelaciones ridículas, visiones indignas... y considerado las qualidades y circun-stancias de la persona melancólica, assí por el natural como por los muchos trabajos que tiene ymaginatiba [*sic*] y con falta de sueño y comida como él mismo confiessa en estos escritos, y la mucha edad, y ha leído y mal entendido doctores, theólogos y místicos, y es persona que affecta espíritu de oración-juzgamos que todas sus porposiciones y rebealciones son debaneos procedidos de las cirunstancias dichas... de suerte que aunque el dicho libro y quadernos contengan proposiziones... damnables... por colligirse del mismo libro y de las explica-ciones que da... nos parece que tiene más necesidad de medios medizinales para reparar la naturaleza y flaqueza de cabeza que de otros que merescan condemnación" (Edict of the Inquisition, 24 April 1624, as cited in ibid., 118–119).

50. "Su vida era espejo de virtud" (Hansen, *Santa Rosa*, 91v).

51. See Iwasaki's important article "Mujers al borde"on Malgarejo and the other women following Rosa. He quotes the Inquisition's notice that the notebooks had been falsified because of her confessor's censorship (p. 96).

52. See Mujica Pinilla, "El ancla," 58–61 and 202n28.

53. Although punishments were not severe, Galve and Iwasaki have read this search for *alumbrados* among Rosa's circle as a smokescreen to deflect negative attention from Rosa's own possible heterodoxy and to improve her chances for sainthood. Neither critic, however, addresses the fact that Rosa's close connection to people examined for hetero- doxy might also implicate her. As Mujica Pinilla notes (ibid., 59), Rosa had the same confessor as one of the women and exchanged letters with another. He also notes that many wrote spiritual notebooks (pp. 58–62). For more on the trials, see Galve, "Santa Rosa"; Iwasaki, "Mujeres al borde"; and Medina, *Historia*, 27–32.

54. See the reproduction of the letters in Angulo, *Santa Rosa*, 334–339. See Getino, *La patrona*, for reproductions of the collages and some of the poetry and prayers. The *procesos* also record transcriptions of reported speech—that is, of the witness recalling Rosa's speech and citing it in the first person. One such example is the testimony by Juan del Castillo that cites Rosa's words during one of her raptures, as quoted in Getino, *La patrona*, 52–55. The *proceso* also includes a list of hers, given to Gonzalo de la Maza, who had it transcribed in his testimony (it deals with the proper dressing of the Christ child), as cited in Millones, *Una partecita*, 188–189.

55. "Como en varias ocasiones tengo escrito para gloria de Dios; A las mercedes q he escrito así en los cuadernos como. . . " (Rosa de Santa Mária, *Las Mercedes*, f. 1).

56. The *proceso* includes the requests for Rosa's "papeles y particulas de sus habitos, huesos, o otras cosas tocantes a su persona," as well as the replies that state that the material had already been turned over (*Proceso ordinario*, fol. 217–218). The request came from the Dominican Fray Luis de Bilbao, who was both one of Rosa's confessors and a censor for the Inquisition. Iwasaki ("Mujeres," 594–595) also discusses the possibility of an autobiography having been written. Rosa herself mentions her notebooks when explaining her collages; see Getino, *La patrona*, 51, and Mujica Pinilla, "El ancla," 96. Wuffarden and Pérez ("Esplendor," 27–28) cite the records that discuss the censoring of her book of religious poetry.

57. In 1624, Fray Gabriel Zarate, prior of the Dominican monastery, reports turning Rosa's possessions and papers over to the Inquisition (letter appended to the *Proceso ordinario*, fol. 217).

58. Archivo Histórico de la Nación (Madrid), Inquisición de Lima, Leg. 353, fol. 167 r.v., as quoted by Wuffarden and Pérez, "Esplendor," 27–28. My research at the Archivo General de la Nación and the Secret Archives of the Vatican turned up no such autobio- graphical documents.

59. Several Peruvian scholars made this suggestion at a recent conference organized by Frank Graziano and held at the John Carter Brown Library, Providence, Rhode Island (May 1999).

60. "Carta de Santa Rosa de Santa María al P. Fr. Gerónimo Bautista," in Angulo, *Santa Rosa*, 237–239. Rosa's two other letters are a note of thanks and a discussion of a spiritual topic.

61. See Getino's reproduction of these in *La patrona*, 15–55 and 73. The reproduction in this chapter is courtesy of Ramon Mujica Pinilla and taken from "El ancla," 104–105.

62. Hansen, "Niñez, natural, educación y voto de viriginidad," *Vida*, chap. 2.

63. "Cosa es de maravillar que en cuerpo tan flaco, y consumido con tantos ayunos, hubiesse lugar donde recibir azotes, y sangre que derramar con ellos. No obstante era tan

grande el deseo, y cuydado que Rosa tenia de castigar su cuerpo que fue necesario que sus confessores le fuessen a la mano en esto" (ibid., 43r, 37r).

64. "Déjame la avecilla, / huye el veloz cantor, / mas siempre está conmigo / mi dulce Redentor. / Pajarillo ruiseñor, / alabemos al Señor; / tú alaba a tu Creador, / yo canto a mi Salvador (as cited in Getino, *La patrona*, 66; also see Loayza, *Vida*, chap. 19).

65. "Oh, Jesús de mi alma! / Qué bien pareces / entre Flores y Rosas / y Olivas verdes" (as cited in *Proceso ordinario*, 45r).

66. Other prayers attributed to her included "Alabanzas de Dios," which is also quoted in the *proceso*, and in *Actos de contrición*. Several of these were published with some frequency in the latter part of the seventeenth century and the beginning of the eighteenth. See, for example, *Exercicio angelico* (1723) held at the Lilly Library, Bloomington, Indiana.

67. "Favores que recibió N.M. y Patrona Santa Rosa de Santa María, como lo significan estos escritos de su letra y puño" (Rosa de Santa Mariá, *Las meredes*, 69). Getino (*La patrona*, 18) suggests that this note may have been written by a nun at the convent. More typically, confessors made written comments in religious women's texts. For other reproductions of the *Mercedes*, see the dissertation theses by Ibañez-Murphy, "¿Primera escritora?," and López, "The Roots of the Rose."

68. "Lo que remito a Nuestro Padre como a mi único Padre espiritual, para que corrija mis yerros, y enmiende lo que en dicha obra faltare por mi ignorancia. Muchos yerros y faltas hallará por ser explicada de mi mano y si se hallare que es bueno, será sólo por haber sido las mercedes de Dios" (ibid., 69).

69. "Confieso con toda verdad en presencia de dios que todas las mercedes que he escrito así en los cuadernos como esculpinadas y retratadas en estos dos papeles ni las he visto ni leído en libro alguno, solo í obradas en esta pecadora de la poderosa mano del Señor en cuyo libro leo que es Sabiduría Eterna" (ibid., 69).

70. "Estas tres mercedes recibí de la piedad divina antes de la gran tribulasión que padecí en la confesión general por mandado de aquel confesor que me dio tanto en que merecer depués de haber hecho la confesión general y de haber padesido cerca de dos años de grandes penas, tribulaciones, desconsuelos, desamparos, tentaciones, batallas con los demonios, calunias de confesores y de las criaturas. Enfermedades, dolores, calentura y para decir lo todo las mayores penas de infierno que se puedan imaginar en estos años últimos habrá unos cinco años que recibo del Señor las mercedes que en ese medio pliego de papel he puesto, por inspiración del corazón aunque indigno" (ibid., 70).

71. See Weber's important work on the topic, *Teresa of Avila and the Rhetorics of Femininity*.

72. See Mujica Pinilla's quotes from biographies and *procesos* in "El ancla," 114–115.

73. For a list of Rosa's confessors, see Iwasaki, "Mujeres," 591; Vargas Urgarte, *La flor de Lima*, 27; and Mujica Pinilla, "El ancla," 51.

74. One scholar notes Hildegard of Bingen's illuminated works about her visionary life and John of the Cross's sketches of his visions, but neither of these authors place word and image in an intimate emblematic relationship. See Ibañez-Murphy, "¿Primera escritora?", 128–134. See also the studies of heart imagery in the late fifteenth and early sixteenth century in Hamburger, *Nuns as Artists*.

75. Catherine of Siena used the imagery of the ladder as well; see Noffke's introduction to her translation of Catherine of Siena's works, in *The Dialogue*.

76. See Ibsen's (*Women's Spiritual Autobiography*, 102, 114) work on the link between vision, meditation, and prayer in this period, and the popularity of the heart as an emblem. For more on emblem books in this period, see Campa's *Emblemata Hispanica*, a study of Spanish emblem books.

77. In *Vida,* chap. 14, Hansen notes Castillo's use of Paz's work.

78. For more on this topic, see Astell's study, *The Song of Songs.*

79. "Herido con flecha de amor"; "eferma de amores, que muero de ella"; "harpón de fuego"; "dardo de amor divino"; "la vida es cruz"; "deposorio espiritual" (Rosa de Santa María, Steps 5–14). For a more complete discussion of these steps and hearts, see López, "The Roots of the Rose," 544–554; Getino, *La patrona,* 15–55; Mujica Pinilla, "El ancla," 98–107; and Ibañez-Murphy, "¿Primera escritora?", 182–205.

80. "Arrobo. Embriaguez en la bodega. Secretos del amor Divino. ¡Oh dichosa unión, abrazo estrecho con Dios!" (Rosa de Santa Mária, Step 15).

81. "Teólogo muy hecho y consumado" (Cited in Pinilla Mujica, "El ancla," 113–114).

82. For more about the politics of sanctity and the careful representation of Teresa's life and works, see Alhgren, *Teresa of Avila,* and Slade, *Teresa.*

83. Van Deusen, "Instituciones religiosas"; Iwasaki, "Mujeres."

84. "Hasta oy... aunque aviéndose levantado en esta dicha ciudad ciertas mujeres que se dezía trataban de espíritu lo qual paresció después no ser encaminado al servicio de Dios porque algunas fueron castigadas esas comunicaban a la dicha Soror Rossa por ventura para acreditar sus acciones y como se descubrió el pecado de aquellas se resfrió algo el crédito de la dicha Rossa... y después que cessó el ruydo y castigo a las dichas mugeres volvió a prevalecer el buen crédito de la dicha Soror Rossa" (Ramírez de Baldéz, *Proceso apostólico,* as cited in Mujica-Pinilla, "El ancla," 63).

85. See Scott, "Urban Spaces, Women's Networks," 64–105.

86. "Siendo para una Virgen el lugar mas apto la clausura de un monasterio" (Santander y Torres, *Sermón,* 4–6).

87. For more on the creation of Teresa as a saint, see the studies by Alghren, *Teresa of Avila,* and Bilinkoff, *The Avila of Saint Teresa.* Also see Scott ("Catherine of Sienna," 44), who argues that the Council of Trent successfully promoted Catharine of Siena as a model Counter-Reformation saint by altering certain biographical details.

Chapter 2

This chapter is based on my previously published article "Testimony for Canonization or Proof of Blasphemy? The New Spanish Inquisition and the Hagiographic Biography of Catarina de San Juan," published by the Johns Hopkins University Press (1999). I have revised several important elements: I include here an analysis of the third part of Ramos's work and have reworked my observations on the role of race and hagiography. My sincere gratitude goes to Grady Wray and Antonio Rubial for their help in locating archival material, and to Jodi Bilinkoff and Mary E. Giles for their useful suggestions in revising this manuscript.

1. The Cabildo's scribe writes a juridical testimony of the event: "Fue tan excessivo el consurso de gente de todos estados, y calidades, que con gravissima dificultad pude conseguir la entrada en dicha cassa." He goes on to list the high-ranking officials present at the event, "Dos testimonios juridicos," in Ramos, *De los prodigios,* vol. 3, 113–114.

2. Greenleaf, *Mexican Inquisition.*

3. When compared with its Spanish counterpart, the New Spanish Inquisition played a more passive role—mostly receiving *denuncias* without prosecuting a large percentage of cases because of the overwhelmingly large territory it had to cover and the relatively few subjects it had jurisdiction over. See Alberro, *La actividad del Santo Oficio,* 82–84.

4. For a general overview of the role of books and the Inquisition in New Spain, see Leonard's *Books of the Brave,* and the work edited by González Obregón, *Libros y libreros en el siglo XVI.*

5. Ramos, *De los prodigios . . .* , 3 vols.

6. Graxeda, *Compendio de la vida.*

7. For a more thorough historical sketch of her life story, see Morgan, "Saints, Biographers and Identity," chap. 5.

8. *Testamento* in Ramos, *De los prodigios,* vol. 3, 116.

9. For a fuller discussion of these biographies and their role in New Spanish society, see Rubial, *La santidad controvertida,* and Destefano, "Miracles and Monasticism."

10. Ramos goes so far as to say that María Jesús was Catarina's "spiritual twin" (*De los prodigios,* vol. 3, 110). For hagiographic biographies of these two nuns, see Salmerón, *De la vida de la venerable Madre Isabel de la Encarnación,* and Lemus, *Vida, birtudes, trabajos, fabores y milagros.*

11. "No podia Señor dedicarse el fin, y corona de esta obra sino a la Muy Illustre e Imperial Ciudad de la Puebla de los Angeles; porque si el grande Emperador Carlos V... la quiso ennoblecer con sus mismas armas... Desde que la Sierva de Dios entró en esta Cuidad tuvo a pares las armas, las del Emperador, que la ennoblecen, y las de Catharina, que la defienden; fue la Venerable Sierva de Dios, las armas mas eficaces de la Puebla pues tantas veces la defendio de los enemigos" (Ramos, "Dedicatoria," *De los prodigios,* vol. 3).

12. See, for example, the *vidas* of the Carmelite Indian woman Francesca de Miguel (cited in Rivas, "Gran cosa," 111); one studied by Lavrin in "Indian Brides," 232; the short sketches of several *indias* in the Convento of Jesús María, *El paraiso occidental* by Sigüenza y Góngora; and, of course, those in the *Las indias caciques de Corpus Christi,* edited by Muriel. A new study by Díaz, "Género, raza," examines this question further.

13. This is based on my own searches through catalogues of works published and a consultation with Antonio Rubial.

14. Destefano ("Miracles and Monasticism," 68) finds reference to its continued prohibition in a 1790 index of books that also includes all three volumes of Ramos's biography.

15. See Rubial, "Mariofanías" (17), in which he explains church doctrine regarding the different manifestations of the Virgin Mary.

16. "Mira esta blanca, y hermosa es Santa Inés; esotro hermosa, y blanca es Santa Catharina Martyr, esta trigueña eres tu. Tu eres la mas hermosa" (Aguilera, *Sermón,* 103).

17. As cited in the opening to the chapter: "No podia Señor dedicarse el fin, y corona de esta obra sino a la Muy Illustre e Imperial Ciudad de la Puebla de los Angeles; porque si el grande Emperador Carlos V... la quiso enoblecer con sus mismas armas añadiendoles el *Plus Ultra* en las dos columnas, y dos Angeles, que las sustentan, desde que la Sierva de Dios entró en esta Ciudad tuvo a pares las armas, las del Emperador, que la ennoblecen, y las de Catharina, que la defienden; fue la Venerable Sierva de Dios, las armas mas eficaces de la Puebla pues tantas veces la defendio de los enemigos" (Ramos, "Dedicatoria," *De los prodigios,* vol. 3).

18. In the transcription of Ramos's text, I have maintained period spelling and accentuation except for v for u, v for b, and tildes, which replace constants following vowels (often for nasalized *n*) or are used to abbreviate *que.*

"Cresció tanto la dissension, y porfia entre los Pyratas; que divididos en Bandos llegaron a esgirmir las espadas, y jugar las Lanzas; hasta, que uno de los Soldados, viendo tan ensagrentada la riña: dixo (hablando con sus Compañeros) muera una porque no perescamos todos: semejante voz dixo Caiphas Pontifice a los Judios en el Concilio, que formó su malicia contra Christo; pero este Soldado sin consejo, diciendo, y haciendo, arrojó un Chuzo, O Lanza a esta innocente niña con animo de quitarla la vida; para que la vida de una innocente Cordera fuesse Arco de Paz entre tantos delinquentes. Pero no sucedió lo que pretendia el inadvertido, y cruel Pyrata; porque huyendo el cuerpo la niña, o declinando el impulso de la Lanza la superior mano, le atravesó solo un muslo; y la Sangre, que salió de la herida, bastó para que lastimados, y compassivos, cessassen en la colera, y la pendencia; y que dejando todos las armas, acudiessen a curarla; y assi fuesse lazo de union, y Concordia su innocente Sangre vertida. Volvieronse luego a los Bageles, y se quedó con la prisionera uno de los principales Capitanes, que la havia ganado, con obligacion de curarla, y tratarla como a hija y no como a esclava" (Ramos, *De los prodigios*, vol. 1, 17).

19. The referent of "she" and "her" switches back and forth without notice between the Mogul lady and Mirrha, in the original as in the translation.

"Determinó esta zelosa desaogar su ira con la belleza, que juzgaba causa, u occassion de su desprecio; procurando quitarle su natural hermosura; maltratabala con palabras, y con obras: pretendiendo muchas vezes consumirla, desgreñandola a repelones; arrastrabala de sus cabellos, azotabala, aporreabala, y afeaba sus mexillas, con la Sangre, que derramaba por las heridas. Procuraba que la hambre marchitasse el color, y gracias de su rostro: y finalmente fue el yunque de una muger vengativa sobre zelosa sin mas delito que ser hermosa, y amada Myrrha; y sin mas occassion que ser objepto de un aborrescimiento invidioso. Crecio este tan hasta lo summo, que no satisfaciendose bastantemente su ira, ni templandosse su rabia con la sangre de una innocente cordera; trató de quitarle muchas vezes la vida. Prevenia los cuchillos su enojo, con determinacion de matarla: pero el temor, de que la Sangre vertida diesse vozes, como la de Abel, que clamó contra el invidioso fratricida, la cortaba, y detenia. Pareciole que matandola sin Sangre, y a escondidas quedaria su maldad occulta; y asi se resolvio a otro hecho mas aleboso; que fue arrojarla al mar con el peso de una piedra, para que se atribuyesse a contingente desgracia, lo que era estudiada malicia de su rabia. Executó ayrada la traycion, pero por dicha de Myrrha tubo prevenida la Providencia Divina una Ancla en el puesto donde cayó, para que assiendose de su Cable pudiesse sacar la cabeza del agua; y pedir a vozes ayuda, favor y el Baptismo, que era ya su principal, y unico cuydado, socorriola un hidalgo Portugues que estaba cerca del mar, como prevenido instrumento de la Omnipotencia Divina, para que la librasse del naufragio, y guardasse como en otros riesgos la vida. Con esta feliz desgracia depositaron en otra casa a esta Niña; donde viendola el amante Mogor macilenta y desfigurada su hermosura, y belleza, passo su amor a la dama Mogora, que con tantas ansias le pretendia" (Ramos, *De los prodigios*, vol. 1, 18).

20. Ramos's narrative in volume 1 comprises 136 folios and in volume 2, 177 folios; recall that the total number of pages is double the number of folios. In addition, both volumes have rather lengthy indexes.

21. "Un monstruo Pez, cuya fealdad, y fiereza la causaba horror, y que no podia explicar, llamadole ya Tiburon, ya Cayman, ya Monstruo Marino; porque su forma era extraordinaria, y abominable, y sus escamas con tales pintas, y manchas, que le hacian horrible a la vista" (Ramos, *De los prodigios*, vol. 2, 119).

22. "Lector, que era digna esta vission de mas profundas, y estendidas glosas, comparala con lo que nos dejo escrito el Evangelista San Juan en el capitulo doze de su Apocalysis, y hallaras, quan uniforme es Dios en hablar, y comunicar sus secretos en todos los tiempos a sus Siervos y escogidos, veras tambien, que como no pudo dexar de verificarse todo lo que mostro a su Sagrado Benjamin de la Catholica Iglesia, siempre perseguida, y siempre vencedora en figura de una prodigiosa muger" (ibid., 120).

23. For example: "Sucediame algunas vezes, entre asombros, y admiraciones, ponderar conmigo mismo, la grandeza de la divina Luz, que ilustra a esta esclarecida Virgen, admirandome, de que siendo en lo natural vozal, y muy cerrada, se explicase con tanta

eloquencia, con tal energia, y con expresiva tan propria en materias tan profundas, y tan varias, que parecia estaba debaxo de la Esphera de su vista todo el universo, sin que se le servasen los secretos del Cielo, ni los pensamientos, y secretos de los corazones de los hombres. Con esta admiracion, la dije un dia: 'Catharina, que necesidad ay, de que te manifieste Dios tantos, y tan desacostumbrados secretos, y mysterios?' A esta pregunta, me respondio con sinceridad, e innocencia: 'No se, que responderle, Padre y señor mio, no se si esto es malo o si es bueno; yo digo lo que me pasa, y se lo dejo a mis Confessores, para que como doctos, y esperimentados, lo apruebaen; pero lo que ahora entiendo es; que me trata, y comunica Jesus, como se pueden tratar, y comunicar aca en lo humano los dos mas tiernos amantes: y como no permite el amor, que entre dos amigos aya cosa oculta, en secreta: assi Dios se muestra Amante, comunicandome lo mas oculto de sus Mysterios.' Esta respuesta de Catharina, es el estilo, que a guardado dios con sus amigos en todos los tiempos" (ibid., 69).

24. "En una occasion, se le dexó ver el Señor, en la misma forma de Niño, pero casi desnudo, al modo, que solemos vestir sus Imagenes en la Solemnidad de su Resurrecion, o Natividad en el Pesebre: Andaba en aquel tiempo, muy cuydadosa Catharina de vestir a Christo desnudo en su Santissimo Nacimiento, y con la dicha apparicion parece le respondió al Señor a sus desseos, diciendole, como quien se le queria arroja a su regazo, y castos abrazos: Catharina visteme? La charidad, y amor de esta su amada, y querida Esposa, creció con esta vision, casi hasta causar excesso mental en el corazon, y la hubiera arrebatado su impulso, a coger al Niño Dios entre sus brazos, a no detenerla las prisiones de su Virginal recato, dandola temor la desnudez de su Unico, y Divino Amante: y assi le dixo, o preguntó que porque no venia vestido? Que si le faltaban Angeles, y Madre, que cubriessen con preciosa telas la Hermosura, Y Belleza, en que se miraban, y gozaban los Cortesanos del Cielo? Respondiola, que queria fuesse ella quien lo vistiesse, y adornase. Replicó Catharina, que ella no tenia con que vestirle, ni manos para tocarle, ni aun ojos para mirarle desnudo, y procurando apartar la vista de aquel Dios de Pureza, Su Divino Amante, quisiera esconderse, y rehundirse en el centro de la tierra... Pero quando mas descuydada, se hallaba otra vez con el mismo objecto, y con demostraciones, y con mas cariñosas ansias de recibir de mano de su Amada, el vestido, que la pedia. Aunque respondia Catharina, con nuevas, mayores, y mas cumplidas repugnancias de su amorosa Pureza; la dexase, que se fuesse, que se ausentarse; porque la rredraba, y acobardaba aquel desnudez de su Divinidad Humanada; y que no se hallaba con fuerzas para abrazarle; viendole tan desnudo, que la causaba no menos confusion, que Divino horror, hasta que le viesse decentemente a los ojos humanos vestido. Duró esta amorosa lucha, entre el Divino Amor, y su querida Esposa, mas de dos años" (ibid., vol. 1, 98–99).

25. For example, in the third volume, Ramos includes the doctor's full report upon Catarina's death (ibid., vol. 3, 83).

26. "Hasta aqui el hecho, y vission historica, en la qual, aunque extraordinaria remirandola con la debida consideracion, no hallo cosa opuesta, o dissona a la Doctrina Christiana, y Catholica Theologia del Baptismo; pero porque puede hacer alguna fuerza, y ocasionar varios discursos esta noticia divulgada entre hombres Doctos, e indoctos, me ha parecido conveniente explicarla, diciendo primero mi sentir, y despues lo que se puede discurrir careando toda la vission; y su significacion con las luzes de la Fee Catholica, con las sentencias de los Santos, y Theologos, que son interpretes de La Ley de Christo en su Santa Iglesia" (ibid., 55).

27. "Como hasta entonces no la entendió, quiso valerse ya de caricias, ya de amenazas, ya de rigores, pero ella sólo se valía de la verdad con que lo amonestó y se valía de las voces que a su Divino Esposo daba, y se valía de muchas y devotas ansias con que llamaba

a la Virgen María. A estas resistencias de Catarina, si crecían en él los enfados, las irascibles y los malos tratos, en ella crecía más la fijeza de su prometimiento y voto" (Graxeda, *Compendio*, 59).

28. Fue siempre esta venerable y devota mujer compuesta en sus acciones, medida en sus palabras, cuerda en sus respuestas, recatada en sus obras, discreta sin afectos, política sin ceremonias, silenciosa sin demasías" (ibid., 50).

29. "Antes de pasar adelante quiero prevenir con acuerdo una pregunta que pueda pulsar con viveza a cualquiera persona, y sea el decir que por qué causa refiero virtudes de Catarina, que ejercitó en aquella temprana edad en que vivía? Y cómo doy razón tan por extenso de lo que yo no vi por entonces? Y además de esto si no lo vi? Luego ella me las refería cuando la comuniqué, repugnancia que hace al buen espíritu porque éste sólo dice sus faltas, no sus virtudes, pues éstas se dejan al conocimiento de quien dirige" (ibid., 49).

30. "No averiguo de esta merced el modo con que recibió, si fue enajenada de los sentidos y potencias o si fue visión imaginaria o si la recibió visiblemente, pues queriendo yo saber de la suerte de que le pasó me solía decir" (ibid., 28).

31. According to Rubial (Ramo Inquisition, v. 678) this edict is in the Archivo General de la Nación in Mexico. I quote it from de la Maza's excerpt, *Catarina de San Juana*, 116. See Rubial, "Mariofanías," 17n6.

32. "Por contenerse en él, revelaciones, visiones y apariciones inútiles, inverosímiles, llenas de contradicciones y comparaciones impropias, indecentes y temerarias, *que sapiunt blasphemias* (que casi son blasfemias), abusando del Misterio Altísimo e Inefable de la Encarnación del Hijo de Dios, y otros lugares de la Sagrada Escritura, y doctrinas temerarias, peligrosas y contrarias al sentir de los Doctores, y práctica de la Iglesia Universal, sin más fundamento que la vana credulidad del autor" (as quoted by León, *Catarina de San Juan*, 89–91).

33. His first volume opens with the largest amount of prefatory material I have seen in any period text published in New Spain. Ramos opens with a long dedication to Bishop Fernández de Santa Cruz, in which he highlights how Catarina de San Juan herself bestowed him with the authority to write her life story, and he extends that privilege to the bishop, as pastor of the flock that includes Catarina (and who, of course, had the power to approve the biography). Listed in narrative order, the remaining preforatory material includes a lengthy letter by Núñez de Miranda, three "Aprobaciones" by two calificadores and a theologian, a license from the Viceroy Conde de Galve, four "Aprobaciones" or "Pareceres" written by some of the leading ecceliastical figures in Puebla upon the request of Bishop Santa Cruz, a license by Santa Cruz himself, and, finally, the necessary license by Ramos's Jesuit superior, the provincial of the order in New Spain.

34. Two letters address more specifically what lies at the heart of the book's trial: the church's efforts to control both heresy and sanctity. Villa mentions Pope Urban VII's edicts in 1625, 1631, and 1640 regulating the process for canonization of holy people; from then on, it was to be centralized, under the domain of Rome. Vaca also acknowledges the pope's authority for having the final word and, meanwhile, makes a case for the truth of Catarina's case and the need for a saint like her. Aware of the concerns about her "prodigiosa" life (that is, the abundance of miracles and visions), he enumerates evidence for its credibility.

35. The licenses include Bishop of Mexico Francisco Aguiar y Seijas (not Bishop Santa Cruz, since the second volume is published in Mexico City) and the provincial of the Jesuit order (Ambrosio Oddon), as well as two brief "pareceres" from a well-known Dominican friar (Juan de Gorospe) and another Jesuit (Josep Vidal).

36. The prefatory material to volumes 2 and 3 includes a long personal letter to Ramos, in which Ambrosio Oddon responds to Ramos's inquiry about the doctrinal content in volume 2. Ostensibly a parallel to Núñez's letter in the first volume, Oddon's is not as privileged in narrative order as it is placed at the end of the published material, and it contains none of the seriousness of tone or concern found in Núñez's. Rather, Oddon exuberantly praises the wonder of Catarina's life and the manifestation of divine grace in it.

37. "En obediencia del decreto de Nuestro Santissimo Padre Urbano VIII, de feliz recordacion, Expedido de la Sagrada Congregacion de la Universal Inquision de la Iglesia a 13 de marzo de 1675, declarado por su Santidad en 5 de junio del año de 1631, y confirmado en 5 de julio de 1634 en que se prohibe dar culto de Santidad a las personas no Canonizadas Protesto que todas las veces, que en esta Historia uso las palabras Santa Bienabenturada, Venerable, Esclarecida, o qualquiera otra, que insinue virtud resebrante, assi de la persona que es assumpto de esta obra; como de qualquiera otra, que con esta occasion nombro con estos, o semejantes epitetos, no es mi intento cayga sobre la persona, dandole el culto debido a los Santos, que con defincion de la Santa Iglesia esta en el Cielo; sino sobre las costumbres, y opinion. Item protesto, que todas las cosas, que refiero con nombre de Ilustraciones, Revelaciones, Raptos, Extasis, Prophecias, Milagros, y otros favores extraordinarios, no tienen mas authoridad que la humana, fundada en motivo, humanos, expuestos a la falibilidad, reservando siempre la infalible decision al Oraculo del Espiritu Santo el Romano Pontifice en su Canonica declaracion a que me sujeto en todo; como Hijo obediente de la Santa Iglesia Catholica Romana, Nuestra Madre" (Ramos, *De los prodigios*, vol. 3, 129).

38. "Que se sepa y entienda que cuanto yo referiere en este escrito, lo ví, lo experimenté y hice aquellas pruebas que tales materias piden para la verificación de su fidelidad, verdad y legalidad, y puesta la mano en el pecho, haciendo la señal de la santa cruz, *Iuro in verbo Sacerdotis* decir verdad en todo" (Castillo Graxeda, *Compendio*, 16).

39. "Solo el que aquí referiré basta para comprobarlos todos, y por haber sido notorio a muchas personas que lo vieron, de que pueden dar fe, que yo los demás los dejo porque en materias de milagros, como son puntos de suyo tan difíciles de averiguar y tan reservados al conocimiento de la iglesia por los que tienen este ministerio de oficio, no quiero que sirvan de embarazo para el crédito de las virtudes de esta sierva de Dios, ni tampoco para alargar esta historia que sólo sirve de despertar y conmover la devoción de los fieles" (ibid., 199).

40. Ibid., 200.

41. Ibid., 201–202.

42. See Castillo Graxeda, *Compendio*, "Introduction."

43. [Catarina] *"En verdad ángel mío, que vuesastedes dicen el verdad, y así echen ruego a Dios no me perda."*

[Graxeda] Que quiso decir: "En verdad que dicen vuestras mercedes la verdad y sienten lo que yo soy, que soy una embustera y aun por eso pido por amor de Dios rueguen por mí, no se pierda mi alma; ya conozco que soy china, ya veo que soy basura, que soy una inmundicia y que soy una perra, pero por el mismo caso, así de lo que consideráis como de lo que me decís, por eso propio os suplico hagáis especial petición para que yo tenga buen fin" (Castillo Graxeda, *Compendio*, 112).

44. See Burke, "How to Be a Counter-Reformation Saint," 46.

45. The concept of decorum was important to the period and is evident in other works. For example, Mercado writes a brief biography about a Philippine servant for the Jesuits and uses a direct simple style in *El cristiano virtuoso*; and Sigüenza y Góngora discusses the need to write in a non-florid style because he is writing a history "de mugeres

y para mugeres" in his chronicle of a Mexican convent, *Paraíso occidental.* For a discussion of the former, see Myers, "La influencia mediativa"; for the latter, see Ross's *The Baroque Narrative of Carlos de Sigüenza y Góngora,* chap. 2.

46. Barnes-Karol, "Religious Oratory."

47. I have been unable to locate the list of rules in effect in the 1690s, but these 1707 rules would have been similar.

48. For a full reproduction of the rules and an interesting study of them, see Pérez-Marchand, *Dos etapas ideológicas*; see also Ramos Soriano, "Critierios inquisitoriales."

49. As mentioned, Palafox was another Puebla figure who had a popular following because he was considered to have died in the odor of sancity; he had also known Catarina. The edict must have been thoroughly carried out, because even the portrait of Catarina in Ramos's work has been removed from most extant copies. The edict is cited in Destefano, "Miracles and Monasticism," 27 and 72n19.

50. All three biographies note that in her lifetime and soon after her death, Catarina de San Juan had throngs of people seeking her intercessory powers. Others traveled as many as 300 leagues to consult with Catarina (Ramos, *De los prodigios,* vol. 3, 44) and others were cured by holding tightly to her portrait (Graxeda, "Compendio," chap. 30).

51. To date, Francisco de la Maza and León are among the few that have worked with archival material and pieced together the series of events and edicts that help provide a fuller picture of the dynamics of religious belief, literary representation, and institutional rules.

52. Letter from the Mexican Inquisition to the Spanish Inquisitor General, December 15, 1695, quoted in Toribio Medina, *Historia del tribunal,* 321.

53. See Francisco de la Maza, *Catarina de San Juan,* 118–119.

54. Finding historical records in which Catarina is named in the late eighteenth or nineteenth centuries—such as the reprinting of Graxeda's biography—would support the conclusion that a cult may have not been entirely averted. According to de la Maza (*Catarina de San Juan,* chap. 3), a mid-eighteenth-century edition of Graxeda is noted by a bibliographer, but he has been unable to find this edition.

55. My thanks go to Antonio Rubial for this observation.

56. Burke, "How to Be a Counter-Reformation Saint," 49.

57. The Catholic Church's change in policy is seen when in the 1960s it canonized a sixteenth-century Peruvian man of African descent, Martín de Porres.

58. For more on this convent and the role of race, see works by Díaz, "Género, raza," Lavrin, "Indian Brides," and Meléndez, "El perfil económico."

59. See Greer, "Iroquois Virgin."

60. I was unable to find any record of it at the Secret Archives of the Vatican.

Chapter 3

Much of the material for this chapter draws on the lengthy studies of María de San José's life and journals in Myers and Powell, *A Wild Country out in the Garden.* Consult chapters 1–2 for more detailed analyses of her family and writings. The original manuscript by María de San José does not have folios consistently marked throughout the twelve volumes, so references to it in this chapter note only the volume number or the page number in our translation, *A Wild Country.*

1. Santander y Torres, *Vida,* 53, 56, 273, and 283.

2. Over a period of approximately twenty-five years (1691?–1717), María de San José produced over two thousand pages recounting her secular and religious life. The autobiographical manuscript (Spanish Codex 39–41), owned by the John Carter Brown Library,

Providence, Rhode Island, totals 1,102 folios. In most cases, if the individual volumes have been numbered, either by María or her confessors, it is by folio (therefore every other page) and also by *quaderno* (which we have translated by its modern Spanish equivalent, "notebook"). The quaderno consists of a unit of three or four large sheets of paper folded into quartos, thus producing either twelve or sixteen folios and twenty-four or thirty-two pages per quaderno. These quadernos were doled out by her confessor and, when filled, returned to him. They are, therefore, significant units of composition, and the author herself often refers to her own writing by quaderno. For more on the nature of the manuscript and its contents, consult Myers and Powell, *A Wild Country*, appendices A and B.

3. If the manuscript was returned to the archives at the Convent of La Soledad in the 1720s, it most likely remained there until the Juárez Reforms (1860s), when many convents were secularized. During the last decades of the nineteenth century and the first decades of the twentieth, conventual archives often were maintained for a time by patrons; but sometimes they later passed into private hands and were sold. Indeed, few Mexican conventual archives remained intact by the end of the Mexican Revolution. Because there is no acquisition record for the manuscript at the John Carter Brown Library (complete records were not kept until 1920), we can only conjecture that the manuscript left La Soledad sometime after 1865 and arrived at the library before 1920.

4. In *Cultura feminina* (320–321), Muriel says this manuscript is lost.

5. Arenal and Schlau, Franco, and Muriel all use Santander y Torres's rewritten passages of María's text as though they were entirely her own words. See selections in Arenal and Schlau, *Untold Sisters*; Franco, *Plotting Women*, chap. 1, and Muriel, *Cultura feminina*, 360–365. While twentieth-century scholars' use of these quotes raised awareness of the existence of dozens of women like Madre María who wrote in the convent, their works typically assumed that biographers like Santander y Torres followed rigorous twentieth-century scholarly standards for quoting sources verbatim.

6. See chronology for a complete listing of these documents.

7. Kate Greenspan explains her borrowing of this term and its reference to medieval and early modern women's mixture of confessional and hagiographic narratives in "The Autohagiographic Tradition."

8. See Destefano, "Introduction" in "Miracles and Monasticism," and Rubial, "Introducción" in *La santidad controvertida*.

9. The women were María Magdalena, famous for her heroic tolerance of forty-four years of being bed-ridden; the Carmelite nun Isabel de la Encarnación; and María de Jesús, who had worked with Catarina de San Juan and later became the city's patron. Bishop Santa Cruz initiated an assertive campaign in an attempt to canonize María de Jesús. See Rubial, *La santidad controvertida*, 161–198.

10. María discusses this relationship in volume 1.

11. For a thorough biographical study of María de San José's secular and religious life, see Myers and Powell, *A Wild Country*, chap. 1.

12. All quotes are taken from Myers and Powell, *A Wild Country*. This one is from p. 15.

13. In the mid-1670s María's sister Leonor entered the Carmelite Convent of San José, and Francisca entered the Convent of San Jerónimo—both in Puebla. The three Palacios sisters who married—María, Isabel, and Catarina—made important social and economic family alliances with elite landowners and a bureaucrat; one (Isabel) eventually became a widow who used her legal right to initiate court proceedings in order to keep her property. The marriages of these Palacios sisters reflect both the limited circle of eligible men among their cousins and the neighboring landowners and a policy of marital alliances calculated to maintain the family estates. See Myers and Powell, *A Wild Country*, 256–258.

14. Myers and Powell, *A Wild Country*, 267.

15. Ibid., 68.

16. Ibid., 91.

17. Ibid., 86.

18. Letter from Bishop Fernández de Santa Cruz to María's confessor, in Santander y Torres, *Vida*, unnumbered preliminary pages.

19. For more on this incident, see Myers and Powell, *A Wild Country*, 274–276.

20. All of María de San José's visions fall into orthodox, doctrinal categories for such passive spiritual activity: a vision could be one of three types or a combination of several. The first type, corporeal visions, produced specific knowledge via the physical senses, being seen or perceived with the body's own eyes, ears, touch, smell, or even taste. The second type of vision, classified as imaginary, stemmed from the *imago* or image of God and bypassed the physical senses, imprinting itself directly on the imagination, in the mind's eye. Although the third type of vision is the least frequent, María de San José also describes experiences with this highest type of vision, the spiritual or "intellectual" vision. Neither seen nor heard, but taking the form of inspiration, intuition, or revelation, they were considered the least likely to be caused by delusion and could serve, it was held, as great aids for understanding God. Visionaries traditionally describe a deepening of love, compassion, and understanding after the close of the experience, which, in turn, results in increased *caritas*, or spiritual activity in service of the human world. For more on this topic, and more specifically in María's writings, see Myers and Powell, *A Wild Country*, 282–283.

21. Myers and Powell, *A Wild Country*, 210.

22. See Rubial, *La santidad controvertida*, 86.

23. Even before it was published, Teresa's *Vida* circulated in manuscript form throughout Spanish convents and was widely influential. Mariana de San Joseph (*Vida*, 27) writes of the influence Teresa's work had on her before Teresa died. Maríana (*Vida*, 12) also mentions reading St. Jerome's letters, meditation books by Luis de Granada and Peter of Alcántara, and Catherine of Siena's letters, as well as Catherine's life story written by her confessor, Raymond da Capus. As a young girl, Mariana imitated the life depicted in Catherine's biography; later, as a mature woman writing about her own life, she imitated its narrative format. For an excellent article on Catherine's and other medieval women's biographies, see Coakley, "Friars as Confidants."

24. Mariana de San Joseph, *Vida de la Venerable M. Mariana de San Joseph*. Some of Madre María's visions also may have been influenced by reading the story of another Augustinian Recollect, Isabel de Jesús (1586–1648), whose account reflects Augustinian devotion to Christ, prayers for souls, and the concept of suffering entailing blood and tears; see Isabel de Jesús, *Vida de la venerable Madre Isabel de Jesús*. In fact, the parallels between María's and Rosa de Lima's lives may have been filtered through the founder's autobiography; they all talk of mystic marriage, family conflict, extreme asceticism, union with Christ on the cross, and prayers for souls in purgatory.

25. Myers and Powell, *A Wild Country*, 8.

26. Ibid., 9.

27. Ibid., 20, 15.

28. Ibid., 43.

29. Among others, these included Bishops Santa Cruz and Maldonado, as well as the renowed Francisco de Vera. For a full list, see Myers and Powell, *A Wild Country*, 2–9.

30. Myers and Powell, *A Wild Country*, 6.

31. Other writers, such as María de la Antigua and Teresa's Carmelite companion Ana de San Bartolomé, recount sudden, miraculous abilities to read and write.

32. Myers and Powell, *A Wild Country*, 53

33. Ibid., 16.

34. For a study of these different confessors, see Myers and Powell, *A Wild Country*, 316–324.

35. See Chicharro, *Libro de la vida*, 66–69, and Espósito, *La mística ciudad*, 42.

36. Myers and Powell, *A Wild Country*, 75.

37. A good contrast to Santander y Torres is the *Vida* written by Sánchez y Castro about another nun in Madre María's convent, Antonia de la Madre de Dios. In the four-hundred-page biography, the author never cites more than one paragraph of Antonia's own writings per chapter. Of course, this may also reflect differing amounts written by the two nuns. Antonia's biographer never mentions the quantity of her accounts, and we do not know if the originals are extant.

38. Both Coakley, "Friars as Confidants of Holy Women," and Bynum, "The Female Body and Religious Practice," mention this difference between medieval men's and women's views of women's spiritual experiences.

39. Myers and Powell, *A Wild Country*, 54–55.

40. Santander y Torres, *Vida*, 112.

41. Bishop Maldonado delivered a sermon in 1707 urging his congregation to support Philip V's monarchy. See Maldonado, *Oración evangelica*, 15–26.

42. María de San José, *Estaciones que la Soberana Emperatriz de los Cielos María Santissima Nuestra Señora anduvo y enseñó a la Venerable Madre María de San Joseph.*

43. Santander y Torres, *Oración funebre.*

44. See the bibliography for dates of the printings. The three oil portraits of María de San José include one currently on display at the Museum of the ex-Convent of Santa Mónica (reproduced in Muriel's *Retratos de monjas*, plate 15), another at the Museum of the ex-Convent of Nuestra Señora de la Soledad, and a third at the Museo Nacional del Virreinato, Tepozotlán (reproduced in Muriel's *Cultura femenina*, plate 17). All three portraits contain information about María's life, such as dates of birth (the Tepozotlán portrait erroneously states that she was born May 4, 1656, which was probably the date of her baptism) and entrance into the convent; her role as founder; and her secular name (Palacios y Solórzano, which Muriel—probably due to the illegibility of the first letters of the surname—erroneously transcribes from the Santa Mónica portrait as Ygnacio y Solórsano). The Santa Mónica portrait also includes a poem about María de San José's conversion experience.

45. See Gómez de la Parra, *Fundación y primer siglo*, 456, and Sánchez y Castro, *Vida de Antonia de la Madre de Dios*, 103.

46. My thanks go to the Reverenda Madre Priora Guillermina Sánchez for describing the convent's tradition.

Chapter 4

My thanks to Amanda Powell, Georgina Sabat-Rivers, and Nina M. Scott for their valuable suggestions on this chapter.

1. Anne Bradstreet was the other colonial woman author who was published.

2. Translations for these two poems are from Trueblood's *A Sor Juana Anthology*. The first is from "Romance," p. 92; the second is from "The Divine Narcissus," p. 155.

3. Fernández de Santa Cruz, "Prologue." Translation from Trueblood, *A Sor Juana*, 202.

4. Trabulse in *Carta de Serafina* notes the many changes introduced into the 1692 version.

5. For details about these early editions, see Sabat-Rivers's introduction to her edition of *Inundación castálida.*

6. For a full study of these final years of Sor Juana's life, see Trabulse, "El silencio final." Alatorre and Tenorio debate some of Trabulse's conclusions about the events in Sor Juana's final years in *Serafina y Sor Juana*, chap. 6 and appendix 2. For a more detailed summary of this debate, see note 41 below.

7. See Brading, *Orbe indiano*, 405. Glantz (in *Sor Juana*, 58) describes an omnipresent "yo". Lavrin ("Sor Juana") argues that this first-person narrative presence stems from the amount of personal will in Sor Juana's work (verus the conventional humble nun), and Merrim ("Narciso," 111–117, "Toward a Feminist Reading," 27) discusses Sor Juana's always strategic use of "yo."

8. See Glantz, *Sor Juana*, chaps. 1–2, and Maza, *Sor Juana ante la historia*.

9. Translated by Margaret Sayers Peden. A companion volume of Sor Juana's poetry was also translated into English by Alan S. Trueblood.

10. For overviews of this history, see, for example, Buxó, "Prefacio" in Bravo Arriaga, *La excepción*, 9–23; Merrim, introduction to *Early Modern Women*; and Poot Herrera, "Sor Juana y su mundo," 1–32. The analysis of the themes of obedience and free will has emerged in scholarship that examines both Sor Juana's poetry and prose. See, for example, Buxó, "Sor Juana"; Sabat-Rivers, "Loa del auto"; Wissmer, *Las sombras*; Glantz, *Sor Juana*; and Lavrin, "Sor Juana."

11. For an overview of the documents that have been found since 1968 and a study of their significance in interpreting Sor Juana's life, see Poot Herrera, *Los guardaditos*, 307–332.

12. As Sabat-Rivers (*En busca de Sor Jeana*) has noted, Sor Juana was clearly familiar with the most popular model for the feminine *vida*, Teresa of Avila's *Libro de su vida*. Bénassy-Berling, *Humanismo y religión*, Franco, *Plotting Women*, Glantz, *Sor Juana*, Merrim, *Early Modern* and Powell "Making Use;" all note this same parallel. See also Myers, "Sor Juana's *Respuesta*," on the topic; this chapter builds on and revises that article.

13. Scholars are debating the authorship of a relatively recently found letter, *Carta de Serafina de Cristo* (1691). Trabulse maintains that it is penned by Sor Juana; see his introduction to *Carta de Serafina*.

14. The family members were small landholders on the Hacienda San Miguel de Nepantla, southeast of Mexico City. It is important to note that Sor Juana's birth year was earlier established as 1651, but it was revised by most scholars in the 1980s when a baptismal record was found. Several scholars still maintain that Sor Juana was born in 1651. Such contradictions in documents about birth years and ages is frequent in colonial records. For example, we have several different birth years recorded for two other women studied in this book: María de San José and Catalina de Erauso.

15. See Quijada and Bustamante, "Las mujeres."

16. Recall that María de San José's brother and sister had moved from the hacienda to relatives' houses in Puebla for similar reasons.

17. "Que a la manera que un Galeón real se defendería de pocas chalupas, que le embistieran, así se desembarazaba Juana Inés de las preguntas, argumentos, y réplicas, que tantos, cada uno en su clase, la propusieron" (as quoted in Glantz, *Sor Juana*, 180).

18. Fernández de Santa Cruz, *Regla*. In fact, this rule was first written for the Hieronymite convent in Puebla, in which María de San José's sister, Francisca de la Encarnación, had professed her vows.

19. For a study of Sor Juana's reading, see Bénassy-Berling, *Humanismo y religión*, part 2, chap. 1.

20. Turning convention on its head, for example, Sor Juana queries the logic of a coral-lipped woman: "Digo, pues, que el coral entre los labios/ se estaba con la grana en los labios/ y las perlas, con nítidos orientes,/ andaban enseñándose a ser dientes; y alegaba

la concha, no muy loca,/ que si ellas dientes son, ella es la boca." Sor Juana jokes about the worn-out poetic conventions for describing women as an ideal: "Es, pues, Lisarda; es, pues . . . Ay Dios, qué aprieto!/ No sé quién es Lisarda, les prometo;/ que mi atención sencilla,/ pintarla prometió, no definilla./ Digo, pues… Oh qué *pueses* tan soeces!/ Todo el papel he de llenar de *pueses*. Jesús, qué mal empiezo!" ("El Pintar Lisarda la belleza," Ovillejos, 214, in Johnson 67, trans). See also Johnson, *Satire*, 66–73; Rabin, "Mito petrarquista"; and Sabat-Rivers, *En busca*, 57–78.

21. "Y sólo sé que mi cuerpo,/sin que a uno u otro se incline,/es neutro, o abstracto, cuanto sólo el alma desposite." "Romance," 48 (translated by Trueblood, *A Sor Juana Anthology*, 31).

22. For a variety of studies on Núñez, see Bravo Arriaga, *La excepción*.

23. "Por el [voto] de obediencia [sacrifica] su propia voluntad, albedrío y toda su alma" (quoted in Glantz, *Sor Juana*, 55).

24. Sor Juana reminds Núñez in her letter to him that he did not pay the dowry; Núñez's biographer Oviedo, however, asserts that he did.

25. For a history and study of this manuscript, see Scott, "If You Are Not Pleased," and Alatorre, "La carta."

26. All translations of the *Carta al Padre Núñez* are from Scott, *Madres del verbo*, 71–82. "¿Quál era el dominio directo que tenía V.R. para disponer de mi persona y del alvedrío (sacando el que mi amor le daba y le dará siempre) que Dios me dio?" (Scott, *Madres del verbo*, 77).

27. "Santos sólo la gracia y auxilios de Dios saven hacerlos" (ibid.).

28. "Dios que me crió y redimió, y que usa conmigo tantas misericordias, proveherá con remedio para mi alma, que esper[o] en su vondad no se perderá aunque le falte la dirección de V.R., que a el cielo hacen muchas llaves, y no se estrechó a un solo dictamen, sino que ay en él infinidad de manciones para diversos genios… ¿Qué precisión ay en que esta salvación mía sea por medio de V.R.: ¿No podrá ser por otro? ¿Restringióse y limitóse la misericordia de Dios a un hombre…?" (ibid., 79).

29. Demitrious, as cited in Trueba Lawand, *El arte*, 23.

30. "La cristiandad se había introducido al mundo bajo la forma epistolar. La importancia de las epístolas de San Pablo… no puede ser exagerada. La religión de Jesús había acentuado el sentido de la persona o circunstancia individuales al enfatizar la relación única y privada del alma humana con su Creador. Además, el desarrollo de la teología cristiana había exigido de los Padres una exposición clara y estrecha de punto de vista por medio del refinamiento de creencias ortodoxas y el combate contra opiniones heréticas. No es sin razón que Gregorio Nacianceno, Gregorio de Nisa, Basilio, y Crisóstomo se incorporan en un canon cristiano de epistolografía y son citados frecuentemente por retóricos de siglos posteriores junto con sus predecesores paganos" (George Kustas, as quoted in Trueba Lawand, *El arte*, 18).

31. Even the Jesuits had a treatise that was widely used in their curriculum; see Trueba Lawand, *El arte*, chap. 6.

32. See Trueba Lawand, *El arte*, 109, 119.

33. For a study of Núñez's *Cartilla* and Santa Cruz's letters published by Miguel de Torres in his biography of the bishop, see Bravo Arriaga, *La excepción*, 55–63 and 101–111.

34. See Lavrin, "Sor Juana," 605–622.

35. See Juana Inés de la Cruz, *Obras*, 813–814.

36. "Vuelvo a poner todo lo dicho debajo de la *censura* de nuestra Santa Madre Iglesia Católica, como su más obediente hija" (ibid., 827).

37. Rebelo Gomes in "Para una nueva lectura" convincingly argues that the title may have a double meaning: it may refer to Athenagoras rather than Athena. It is also worthy

of note that when this letter was republished in her second volume of collected works, it was retitled as *Crisis sobre un sermón* (1692); we do not know if this was Sor Juana's original title for the letter, or if it was imposed later by the publisher. My thanks to Georgina Sabat-Rivers for pointing this out to me.

38. "Toda la profesión religiosa consiste en no quitarle a Dios cosa alguna de lo mesmo que le dio, porque quién hay que quite a Dios lo que ya le tiene dado?" (Fernández de Santa Cruz, *Regla*, as quoted in Glantz, *Sor Juana*, 77).

39. According to a study by Trabulse, Núñez had just published a small pamphlet, *Comulgador penitente* (Puebla 1690), in which he corroborates Vieira's sermon and further elaborated on the theory of Christ's *finezas*, arguing that Christ's greatest gift was his embodiment in the form of the Eucharist. To attack and correct Vieira, then, was to attack and correct the influential Núñez (Trabulse, "El silencio final," 11). Alatorre and Tenorio dispute this reading of the *Comulgador* in their *Serafina y Sor Juana*, 77–83.

40. For more on the general dynamic, see, for example, Bénassy-Berling, "Más sobre la conversión"; Bravo Arriaga, "Sobre dos" in *La excepción*; and Trabulse, "El silencio."

41. A second letter, *Carta de Serafina de Cristo*, written soon after the *Carta atenagórica*, but before the *Respuesta*, may provide a partial key to the polemic. Trabulse argues in his study and transcription and discussion of this letter that it was written by Sor Juana and addressed to Bishop Santa Cruz: in it she reveals that Núñez had been the target of her previous letter, not his Portuguese predecessor Vieira; the letter talks of the Castilian (not Portuguese) soldier (Jesuits were the "soldiers of Christ"). See Trabulse's transcription and study, *Carta de Serafina de Cristo, 1691* (1996).

Recent scholarship, however, has questioned the authenticity of this letter. Alatorre and Tenorio's recent book, *Serafina y Sor Juana*, refutes Trabulse's findings and argues that the *Carta de Serfina* may not be written by Sor Juana but by Castareña Ursúa, the publisher of *Fama y obras posthumas*. Their arguments about the authenticity of the document (as being an autograph manuscript by Sor Juana) are convincing, but other aspects of their book ignore certain parts of Trabulse's thesis. Poot Herrera (*Los guardaditos*, 326–327) argues in a more measured manner that while Sor Juana may not have been the "material author" of the *Carta de Serafina*, she was the "intellectual author:" the letter reflects Sor Juana's arguments and was produced in her convent. The complexity and authenticity of the letter is still unfolding, particularly with Poot Herrera's (*Los guardaditos*) recent archival searches in which she has traced other players involved in the polemic. After this chapter went to press, I discovered that Trabulse had published another book, *La muerte de Sor Juana* (1999) in which he revises and expands on his earlier studies.

42. Addressed to Bishop Santa Cruz, the letter uses his own female pseudonym with which he signed the prologue to the *Carta atenagórica*, "Sor Filotea," which, in turn, was probably taken from St. Francis de Sales's popular guide for nuns.

43. The *Respuesta* has been most frequently studied for clues to Sor Juana's psyche and poetic production and, more recently, for its dialogue with church rules and history, dealing in particular with themes of obedience and institutional hierarchy. Some scholars have extended this idea of dialogue to the highly intertextual nature of the *Respuesta*, highlighting Sor Juana's careful rewriting of authors mentioned. Scott ("La gran turba") for example, examines the catalogue of women included, while Luciani ("Anecdotal Self-Invention") argues that the anecdotes included in her self-portrait are highly metaphorical and emblematic in their rewriting of St. Paul's letters and Aristotelean theory. See also the studies on obedience and free will by Sabat-Rivers, "En busca de Sor Juana (309–332)"; Wissmer, *Las sombras*; Glantz, *Sor Juana*; Lavrin, "Sor Juana"; and Powell, "Making Use of the Holy Office."

44. Perelmuter, "La estructura," 152.

45. All translations of the *Respuesta* are from Arenal and Powell, *The Answer/La respuesta*, 38–105. "¿Por ventura soy más que una pobre monja, la más mínima criatura del mundo y la más indigna de ocupar vuestra atención?" (Arenal and Powell, *The Answer/La Respuesta*, 41).

46. "Bendito seáis vos, Señor, que no sólo no quisisteis en manos de otra criatura el juzgarme, y que ni aun en la mía lo pusisteis, sino que lo reservasteis a la vuestra" (ibid.).

47. "Dejen eso para quien lo entienda, que yo no quiero ruido con el Santo Oficio, que soy ignorante" (ibid., 47).

48. "vuestra doctísima, discretísima, santísima y amorosisma carta" (ibid., 39).

49. "El escribir nunca ha sido dictamen propio, sino fuerza ajena, que les pudiera decir con verdad: *Vos me coegistis*. Lo que sí es verdad que no negaré... que desde que me rayó la primera luz de la razón, fue tan vehemente y poderosa la inclinación a las letras, que ni ajenas represiones —que he tenido muchas— ni propias reflejas —que he hecho no pocas— han bastado a que deje de seguir *este natural impulso que Dios puso en mí*: Su Majestad sabe por qué y para qué" (ibid.).

50. This reference is found much earlier in 2 Corinthians 12:11.

51. "Sabe también Su Majestad que no consiguiendo esto, he intentado sepultar con mi nombre mi entendimiento, y sacrificárselo sólo a quien me le dio; y que no otro motivo me entró en religión" (Arenal and Powell, *The Answer/La respuesta*, 47).

52. "Prosiguiendo en la narración de mi inclinasión, de que os quiero dar entera noticia" (ibid., 48).

53. "Y en fin, cómo el Libro que comprende todos los libros, y la Ciencia en que se incluyen todas las ciencias, para cuya inteligencia todas sirven; y despúes de saberlas todas (que ya se ve que no es fácil, ni aun posible), pide otra circunstancia más que todo lo dicho, que es una continua oración y pureza de vida, para impetrar de Dios aquella purgación de ánimo e iluminación de mente que es menester para la inteligencia de cosas tan altas, y si esto falta, nada sirve de lo demás" (ibid., 55–57).

54. "Todas las cosas salen de dios que es el centro a un tiempo y la circunferencia de donde salen y donde paran todas las líneas criadas" (ibid., 59).

55. "Ya se ve cuán duro es estudiar en aquellos caracteres sin alma, careciendo de la voz viva y explicación del maestro; pues todo este trabajo sufría yo muy gustosa por amor de las letras" (ibid., 55).

56. "En todo lo dicho, venerable señora, no quiero ...decir que me han perseguido por saber, sino sólo porque he tenido amor a la sabiduría y a las letras, no porque haya conseguido ni uno ni otro" (ibid., 71).

57. See ibid., 60–71.

58. Ibid., 75.

59. "Si Aristóteles hubiera guisado, mucho más hubiera escrito" (ibid., 75).

60. "Y así remito la decisión a ese soberano talento, sometiéndome luego a lo que sentenciare, sin contradicción ni repunancia" (ibid., 77).

61. "Veo aquella egipcíaca Catarina, leyendo y convenciendo todas las sabidurías de los sabios de Egipto. Veo una Gertrudis leer, escribir y enseñar" (ibid., 79).

62. "¿Cómo vemos que la Iglesia ha permitido que escriba una Gertrudis, una Teresa, una Brígida, la monja de Agreda y otras muchas?... y ahora vemos que la Iglesia permite escribir a las mujeres santas y no santas, pues la de Agreda y María de la Antigua no están canonizadas y corren sus escritos; y ni cuando Santa Teresa y las demás escribieron, lo estaban" (ibid., 91).

63. "Tales fueron las Divinas Letras en poder del malvado... Lutero y de los demás heresiarcas... a los cuales hizo daño la sabiduría" (ibid., 83).

64. "¡Oh cuánto daños se excusaran en nuestra república si las ancianas fueran doctas como Leta y que supieran enseñar como manda San Pablo y mi Padre San Jerónimo!" (ibid., 85).

65. For more on this debate in the context of Sor Juana's work, see Arenal and Powell, *The Answer/La respuesta*, 254–256, and Merrim, *Early Modern Women*, introduction.

66. "Y protesto que sólo lo hago por obedeceros; con tanto recelo, que me debéis más en tomar la pluma con este temor... Pero, bien que va a vuestra corrección; borradlo, rompedlo y reprendedme" (Arenal and Powell, *The Answer/La respuesta*, 83).

67. "Si el crimen está en la Carta Atenagórica, fue aquella más que referir sencillamente mi sentir... Si es, como dice el censor, herética, por qué no la delata? Y con eso él quedará vengado y yo contenta,... pues como yo fui libre para disentir de Vieira, lo será cualquiera para disentir de mi dictamen" (ibid., 93).

68. "¿Pero, dónde voy, Señora mía? Que esto no es de aquí,... insensiblemente se deslizó la pluma" (ibid.).

69. "Que no sólo es lícito, pero utilísimo y necesario a las mujeres el estudio de las sagradas letras, y mucho más a las monjas" (ibid.).

70. "Confieso desde luego mi ruindad y vileza"; "yo nunca he escrito cosa alguna por mi voluntad, sino por ruegos y preceptos ajenos"; "los torpes borrones de mi ignorancia" (ibid., 97–103).

71. Víctor, víctor Catarina,
    que con su ciencia divina
    los sabios ha convencido,
    y victoriosa ha salido
    —con su ciencia soberana—
    de la arrogancia profana
    que a convencerla ha venido!
    víctor, víctor, víctor!
    ... Nunca de varón ilustre
    triunfo igual habemos visto;
    y es que quiso Dios en ella
    honrar el sexo femenino.
    Víctor, víctor!
    ... Tutelar sacra Patrona, es de las Letras Asilo;
    porque siempre ilustre Sabios,
    quien Santos de Sabios hizo.
    Víctor, víctor!

(From *Villancicos a Santa Catarina*, trans. Arenal and Powell, *The Answer/La respuesta*, 161–162)

72. As *calificador*, Núñez de Miranda wrote an "Aprobación" to Pedro de la Vega's life of Catherine: *La rosa de Alexandria entre flores humanas y divinas letras, Sta Catalina, Virgen, Regia, Doctora, Ilustre martyr, virtudes de su vida, triunfo de su muerte*, 1671. In the license he praises St. Catherine's erudition.

73. See Trabulse's "El silencio final," 13.

74. The *Enigmas* were rediscovered in 1968. Apparently the title page was published, but the text was not; it had been blocked from publication by the archbishop of Mexico. See Alatorre, *Sor Juana*, and Trabulse, "El silencio," 13. Poot Herrera (*Los guardaditos*, 343) also discusses the content of a series of romances written during these same years and argues that they provide further evidence of Sor Juana's continued literary activity.

75. As Trabulse's careful chronology elucidates, within weeks of the publication of the *Carta Atenagórica*, Palavicino had preached a sermon, *La fineza mayor* (January 1691) in Sor

Juana's own convent. He declared Sor Juana a wise "monja teóloga." Within the month the Inquisition blocked the publication of Palavicino's sermon, and Sor Juana wrote her *Respuesta*. By April 1691, the case against Palavicino was dropped, but it was reinitiated about a year later, coinciding with the probable initiation of a *proceso espiscopal secreto* against Sor Juana (1693) (Trabulse, "El silencio final," 12). Within days of Palavicino's sermon, someone in Sor Juana's camp wrote the *Carta de Serafina de Cristo*.

76. Poot Herrera (*Los guardaditos*, 332) mentions a document and study that reveals that Núñez was "a censured censor."

77. Ibid.

78. "Abjurar de sus errores, a confesarse culpable, a desagraviar a la Purísima Concepción, a no publicar más y a ceder su biblioteca y sus bienes al arzobispo" (as quoted in Trabulse "El silencio final," 13). It is important to note that Sor Juana did not take issue with the dogma of the Holy Conception here but, rather, to ideas put forth by Núñez and his followers.

79. There were 185 books and 15 manuscript *legajos* (Trabulse, "El silencio final"). See also Poot Herrera, *Los guardaditos*, 329. "Las monjas," a study by Rubial, reveals that Sor Juana continued to be active in the financial world of the convent as well.

80. See Trabulse, "El silencio final," 12–13.

81. Ibid., 15.

82. "La vida de esta *rara* Muger, que nacio en el Mundo a justificar a la naturaleza las vanidades de prodigiosa" (Calleja, "Aprobación," in *Fama y obras*, unnumbered preliminary pages).

83. "Quien a las objeciones de los que passan la simple aprehension por juizio hecho, quisiere ver vna cabal satisfacion... alli vera, que la Madre Juana Ynes no destino este escrito para notorio... Alli vera, que con la satisfacion, que da la Poetisa al Padre Vieira, queda mas ilustrado, que con la defensa que le hizo quien lavo con tinta la nieve. Y alli finalmente vera en esta Muger admirable vna humilidad de candidez tan mesurada, que no rehusa dar satisfaciones de su misma ofensa" (Calleja, "Aprobación," *Fama*).

84. Oviedo, *Vida exemplar*.

85. "Tan lejos esta señora de amar o desear estos favores de Dios extraordinarios, que temblaba y se horrorizaba sólo con su memoria; alli por juzgarse indigna e incapaz de todos ellos; como por temer el riesgo y peligro que ocasionan, y de que han sido ejemplo espantoso tantos Icaros... suplicaba instantemente a dios, que la librase de ese camino la llevase sólo por la segura senda del padecer, asistida de vivísima fe, de firmísima esperanza y de ardientísma caridad" (as quoted in Glantz, *Sor Juana*, 97).

86. Glantz (*Sor Juana*, chap. 1 and page 121) notes many of these references to Sor Juana during the colonial period.

87. "Y si por ser primero/ Colón, el que valiente/descubrió nuestros polos/ antes que a ellos Américo viniese,/ se mandó que estos orbes,/que en sí tantos contiene,/ no América, como antes,/ sino sólo Colonia se dijesen./ Con cuánta más justicia,/ si a la tuya atiende,/ desde hoy mudando nombre/ o Nísida o Nisea llamarse deben" (as quoted in Glantz, *Sor Juana*, 34n31).

88. "Esta América Septentrional, tan celebrada por sus ricos minerales, puede gloriarse de haber sido patria de una mujer tan heroica que podemos aplicarle el epíteto de la mujer fuerte" (as quoted in ibid., 38).

89. For a study of these, see Sabat-Rivers, "Blanco, negro, rojo: Semiosis racial en los villancicos."

Chapter 5

My thanks to Asunción Lavrin for first introducing me to Ursula's text and to Mary E. Giles, Catherine Larson, and Kristin Routt for their valuable suggestions for this chapter. My thanks also to Pascale Bonaforte and René Millar for their help in tracking down archival materials in Santiago. This chapter is a greatly expanded and revised version of my 1990 article on Ursula Suárez "Miraba las cosas." In particular, I examine the historical context that may have been a key factor in the writing of the *Relación*.

1. See *Los empeños de una casa* by Sor Juana, the character Castaño, Act III.

2. "Vestía de monja al mulato del convento, llevándolo a los tornos y locutorio de hombres, que tras mí entrase para que con algunos se endevotase; y con tal gracia lo hasía que me finaba de risa, y más cuando le pedían la manita, y el mulato la sacaba lleña de callos; y estaban ellos tan embelesados, que no reparaban en lo áspero y crecido. En fin, ellos le daban sus realillos y cajetas de polvillo y era tan disparatado el mulato que, después de agarrada la plata, les dejaba las manos arañadas, habiendo estado con mil quiebros hablando de chifillo; yo a su oído, hecha el enemigo. En estas cosas se ocupaba la provisora [Ursula]: ojalá no lo fuera, si había de ser tan perversa" (Suárez, *Relación*, 161).

3. "Tengo de haser milagros, y han de pagarlos; ¿habrán visto santos ni santas interesados?: yo he de ser ésa, porque si sano enfermos o doy vista a siegos, han de venir a servir al convento, y ustedes [las monjas] se llevarán el provecho; yo, el trabajo: que me estarán atormentando, y tengo de ser una santa muy alegre" (ibid., 246).

4. "No he tenido una santa comedianta, y de todo hay en los palacios; tu has de ser la comedianta" (ibid., 230).

5. "predicar como San Pablo" (ibid., 202).

6. As in the case of many of these texts, the original title is telling of its genric origins; it echoes to a degree Teresa. Ursula's title is: "Relación de las singulares misericordias que ha usado el Señor con una religiosa, indigna esposa suya, previniéndole siempre para que sólo amase a tan Divino Esposo y apartase su amor de las criaturas; mandada escrebir por su confesor y padre espiritual" (ibid., 89).

7. My dates are based on Ramón and Podestá's informative preliminary study to the *Relación*, but my interpretation takes into account the important fact that only the first eight notebooks are written as a *vida*, while four of the remaining six are written as discrete narrative units and notebooks 13–14 are written as a single unit. For this reason, dates, addressees, and—perhaps most importantly—narrative order are difficult to establish. In fact, the editor changes the order of several notebooks from both the original autograph manuscript held at the Archives of the Convento Santa Clara de la Victoria and the nineteenth-century copy at the Archivo Nacional (Ramón, "Introducción," 17–22). Ramón (ibid., 39–40) argues that the manuscript was written in four stages: 1708; ca. 1710–1712; ca. 1726; and ca. 1730–1732.

8. A master's thesis by Mac Keller, "La relación autobiográfica," outlines the contents of these notebooks, 18–22. My thanks to René Millar for providing me with a copy of the thesis.

9. As in the case of most nuns' writings, they were probably bound by Ursula herself or one of her confessors.

10. Canovás, "Ursula Suárz"; Montecinos, "Identidad feminina"; Valdés, "Escritura de monjas"; Lagos, "Confessing"; Routt, "Authorizing Orthodoxy" and Ibsen, *Women's*.

11. Francisco and María were married around 1663; for a thorough study of the family, see Ramón, "Introducción," 54–60.

12. Ursula's grandmother had arranged for her son's marriage and asked for Ursula's mother "desnuda"—that is, she needed no dowry, not even, as the autobiographer informs

us, the clothing she wore or a bed to sleep on. For further historical detail, see Ramón, "Introducción,", 58–61. For more on marriages in colonial Chile, see Salinas Meza, "Uniones ilegítimas." For a good general study of women in colonial Chile, see Salinas, *Las chilenas*, chap. 4. Salinas bases some of her conclusions about marriage and feminine education in colonial Chile on Ursula's account.

13. Ursula's grandmother alone had five domestic slaves (Salinas, *Las chilenas*, 31).

14. Suárez, *Relacion*, 112, 232.

15. Ibid., 105. The "Aprobación" to the biography of María de San José, for example, talks of the nun's convents as "donde tantas Sagradas Virgines se desatan en olorosas suavidad y se exhalan en fragantes humos" and "Viviente confección de Aromas" (Santander y Torres, *Vida*, unnumbered preliminary pages).

16. "Si tomaba un libro era por entretenimiento y no para aprovecharme de ello; y los buscaba de historias o cuentos, novelas o comedias... también leí en esos tiempos de noviciado de la Escritura algo, y también vidas de santos, y en no siendo trágicas, las dejaba" (Suárez, *Relación*, 148–149).

17. "Hise la intención de no perder ocasión que no ejecutase engañar a cuantos pudiese mi habilidad, y esto con un entero, como si hisiese Dios en el estado presente servicio muy bueno" (ibid., 113–114).

18. For a history of the convent and role of Ursula's grandfather, Alonso del Campo, see Guernica, *Historia*, chaps. 1–2. The money was donated as early as 1629, but years of conflict within the Franciscan order, economic concerns, and a major earthquake delayed the founding for nearly half a century.

19. See Salinas, *Las chilenas*, 162.

20. See Ramón, "Introducción," 68.

21. Ibid., 56.

22. "No ha habido noviciado más rígido, porque tuvimos una maestra muy recta y de condición recia, la cual nos tenía debajo de llave todo el día en una seldita que apenas cabían las treinta novisias, porque no tenía la selda ni corral, ni huerta" (Suárez *Relación*, 142).

23. Ramón, "Introducción," 41. A 1690 document records the sale of a house to María de Escobar (Ursula's mother): "Una celda con su huertecita que están los claustros de este Monasterio, de ocho varas de frente y el largo desde dicho frente hasta topar con las paredes de la casa que posee la viuda del Capitán D. Jorge Blander" (as quoted in Guernica, *Historia*, 114).

24. Suárez, *Relación*, 171.

25. Guernica, *Historia*, 214–217.

26. For a list of these men, see Ramón, "Introducción," 37 and 78.

27. For more on documentation dealing with Ursula's profession, see Ramón, "Introducción," 77–78.

28. Suárez, *Relación*, 63, 239–241.

29. For a history of this conflict, see Guernica, *Historia*, 51–52.

30. "Fue el tenor de la sentencia que a doña Ursula Suares, porque alborotaba el convento y perdía el respeto y obediencia a las preladas, dando escándalos y causando insendios a las relgiosas, quitándoles el habla porque no la habían hecho abadesa y prelada, por tantos delitos y levantamientos, mandaba su señoría ilustrísima se me diese diciplina de rueda; que junta toda la comunidad cada una me asotase, y luego besase los pies a todas las religiosas, y comiese en tierra, y estuviera reclusa en mi selda, sin salir de ella; y esto se ejecutase por nueve días, que así lo había proveído y mandado su ilustrísima ante su notario, y así se había firmado" (Suárez, *Relación*, 261).

31. Ibid., 270.

32. "Onse años antes que me eligiesen de abadesa, me dijo su Majestad: 'Favo[re]seré tu convento si admites su gobierno'" (ibid., 239).

33. See note 7 for information on the chronology of composition.

34. As quoted in Ramón, "Introducción," 80.

35. Guernica's history of the convent, for example, culls many of the convent records and finds instances in which Ursula's name is mentioned. On one occasion, it is because she is sick and funds are allotted for buying her more food (*Historia*, 163). In another, she signs off on a document dealing with a *celda* (*Historia*, 126). More detailed accounts about her life are not mentioned by Guernica or Ramón.

36. Our only clue to Gamboa being the addressee of these eight notebooks is when Ursula (*Relación*, 163) refers to María de Gamboa as "hermana de Vuestra Paternidad." This occurs in the middle of the *vida* sequence.

37. Ibid., 165, 166, 167, 169–170.

38. "Desía por las demás: '¿Cómo podrán tener oración larga, que a mí luego se me acaba?' Daban todas risadas, disiendo: '¿Cómo se le acaba?'; desíales: "Yo no lo entiendo bien: lo tengo de memoria, pero con él no hago cosa;' desíanme: 'Divertiráse en otras cosas'; desíales: "no es eso, que el punto lo estoy disiendo'; reíanse también desto. Mas no dejaba de ira mi oración a tiempos" (ibid., 166–167).

39. I owe a debt of gratitude to Kristine Ibsen and Kristin Routt for bringing to my attention the connection between the *comedia* and the *Relación*. See Ibsen, *Women's*, chap. 6, and Routt, "Authoring Orthodoxy," chap. 4.

40. Popular dramatists, such as Lope de Vega, set dozens of saints' lives to dramatic form.

41. The *mujer varonil* was a constant favorite in Spanish theatre from 1590 to 1600, with at least one new play produced each year. As McKendrick's (*Woman and Society*, 43) important study of women in Golden Age theatre notes, the *mujer varonil* represented a woman who " through inclination or through circumstance, departed from the feminine norm of the society in which they lived, or which had, at least, nurtured them." Moreover, her revolt "is against Society and convention, and woman's inferior position in them, not against her sexual role vis-à-vis man" (*Woman and Society*, 317). Typically this rebellion was considered virtuous because the woman aspired to transcend the limitations of her sex. For more on this argument, see Ibsen, *Women's*, 122–130.

42. Weber studies Teresa's writings in *Teresa*, 128–134; Ross points to Sigüenza y Góngora's use of this structure in *The Baroque Narrative*, chap. 4; Johnson mentions several elements in Sor Juana's *Respuesta* in *Satire*, 76–87; and Sánchez Lora examines a variety of religious women's life stories in *Mujeres*, 351–357, 404–405.

43. Rabell, "La confesión," 20.

44. Interestingly, after writing his picaresque novel, Alemán went on to write two hagiographic biographies—one on Saint Anthony of Padua and one on the archbishop of Mexico.

45. Howard Mancing brought to my attention another case in which the *pícara* clearly deviates from a nun's confession. The anonymons seventeenth-century *Vida y costumbres de la Madre Andrea* recounts the life of woman who is a madre only by title, not profession. In fact, she is the antithesis of a model nun.

46. Friedman elaborates this idea in "The Picaresque as Autobiography: Story and History," 119–128.

47. Ramírez Leyva (*María Rita Vargas*, 39), for example, links *beatas* and *pícaras*, with both generally pertaining to the lower class. See also Huerga, "La picaresca de las beatas," and Perry, *Gender and Disorder*.

48. Suárez, *Relación*, 91. There is an echo here of the picaresque as well: the *pícaro* moves from one master (*amo*) to another.

49. Ibid., 98.

50. "En una ocasión se empesó [mi madre] a lamentar que no tenía con qué poder trabajar, y que mi abuela, teniendo tanto trigo, no le daba una fanega, y a mí me dijo: 'Dirásle, piquito, para que diga tu abuela que la murmuro y que soy nuera.' Yo busqué ocasión de desirlo a mi abuela, porque aunque era tan chiquilla, que ni sinco años tenía, miraba las cosas que desía; y un día que en la cama me tenía, le dije: 'Abuelita, la pobre de mi mamá no tiene con qué trabajar: ¿por qué vuestra mersed no le da?'; respondió: '¿No tiene tres negras esclavas?: ¿por qué no las hase trabajar?: ¿cómo las envía alquilar?: y le he dicho que [s]e han de enfermar con los alquileres, y tu madre no quiere'. Así hablaba conmigo como si yo fuera gente. Díjele: 'Déle trigo, y con eso hará sus amasijos'. '¿Ella te lo dijo?' 'Mi mamá habla conmigo —le respondí yo—; déle el trigo'... Yo empesé a llorar y a darle quejas, disiendo: '¿Ve cómo no me quiere abuela?: ¿esas son sus finesas, no quererme dar la llave de la espensa?' Tantas bachillerías le desía, que dijo: 'Toma la llave, niña; da dos fanegas'. Fui a mi madre muy contenta; díjele: 'Vamos a la espensa, que ya le da trigo mi abuela'. '¿No te dije que no se lo dijeras?; hay desvergüensa; ¿par qué se lo contastes a tu abuela?: que delante de ti no se puede hablar'. Yo empesé a temblar, jusgando me había de asotar. Entonses le dijo mi tía: 'No seas así, Marucha, con tu hija: sobre buscarte la vida y con qué poder trabajar, haséis a este angelito temblar, en ves que la habías de halagar. No seas necia con ella, que es tan donosa y descreta'" (ibid.).

51. Ibid., 94–95.

52. "Seráslo [monja] con toda comodidad, si Dios me quisiere guardar hasta que tu tengas edad, que no habrá monja de más comodidad, con tu selda alhajada, muy bien colgada, escaparate y tu plata labrada, que del Perú se traerá, y los liensos del Cusco, y todo lo nesesario a Lima enviaré emplearlo. Tendrás tu esclava dentro y otra fuera, y cuatro mil pesos de renta; esto fuera de tu herencia, que de por si te la darán" (ibid., 101).

53. Ibid., 119,104. "Se me ponía en la cabesa que todas las que se casaban estaban muertas" (ibid., 126).

54. "¿Pues, yo había de consentir que con hombre me acostasen?: primero he de horcarme, o con una daga degollarme, o el pecho atravesarme" (ibid., 123–124).

55. For a study of the folkloric elements in Suárez's *Relación*, see Cánovas, "Ursula Suárez," 100. As Ramón ("Introducción," 76) notes, this incident probably plays on the confusion of a child who knows the Chilean tradition of displaying the marriage bed at weddings.

56. "Había oído contar de una varilla de virtud, que con ella se hasían maravillas. Creíalas, y así buscaba esta varilla con ansias: salía de casa y seguíame por una sequia que sale de las monjas agustinas, y llegaba tan abajo donde la sequía se batía, que tiraba a la campaña... Habían unos cuartos vasíos y sin puertas, donde se cometían tantas desvergüensas que era temeridad ésta, siendo de día, y no solas dos personas habían en esta maldad, sino 8 ó 10; y esto no había ojos que lo viesen, sino los de una inosente, que no sabía si pecado cometían. Yo pensaba eran casamientos, y así todos los días iba a verlos" (Suárez, *Relación*, 107–108).

57. "Yo le desía [a mi tía]: 'Cuando grandesilla seré la rosa entre las espinas, que he de ser monjita'; ella me desía: '¿Vos habías de ser monja?: tan perversa y de tan mala casta, enemigos de ser monjas' y le respondía yo: 'Yo, tía, he de ser la corona de la generación'; desíame: 'Calla, loca, que tu vivesa no es para monja, aunque de chiquitita en mantillas te estaba bañando un día en medio del patio, y me causastes espanto, porque, teniéndote en cueritos... agarrada de las trensas de mis cabellos empesastes a repicar con gran compás, y

hasías el tañido de las campanas con la boca.' Yo, espantada, llamé a tu madre y le dije: 'Gata, ven a ver a tu hija, que ha de ser monja: mira cómo repica'. Mi madre y todas las de la casa salieron a selebrar tu gracia: no sé que será, porque tú eres gran bellaca'. Yo le desía: 'Tía, vuestra mersed lo verá cómo soy monja'" (ibid., 91–92).

58. For an excellent analysis of this topic in Suárez, see Routt, "Authorizing Orthodoxy," chap. 4.

59. Suárez, *Relación*, 181.

60. See Rabell, "La confesión."

61. "En conclusión, hise la intención de no perder ocasión que no ejecutase engañar a cuantos pudiese mi habilidad, y esto con un entero, como si hisiese a Dios en el estado presente servicio muy bueno; no se pasarían cuatro días que no ejecuté mi intento" (Suárez, *Relación*, 113–114).

62. "Después de completas, parecióme buena ocasión esta para poder engañar. Fui a la caja de mi tía; como mica empéseme [a] aliñar con mucho afán, y desía: 'Cuando suben a la ventana van aliñadas'. Saqué el solimán y sin espejo me lo empesé a pegar, y muy buena color; no sé si me puse como mascarón: a esto no atendía yo, sino al aliño que a las mujeres había visto... y saqué una mantilla... que me tapara la cara: bien lo discurría, que viesen que era blanca y no conosiesen era niña. Fuime así a la ventana... Yo que estoy ya sentada, vi venir un hombre de hasia la plasa y dije: 'Gracias a Dios, ahora te engaño a vos'. Así susedió, que el hombre se llegó a la ventana y me empesó [a] hablar. Ni yo sabía lo que e[l] hombre me desía ni lo que yo le respondía . . . pedíame la mano; yo hise reparo que si me la veía había de conoser por ella que era niña. Sacó un puñado de plata y me la daba; y porque no me viera la mano me acobaraba, no porque me alborotó la plata. Por último díjele: 'Si me da la plata, entre la mano en la ventana'; yo todo lo hasía por asegurarla y arrebatársela; entró el puñado de plata como se lo mandaba y doyle una manotada dejándome juntamente caer de la ventana, con un patacón que sólo le pude arrebatar, que no cupo en mi mano más. Y así que estuve abajo, lo empesé a llamar de caballo, disiéndolo: 'Te [he] engañado, tontaso; tan mal animal que de mí se dejó engañar'... Serré la ventana de presto y fuime dentro a guardar los aseos y lavarme la cara porque no me viese mi tía afeitada" (ibid., 114–115).

63. Ibid., 115, 127, 134.

64. "Selebraban la gracia y desían que debía de ser gran bellaca y resabida" (ibid., 141).

65. "Yo estuve disgustada de principio en el convento, echando menos los aseos de mi casa y el no comer en plata labrada" (ibid., 140).

66. Criticism of the *devoto* system was broadly based: Teresa of Avila attacked it, and picaresque novelists such as Quevedo and Alemán criticized it. For more information on the practice, see Ramón, "Introducción," 71–72, and Perry's discussion of *devotos* and satire in *Gender and Disorder*, 80n18.

67. "Yo digo que, como le daba, no sólo gran religiosa me pronosticaba sino santa, porque este dar era cono[n]isar" (Suárez, *Relación*, 142).

68. "Llegaba el tiempo de confesarme y hasía esamen de tantas maldiciones" (ibid., 165).

69. "Pues este hombre, ¿no era un necio, que a tales disparates daba crédito?; pues ¿había de irme con hombre casado, ya que salía del convento, y más teniendo él conosimiento de mis parientes y quién era?: suya fue la simplesa en creeerme, cuando desía que yo paresía perversísima, que tenía trasa de al diablo engañarlo: ellos mesmos lo desían, y ensima les caía; con que ahora pienso que los diablos para las mujeres son ellos que han sido los engañados" (ibid., 186–187).

70. Ibid., 192–200. "Yo puse en vos las palabras de san Pablo, porque quiero prediques como él" (ibid., 203). Ursula's first discussion of St. Paul and theology is couched between two accounts of prayer (ibid., 186–189).

71. "[Padre Viñas] díjome no dije[se] lo que dijo san Pablo, sino lo que Samuel, también las palabr[a]s de la Virgen Santísima: *Ece ancila*; yo, como no sabía, desía lo que se me ofrecía... y par[e]se que esto [n]o salía de mi alma, sino que con la boca sólo lo hablaba; yo lo desía porque el padre lo había mandado, no con la eficasia que había dicho las de san Pablo, porque estas las digtó mi corasón. En otra ocasión... me dijo esta vos en el interior: 'Yo quiero manifestar la fuersa de mi poder en vos'" (ibid., 200).

72. Ibid., 214–216, 209, 212, 196.

73. These notebooks open and close with clearly marked narrative formula.

74. For more on composition of the notebooks see Podestá, "Editor's note to *Relación*," 17–22, and Ramón, "Introducción," 37–43.

75. For studies of language and its role in the picaresque novel, see Friedman, *The Antiheroine's Voice*.

76. This confusion, as we saw in the chapter on Catarina de San Juan, may reflect the fact that all people of Asian descent were called "chinos."

77. Suárez, *Relación*, 218–220, 231. "Preguntéles por qué no estaban bautisados antes; dijeron no sabían resar: 'Vos —me dijeron— enseñastes a nosotros.' Yo me reí de su tontería de desir que no habían podido aprender con los padres, sino de mí" (ibid., 232).

78. "Soy tan habladora que me buscaban las religiosas que las divertiera, y me llamaban la historiadora" (ibid., 245).

79. "[El obispo] padesía de hipocondría; yo, por divertírsela, le desía bufonadas y hasía dar risadas:... se divertía de mis frioneras" (ibid., 243).

80. "Dile al obispo que el haberte dado el pie no le paresca fue acaso, sino para que te dé la mano, que hartos tiempos te han hollado, y como trigo acribado, que trese años has estado en el lago, que te dé la mano y que se acuerde bien si ha dado el pie [a] alguna mujer, que para ti lo guarde y para eso lo consagré" (ibid., 244).

81. "Díjome mi Señor y Padre amantísimo: 'No he tenido una santa comedianta, y de todo hay en los palacios; tu has de ser la comedianta'; yo le dije: 'Padre y Señor mío, a más de tus beneficios y misericordias, te agradesco, que ya que quieres haserme santa, no sea santa friona': díjome: 'Ya no envidiarás a doña Marina y a la Antigua'" (ibid., 230). For a more complete identification of these two women, see Ramón, "Introducción," 34.

82. "Han de saber que he de ser santa, y no así como quiera, que no ha de haber en la Iglesia de Dios santa tan disparatada" (Suárez, *Relación*, 245).

83. Significantly, men who are not portrayed in this light are depicted as effeminate. The loving father is called a pansy (*marica*) by his wife, and one kind *devoto* is portrayed as both mother and father to Ursula.

84. Cánovas ("Ursula Suárez," 114) keenly observes that Ursula's account is "un testimonio que reorienta (o cuestiona) la literatura edificante de la época." He suggests that she reorients it by including "la voz tradicional (el folklore), de raigambre hispánica" and a feminine voice. He does not, however, posit a convincing argument to explain why Ursula would question didactic literature. As Routt ("Authorizing Orthodoxy," chap. 4) explains, Ursula flaunts her own voice—whether in dialogue with God, making jokes, or teaching. She rejects the serious, silent, self-mortifying saintly paradigm and offers a new role.

85. See Cruz, "The Picaresque as Discourse of Poverty," 90.

86. The dream is told to Padre Viñas, who died in 1719, so it took place sometime before that.

87. See a parallel symbolism of a dove and serpent in Santander y Torres, "Aprobación," *Vida*.

88. "Cuando referí esto al padre Viñas, me dijo: 'Y no tiene güesos'; yo le dije: 'Si se lo oí sonar.' 'No tiene güesos,' volvió a replicar. Yo callé y no le pugné más" (Suárez, *Relación*, 270).

89. "Díjome su Majestad: 'Repique ha de haber,' yo le dije: 'Y truenos también, para que esté buena la fiesta'" (ibid., 263).

90. "No me hables en latín ni me nombres a san Pablo ni me tomes en la boca la Biblia" (ibid., 262).

91. "Viendo tantas misericordias como de su inmensa bondad resebía, le dije: 'Señor y dueño de todo mi ser, mi solo amor y todo mi bien, parese quieres haser verdaderas mis locuras'; respondió: 'Profetisabas en ti'; díjele: 'Yo profeta en mi tierra?'; díjome: 'Contigo todo se dispensa'; díjele: 'Y cuando tengo de ser santa?'; respondió: 'Cuando estés callada'; díjele: 'Mucho me falta, que no puedo estar callada'" (ibid., 245).

92. Recall that María de San Jose's notebooks are carefully reordered and do not follow the chronology of composition; her *Stations* were recopied and circulated in manuscript form during her own life. Both were used later for the hagiographic *vida*. In Ursula's case, the opening title and chapter heading are clearly in a formal hand, and talks of Ursula are in third person: "Relación de las singulares misericordias que ha usado el Señor con una religiosa, indigna esposa suya, previniéndole siempre para que sólo amase a tan Divino Esposo y apartase su amor de las ciraturas; mandaba escrebir por su confesor y padre espiritual." The main body of the text is in a less careful hand, typical of many nuns' handwriting. Besides the paleography, the theory that the notebooks might be in Ursula's original hand is convincing, since there are blank pages in the manuscript that would typically not be in a manuscript copy.

93. There surely were written works after that date, as Abbess Ursula wrote many letters and Ramón conjectures that her extant notebooks probably represent a small portion of what she actually wrote. There is some discrepancy about the order of notebooks 10–13: they were composed as separate narrative units and have been ordered in several ways. I believe that the twentieth-century edition has misplaced the twelfth notebook, which contains a single anecdote about Ursula's wimple. The editors placed it in the middle of the chronological story about the 1711 election of the abbess (notebook 11), subsequent difficulties with the abbess and confessors (notebook 13), and the bishop's 1715 *sentencia* (notebook 14). The nineteenth-century copy places the twelfth notebook before this sequence (between notebooks 10 and 11), and it seems less disruptive there. See Podestá, "Editor's note to *Relación*," 21.

94. Ibsen, for example, argues: "Like the *mujer varonil*, Ursula in the end is forced to defer to male authority, although with a decidedly unhappy, if not tragic, ending. Ursula Suarez's decision to end her narration with a dream that predates the time of writing by at least twelve years suggests the enormous pain of realization when this 'very happy saint' was forced by circumstances into silence" (*Women's*, 136).

95. Ibsen (in *Women's*, 134) discusses the role of a controversial Inquisition trial and Romero's transfer to Quito. In "Introducción," 36–43, Ramón argues that later notebooks were probably destroyed. My reading is based on the fact that in notebook 10 each of Ursula's previous confessors, and therefore possible addressees, are named.

96. "Díjome: '¿No se han leído casos de obispos que han tenido hijos?'" (Suárez, *Relación*, 234).

97. See Myers and Powell, *A Wild Country*, 217–226.

98. For example, a period notary cites in a 1735 document about a sale of property that Ursula was present with the abbess at the time of the purchase (Guernica, *Historia*, 126).

99. Although, the nun who won the position of abbess on two occasions did not die until 1745 (Guernica, *Historia*, appendix 1).

100. See Ibsen, *Women's*, 134.

101. "Señor mío, ¿por qué cuando usas de tus misericordias con las mujeres, anda la Inquisición conosiendo de ellas?" (Suárez, *Relación*, 252).

102. Ursula's confessor was fearful; she reports: "Teme por lo que susedió a fray Luis de Granada, y en estos tiempos de la Carransa" (ibid., 253).

103. See Guernica, *Historia*, 303 and 210–227. The bishop who was in power during Ursula's time as abbess, Fernández Rojas, also reinforced guidelines from the Council of Trent on enclosure of nuns and focusing on the spiritual life.

104. See Ibsen, *Women's*, 134.

105. For information about the 1730 earthquake, see Guernica, *Historia*, 115; for the position of abbess in 1732, see ibid., 241–243.

106. A funerary sermon of Madre Castillo was written, but there was no hagiographic biography. See McKnight's important study, *The Mystic of Tunja*, 125.

107. Routt, "Authoring Orthodoxy"; Arenal and Schlau, *Untold Sisters*.

Chapter 6

My thanks to Mary E. Giles, Amanda Powell, and Linda Curcio-Nagy for their valuable comments on an early draft of this paper, read at the Modern Languages Association in San Francisco, 1998. An abbreviated version of this chapter was published in Kathleen Ann Myers, *Writing of the Frontier*, ed. Santa Arias and Mariselle Meléndez (Lewisburg, PA: Bucknell University Press, 2002). All translations of Catalina's *Vida* are courtesy of Nina M. Scott.

1. "The nuns were beside themselves when they took their leave of me, and I was carried off in a litter with a retinue of six priests, four friars, and six swordsmen" (Stepto and Stepto, *Lieutenant Nun*, chap. 21). The translation of Catalina's title from "alférez" into lieutenant is problematic. According to the second *Relación* (1625), Catalina was promoted to Sargento Mayor, but Vallbona (*Vida i sucesos*, 165n12) says that official documents show she only received the title of *alférez*, or ensign.

2. During much of this time, she went by the alias of Alonso Díaz Ramírez de Gúzman.

3. The petitions are reproduced, along with notarized testimony from witnesses, in Vallbona's edition of *Vida i sucesos*, appendix 2. These documents, among others, are also reproduced in Tellechea Idigoras, *Doña Catalina de Erauso*. Both editions draw on Ferrer's *Historia de la Mónja Alférez* and Medina's *Biblioteca Hispano-Chilena*, as well as new archival material. The petitions include two separate ones to the Crown: one for remuneration for Catalina's military services and the other for compensation for a robbery that occurred when she traveled to Rome in 1626. See Merrim, "Petition of Catalina de Erauso" for a translation and study of the petition, which recounts her decision to cross-dress and be a soldier. The memoirs have been edited on a handful of occasions. The most recent, complete Spanish edition is Vallbona's *Vida i sucesos de la Monja Alférez.* See the bibliography in Vallbona for a complete listing of previous editions in English and Spanish. The only one not listed that is of some importance is Pedro Rubio Merino's recent *La Monja Alférez* (1995). The document about Catalina's share of her family estate is cited by Stepto from Lucas G. Castillo Lara, *La asombrosa historia de Doña Catalina de Erauso*, xlii (Castillo 318); · Tellechea Idigoras's *Doña Catalina* reproduces many of the family's wills and estate documents.

4. One of the few documents that describes Catalina during these years is reproduced in Vallbona, *Vida i Sucessos*, 155. Another is the *Tercera relación* (Mexico 1653), discussed later in this chapter.

5. For more about cross-dressing in seventeenth-century Spain, see Perry, *Gender and Disorder*, chap. 6, and Merrim, "Catalina de Erauso: From Anomoly to Icon." See also Velasco's important new book, *The Lieutenant Nun*, chaps. 1–2.

6. This is Merrim's central argument in her study and translation of this document; see "Petition."

7. For a history of the manuscript and its nineteenth-century publication, see Vallbona, *Vida i sucesos* 2–3.

8. Bynum's *Holy Feast and Holy Fast* has been one of the landmark works on this topic. In the context of colonial Spanish America, see Routt's "Authorizing Orthodoxy" and Ibsen's *Women's Spiritual Autobiography*. For lengthier discussions of this topic with regard to Catalina de Erauso in particular, see Merrim, *Early Modern Women's Writing*, 13–18, and Velasco, *The Lieutenant Nun*, chap. 1.

9. For extensive, and often new, documentation on Catalina's family, see Tellechea Idigoras's *Doña Catalina*. Also consult my chronology and note there for more information about discrepancies about many dates for Catalina's life.

10. Captain Miguel de Erauso was part of the Armada, and served in various other positions as scribe and mayor; for more historical details on Catalina's family, see Tellechea Idigoras, *Doña Catalina*.

11. "Era mi inclinasión andar i ver el mundo" (Vallbona, *Vida i Sucesos* chap. 5).

12. For the full names of the sisters who entered the convent with Catalina and the brothers who went to America, see Tellechea Idigoras, *Doña Catalina*.

13. "Y también hay pobres soberbios que ya que no pueden morder ladran, y siempre andan con la cabeza baja mirando donde pueden hacer presa, ni se quieren sujetar ni hay razón con ellos. A esta gente tal llaman soldados no porque lo sean, sino porque son bien andantes de unos lugares para otros, siempre con los naipes en las manos, por no perder ocasión de jugar con cuantos topan, y por si acaso topan con algún novicio o chapetón que no está diestro y bien disciplinado en su malicia, o que no alcance su malicia con naipes falsos les dan mates y les quitan el dinero y la hacienda... Son grandísimos fulleros que su cuidado no es otro más que entender en el arte de engañar. Esta gente es mucha la que anda por el Perú. Y todos por la mayor parte son enemigos de la gente rica y no desean sino novedades y alteraciones y alborotos en el Reino, por robar en y meter en los codos en los bienes de que no pueden alcanzar parte sino con guerra y disensiones. Es gente que no quieren servir. Todos andan bien vestidos, porque nunca les falta una negra o una india y algunas españolas, y no de las más pobres... Es más la gente vagabunda que tiene el Perú . . . y busquen su vida como mejor pudieron. A otra suerte de gente de menor cuantía y que no puede usar tan bien ni con tanta libertad la arte de la adulación ni tienen caudal para andar en vagabundos de unas tierras a otras, y también porque se inclinan más al trabajo y al ejercicio de las armas y a comer a cuenta del rey, estos tales se meten soldados, porque todos los años se hace en Lima gente para el Reino de Chile. Y los llevan debajo de sus banderas a pelear con los araucanos. Y les dan en Lima doscientos pesos, con que se visten. Con esto limpian la tierra y envían gente contra los indomables araucanos. Y pocos destos soldados vuelven a Perú" (*La inedita*, 69–70).

14. "Hallándola, la truxeron ante Su Señoría [el obispo], vestida [de] calzón y ropilla de perpetuam failesco y un ferruelo de cordellate pardo, sombrero blanco guarnecido de trencilla de oro la halda y el cayrel, valon de puntas, jubón de raso blanco trencillado,

coleto de ante guarnecido, espada y daga dorada" (as quoted in Tellechea Idigoras, *Doña Catalina*, 61).

15. By most accounts these events took place around 1619, although the document that records some of the inquiry made by the bishop is dated 1617. Perhaps this is merely an error in the transcription of the document (see Tellechea Idigoras, *Doña Catalina*, 60–64). This document is particularly interesting because there are several discrepancies about Catalina's life, and it illustrates the sort of question and answer format of much period inquiry that informed autobiographical narrative structures, as discussed in the introduction to this book.

16. "La prosecución honesta en adelante, i la abstinencia en ofender al próximo, temiendo la ulción de Dios sobre su mandamiento, *non occides.*" (Vallbona, *Vida i sucesos*, chap. 25).

17. See Rubial, "Catalina de Erauso," 115–117.

18. The anonymous satirist exclaims: "Vive Apolo, que será/ un lego quien alabare/ desde hoy a la Monja Alférez/ sino a la Monja Almirante" (Romance 48 in Sor Juana Inés de la Cruz, *Obras*, 309).

19. For transcriptions of three broadsides—selections from a history, a play, and a poem—as well as information about the Italian translations, see Valbona, *Vida i sucesos*, appendices. Both Merrim, "Catalina de Erauso," and Perry, *Gender and Disorder*, analyze some of these works.

20. "Tenga fin aqui/ este caso verdadero/ donde llega la Comedia/ han llegado los sucesos;/ que oy está el Alferez Monja/ en Roma." For analyses of Montalbán's treatment of the manly woman character type in this play, see Velasco, *The Lieutenant Nun*, 60–70, and Perry, "La Monja Alférez."

21. *Relación prodigiosa* (Madrid 1625), *Segunda parte de la relación* (Madrid 1625), and Fray Diego de Rosales, *Historia general del Reino de Chile* (chap. 37). These are all reprinted in Vallbona's Appendixes. The broadsides also were reprinted in Mexico.

22. There are three versions of these memoirs; I use Vallbona's edition of the standard version, which is based on Ferrer's (*Historia*) first edition of the text. Ferrer, in turn, worked with Múñoz's eighteenth-century copy of a document in Seville; see Rubio Merino, *La monja*, 18. Múñoz's version is housed at the Real Academia de Historia in Madrid. This is a 1784 copy, which has eighteenth-century calligraphy but seventeenth-century orthography and morphosyntax. According to most critics, the account was completed between 1624 and 1626, then deposited in the publishing house of Bernardino de Gúzman in Madrid. Two alternate versions of the *Vida* were published for the first time in 1995 by Rubio Merino and are based on late-seventeenth-century copies housed at the Cathedral Archives in Seville. Of the two versions, M-I and M-II, only the first is complete. It covers the same years and anecdotes as Vallbona's edition, but there are significant changes in the narration of certain events. I discuss one of the most significant, the moment of confession to the bishop, later in this chapter (M-I, Rubio Merino; chap. 20 Vallbona). For more on the history of the manuscripts, see Medina, *Biblioteca Hispano-Chilena*; Rubio Medina, *La Monja Alférez*; and Vallbona, *Vida i sucesos*.

23. Several theories exist about the extent to which Catalina de Erauso had a hand in the writing of her own memoirs. Most critics agree that she was extensively involved but that the transcriber probably elaborated on her story either at the time of the original composition or later when it was copied. Vallbona sets out her theories in *Vida i sucesos*, 2–11, and Merrim in "Catalina de Erauso," 196.

24. See Merrim, "Catalina de Erauso," 195.

25. Vallbona, *Vida i sucesos*, 11.

26. *El Carnero* (1636–1638) by Rodriquez Freile and The *Historia de Potosí* by Arzans de Orsua (first part of the eighteenth century) for example, have been studied for their novelesque retelling of scaborous tales. Likewise, scholars point out the blurring of Sigüenza y Góngora's voice as transcriber with the first-person accounts of Ramírez's shipwreck in *Naufragios* and of nuns retelling the history of their convent in *Paraíso occidental*. For a more thorough discussion of these hybrid genres, see Ross, *The Baroque Narrative*. Many colonial scholars, such as González-Echevarría in "The Law of the Letter," note that period accounts often defy traditional definitions of literary and historical genres; the texts created a new type of writing.

27. See, for example, the documents in Vallbona, *Vida i sucesos*, appendix 2, and Merrim, "Petition," 37.

28. Garber, "Preface to Lieutenant Nun"; Juárez, "La mujer militar"; Merrim, "Catalina de Erauso"; Perry, "La Monja Alférez"; Velasco, *The Lieutenant Nun*; and Vallbona, *Vida i Sucesos*.

29. Perry, *Gender and Disorder*, chap. 6 "Sexual Rebels."

30. Merrim, *Early Modern*, 13–15.

31. See also the case discovered by Velasco and her overview of the popularity of female transvestitism in historical and literary works of the period, *The Lieutenant Nun*, 22–23, 32–40.

32. The painting is in the colonial art collection at CONDUMEX, Mexico City. My thanks to Manuel Ramos Medina for showing this to me.

33. Merrim, for example, briefly mentions the influence of the picaresque tone, the theatricality of the narration, and the lack of interiority or remorse characteristic of the soldier's life in "Catalina de Erauso," 181, 195. Garber mentions the complex mixture of literary forms from autobiography to pilgrimage and picaresque narrative structures in Preface to *Lieutenant Nun*, xxiii, xxxiv; and Rubio Merino does as well in *La Monja Alférez*, 43–44, 50, 88. In the most extensive study of genre, Vallbona divides the narrative according to the echoes from the picaresque (chaps. 1–5), the chronicle of conquest (chap. 6 and others), and cloak and dagger theatre and travel literature (chaps. 6, 11–20), as well as various popular story-telling influences throughout (chaps. 9–11). She also carefully footnotes passages reminiscent of these genres.

34. For how this type of writing derived from bureaucratic, legal, and ecclesial models, see González-Echevarría, "The Law of the Letter," 107–109; and Fernández, *Apology to Apostrophe*, chap. 1.

35. This is a term used by Fernández in his study of Hispanic autobiography, *Apology*, 22.

36. These categories also correspond to the three that Levisi in *Autobiografías del siglo de oro* says are the predominant forms during Spain's Golden Age (the memorial, picaresque, and confession).

37. Although generally they were not published until the twentieth century, these soldiers' accounts may have circulated in manuscript form. For twentieth-century editions of some of these, see Cossío, *Autobiografías*.

38. The text states her birth year as 1585, but the baptismal record states 1592; see Vallbona, *Vida i sucesos*, 151.

39. Ginés de Pasamonte's *Vida* (ca. 1604) (in Cossío, *Autobiografías*) is one of the few soldier's accounts that describes having a religious calling yet becoming a soldier because he did not have the necessary background and money to enter the religious life.

40. Levisi uses this term in her book that examines three soldiers' accounts, *Auto-biografías*, 141.

41. Garber emphasizes the memoirs' frequent description of clothes and argues that Catalina is a transvestite; she fails to place this emphasis, however, in the broader context of soldiers' accounts, which often talk of clothing as it related to status. See Garber's preface to *Lieutenant Nun*. It should be noted here that the descriptions of cities in the memoirs often echo period chronicles, a genre not studied in this essay because it does not fit into the life-writing focus.

42. "Juntámonos otros quantos con él, i alojámonos en los llanos de Valdivia en campaña raza, cinco mil hombres con harta incomodidad. Tomaron i asolaron los Yndios la dicha Valdivia... Viéndola [bandera] llevar, partimos tras ella yo i dos Soldados de caballo por medio de grande multitud, atropellando i matando, i recibiendo daño: en breve cayó muertos uno de los tres. Proseguimos los dos. Legamos a la vandera, cayó de un bote de lanza mi compañero. Yo recibí un mal golpe en una pierna. Maté al Cacique que la llevaba i quitésela, i apreté con mi caballo, atropellando, matando i hiriendo a infinidad, pero mal herido, i pasado de tres flechas, i de una lanza en el ombro izquierdo que sentía mucho. En fin, llegué a mucha gentre i caí luego del caballo... quedé Alférez de la compañía de Alonso Moreno... i holgué mucho" (Vallbona, *La Monja*, Chap. 6).

43. "Mass was held in the jail, and when the priest had taken communion he gave it to me and turned back to the altar, and I instantly spat the wafer out into my right hand, shouting madly, 'I call on the church! I call on the church!' Complete bedlam ensued. The brothers were scandalized and kept shouting, 'Heretic! Heretic!' ... The priests circled round me, along with a great number of townspeople—they lighted candles, unfurled a canopy over my head, and carried me in procession into the sacristy, where everyone got down on their knees and a priest pried the wafer from my hand and placed it in the tabernacle.... This was a scheme I had come up with thanks to a pious Franciscan, who gave me some words of wisdom when I was in jail, and took my last confession. The governor kept the church surrounded, with me under lock and key" (chap. 15). According to Catholic belief, the consecrated host became the actual body of Christ in the process of transubstantiation and could only be touched by the hands of a priest. Similar treatment of the church can be seen in Miguel Castro's parody of the canonical hours; see Pope, *La autobiografía española*, 197.

44. Catalina, *Vida*, chap. 9.

45. As we will see, Alonso de Conteras is the closest in tone. Others, such as Castro's *Vida* (ca. 1609) and Pasamonte's *Vida i trabajos* (ca. 1605) (in Cossio, *Autobiografías*), have elements of the picaresque, especially Castro's retelling of amorous encounters, but they also include a structure based on trials (and, therefore, deserving of merit). For more on the development of the genre, see Pope, *La autobiografía*, and Levisi, *Autobiografías*.

46. As an example of the first, Pope studies the account by Charles V's soldier Diego García de Paredes (1468–1533). Examples of more roguish accounts are Miguel Castro's story (ca. 1612) of swordfights and brawls, and the duke of Estrada's contradictory *Comentarios de el desengañado* (1614, 1633, 1642). According to Pope, by as early as the first decade of the seventeenth century in Diego Suárez Montañez's *Discurso verdadero* (ca. 1610), the soldier-autobiographer wished to satisfy the reader's curiosity, and thus the narrator incorporated elements of the popular picaresque form; he recounts his "naturaleza y inclinasión y curso de la vida, para enterar a los lectores de mis partes y vivienda, en el curioso que lo quisiere, aberigurar lo hallará así sin discrepar punto de verdad" (quoted in Pope, *La autobiografía*, 123).

47. Quoted in Serrano y Sanz, *Apuntes*, 485.

48. Estebanillo González, *La vida y hechos de Estebanillo González, hombre de buen humor, compuesta por él mismo*, Antwerp 1646; there were at least five other editions published in Madrid during the next hundred years. See Pope, *La autobiografía*, chap. 4.

49. Pope (*La autobiografía*, 140) sees this as manifesting itself as "la desadaptación" that was increasingly expressed after 1600, as a "perplejidad ante las nuevas condiciones sociales que los autobiógrafos que siguen resolverán adecuadamente con una abierta aceptación de la inseguridad y la aventura."

50. Catalina resubmitted her petition to the Consejo de Indias in August 1625, and in April 1626, after presenting a case to the king, she was granted remuneration for her services. For the chronology of these documents, see Vallbona, *Vida i sucesos*, 119, 121.

51. According to his own *Vida* (ca. 1630), Contreras (in Cossío *Autobiografías*) left home at a young age after killing a boy; he served in the army, was promoted to alférez and later captain, met both the king and pope, and became the subject of a famous playwright's drama. He also was a rogue, killed to protect his honor, and gambled. See the edition of his *Vida* in Cossío's *Autobiografías de soldados*. Lope de Vega's *El rey sin reino* is very loosely based on Contreras's life. Contreras lived with Lope from 1622 to 1623.

52. Only in later additions, once things no longer were going his way, is there evidence of a petition. Levisi (*Autobiografías*, 129, 130) discusses the 1633 and 1641 additions. See also Pope, *La autobiografía*, 148–164.

53. Stepto and Stepto, *Lieutenant Nun*, xl.

54. According to Vallbona's division in *Vida i sucesos*, 9, chapters 1–5 correspond to the picaresque.

55. "Es de saber que esta Doña Beatriz de Cárdenas era Dama de mi amo, i él mirava a tenernos seguros, a mí, para servicio, i a ella, para gusto… una noche me encerró i se declaró en que a pesar del diablo havía de dormir con ella… i dixe luego a mi amo que de tal casmiento no havía que tratar, porque por todo el mundo yo no lo haría. A lo qual él porfió, i me promtetió montes de oro" (Vallbona, *Vida i sucesos*, chap. 3).

56. See Cruz's use of the term, "The Picaresque as Discourse of Poverty," and Mandrell's discussion of sexual desirability in "Questions of Genre and Gender," 152.

57. In "La confesión en jerigonza," Rabell argues that much of the slang used in the Lazarillo text has sexual innuendos.

58. See the documents in Tellechea Idigoras, *Doña Catalina*, and Vallbona, *Vida i sucesos*.

59. See Stepo and Stepto, *Lieutenant Nun*, xl–xli, and Perry, *Gender and Disorder*, 135.

60. For a discussion of this dynamic in the Lazarillo de Tormes text, see Rosenberg, *The Circular Pilgrimage*, 75, 81–86.

61. Like many of the dates associated with Catalina's life, there is a discrepancy in different accounts. A letter recording the encounter with the bishop is dated in Tellechea Idigoras as 1617 (*Doña Catalina*, 61–65), but by other accountings this would have had to take place around 1619 because the *Vida* says the bishop died five months later.

62. For a study of these differences between men's and women's spiritual *vidas*, see Myers and Powell, *A Wild Country*, chap. 2, and McKnight, *The Mystic of Tunja*, 54–59.

63. It is interesting to note that in the last chapter, Loyola's transcriber mentions that he has added some of his own comments to the narrative.

64. It is important to note that one of the manuscript versions that Rubio Merino published in 1995 renders this scene in a very different light. The same biographical elements are present, but the more literary reworking of it is absent: "Preguntóme [el obispo] en forma quien era. De dónde. Hija de quien. Fuy respondiendo. Apartóme un poco y preguntóme si era Monja y la causa y modo de la salida del convento. Díxesela. Porfióme con preguntas sobre esto, porque no se podía a ello persuadir. Tornóme a decir que le dixesse la verdad y que ya veía yo que podía fiarme. Díxele: Illmo. Señor, no hay más que lo que he dicho y si V.S. illma. Es servido, nombre personas honestas que me vean, que llana estoy." She goes on to report the medical examination: "Yo me manifesté.

Ellos me miraron y se satisficieron de que verdaderamente estaba virgen" (Rubio Merino, *La Monja Alférez*, M-I, 86).

65. "Señor... la verdad es ésta: que soi muger; que nací en tal parte, hija de fulano i sutana; que me entraron de tal edad en tal Convento con fulana mi tía; que allí me crié; que tomé el hábito; que tuve noviciado; que estando para profesar, por tal ocasión me salí; que me fui a tal parte, me desnudé, me vestí, me corté el cabello; partí allí i acullá me embarqué, aporté, trahiné, maté, herí, maleé, correteé, hasta venir a parar en lo presente i a los pies de Su Señoría Ilustrísima."

66. Catalina, *Vida*, chap. 2.

67. Ibid.

68. "Corrió la noticia de este suceso por todas partes, y los que antes me vieron y los que antes y despues supieron mis cosas en todas las Indias, se maravillaron" (chap. 20).

69. "Dame otra Monja Alférez, y le concederé lo mismo" (Vallbona, *Vida i sucesos*, 171).

70. Merrim, "Catalina de Erauso," discusses the role of fame in this construction.

71. For example, Ursula Suárez went to China, Madre de Agreda bilocated to New Mexico, and Madre María de San José had a vision of being in Rome.

72. "En hábito de hombre, con espada y daga, guarniciones de plata, algunos malos pelillos por varba, Y era el guapo de los guapos. Tenía una gran aria de mulas y negros con que conducía ropa a México" (letter from Fray Diego de Sevilla, as quoted by Rubio Merino, *La Monja Aférez*, 133).

73. Vallbona restored the fluctuation between feminine and masculine adjectives that is found in the original manuscript copy; the use of masculine adjectives, however, dominates. She also notes that the first two broadsides use the feminine, but there is fluctuation between the masculine and feminine in the third *Relación*. See Vallbona, *Vida i sucesos*, 2–5, 161n5.

74. These broadsides are reproduced in Vallbona, *Vida i sucesos*, appendix 3.

75. Vallbona, *Vida i sucesos*, 173, 174.

76. Palafox might have known Catalina, since she would probably have passed through Puebla as she transported goods from the Port of Veracruz along the Royal Road to Mexico City.

77. Rosales's history is based on Domingo Sotelo Romay's notes for a history of Chile. As a Jesuit chronicler, Romay had been chosen to write the history, but he never completed it. The history apparently was not published until the nineteenth century. According to Vallbona, this is the only document that completely changes Catalina's life; see Vallbona, *Vida i sucesos*, 181n4 and 183n5, and Medina, *Biblioteca Hispano-Chilena*, 221–225.

78. "Desecha en lágrimas como otra Magdalena se fue determinada a no hazer caso de la murmuración del fariseo, el mundo, a postrarse a los pies de Christo y labárselos con las lágrimas de sus ojos y limpiarlos con sus cabellos, y se echó a los pies del Licenciado... y le pidió con muchas lágrimas le oyesse de confesión, y descubriéndole todo el discurso de su vida, resulta en lágrimas, se resolvió a no apartarse hasta salir para el Convento" (Vallbona, *Vida i sucesos*, 182–183).

79. Merrim, *Early Modern*, 21. If the *Vida i sucesos* can be relied on, the priest to whom Catalina first confessed not only allowed her to continue being dressed as a man, but helped her escape, once he saw she was not inclined to return to the cloister (chap. 18).

80. Perry, *Gender and Disorder*, 131, 135.

81. Vallbona reproduces a document that includes a description of the patriotic roles of Catalina's brothers and father: "Alférez Miguel de Herausso y Francisco de Herausso que sirvió en la armada de Lima con don Rodrigo de Mendoza, y Domingo de Herauso, se fue en el armada que salió para el Brassil, y bolbiendo de allá fue uno de los que

perecieron en la Almirata de las Quatro Villas, que se quemó, que todos tres fueron sus hermanos" (1626 Petition, *Vida i sucesos*, 133). Stepto and Stepto (*Lieutenant Nun*, xxvii) also note that Catalina's father, a military captain, may have served in the American colonies and that Mariana Erauso married, while the other three sisters—Mari Juana, Isabel, and Jacinta—became nuns at the Convent of San Sebastian.

82. Perry, *Gender and Disorder*, 131–133; Merrim, "Catalina de Erauso, 185. Both studies base many of their conclusions on a variety of recent studies that examine the topic.

83. Merrim, "Catalina de Erauso," 185–186, cites Dugaw's work, *Warrior Women and Popular Balladry*. Wheelright, *Amazons and Military Maids*, and Shepherd, *Amazons and Warrior Women*, also touch on the topic. Davis, "The Reasons for Misrule," in *Society and Culture*, examines the extent of cross-dressing found in France during Carnival. See also Velasco's important new study on the topic, *The Lieutenant Nun*.

84. Juárez, "La mujer militar," 151. Socolow, "The Women" and Pumar Martinez, *Españolas en Indias*.

85. See Pumar Martínez, *Españolas en Indias*, 78–84, 85–94.

86. See McNamara, *Sisters in Arms*, 540–541.

87. Arzáns de Orsua, *Historia de la villa imperial de Potosí*, L. VI, c. 6; L. IX, c. 6.

88. Wheelright, *Amazons*, 18; Dugar, *Warrior Women*. "Fuimos bien recibidos por la falta de gente que había en Chile" (chap. 6).

89. Diego de Rosales complains, "como si en otras partes no se hiciese la guerra sin mujeres y sin ciradas, que si solamente sirvieran de criadas fuera tolerable; pero ni ellas ni ellos se contentan con eso, sino que usando de ellas para sus apetitos desordenados, va el ejército cargado de pecados... uno de las prinicpales desgracias y azotes de este Reyno es este desorden de amancebamiento con las criadas" (quoted in Salinas, *Las chilenas*, 19). In 1602 the governor of Chile, Alonso de Ribera, set up new rules for the military which aimed at standardizing the army and doing away with such practices, but they were not followed on the frontiers to the south of Santiago (see Salinas, *Las chilenas*, 19).

90. "Que estos milagros suelen acontecer en estos conflictos i más en Yndias. Gracias a la vela industria" (Vallbona, chap. 10).

91. See Merrim, "Catalina," 190. Interestingly, Christine of Sweden, who had helped the Counter-Reformation with her conversion to Catholicism and abdication of her throne, later caused the Catholic Church great embarrassment for her transvestite tendencies in Rome, but the church apparently did little to stop her.

92. "The Ensign Doña Catalina de Erauso, resident and native of the town of San Sebastián, in the province of Guipúzcoa, says that of the last 19 years, she has spent 15 in the service of Your Majesty in the wars of the kingdom of Chile and the Indians of Peru, having traveled to those parts in men's garb owing to her particular inclination to take up arms in the defense of the Catholic faith and in the service of Your Majesty, without being known in the aforesaid kingdom of Chile, during the entire time she spent there as other than a man" (as translated by Merrim, "Petition," 37).

93. "I would prefer, my daughters, that in no way you be women, nor resemble them in the least, but rather strong men, for if women behave as they should the Lord will make them so manly that they will inspire terror even in men" (as quoted in Merrim, "Catalina de Erauso," 188).

Conclusions

1. My thanks to Asunción Lavrin for explaining this practice to me.
2. For a study of this period, see Rubial *La santidad*, 42.
3. Rivas, "Gran cosa," 123n57.

4. See Rubial's excellent study of this process of secularization, in *La santidad*, 15–16.

5. In the case of Madre María de San José's convents, for example, they were affected by the reforms implemented by Benito Juárez in the 1860s. Nevertheless, her first convent in Puebla continued to operate in secret until the 1920s. See *Word from New Spain*, 10–11.

6. Rivas, "Gran cosa," 113–126.

7. Rubial *La santidad*, 86–87.

Bibliography

Introduction

Ahlgren, Gillian T. W. *Teresa of Avila and the Politics of Sanctity*. Ithaca, NY: Cornell University Press, 1996.

Alberro, Solange. *Inquisición y sociedad en México 1571–1700*. México: Fondo de Cultura Económica, 1993.

Arenal, Electa, and Stacey Schlau. *Untold Sisters: Hispanic Nuns in Their Own Works*. Trans. Amanda Powell. Albuquerque: University of New Mexico Press, 1989.

Bell, Rudolph, and Donald Weinstein. *Saints and Society: The Two Worlds of Western Christendom, 1000–1700*. Chicago: University of Chicago Press, 1982.

Bilinkoff, Jodi. "Confessors, Penitents, and the Construction of Identities in Early Modern Avila," in *Culture and Identity in Early Modern Europe (1500–1800)* (83–102), ed. Barbara Diefendorf and Carla Hesse. Ann Arbor: University of Michigan Press, 1994.

Bordas, Andrés de. *Práctica de confessores de monjas, en que se explican los quatro votos de obediencia, pobreza, castidad y clasura, por modo de diálogo*. Mexico, 1708.

Burke, Peter. "How to Be a Counter-Reformation Saint," in *Religion and Society in Early Modern Europe 1500–1800* (45–55), ed. Kaspar von Greyerz. London: George Allen and Unwin, 1984.

Bynum, Caroline Walker. *Holy Feast and Holy Fast: The Religious Significance of Food to Medieval Women*. Berkeley: University of California Press, 1987.

Coakley, John, "Friars as Confidants of Holy Women in Medieval Dominican Hagiography," in *Images of Sainthood in Medieval Europe* (221–246), ed. Renate Blumenfeld-Kosinski and Timea Szell. Ithaca, NY: Cornell University Press, 1991.

Davis, Natalie Zemon. *Women on the Margin: Three Seventeenth Century Lives*. Cambridge, MA: Harvard University Press, 1995.

Destefano, Michael T. "*Miracles and Monasticism in Mid-Colonial Puebla, 1600–1750: Charismatic Religion in a Conservative Society*." Ph.D. diss., University of Florida, 1977.

Fernández, James D. *Apology to Apostrophe: Autobiography and the Rhetoric of Self-Representation in Spain*. Durham, NC: Duke University Press, 1992.

Franco, Jean. *Plotting Women: Gender and Representation in Mexico*. New York: Columbia University Press, 1989.

Galve, Luis Miguel. "Santa Rosa de Lima y sus espinas: La emergencia de mentalidades urbanas de crisis y la sociedad andina (1600–1630)," in *Manifestaciones religiosas en el mundo colonial americano*. (vol. 1, 53–70), ed. Clara García Aylurado and Manuel Ramos. Medina. Mexico: La Galera, 1993.

Giles, Mary E. *The Book of Prayer of Sor María of Santo Domingo: A Study and Translation* Albany: State Universities of New York Press, 1990.

Greenspan, Kate. "The Autohagiographical Tradition in Medieval Women's Devotional Writing." *Auto/Biography Studies* 6 (1991): 157–168.

Herpoel, Sonja. *A la zaga de Santa Teresa: Autobiografías por mandato*. Amsterdam: Rodopi, 1999.

Huerga, Alvaro. *Historia de los alumbrados*, vol. 3. Madrid: Fundación Universitaria Española, 1986.

Ibsen, Kristine. *Women's Spiritual Autobiography in Colonial Spanish America*. Gainesville: University Press of Florida, 1999.

Kamen, Henry. *Inquisition and Society in Spain in the Sixteenth and Seventeenth Centuries.* Bloomington: Indiana University Press, 1985.

Kieckhefer, Richard. "Imitators of Christ: Sainthood in the Christian Tradition," in
   Sainthood: Its Manifestions in World Religions. (1–42), ed. Richard Kieckhefer and George
   D. Bond. Berkeley: University of California Press, 1998.

Lavrin, Asunción. "In Search of the Colonial Woman in Mexico: The Seventeenth and
   Eighteenth Centuries," in *Latin American Women: Historical Perspectives* (23–59), ed. A.
   Lavrin. Westport, CT: Greenwood, 1978.

———. "La vida femenina como experiencia religiosa: Biografía y hagiografía en
   Hispanoamérica colonial." *Colonial Latin American Review* 2 (1993): 27–52.

Lerner, Gerda. *The Creation of Feminist Consciousness: From the Middle Ages to 1870.* New York:
   Oxford University Press, 1993.

McKnight, Kathryn Joy. *The Mystic of Tunja: The Writings of Madre Castillo, 1671–1742* Amherst:
   University of Massachusetts Press, 1997.

McNamara, Jo Ann. *Sisters in Arms: Catholic Nuns through Two Millennia.* Cambridge: Harvard
   University Press, 1996.

María de San José. *Oaxaca Manuscript.* Spanish Codex 39–42. The John Carter Brown
   Library, Providence, Rhode Island.

Martin, Luis. *Daughters of the Conquistadores. Women of the Viceroyalty of Peru.* Albuquerque:
   University of New Mexico Press, 1983.

Maza, Francisco de la. *Catarina de San Juan* [1970]. Mexico: Cien de México, 1990.

Montero, Joseph. *Sermón.* Puebla, Mexico, 1693.

Muriel, Josefina. *Cultura femenina novohispana.* Mexico: Universidad Nacional Autónoma de
   México, 1982.

Myers, Kathleen Ann. *A Word from New Spain: The Spiritual Autobiography of Madre María de San
   José (1656–1719).* Liverpool: Liverpool University Press, 1993.

Myers, Kathleen Ann, and Amanda Powell. *A Wild Country out in the Garden: The Spiritual
   Journals of a Colonial Mexican Nun.* Bloomington: Indiana University Press, 1999.

Nos los inquisidores. Edict of the Mexican Inquisition, 1621. Lilly Library Collection,
   Bloomington, Indiana.

Petroff, Elizabeth. *Medieval Women's Visionary Literature.* New York: Oxford University Press,
   1986.

Poutrin, Isabelle. *Le Voile et la plume: Autobiographie et sainteté féminine dans l'Espagne moderne.*
   Madrid: Casa de Velázquez, 1995.

Ragon, Pierre, "Libros de devoción y culto a los santos en el México colonial (siglos XVII
   a XVIII)," in *Actas del XI Congreso Internacional de AHILA* (210–223), ed. John R. Fisher.
   Liverpool: Liverpool University, 1998.

Ramos, Alonso, "Dedi De los prodigios de la omnipotencia y milagros de la gracia en la
   vida de la venerable Sierva de Dios Catharina de S. Joan. Puebla, Mexico, 1692.
   Vol. 13, "Dedicatoria."

Ribadeneyra, Pedro de. *Flos Sanctorum.* Vols. 1–7. Madrid: La Imprenta Real, 1716.

Rivas, Emma, "'Gran cosa es el buen exemplo que muebe con mucha facilidad': Lecturas
   ejemplares novohispanas del siglo XVII," *Historias* 31 (1994): 113–126.

Rosenberg, John R. *The Circular Pilgrimage: An Anatomy of Confessional Autobiography in Spain.*
   New York: Peter Lang, 1994.

Rubial, Antonio. *La santidad controvertida.* Mexico: Fondo de Cultura Económica, 1999.

Santander y Torres, Sebastián de. *Vida de la venerable madre María de S. Joseph, religiosa augustina
   recoleta, fundadora en los Conventos de Santa Monica de la Ciudad de Puebla, y despues en el de la
   Soledad de Oaxaca.* Mexico, 1723.

Scott, Karen. "Catherine of Sienna in Lay Sanctity in the 14th Century," in *Lay Sanctity* (77–90), ed. Anne Astell. South Bend, IN: University of Notre Dame Press, 2000.

Slade, Carol. *St. Teresa of Avila: Author of a Heroic Life*. Los Angeles: University of California Press, 1995.

Surtz, Ronald E. *The Guitar of God: Gender, Power, and Authority in the Visionary World of Mother Juana de la Cruz (1481–1534)*. Philadelphia: University of Pennsylvania Press, 1990.

Tambling, Jeremy. *Confession: Sexuality, Sin, the Subject*. New York: Manchester University Press, 1990.

Tentler, Thomas N. *Sin and Confession on the Eve of the Reformation*. Princeton, NJ: Princeton University Press, 1977.

Teresa de Jesús, Santa. *Libro de la vida*. Ed. Dámaso Chicharro. Madrid: Cátedra, 1982.

Weber, Alison. *Teresa of Avila and the Rhetoric of Femininity*. Princeton, NJ: Princeton University Press, 1990.

Zimmerman, T. C. Price. "Confession and Autobiography in the Early Renaissance," in *Studies in Honor of Hans Baron* (119–140). Florence: Sansoni Editore, 1971.

Chapter 1

Primary Texts

Bilboa, Luis. *Sermón*. In *Prodesa ordinario*, 1617. unnumber folios.

Gonzalez de Acuña, Antonio. *Rosa mística: Vida y muerte de Santa Rosa de Santa María*. Rome, 1671.

Hansen, Leonard. *Vida admirable de Sta. Rosa de Lima: Patrona del Nuevo Mundo*. Trans. Jacinto Parrra. Manila 1671 [1664].

Loayza, Fray Pedro de. *Vida de Santa Rosa de Lima*. Ed. Carlos Aníbal Alvarez. Lima: Iberia, S.A., 1965 [1619].

Millones, Luis. *Una partecita del cielo: La vida de Santa Rosa de Lima narrada por don Gonzalo de la Maza a quien ella llamaba padre*. Lima: Editorial Horizonte, 1993 [1617].

Proceso apostólico, 1630–1632. Archivo Secreto Vaticano, *Riti*. Vols. 1573, 1574, 1575, 1576.

Proceso ordinario, 1617–1618. Archivo Secreto Vaticano, *Riti*. Vols. 1570, 1571, 1572. Lilly Library copy, Bloomington, Indiana.

Ribero Leal, Manuel de. *Oración evangélica*, Lima, 1675.

Rosa de Santa María (de Lima). *Exercicio Angelico, empleo Celestial de Alabanzas a Dios por sus infinitas perfecciones... que inventó Santa Rosa de Santa María y pueden imitar las almas deseosas de aagradar a Nuestro Señor. Pr un Padre de la Compañia de Jesús*. Lima, 1728.

———. *Las mercedes* and *Escala mística*, in *La patrona de América*, ed. Luis Getino. Lima, 1937.

Secondary Sources

Ahlgren, Gillian T. *Teresa of Avila and the Politics of Sanctity*. Ithaca, NY: Cornell University Press, 1996.

Angulo, Padre Domingo. *Santa Rosa de Santa María: Estudio bibliográfico*. Lima, 1917.

Araoz, José Flores et al. *Santa Rosa de Lima y su tiempo*. Lima: Banco de Crédito del Perú, 1995.

Astell, Ann. *The Song of Songs in the Middle Ages*. Ithaca, NY: Cornell University Press, 1990.

Bilinkoff, Jodi. *The Avila of Saint Teresa: Religious Reform in a Sixteenth-Century City*. Ithaca, NY: Cornell University Press, 1989.

Bouza Alvarez, José Luis. *Religiosidad contrarreformista y cultura simbólica del barroco*. Madrid: Consejo Superior de Investigaciones Científicas, 1990.

Brading, David A. *The First America: The Spanish Monarchy, Creole Patriots and the Liberal State, 1492–1867*. Cambridge: Cambridge University Press, 1991.

Bruno, Cayetano. *Rosa de Santa María: La sin igual historia de Santa Rosa de Lima, narrada por los testigos oculares del proceso de su beatificación y canonización*. Lima: Editorial Salesiana, 1992.

Burke, Peter. "How to Be a Counter-Reformation Saint," in *Religion and Society in Early Modern Europe 1500–1800* (45–55), ed. Kaspar von Greyerz. London: George Allen and Unwin, 1984.

Campa, Pedro F. *Emblemata Hispanica: An Annotated Bibliography of Spanish Emblem Literature to the Year 1700*. Durham, NC: Duke University Press, 1990.

Catherine, of Siena, Saint. *The Dialogue*. Trans. Suzanne Noffke. New York: Paulist Press, 1980.

Cussen, Celia L. "La fe en la historia: Las vidas de Martín de Porras," in *Historia, memoria y ficción* (281–301), ed. Moises Lemlij and Luis Millones. Lima: Seminario Interdisciplinario de Estudios Andinos, 1996.

Galve, Luis Miguel. "Santa Rosa de Lima y sus espinas: La emergencia de mentalidades urbanas de crisis y la sociedad andina (1600–1630)," in *Manifestaciones religiosas en el mundo colonial americano* (1, 53–70), vol. 1, ed. Clara García Aylurado and Manuel Ramos Medina. Mexico: La Galera, 1993.

Getino, Luis. *La patrona de América ante los nuevos documentos*. Madrid: Revista de las Españas, 1937.

Graziano, Frank. "Una verdad ficticia: Santa Rosa de Lima y la hagiografía," in *Historia, memoria y ficción* (302–311), ed. Moises Lemlij and Luis Millones. Lima: Seminario Interdisciplinario de Estudios Andinos, 1996.

———. *Wounds of Love: The Mystical Marriage of Saint Rose of Lima*. New York: Oxford University Press, forthcoming.

Hamburger, Jeffrey F. *Nuns as Artists: The Visual Culture of a Medieval Convent*. Berkeley: University of California Press, 1997.

Ibañez-Murphy, Carolina. "¿Primera escritora colonial? Santa Rosa de Lima: Las mercedes y la Escala mística." Ph.D. diss., University of Arizona, 1997.

Ibsen, Kristine. *Women's Spiritual Autobiography in Colonial Spanish America*. Gainesville: University of Florida Press, 1999.

Iwasaki, Fernando. "Mujeres al borde de la perfección: Rosa de Santa María y las alumbradas de Lima." *Hispanic American Historical Review* (1993): 581–613.

Kieckhefer, Richard. "Imitators of Christ: Sainthood in the Christian Tradition," in *Sainthood: Its Manifestions in World Religions* (1–42), ed. Richard Kieckhefer and George D. Bond. Berkeley: University of California Press, 1998.

LaValle, Bernard. *Las promesas ambiguas: Ensayos sobre el criollismo colonial en los andes*. Lima: Pontífica Universidad Católica del Perú, 1993.

Lewin, Boleslao, ed. *Descripción del virreinato del Peru: Crónica inedita de comienzos del siglo XVII*. Rosario, Peru: Universidad Nacional del Litoral, 1958.

López, Alfred Anthony Brichta. "The Roots of the Rose: A Sociohistorical Biography of St. Rose of Lima (Rosa de Santa Maria), 1586–1617." Ph.D. diss. University of New Mexico, 1995.

Loreto López, Rosalva. "La fiesta de la concepción y las identidades colectivas, Puebla (1619–1636)," in *Manifestaciones religiosas en el mundo colonial americano*. (Vol. 2, 87–105), ed. Clara García Ayluardo and Manuel Ramos Medina. Mexico: Condumex, 1993.

Mannarelli, María Emma. "Fragmentos para una historia posible: Escritura/crítica/ cuerpo en una beata del siglo XVII," in *Historia, memoria y ficción* (266–280), ed. Moises Lemlij and Luis Millones, 1996.

Martin, Luis. *Daughters of the Conquistadores: Women of the Viceroyalty of Peru*. Albuquerque: University of New Mexico Press, 1983.

Martínez Hampe, Teodor. *Santidad e identidad criolla: Estudio del proceso de canonización de Santa Rosa*. Cuzco, Peru: Centro de Estudios Regionales Andinos Bartolomé de las Casas, 1998.

Medina, José Toribio. *Historia del tribunal de la inquisición de Lima (1569–1820)*. Vols. 1–2. Santiago, Chile: Fondo Histórico, 1956.

———. *Biblioteca extranjera de santos y venerables*. Mexico, 1919.

Meléndez, Juan. *Festiva Pompa, culto religoso, veneracion reverente, fiesta, aclamación y aplauso: A la feliz beatificación de la bienaventurada virgen Rosa de S. María*. Lima, 1671.

Mills, Kenneth, and William B. Taylor. *Colonial Spanish America: A Documentary History*. Wilmington, DE: Scholarly Resources, 1998.

Mujica Pinilla, Ramon. "El ancla de Santa Rosa de Lima: Mística y política en torno a la patrona de América," in *Santa Rosa y su Tiempo* (54–215), ed. José Flores Araoz et al. Lima: Banco de Credito, 1995.

Oviedo y Herrera, Luis Antonio de. *Vida de la esclarecida virgen Santa Rosa de Santa María, natural de Lima y parona de el Perú: Poema heroyco*. Madrid, 1711.

Ribero Leal, Manuel de. *Oración evangelica en la beatificacion de Rosa de Santa Maria*. Lima, 1675.

Ross, Waldo. "Santa Rosa de Lima y la formación del espíritu hispanoamericano." *Mercurio Peruano* 462 (1966): 165–212.

Sánchez, Ana. "Angela Carranza, alias Angela de Dios: Santidad y poder en la sociedad virreinal peruana (s.XVII)," in *Catolicismo y extirpación de idolatrías: Siglos XVI–XVII* (263–292), ed. Gabriela Ramos and Henrique Urbano. Cuzco: Centro de Estudios Regionales Andinos "Bartolomé de las Casas," 1993.

Santander y Torres, Sebastián de. *Sermón panegirico*. Puebla, Mexico, 1692.

Scott, Karen. "Urban Spaces, Women's Networks, and the Lay Apostolate in the Siena of Catherine ," in *Creative Women in Medieval and Early Modern Italy: A Religious and Artisitic Renaissance* (105–119), ed. E. Ann Matter and John Coakley. Philadelphia: University of Pennsylvania Press, 1994.

———. "Catherine of Sienna in Lay Sanctity in the 14th Century," in *Lay Sanctity* (77–90), ed. Anne Astell. South Bend, IN: University of Notre Dame Press, 2000.

Sebastián, Santiago. *Contrarreforma y barroco: Lecturas iconográficas e iconológicas*. Madrid: Alianza Editorial, 1981.

Slade, Carol. *St. Theresa of Avila: Author of a Heroic Life*. Los Angeles: University of California, 1995.

Van Deusen, Nancy E. "Instituciones religiosas y seglares para mujeres en el siglo XVII en Lima," in *Manifestaciones religiosas en el mundo colonial americano* (Vol. 2, 65–86), ed. Clara García Ayluardo and Manuel Ramos Medina. Mexico: Condumex, 1993.

Vargas Ugarte, Ruben. *La flor de Lima: Santa Rosa*, 4th ed. Lima: Ediciones Paulinas, 1983.

Weber, Alison. *Teresa of Avila and the Rhetoric of Femininity*. Princeton, NJ: Princeton University Press, 1990.

Wuffarden, Eduardo, and Pedro Guibovich Pérez. "Esplendor," in *Santa Rosa de Lima y su tiempo* (4–53), ed. José Flores Araoz et al. Lima: Banco de Crédito del Perú, 1995.

Chapter 2
Primary Texts

Aguilera, Francisco de. *Sermón en que se da noticia de la vida admirable, virudes heroicas y preciossa muerte de la venerable señora Chatharima de San Joan, que florecio en perfeccion de vida y murio con acclamacion de santidad en la ciudad de la Puebla de los Angeles a 5 de enero de el año de 1688*. Puebla, Mexico, 1688.

Graxeda, José del Castillo. *Compendio de la vida y virtudes de la venerable Catarina de San Juan*. Puebla, Mexico: Bibliotheca Angelopolitana, 1987. [1692].

Ramos, Alonso. *De los prodigios de la omnipotencia y milagros de la gracia en la vida de la venerable sierva de Dios Catharina de S Joan.* Vol. 1, Puebla, Mexico, 1689; Vol. 2, Mexico, 1690; Vol. 3, Mexico, 1692.

Secondary Sources

Alberro, Solange. *La actividad del Santo Oficio de la Inquisición en Nueva España 1571–1700.* Mexico. Instituto Nacional de Antropología e Historia (Colección Científica), 1981.

————. "Herejes, brujas y beatas: Mujeres ante el tribunal del santo oficio de la inquisición en la Nueva España," in *Presencia y transparencia: La mujer en la historia de México* (79–94). Mexico: El Colegio de México, 1987.

Arenal, Electa, and Stacey Schlau. "Thin Lines, Bedeviled Words: Monastic and Inquisitorial Texts by Colonial Mexican Women," in *Estudios sobre escritoras hispanas en honor de Georgina Sabat Rivers* (31–44), ed. Lou Charnon-Deutsch Madrid: Castalia, 1992.

Barnes-Karol, Gwendoln. "Religious Oratory in a Culture of Control," in *Culture and Control in Counter-Reformation Spain* (51–77), ed. Anne Cruz and Mary Elizabeth Perry. Minneapolis: University of Minnesota Press, 1992.

Bilinkoff, Jodi. "Confessors, Penitents, and the Construction of Identities in Early Modern Avila," in *Culture and Identity in Early Modern Europe 1500–1800* (83–102), ed. Barbara Diefendorf. Ann Arbor: University of Michigan Press, 1994.

Burke, Peter. "How to Be a Counter-Reformation Saint," in *Religion and Society in Early Modern Europe 1500–1800* (45–55), ed. Kaspar von Greyerz. London: George Allen and Unwin, 1984.

Burns, Kathryn. *Colonial Habits: Convents and the Spiritual Economy of Cuzco, Peru.* Durham, NC: Duke University Press, 1999.

Destefano, Michael Thomas. "Miracles and Monasticism in Mid-Colonial Puebla, 1600–1750: Charismatic Religion in a Conservative Society." Ph.D. diss., University of Florida, 1977.

Díaz, Mónica. "Género, raza y género literario en los conventos para mujeres indigenas en el México colonial." Ph.D. diss., Indiana University, 2001.

González Obregón, Luis, ed., *Libros y libreros en el siglo XVI.* Mexico: Archivo General de la Nación, 1914.

Greenleaf, Richard. *The Mexican Inquisition of the Sixteenth Century.* Albuquerque: University of New Mexico Press, 1969.

Greer, Allan. "Iroquois Virgin: The Story of Catherine Tekakwitha in New France and New Spain," in *Colonial Saints* (235–250), ed. Jodi Bilinkoff and Allan Greer. New York: Routlege Press, 2003.

Huerga, Alvaro. *Historia de los alumbrados,* vol. 3. Madrid: Fundación Universitaria Española, 1986.

Lavrin, Asunción. "Indian Brides of Christ: Creating New Spaces for Indigenous Women in New Spain." *Mexican Studies/Estudios Mexicanos* 15 (1999): 225–260.

Lemus, Diego de. *Vida, birtudes, trabajos, fabores y milagros de la venerable madre Sor Maria de Jesús angelopolitana religiosa en el insigne convento de la limpia concepción de la ciudad de los Angeles.* León, 1685.

León, Nicolás. *Catarina de San Juan y la china poblana.* Mexico: Altiplano, 1971 [1921–1922].

Leonard, Irving A. *Books of the Brave.* New York: Gordian Press, 1964.

Libro primero de votos de la inquisición de México, 1573–1600. Mexico: Imprenta Universitaria, 1949.

Luis de Granada, Fray. *Historia de Sor María de la visitación y sermón de las caídas públicas.* Barcelona: Juan Flors, 1962.

Maza, Francisco de la. *Catarina de San Juan.* Mexico: Cien de México, 1990 [1970].

Medina, José Toribio. *Historia del tribunal del Santo Oficio de la Inquisición en México.* Ed. Julio Jiménez Rueda. Mexico: Ediciones Fuente Cultural, 1952.

Meléndez, Mariselle. "El perfil económico de la identidad racial en los *Apuntes* de las indias caciques del Convento Corpus Cristi." *Revista de Crítica Literaria Latinoamericana* 46 (1997): 115–132.

Mercado, Pedro. *El cristiano curioso.* Madrid, 1673.

Morgan, Ronald J. "Saints, Biographers and Identity Formation in Colonial Spanish America." Ph.D. diss., University of California–Santa Barbara, 1998.

Muriel, Josefina., ed. *Las indias caciques de Corpus Christi.* Mexico: Universidad Autónoma Nacional de México, 1963.

Myers, Kathleen A. "La influencia mediativa del clero en las *Vidas* de religiosos y monjas." *Revista de Literatura* 61, no. 121 (1999): 35–59.

Pérez-Marchand, Monelisa Lina. *Dos etapas ideológicas del siglo XVIII en México a través de los papeles de la inquisición.* Mexico: Colegio de México, 1945.

Ramos Soriano, José Abel. "Critierios inquisitoriales en la prohibición de literatura relacionada con la comunidad doméstica en la Nueva España," in *El placer de pecar y el afán de normar* (353–376), ed. Seminario de Historia de las Mentalidades. Mexico: Institute Nacional de Antropología e Historia, 1987.

Rivas, Emma. "'Gran cosa es el buen exemplo que muebe con mucha facilidad.' Lecturas ejemplares novohispanas del siglo XVII." *Historias* 13 (1994): 113–126.

Ross, Kathleen Ann. *The Baroque Narrative of Carlos de Sigüenza y Góngora: A New World Paradise.* Cambridge: Cambridge University Press, 1993.

Rubial García, Antonio, "Espejo de virtudes, sabrosa narración, emulación patriótica: La literatura hagiográfica sobre los venerables no canonizados en la Nueva España," in *La literatura novohispana* (89–110), ed. José Pascual Buxó. Mexico: UNAM, 1994.

———. *La santidad controvertida.* Mexico: Fondo de Cultura Ecónomica, 1999.

———. "Mariofanías extravagantes: Las visiones de Catarina de San Juan." *Universidad de México* (1992): 15–17.

Salmeron, Pedro. *De la vida de la venerable madre Isabel de la Encarnacion, Carmelita Desclaza, natural de la ciudad de los Angeles.* Puebla, Mexico, 1640.

Schlau, Stacey. "Yo no tengo que me lleven a la inquisición: Las ilusas María Rita Vargas y María Lucía Celis," in *Mujer y cultura en la colonia hispanoamericana* (183–194), ed. Mabel Moraña. Pittsburgh, PA: Biblioteca de América, 1996.

Sigüenza y Góngora, Carlos de. *El paraíso occidental.* Mexico: Universidad Nacional Autónoma de Mexico, 1995.

———. *Los infortunios de Alonso Ramirez.* Madrid: Espasa-Calpe, 1941.

Chapter 3
Primary Texts

Maldonado, Angel. *Santissimo Patri Excelso in verbo Gloriae Benedicto XIII Pontifici Maximo. Gratum existimo Sanctitati vestrae, aptum ad vestram gloriam, coronam scribere, mittere ad vos Venerabilis Virginis Maria a San Joseph.* Puebla, Mexico (?), ca. 1726.

María de San José. *Estaciones que la Soberana Emperatriz de los Cielos María Santissima Nuestra Señora anduvo y enseñó a la Venerable Madre María de San Joseph... sacadas de lo que escribe en su vida.* Puebla and Seville, 1723; Mexico, 1743, 1773; Puebla, 1782.

———. *Oaxaca Manuscript.* Spanish Codex 39–41. The John Carter Brown Library, Providence, Rhode Island.

Kathleen A. Myers, ed. *Word from New Spain: The Spiritual Autobiography of María de San Joseph (1656–1719).* Liverpool: Liverpool University Press, 1993.

————. *A Wild Country out in the Garden: The Journals of a Mexican Nun.* Kathleen Ann Myers and Amanda Powell, eds. and trans. Bloomington: Indiana University Press, 1999.

Santander y Torres, Sebastián de. *Oración funebre que predicó el M. R. P. M. Fray Sebastian de Santander, del orden de Predicadores de N. P. Santo Domingo: En las honras de la V. M. María de San Joseph.* Puebla, Mexico, 1719.

————. *Vida de la venerable madre María de S. Joseph, religiosa augustina recoleta, fundadora en los Conventos de Santa Monica de la Ciudad de Puebl, y despues en el de la Soledad de Oaxaca.* Mexico, 1723.

Secondary Sources

Arenal, Electa, and Stacey Schlau. *Untold Sisters: Hispanic Nuns in Their Own Works.* Trans. Amanda Powell. Albuquerque: University of New Mexico Press, 1989.

Bynum, Carolyn Walker. *Fragmentation and Redemption: Essays on Gender and the Human Body in Medieval Religion* (181–238). New York: Zone, 1991.

Chicharro, Dámaso, ed. *Libro de la vida de Santa Teresa de Jesús.* Madrid: Cátedra, 1982.

Coakley, John, "Friars as Confidants of Holy Women in Medieval Dominican Hagiography," in *Images of Sainthood in Medieval Europe* (222–246), ed. Renate Blumenfeld-Kosinski and Timea Szell. Ithaca, NY: Cornell University Press, 1991.

Destefano, Michael T. "Miracles and Monasticism in Mid-Colonial Puebla, 1600–1750: Charismatic Religion in a Conservative Society." Ph.D. diss., University of Florida, 1977.

Franco, Jean. *Plotting Women: Gender and Representation in Mexico.* New York: Columbia University Press, 1989.

Gómez de la Parra, José. *Fundación y primero siglo del muy religioso Convento de San Joseph de Religiosas Carmelitas.* Mexico: Universidad Iberoamericana, 1992 [Puebla, 1732].

Greenspan, Kate. "The Autohagiographic Tradition in Medieval Women's Devotional Writing." *Auto/hagiography Studies* 6, no. 2 (1991): 157–168.

Isabel de Jesús. *Vida de la venerable madre Isabel de Jesús... Dictada por ella misma.* Madrid, 1675.

Maldonado, Angel. *Oración evangélica predicada en el santuario de N. Señora de la Soledad.* Mexico, 1707.

Mariana de San Joseph. *Vida de la venerable M. Mariana de S. Joseph, fundadora de la recolección de monjas augustinas.* Ed. Luis Muñoz. Madrid, 1645.

Montero, Joseph. *Sermón.* Puebla, Mexico, 1693.

Muriel, Josefina. *Cultura feminina novohispana.* Mexico: Universidad Nacional Autónoma de México, 1982.

————. *Retratos de monjas.* Mexico: Editorial Jus, 1952.

Rubial, Antonio. *La santidad controvertida.* Mexico: Fondo de Cultura Económica, 1999.

Sánchez y Castro, Joseph Gerónymo. *Vida de la venerable madre Sor Antonia de la Madre de Dios, religiosa Agustina Recoleta, y fundadora en el Convento de Santa Mónica de la Puebla de los Angeles, y despues en el de Nuestra Señora de la Soledad.* Mexico, 1747.

Chapter 4
Primary Texts

Alatorre, Antonio, ed. "La Carta de Sor Juana al Padre Nuñez (1682)." *Nueva Revista Filología Hispánica* 335 (1987): 591–673.

Juana Inés de la Cruz. *Obras completas,* 3rd ed. Vols. 1–4. Ed. Alfonso Méndez Plancarte. Toluca: Instituto Mexiquense de Cultura, 1994.

————. *Obras completas.* Ed. Alfonso Méndez Plancarte. Mexico: Editorial Porrua, 1975.

Trabulse, Elías, ed. *Carta de Serafina de Cristo, 1691.* Toluca: Instituto Mexiquense de Cultura, 1996.

Translations

Arenal, Electa, and Powell, Amanda, ed. and trans. *The Answer/La respuesta.* New York: Feminist Press, 1994.

Scott, Nina M., ed. and trans. "Letter to the R. F. M. Antonio Núñez," in *Madres del verbo/ Mothers of the Word: Early Spanish American Women Writers, A Bilingual Anthology* (71–82). Albuquerque: University of New Mexico Press, 1999.

Trabulse, Elías, ed. "Carta de Serafina de Christo, Convento de N.P.S. Gerñonimo de México en 1 de febrero de 1691 años." Trans. Alfonso Montelongo. In *Sor Juana y Vieira: Trescientos años después* (183–193), ed. K. Josu Bijesca and Pablo A. Brescia. Santa Barbara, CA: Anejo de la Revista Tinta, 1998.

Trueblood, Alan S. trans. *A Sor Juana Anthology.* Cambridge, MA: Harvard University Press, 1988.

Secondary Sources

Alatorre, Antonio. "La carta de Sor Juana al Padre Núñez (1682)." *Nueva Revista Filología Hispánica* 335 (1987): 591–673.

Alatorre, Antonio and Martha Lilia Tenorio. *Serafina y Sor Juana.* Mexico: El Colegio de México, 1998.

Bénassy-Berling, Marie-Cécile. *Humanismo y religión en Sor Juana en la Nueva España.* Mexico: Era, 1989 [1982].

———. "Más sobre la conversión de sor Juana." *Nueva Revista de Filología Hispánica* 32 (1983): 462–471.

———. "Sobre dos textos del arzobispo Francisco Aguiar y Seijas," in *Y diversa de mí misma entre vustras plumas ando: Homenaje interancional a Sor Juana* (85–90), ed. Sara Poot Herrera. Mexico: Colegio de Mexico, 1993.

Bijuesca, K. Josu, and Brescia, Pablo A., eds. *Sor Juana y Vieira: Tescientos años después.* Santa Barbara, CA: Anejo de la Revista Tinta, 1998.

Boenig, Robert, ed. *The Mystical Gesture: Essays on Medieval and Early Modern Spiritual Culture in Honor of Mary E. Giles.* Aldershot, England: Ashgate Publishing, 2000.

Brading, David A. *Orbe indiano: De la monarquía católica a la republica criolla, 1492–1867.* Trans. Juan Utrilla. Mexico: Fondo de Cultura Económica, 1993.

Bravo Arriaga, María Dolores. *La excepción y la regla: Estudios sobre espiritualidad y cultura en la Nueva España.* Mexico: Universidad Nacional Autónoma de México, 1997.

Bundgard, Ana. "La ironía principio vertebrador de la 'Respuesta de Sor Filotea de la Cruz.'" Presented at "Sor Juana y Su Mundo," Universidad Claustro Sor Juana, Mexico, D.F., 1995.

Buxó, José Pascual. "Los desatinos de la Pitonisa," in *Mujer y cultura en la Colonia hispano- americana* (217–234), ed. Mabel Moraña. Pittsburgh: Biblioteca de America, 1996.

———. "Prefacio" in María Dolores Bravo Arriaga, *La excepción y la regla.* Mexico: UNAM, 1997.

Calleja, Diego. *Fama y obras póstumas del Fenix de México* by Sor Juana Inés de la Cruz. Madrid, 1700.

Cevallos-Candau, Francisco Javier et al., eds. *Coded Encounters: Writing, Gender, and Ethnicity in Colonial Latin America* Amherst: University of Massachusetts Press, 1994.

Coloquial internacional: Sor Juana Inés de la Cruz y el pensamiento novohispano, ed. Manuel Ramos Medina. Toluca: Instituto Mexiquense de Cultura, 1995.

Duby, Georges, ed. *Historia de las mujeres en Occidente*. Mexico: Taurus, 1992.

Fernández de Santa Cruz, Manuel. *Regla del glorioso doctor de la Iglesia San Agustín, que han de guardar las religiosas del Convento del Maximo Doct. S. Gerónimo*. Puebla, Mexico, 1701.

Franco, Jean. *Plotting Women: Gender and Representation in Mexico* (chap. 3). London: Columbia University Press, 1989.

Glantz, Margo. *Sor Juana Inés de la Cruz: ¿Hagiografía o autobiografía?* Mexico: Editorial Grijalbo, 1995.

Johnson, Julie. *Satire in Colonial Spanish America: Turning the World Upside Down*. Austin: University of Texas Press, 1993.

Lavrin, Asunción. "Sor Juana Inés de la Cruz: Obediencia y autoridad en su entorno religioso." *Revista Iberoamericana* 172–173 (1995): 605–622.

Luciani, Fred. "Anecdotal Self-Invention in Sor Juana's *Respuesta a Sor Filotea*." *Colonial Latin American Review* 4 (1995): 73–84.

Marquet Antonio, ed. *Tema y variaciones de literatura*. Mexico: Universidad Autonóma Metropólitana, 1996.

Maza, Francisco de la. *Sor Juana Inés de la Cruz ante la historia: Biografías antiguas, La fama de 1700. Noticias de 1677 a 1882*. Mexico: Universidad Nacional Autonóma de México, 1980.

Merrim, Stephanie. *Early Modern Women's Writing and Sor Juana Inés de la Cruz*. Nashville, TN: Vanderbilt University Press, 1999.

——. "Narciso desdoblado: Narcissistic Stratagems in *El Divino Narciso* and the *Respuesta a Sor Filotea de la Cruz*." *Bulletin of Hispanic Studies* 64 (1987): 111–117.

——. "Toward a Feminist Reading of Sor Juana Inés de la Cruz: Past, Present, and Future Directions in Sor Juana Criticism," in *Feminist Perspectives on Sor Juana Inés de la Cruz* (11–37), ed. Stephanie Merrim. Detroit: Wayne State University Press, 1991.

Moraña, Mabel. "Orden dogmático y marginalidad en la Carta de Monterrey de Sor Juana Inés de la Cruz." *Hispanic Review* 58 (1990): 205–225.

——, ed. *Mujer y cultura en la colonia hispanoamericana*. Pittsburgh: Biblioteca Americana, 1996.

Myers, Kathleen A. "Sor Juana's *Respuesta*: Rewriting the *vitae*." *Revista Canadiense de Estudios Hispánicos* 14 (1990): 459–471.

Núñez de Miranda, Antonio. *Cartilla de la doctrina religiosa dispuesta por uno de la compañía de Jesús para dos niñas hijas espirituales suyas, que se crían para monjas y desean serlo con toda perfección*. Mexico, 1672(?).

Oviedo, Juan Antonio. *Vida exemplar, heroicas virtudes, y apostólicos ministerios de el V.P. Antonio Núñez de Miranda*. Mexico, 1702.

Paz, Octavio. *Sor Juana Inés de la Cruz or, the Traps of the Faith*. Barcelona: Seix Barral, 1982. Trans. M. Sayers Peden. Cambridge, MA: Harvard University Press, 1988.

Perelmuter, Rosa. "La estructura retórica de la *Respuesta a Sor Filotea*." *Hispanic Review* 51 (1983): 147–158.

——. "Sor Juana Inés de la Cruz ante la crítica," in *Mujer y cultura en la colonia hispano-americana* (273–280), ed. Mabel Moraña. Pittsburgh: Biblioteca Americana, 1996.

Poot Herrera, Sara. "Sor Juana y su mundo, tres siglos después," in *Sor Juana y su mundo* (1–31), ed. Sara Poot Herrera. Mexico: Universidad del Claustro de Sor Juana, 1995.

——. "Sor Juana y Sor Serafina en la boca del lobo," in *Tema y variaciones de literatura* (273–288), ed. Antonio Marquet. Azcapotzalco, Mexico: Universidad Autónoma Metropolitanta, 1996.

——. *Los guardaditos de Sor Juana*. Mexico: UNAM, 1999.

——, ed. *Sor Juana y su mundo*. Mexico: Universidad del Claustro de Sor Juana, 1995.

——, ed. *Y diversa de mí misma entre vuestras plumas ando: Homenaje interenacional a Sor Juana Inés de la Cruz*. Mexico: Colegio de México, 1993.

Powell, Amanda. "Making Use of the Holy Office," in *The Mystical Gesture: Essays on Medieval and Early Modern Spiritual Culture in Honor of Mary E. Giles* (193–216), ed. Robert Boenig. Aldershot, England: Ashgate Publishing, 2000.

———. "Apollo-smiter, Muse-silencer, Sideshow-barker, Scamp: Images of Men in Two Epistolary *Romances* by Sor Juana." Unpublished paper.

Quijada, Mónica, and Jesús Bustamante. "Las mujeres en Nueva España: orden establecido y márgenes de actuación," in *Historia de las mujeres en Occidente* (617–633), ed. Georges Duby. Mexico: Taurus, 1992.

Rabin, Lisa. "Mito petrarquista y transformación criolla en un romance de Sor Juana," in *Tema y variaciones de literatura* (162–174), ed. Antonio Marquet. Mexico: Universidad Autonóma Metropólitana, 1996.

Rebelo Gomes, Florbela. "Para una nueva lectura de la *Carta Atenagórica*, " in *Y diversa de mí misma entre vuestras plumas ando: Homenaje interenacional a Sor Juana Inés de la Cruz* (287–300), ed. Sara Poot Herrera. Mexico: Colegio de México, 1993.

Rubial, Antonio. "Las monjas se inconforman: Los bienes de Sor Juana en el espolio del Arzobispo Francisco de Aguiar y Seijas," in *Tema y variaciones de literatura* (61–72), ed. Antonio Marquet. Mexico: Universidad Autónoma Metropolitana, 1996.

Sabat-Rivers, Georgina. *Bibliografía y otras cuestiunculas sorjuaninas.* Argentina: Biblioteca de Textos Universitarios, 1995.

———. "Blanco, negro, rojo: Semiosis racial en los villancicos de Sor Juana Inés de la Cruz," in *Tema y variaciones de literatura* (85–105), ed. Antonio Marquet. Mexico: Universidad Autónoma Metropolitana, 1996.

———. "Sor Juana: Mujer, barroca, intelectual y criolla," in *Coloquial Internacional: Sor Juana Inés de la Cruz y el pensamiento novohispano* (375–395), ed. Manuel Ramos Medina. Toluca: Instituto Mexiquense de Cultura, 1995.

———. *En busca de Sor Juana.* Mexico: Universidad Nacional Autónoma de México, 1998.

———, ed. *Inundación castálida.* Madrid: Castalia, 1982.

Scott, Nina M. "'If You Are Not Pleased to Favor Me, Put Me out of Your Mind': Gender and Authority in Sor Juana Inés de la Cruz and the Translation of Her Letter to the Reverend Father Maestro Antonio Núñez of the Society of Jesus." *Women's Studies International Forum* 2 (1988): 429–438.

———. "'La gran turba de las que merecieron nombres': Sor Juana's Foremothers in 'La Respuesta a Sor Filotea,'" in *Coded Encounters: Writing, Gender, and Ethnicity in Colonial Latin America* (206–223), Amherst: University of Massachusetts Press, 1994. eds. Francisco Javier Cevallos-Candau et al.

Torres, Miguel de. *Vida, obras y ejemplos del Ilust. y Exc. Señor doctor D. Manuel Fernández de Santa Cruz.* Puebla, Mexico, 1716.

Trabulse, Elías. "El silencio final de Sor Juana." *Universidad de México* 558 (1997): 11–19.

———. *La muerte de Sor Juana.* Mexico: Centro de Estudies de Historia, 1999.

Trueba Lawand, Jamile. *El arte epistolar en el renacimiento español.* Madrid: Editorial Tamesis, 1996.

Wissmer, Jean-Michael. "La última Sor Juana." *Revista Iberoamericana* 172–173 (1995): 639–650.

———. *Las sombras de lo fingido: Sacrificio y simulacro en Sor Juana Inés de la Cruz.* Toluca: Instituto Mexiquense de Cultura, 1998.

Chapter 5
Primary Text

Suárez, Ursula. *Relación autobiográfica.* Ed. Mario Ferriccio Podestá. Intro. Armando de Ramón. Santiago, Chile: Editorial Universitaria de la Universidad de Concepción, 1984.

Secondary Sources

Arenal, Electa, and Stacey Schlau. *Untold Sisters: Hispanic Nuns in Their Own Writings*. Trans. Amanda Powell. Alburquerque: University of New Mexico Press, 1989.

Bataillon, Marcel. *Pícaros y picaresca: La pícara Justina*. Madrid: Taurus, 1969.

Birckel, Maurice. "Picaresca y vida conventual en el Peru del ochocientos." *Historia 16* 26 (1978): 105–115.

Cánovas, Rodrigo. "Ursula Suárez (Monja Chilena, 1666–1749): La autobiografía como penitencia." *Revista Chilena de Literatura* 35 (1990): 97–115.

Casas de Faunce, María. *La novela picaresca latinoamericana*. Madrid: Planeta, 1977.

Colie, Rosalie L. *The Resources of Kind: Genre-Theory in the Renaissance*. Ed. Barabara Lewalski. Berkeley: University of California Press, 1973.

Cruz, Anne J. "The Picaresque as Discourse of Poverty." *Ideologies and Literature* (fall 1985): 90–120.

Friedman, Edward. *The Antiheroine's Voice: Narrative Voice and Transformation of the Picaresque*. Columbia: University of Missiouri Press, 1978.

———. "The Picaresque as Autobiography: Story and History," in *Hispanic Issues: Autobiography in Early Modern Spain* (119–128), ed. Nicholas Spadaccini and Jenaro Talens. Minneapolis: Prisma Institute, 1988.

González, Aníbal. "*Los Infortunios de Alonso Ramírez*: Picaresca e historia." *Hispanic Review* 51 (1983): 189–204.

Guernica, Juan de. *Historia y evolución del Monasterio de Clarisas de Nuestra Señora de la Victoria en sus cuatro períodos*. Santiago, Chile: Sagrado Corazón de Jesús, 1944.

Hanrahan, Thomas. *La mujer en la picaresca española*. Madrid: Porrúa, 1967.

Huerga, Alvaro. "La picaresca de las beatas," in *La picaresca: origenes, textos y estructuras. Actas del I Congreso Internacional sobre la picaresca* (144–148), ed. Manuel Criado de Val. Madrid: Fundación Universitaria Española, 1979.

Ibsen, Kristine. *Women's Spiritual Autobiography in Colonial Spanish America*. Gainesville: University of Florida Press, 1999.

Johnson, Julie. *Satire in Colonial Spanish America: Turning the World Upside Down*. Austin: University of Texas Press, 1993.

———. "Los pícaros y las pícaras en el nuevo mundo: Algunas observaciones," in *Mujer y cultura en la colonia hispanoamericana* (281–294), ed. Mabel Moraña. Pittsburgh: Biblioteca de América, 1996.

Lagos, María. "Confessing to the Father: Marks of Gender and Class in Ursula Suárez *Relación*." *Modern Language Notes* 110 (1995): 353–384.

Mac Keller, Isabel. "La relación autobiográfica de Ursula Suárez: La infacción del orden sagrado y terrenal en el reino de Chile en el siglo XVIII." Master's thesis, Universidad Católica de Santiago, 1990.

McKendrick, Melveena. *Woman and Society in the Spanish Drama of the Golden Age: A Study of the Mujer Varonil*. Cambridge: Cambridge University Press, 1974.

Montecinos, Sonia. "Identidad femenina y escritura en la *Relación autobiográfica* de Ursula Suárez," in *Escribir en los bordes* (105–115), ed. Carmen Berenguer et al. Santiago, Chile: Cuarto Propio, 1990.

Myers, Kathleen Ann. "Miraba La cosas que decía: Convent Writing Picaresque Tales, and the Relación autobiogralica by Ursula Suávez (1666–1749)." *Romance Quarterly* 40 (1993): 1546–172.

Myers, Kathleen Ann, and Amanda Powell. *A Wild Country out in the Garden: the Spiritual Journal of a Mexican Nun*. Bloomington: Indiana University Press, 1999.

Perry, Mary Elizabeth. *Gender and Disorder in Early Modern Seville*. Princeton, NJ: Princeton University Press, 1990.

Rabell, Carmen R. "La confesión en jerigonza del *Lazarillo de Tormes*." *Bulletin of Hispanic Studies* 73 (1996): 19–46.

Ramón, Armando de. "Introducción" to Ursula Suárez's *Relación autobiográfica*. Ed. Mario Ferriccio Podesta. Santiago, Chile: Editorial Universitaria de la Universidad de Concepción, 1984.

Ramírez Leyva, Edelmir. *María Rita Vargas, María Lucía Celis: Beatas embacadoras de la colonia*. Mexico: Universidad Nacional Autonona de Mexico, 1988.

Ross, Kathleen Ann. *The Baroque Narrative of Carlos de Sigüenza y Góngora*. Cambridge: Cambridge University Press, 1993.

Routt, Kristin. "Authoring Orthodoxy: The Body and the *camino de perfección* in Spanish American Colonial Convent Writings." Ph.D. diss., Indiana University, 1998.

———. "'Hablar con dios': Language as Ursula Suárez's *Camino de Perfección*." *Dieciocho* 21, no. 2 (1998): 219–236.

Salinas, Cecilia. *Las chilenas de la colonia: Virtud sumisa, amor rebelde*. Santiago, Chile: LOM, 1994.

Salinas Meza, René. "Uniones ilegítimas y desuniones legítimas: El matrimonio y la formación de la pareja en Chile colonial," in *La familia en el mundo iberoamericano* (173–192), ed. Pilar Gonzalbo Aizpuru and Cecilia Rabel. Mexico: Universidad Nacional Autónoma de México, 1994.

Sánchez Lora, José L. *Mujeres, conventos y formas de la religiosidad barroca*. Madrid: Fundación Universitaria Española, 1988.

Santander y Torres, Sebastián de. *Vida de la venerable María de San Joseph, religiosa augustina recoleta, fundadora en los Conventos de Santa Monica de la Ciudad de Puebla y despues en el de la Soledad de Oaxaca*. Mexico, 1723.

Sieber, Harry. *Language and Society in La vida de Lazarillo de Tormes*. Baltimore: Johns Hopkins University Press, 1978.

Valdés, Adriana. "Escritura de monjas durante la colonia: El caso de Ursula Suárez en Chile," *Mapocho* 31 (1992): 149–166.

Van Praag, V. A., ed. *Vida y costunbres de la Madre Andrea*. *Revista de Literatura* 14 (1958): 111–169.

Vogeley, Nancy. "Defining the 'Colonial Reader': *El periquillo sarniento*." *PMLA* 102 (1987): 784–800.

Weber, Alison. *Teresa of Avila and the Rhetoric of Femininity*. Princeton, NJ: Princeton University Press, 1990.

Chapter 6
Primary Texts

Ferrer, Joaquín María de, ed. *Historia de la Monja Alférez Doña Catalina de Erauso, escrita por ella misma*. Paris: Imprenta de Julio Didot, 1829.

Rubio Merino, Pedro, ed. *La Monja Alférez: Doña Catalina de Erauso. Dos manuscritos inéditos de su autobiografía*. Seville: Cabildo Metropolitano de la Catedral de Sevilla, 1995.

Scott, Nina. *Madres del verbo: Mothers of the Word. Early Spanish America Women Writers: A Bilingual Anthology*. Albuquerque: University of New Mexico Press, 1999.

Stepto, Michele and Stepto, Gabriel, trans. *Lieutenant Nun: Memoir of a Basque Transvestite in the New World. Catalina de Erauso*. Boston: Beacon Press, 1996.

Vallbona, Rima de, ed. *Vida i sucesos de la Monja Alférez: Autobiografía atribuida a Doña Catalina de Erauso*. Tempe, AZ: Center for Latin American Studies, 1992.

Secondary Sources

Arzáns de Orsua y Vela, Bartolomé. *Historia de la villa imperial de Potosí*, vols. 1–3. Ed. Lewis Hanke and Gunnar Mendoza. Providence: Brown University Press, 1965.

Bynum, Carolyn Walker. *Holy Feast and Holy Fast: The Religious Significance of Food to Medieval Women*. Berkeley: University of California Press, 1987.

Cossío, José María de, ed. *Autobiografías de soldados (siglo XVII)*. Biblioteca de autores españoles, vol. 90. Madrid: Real Academia Española, 1956.

Cruz, Anne J. "The Picaresque as Discourse of Poverty." *Ideologies and Literature* (fall 1985): 90–120.

Davis, Natalie Zemon. *Society and Culture in Early Modern France: Eight Essays*. Stanford, CA: Stanford University Press, 1975.

Dugaw, Diane. *Warrior Women and Popular Balladry, 1650–1850*. Cambridge: Cambridge University Press, 1989.

Fernández, James D. *Apology to Apostrophe: Autobiography and the Rhetoric of Self-Representation in Spain*. Durham, NC: Duke University Press, 1992.

Garber, Marjorie. Preface to *Lieutenant Nun: Memoir of a Basque Transvestite in the New World*. Catalina de Erauso. Trans. Michele Stepto and Gabriel Stepto. Boston: Beacon Press, 1996.

González-Echevarría, Roberto. "The Law of the Letter: Garcilaso's *Commentarios* and the Origins of the Latin American Narrative." *Yale Journal of Criticism* 1 (1987): 107–131.

Ibsen, Kristine. *Women's Spiritual Autobiography in Colonial Spanish America*. Gainesville: University Press of Florida, 1999.

Ignacio de Loyola. *Ejercicios espirituales, Autobiografía*. Bilbao, Spain: Mensajero, 1998.

Juana Inés de la Cruz. *Obras completas*, ed. Méndez Plancarte. Mexico: Editorial Porrua, 1975.

Juárez, Encarnación. "Señora Catalina, ¿dónde es el camino? La autobiografía como búsqueda y afirmación de identidad en *Vida i sucesos de la Monja Alférez*," in *LA CHISPA '95 Selected Proceedings* (185–196), ed. Claire J. Paolini. New Orleans: Tulane University Press, 1995.

Juárez, Encarnación. "La mujer militar en la América colonial: El caso de la Monja Alférez." *Indiana Journal of Hispanic Literatures* 10–11 (1997): 147–161.

Lees, Clare A. *Medieval Masculinities: Regarding Men in the Middle Ages*. Minneapolis: University of Minnesota Press, 1994.

Levisi, Margarita. *Autobiografías del siglo de oro*. Madrid: Sociedad General Española de Librería, 1984.

Leush, Boleslao, ed. *Descripción del Virrenato del Perú: Crónica inedita de comicnzos del siglo XVII*. Rosario, Argentia: Instituto de Investigaciones Históricas, 1958.

Mandrell, James. "Questions of Genre and Gender: Contemporary American Versions of the Feminine Picaresque." *Novel* 20 (1987): 149–170.

McKnight, Kathryn Joy. *The Mystic of Tunja: The Writings of Madre Castillo, 1671–1742*. Amherst: University of Massachusetts Press, 1997.

McNamara, Jo Ann. *Sisters in Arms: Catholic Nuns through Two Millennia*. Cambridge, MA: Harvard University Press, 1996.

Medina, José Toribio. *Biblioteca Hispano-Chilena*, vol. 1. Amsterdam: N. Israel, 1956.

Merrim, Stephanie. "Catalina de Erauso: From Anomaly to Icon," in *Coded Encounters: Writing, Gender, and Ethnicity in Colonial Latin America* (177–205), ed. Francisco Javier Cevallos-Candau et al. Amherst: University of Massachusetts Press, 1994.

———. *Early Modern Women's Writing and Sor Juana Inés de la Cruz*. Nashville, TN: Vanderbilt University Press, 1999.

————. "Petition of Catalina de Erauso to the Spanish Crown, 1625." *Review* 43 (1990): 37–41.

Myers, Kathleen Ann. "'Miraba las cosas que desía': Convent Writing, Picaresque Tales, and the *Relación autobiográfica* by Ursula Suárez (1666–1749)." *Romance Quarterly* 40 (summer 1993), Part 2: 156–172.

Myers, Kathleen Ann. "Writing of the Frontier: Blurring Gender and Genre in the Monja Alférez's Account." *Mapping Colonial Spanish American: Places and Commonplaces of Identity, Culture, and Experience,* (181–201), ed. Santa Arias and Mariselle Meléndez. Lewisburg: Bucknell University Press, 2002.

Myers, Kathleen A., and Amanda Powell. *A Wild Country out in the Garden: The Spiritual Journal of a Colonial Mexican Nun.* Bloomington: Indana University Press, 1999.

Ortner, Sherry B., and Harriet Whitehead, eds. *Sexual Meanings: The Cultural Construction of Gender and Sexuality.* Cambridge: Cambridge University Press, 1981.

Perry, Mary Elizabeth. "*La Monja Alférez*: Myth, Gender, and the Manly Woman in a Spanish Renaissance Drama," in *LA CHISPA '87: Selected Proceedings* (239–249), ed. Claire J. Paolini. New Orleans: Tulane University Press, 1987.

————. *Gender and Disorder in Early Modern Seville.* Princeton, NJ: Princeton University Press, 1990.

Pope, Randolph D. *La autobiografía española hasta Torres Villarroel.* Frankfurt: Peter Lang, 1974.

Pumar Martínez, Carmen. *Españolas en Indias: Mujeres-soldado, adelantadas y gobernadoras.* Madrid: Biblioteca Iberoamericana, 1988.

Rabell, Carmen R. "La confesión en jerigonza del *Lazarillo de Tormes*." *Bulletin of Hispanic Studies* 73 (1996): 19–46.

Ribadeneyra, Pedro de. *Flos sanctorum en que se contienen las vidas de los santos,* vols. 1–6. Madrid, 1716.

Rodríquez Freile, Juan. *El Carnero.* Bogotá: Biblioteca Popular de Literatura, 1942.

Rosenberg, John R. *The Circular Pilgrimage: An Anatomy of Confessional Autobiography in Spain.* New York: Peter Lang, 1994.

Ross, Kathleen Ann. "Cuestiones de género en *Infortunios de Alonso Ramírez.*" *Revista Iberoamericana* 61 (1995): 591–603.

————. *The Baroque Narrative of Carlos de Sigüenza y Góngora: A New World Paradise.* Cambridge: Cambridge University Press, 1993.

Routt, Kristin. "Authoring Orthodoxy: The Body and the *Camino de perfección* in Spanish-American Colonial Convent Writings," Ph.D. diss. Indiana University, 1998.

Rubial García, Antonio. "Mariofanías extravagantes: Las visiones de Catarina de San Juan." *Universidad de México* 499 (1992): 15–20.

Salinas, Cecilia. *Las chilenas de la colonia: Virtud Sumisa, Amor Rebelde.* Santiago, Chile: LOM, 1994.

Scott, Joan W. "Gender: A Useful Category of Historical Analysis." *American Historical Review* 91 (1986): 1053–1073.

Serrano y Sanz, Manuel. *Apuntes para una biblioteca de escritoras españolas.* Madrid: Atlas, 1975.

Socolow, Susan Migden. *The Women of Colonial Latin America.* Cambridge: Cambridge University Press: 2000.

Shepherd, Simon. *Amazons and Warrior Women: Varieties of Feminism in Seventheeth-Century Drama.* New York: St. Martin's Press, 1981.

Siqüenza y Góngora, Carlos de. *Los infortunios de Alonso Ramírez* (1690). Madrid: Espasa-Calpe, 1941.

Spadaccini, Nicholas, and Jenaro Talens, eds. *Autobiography in Early Modern Spain.* Minneapolis: Prima Institute, 1988.

Taddeo, Sara. "'Mentís, que no soy mujer mientras empuño este acero': Verdad, engaño, and valor in La Monja Alférez,"in *Looking at the Comedia in the Year of the Quincentennial: 1992 Symposium on Golden Age Drama* (111–120), ed. Barbara Mujica, 1993.

Tellechea Idigoras, J. Ignacio. *Doña Catalina de Erauso, La Monja Alférez.* San Sebastián: Donostia, 1992.

Temprano, Emilio. *Vidas poco ejemplares: Viaje al mundo de las rameras, los rufianes y las celestinas (siglos XVI–XVIII).* Madrid: Ediciones del Prado, 1995.

Wheelwright, Julie. *Amazons and Military Maids: Women Who Dressed as Men in the Pursuit of Life, Liberty, and Happiness.* Boston: Pandora, 1989.

Velasco, Sherry. *The Lieutenant Nun: Transgenderism, Lesbian Desire, and Catalina de Erauso.* Austin: University of Texas Press, 2000.

Conclusions

Rivas, Emma. "'Gran cosa es el buen exemplo que muebe con mucha facilidad': Lecturas ejemplares novohispanos del siglo XVII," *Historias* 31 (1994): 113–126.

Rubial, Antonio. *La Santidad Controvertida.* Mexico: Fondo de Cultura Económic, 1999.

Index

Page numbers in *italics* indicate illustrations.